JEAN-MICHEL WILMOTTE

JEAN-MICHEL WILMOTTE

images
Publishing

Published in Australia in 2018 by
The Images Publishing Group Pty Ltd
ABN 89 059 734 431
6 Bastow Place, Mulgrave, Victoria 3170, Australia
Tel: +61 3 9561 5544 Fax: +61 3 9561 4860
books@imagespublishing.com
www.imagespublishing.com

Copyright © The Images Publishing Group Pty Ltd 2018
The Images Publishing Group Reference Number: 1338

All rights reserved. Apart from any fair dealing for the purposes of private study, research, criticism or review as permitted under the Copyright Act, no part of this publication may be reproduced, stored in a retrieval system or transmitted in any form by any means, electronic, mechanical, photocopying, recording or otherwise, without the written permission of the publisher.

National Library of Australia Cataloguing-in-Publication entry:

Title:	Jean-Michel Wilmotte / Philip Jodidio (Ed.)
ISBN:	9781864707489 (hardback)
Series:	Leading Architects of the World.
Subjects:	Jean-Michel Wilmotte (monograph)
	Architecture, Modern—21st century.
	Architecture, Modern—20th century.
	International style (Architecture)
	Architectural practice, International.
	Architectural design.

Production manager: Nicole Boehringer
Senior editor: Gina Tsarouhas
Assisting editors: Driss Fatih, Bree De Roche (IMAGES); Valérie Valentin (W&A Paris)
Graphic designer: Thais Ometto, Thais Pedroso

Printed on 140gsm GoldEast Matt Art paper by Everbest Printing Investment Limited, in Hong Kong/China

IMAGES has included on its website a page for special notices in relation to this and our other publications. Please visit www.imagespublishing.com

CONTENTS

6 INDISSOCIABLE: PAST AND PRESENT IN THE WORK OF JEAN-MICHEL WILMOTTE

NEW BUILDINGS
16 LEE HOUSE
22 PANGYO RESIDENCE
28 SIGNAL TOWER
34 BRAIN AND SPINE INSTITUTE
40 MONTE CARLO VIEW TOWER
44 EPADESA CORPORATE HEADQUARTERS
48 BARRISTERS TRAINING COLLEGE
54 ARTS CENTER, INTERNATIONAL SCHOOL OF GENEVA
58 ALLIANZ RIVIERA STADIUM
66 QUADRANS BUILDINGS
72 6 PANCRAS SQUARE, GOOGLE HEADQUARTERS
78 DAEJEON CULTURAL CENTER
84 FERRARI SPORTING MANAGEMENT CENTER
90 RUSSIAN ORTHODOX SPIRITUAL AND CULTURAL CENTER
96 PRIVATE CHALET
104 EIFFAGE CORPORATE HEADQUARTERS
110 BLEU CIEL RESIDENTIAL TOWER
114 GIROFLÉES TOWER

RENOVATION PROJECTS
120 LA RÉSERVE HOTEL, RAMATUELLE
128 JEAN PIERRE RAYNAUD STUDIO
134 MANDARIN ORIENTAL HOTEL
140 CHÂTEAU PÉDESCLAUX WINERY
146 SUMMIT HOUSE, JCDECAUX UK HEADQUARTERS
152 STATION F START-UP CAMPUS
162 COLLÈGE DES BERNARDINS

URBAN PROJECTS
172 GREATER MOSCOW PROPOSAL
178 ALLÉES JEAN-JAURÈS

MUSEUMS
186 PAVILLON DES SESSIONS, MUSÉE DU LOUVRE
192 GANA ART CENTER
196 PRESIDENT JACQUES CHIRAC MUSEUM
202 ULLENS CENTER FOR CONTEMPORARY ART
208 MUSEUM OF ISLAMIC ART
214 MUSÉE D'ORSAY REFURBISHMENT
222 SURSOCK MUSEUM
228 THE NEW RIJKSMUSEUM

APPENDIX
236 WILMOTTE & ASSOCIÉS ARCHITECTES
237 ADDRESSES
238 PROJECT DATA
246 MAJOR PROJECTS
248 AWARDS
250 SELECTED BIBLIOGRAPHY
252 EXHIBITIONS DEDICATED TO JEAN-MICHEL WILMOTTE'S WORK
254 CREDITS
255 INDEX OF PROJECTS

INDISSOCIABLE: PAST AND PRESENT IN THE WORK OF JEAN-MICHEL WILMOTTE

Born in 1948 and a graduate of the Ecole Camondo in Paris (1973), Jean-Michel Wilmotte created his own firm, Governor, in 1975. He came to the attention of the public when he won a competition organized in 1987 by the Établissement public du Grand Louvre for the temporary exhibition spaces, bookshop, and restaurants in the new spaces beneath I.M. Pei's Pyramid in the Cours Napoléon of the Louvre. He spoke of these spaces and of his close work with Pei and with Michel Macary in these terms, "The work on the first phase of the Louvre project was undertaken on the basis of an extremely precise and detailed program. It permitted me to have a very interesting dialogue with Pei and Macary. I wanted to go in the same direction they did and to keep the spirit of the Louvre in mind. I think it was appropriate in this instance to keep a reserved attitude once I had fully assimilated the existing architecture. This is not to say that I attempted in any way to dilute the personality of my work with respect to that of my colleagues." Wilmotte returned to the Louvre and to his collaboration with Pei and Macary for the Decorative Arts rooms (51,667 square feet [4,800 square meters]) in the newly refurbished Richelieu Wing of the museum in 1993. As was the case in the new Museum of Islamic Art in Doha, he also was responsible for the display cases and furniture of the entire Richelieu Wing. Here again, Wilmotte showed not only great sensitivity to the objects displayed but also to the historic building.

Seoul, Beirut and even Sarran

Subsequent to his initial work on the Louvre, Jean-Michel Wilmotte became one of the most active and influential interior designers in the museum field in Europe, but as of 1993 he also began to work actively as an architect in his own right, while carrying out numerous urban furniture and design projects, such as the 1994 refurbishment of the Champs-Elysées in Paris. As an interior designer, he has completed boutiques and showrooms for such prestigious clients as Chaumet, John Galliano or Cartier. As an architect, amongst numerous other projects, he completed the Gana Art Center (Seoul, South Korea, 1996–98) and the Insa Art Center in the same city two years later. Wilmotte worked on the refurbishment of the National Museum in Beirut in 1999, and built the Musée Jacques Chirac in Sarran, France (2002/2006, built in two phases) for gifts given to President Chirac during his tenure in office. Though displaying diplomatic gifts might not seem the most interesting type of work for an architect like Jean-Michel Wilmotte, his friendship with the former President of France and above all his understanding of the architecture of the region of Sarran allowed him to create not only a lasting tribute to the President, but also works of architecture that are subtle, in harmony with older buildings on the site, and yet resolutely modern. There is always a balance to be considered in the presence of older architecture between respect and the necessary contemporary presence. Wilmotte has an instinctive grasp of these issues, just as he masters the contrasts between opacity and transparency, or solidity and lightness. It is light that best characterizes his work, penetrating seemingly dense walls with natural ease. The architecture of Jean-Michel Wilmotte tends to assume a somewhat weighty or substantial appearance or feeling as viewed from many angles, and yet, the light is always there, filtering from hidden sources, or coming through a window. While contemporary architecture has often strived for an almost ethereal lightness that also conveys an ephemeral feeling, Wilmotte's buildings are very present, something like the stones of the past even when they are made of concrete and steel. And to this affirmed presence is joined a subtle dosage of translucid, transparent, light-filled spaces. This combination of apparently contradictory elements perhaps best defines the "style" of Wilmotte, one unlike that of almost any other architect. The substantial aspect of his buildings may well be linked to his long experience with the renovation of historic buildings, spaces like the "Arts Premiers" galleries of the Louvre (2000).

Linking the past to the present, again and again

The term "Arts Premiers" can be translated loosely as "first arts" or primal arts, and refers to what is elsewhere called primitive art. It was in collaboration with the noted art-world figure Jacques Kerchache and under the leadership of President Jacques Chirac that galleries in the Pavillon des Sessions on the River Seine side of the palace were set aside in the Louvre for works from Africa, the Americas, Asia, or Oceanic regions. The point was clearly to give these expressions an equal footing with Western art forms already privileged in the Louvre. A total of 108 works of art from the French national collections were put on display in a 15,069-square-foot (1,400-square-meter) place especially redesigned by Jean-Michel Wilmotte. At stake in this instance, there was of course not only the display of unusual works of art, some of which are quite large, but also the fundamental respect of the Louvre itself. A flexible overhead lighting system and what must certainly be described as an innate sensitivity to the works allowed Wilmotte to successfully bridge a gap between civilizations and centuries—no small accomplishment.

Jean-Michel Wilmotte's work in collaboration with I.M. Pei did not end with the 1995 inauguration of the Richelieu Wing of the Louvre; it took up again in an entirely different context with the Museum of Islamic Art in Doha. In his spectacular design for the building, Pei erected what he considered to be an expression of the "essence of Islamic architecture" on an artificial island at the tip of Doha's Corniche road. The Chinese-American architect carried through the design to the main atrium space at the heart of the museum, but left the galleries, essentially in the form of a series of black boxes, to Wilmotte. In these spaces, the French architect devised display cases and a sophisticated use of lighting and materials to truly place the objects of Islamic art held by the museum in a position to be admired from all angles. Whereas the atrium space of Pei is bathed in natural light, Wilmotte's galleries are given over to relative darkness where the objects spring out in all their color and beauty. Mastering a use of rare woods and stones, Wilmotte gives every inch of these galleries a real feeling of being precious, of solidity and power that is restrained to the benefit of the works of art.

Bringing light to *The Night Watch*

One of the most significant projects of Jean-Michel Wilmotte, the new exhibition design for the Rijksmuseum in Amsterdam, completed in 2013, may have attracted less attention than it deserved. The Rijksmuseum was built not far from the center of Amsterdam in 1885 by the Dutch architect Pieter Cuypers (1827–1921), in a Neo-Gothic and Renaissance style. In 2003 the Dutch government implemented a comprehensive restructuring and renovation program for the Rijksmuseum so that it would meet top international museum standards. A total of 129,167 square feet (12,000 square meters) of new exhibition spaces were designed by Wilmotte, with the Spanish architects Cruz & Ortiz doing restructuring work, including the main entrance hall. Wilmotte's brief was to restore Cuyper's original internal architecture and layout, and to design the gallery spaces so that the collection did not touch the building's walls. The architects intervened on four levels of the structure, including Level 2 with such celebrated works as *The Night Watch* by Rembrandt. No less than 220 display cases were designed for the refurbished galleries. These cases are notable because of their transparency, but also the way in which they complete the atmosphere of the galleries, where five shades of gray are complimented by a unique LED-based lighting system, developed with Philips Lighting, called Lightracks, created by Wilmotte for the museum. The wonderful 17th-century Dutch masterpieces of the Rijksmuseum, often bathed in subtle light constrasting with rich shadows, finally found an appropriate place in the galleries redesigned by Wilmotte. Jean-Michel Wilmotte is surely one of the great masters in the world of this kind of intervention, where architecture, interior design, and lighting meet at the service of works of art.

This enumeration gives only a partial indication of the extensive activities of Jean-Michel Wilmotte in such apparently disparate areas as museum interiors, furniture and object design, urban planning, or architecture. Indeed it seems clear that there is an indissociable link between the furniture and object designs of Wilmotte and his architecture. There is no doubt that the same spirit informs both the well-grounded walls of his buildings and the movable world of his objects. As is the case in his architecture, the objects of Wilmotte almost always appear to be substantial, even weighty, and yet they also confer a feeling of comfort, of solidity in the most positive and modern sense of the term. There is a Wilmotte style and it speaks to the substantial links that always exist between the past and the present, between lightness and weight, between opacity and hovering light.

Solidly connected

When it comes to architecture, or whatever the project, his style appears to be respectful of its environment, while retaining a fundamental modernity. Light, and the skilful juxtaposition of transparent, translucent, and opaque surfaces are key elements of his approach. So, too, is his personable, humane manner in dealing with clients and decision-makers. Those who have noticed that Jean-Michel Wilmotte seems to know everybody who counts in the world of architecture, design, and art, also understand that he has similar contacts in the political world of France, in the highest circles of its business elite as well. It is apparent finally that a characteristic of Wilmotte's work in all of the areas he deals with, is the very solidity of his designs. From furniture to architecture, he imbues what he does with a feeling of permanence that is not typical of contemporary buildings or objects. Despite having 250 employees or more, he has managed to continue to be the essential driving force for his office, in obtaining work and in finding appropriate solutions to often very difficult architectural and design problems, where the old stones of Europe come into contact with a desire for contemporary flair.

Although his work on museums has been one of the highlights of the career of Jean-Michel Wilmotte, he has also undertaken, mostly in recent years, a series of large commissions that concern buildings he has designed. This is the case of the Allianz Riviera Stadium, (Nice, France, 2013), which makes use of a large quantity of timber in keeping with the location of the facility in a designated "Eco-District." In fact, it is billed as including the largest wood-metal space frame ever built. Lightness and transparency are the key concepts that guided its design. The stadium has a very large, rounded rectangular opening above the pitch, but otherwise provides protection from the elements or the strong Nice sun for spectator seating. In this way, there is a combination of the presence of the outdoors and a partial covering. The translucent skin of the façade reveals a light skeletal structure beneath, creating a play of light and shadow along its surface. Despite its location in a seismic activity area, stadium includes a 151-foot (46-meter) roof cantilever. During the day, the stadium is filled with diffused natural light, while at night it glows from within. The undulating form of its EFTE membrane gives an impression that the structure is floating, acting like a protective veil that lifts upwards to welcome spectators. An important aspect of Wilmotte's talent is revealed here—his instinctive ability to make the users of his buildings feel at ease. The stadium experiments with lighter forms than many of his other newly built works, but it also retains the sense of logical modernity that imbues the rest of his oeuvre. Inside, the stadium is comfortable and inviting, with light-filled spaces, expansive views of the surrounding landscape, and generously scaled walkways. The stadium was designed to allow for numerous event configurations, including sports, concerts, and other types of large public events.

From the Seine to Barbizon

Even more visible to the general public, the Russian Orthodox Spiritual and Cultural Center (Paris, France, 2016) sits near the banks of the River Seine and not far from the symbolically important Alexandre III Bridge, named after Tsar Alexander III. The complex includes a parish hall, a religious center, a school, and above all the Holy Trinity Cathedral that makes use of five typical gilded domes that signal the presence of the institution to the neighborhood. Using the same stone as the neighboring Trocadero Palace (on the opposite bank of the river), the Center again displays the mastery of Wilmotte in terms of integrating his work into a rather complex architectural and historic context while also projecting a sense of solid modernity. Called in after the Mayor of Paris Bertrand Delanoë rejected a scheme by another architect in 2012, Jean-Michel Wilmotte showed his ability to navigate circumstances that were politically complicated to top off the architectural challenge that he also met with brio.

Other recent work of Jean-Michel Wilmotte has gone from very interesting private houses to office towers. The range of his architectural commissions speaks clearly of the extent of his capacities, from the small to the large, from renovations to new construction. His house for the French artist Jean Pierre Raynaud (Barbizon, France, 2009) is a key example of this versatility. Jean Pierre Raynaud, born in 1939, has sought in his own way in the past to isolate himself from the events and noise of Paris, for a time by living underground in a house essentially of his own design (Le Mastaba, built in collaboration with the architect Jean Dedieu, 1986) in La Garenne Colombes, just 6.2 miles (10 kilometers) from the city center. At La Garenne Colombes, Raynaud created and exhibited his own works, ranging from giant flower pots coated in gold leaf to foreign flags made into works of art by his intervention. More recently, seeking the assistance of his friend Jean-Michel Wilmotte, Raynaud created a new place to work in Barbizon. Thirty-six miles (58 kilometers) from Paris, Barbizon is known as the home of the school of painting of the same name that included such significant 19th-century painters as Théodore Rousseau and Jean-François Millet. Stripping an old house called the Clos d'Hortense of later additions, the architect removed 1960s extensions to the house and added a large glazed interior space and also developed substantial 5,113 square feet (475 square meters) of exterior terraces. A small 100-year old Nordic-style pavilion, which was part of the Universal Exposition of 1889, was painted entirely in black at the request of the artist and is part of the overall composition. The "verrière" also opens the house toward its wooded setting and the artist's own 43,056-square-foot (4,000-square-meter) garden, where Raynaud and Wilmotte worked in collaboration with the landscape designers Neveux-Rouyer to create the kind of unity between art, architecture and nature that he is fond of. Indeed, Jean Pierre Raynaud has long worked at the frontier between architecture and art, making his own house in La Celle Saint Cloud, also near Paris, beginning in 1969, until its demolition 24 years later. With the rubble from the demolition, Raynaud organized a noted 1993 exhibition at the CAPC in Bordeaux. In this exceptional case, the architecture of the artist's atelier can be considered a part of his work in art—here in close collaboration with Jean-Michel Wilmotte.

Bigger and more prestigious

Wilmotte has delved actively into the area of the design and construction of towers; for example, with the Monte-Carlo View Tower (Monaco, 2012) a 20-story high-rise topped by a triplex apartment, and the Giroflées Tower

(Monaco, 2020), a 22-story, 426-foot (130-meter) residential tower on the eastern side of Monaco in the Saint-Roman area with 73 luxury apartments. The architect's extensive network of connections with developers and clients, as well as political officials, has allowed him to design and build where many other architects are not admitted. This is the case in Monaco, but surely also, even more recently, in the United States, where his projects at Harwood Village (in particular Bleu Ciel Residential Tower, Dallas, Texas, 2018) mark a new step for the Paris-based architect, his acceptance in the American market, which is often quite closed to foreign or French designers.

The range and breadth of the activity of the Wilmotte office runs from state-of-the-art lighting design to mixed-use towers, but the architect has also made a point of creating office complexes for major organizations and firms. Two examples published here give an idea of recent work in this area. One of the most talked about official projects in France in recent years has been the installation of the French Ministry of Defence in the Balard area of the 15th arrondissement in Paris. Jean-Michel Wilmotte was tasked with creating buildings for the Quadrans service campus on the site. With a floor area approaching 1,076,390 square feet (100,000 square meters), this substantial complex is set on a landscaped 6.9 acres (2.8 hectares) and could easily have given an impression of heaviness, but Wilmotte succeeds in using an approach that recalls traditional Parisian townhouses that allows the buildings to be at once at home in the city and efficient as office buildings. Planted rooftops and terraces, as well as generous natural light inside make the offices agreeable, while offices can be modulated in size providing for a maximum degree of future flexibility. Outside of Paris in Vélizy-Villacoublay, Wilmotte built the 258,333-square-foot (24,000-square-meter) headquarters for the major French civil engineering firm Eiffage in 2015. The sobriety and functional aspect of this complex is indeed quite characteristic of Wilmotte's work. Though in recent years he has experimented with somewhat more exuberant forms, his style tends toward a rich palette of relatively sober materials arranged in forms that speak openly of solidity in a way that contemporary architecture has sometimes forgotten to do. Here as elsewhere, a garden, in this case arranged like a natural bowl around the building, tempers harder materials like raw-pour in-situ concrete or black metal doors and window frames. The material solidity of Wilmotte's buildings (and perhaps his offices in particular) is always allayed by the presence of natural light or greenery. But these presences, which make the offices more agreeable, sit lightly in and around buildings that are resolutely modern and efficient.

Wilmotte has also found ways to advance with such prestigious clients as Ferrari, for whom he built the Sporting Management Center (Maranello, Italy, 2015). Devoted to the design and assembly of Ferrari Formula 1 racing cars, the Sporting Management Center can be considered an iconic building, with a strong visual identity. Ferrari's signature red, black, and metal, as well as the winding shape of the envelope, contribute to creating the building's strength, character and the impression of movement that it generates. Conveying ideas of speed, performance and acceleration, which are intrinsic to the brand's identity, into a graphic and spatial interpretation, results in the transformation of the building into a glass-clad vessel, as identifiable as the firm's bright-red racing cars. Another area that is imbued with prestige is that of the wineries of France, where Wilmotte has worked extensively. His Château Pédesclaux (Pauillac, 2015) is published here, but he has also worked for Laurent-Perrier champagnes (Tours-sur-Marne, France, 2015), where he was asked to design the facilities for the distinguished Grand Siècle label. Here Wilmotte brings together his knowledge of architectural spaces, but also of lighting and interior design; for example, in the 2,691-square-foot (250-square-meter) tasting room. The essential element for great wines is a capacity to relate their history to the present and future, and in this respect, Laurent-Perrier could not have found a better architect and interior designer than Jean-Michel Wilmotte. Inaugurated in 2015, his complete renovation of the Château Mentone winery (Saint-Antonin-du-Var) involved no new construction, but rather a complete redefinition of existing spaces and a farm structure whose origins lie in the 11th century. Again, the excellence of Wilmotte's work in making the past relevant is here patently obvious.

Also a matter of contacts and being in the right place at the right time, Jean-Michel Wilmotte has been in charge of the renovation of the Halle Freyssinet into Station F start-up campus (Paris, 2017). His client in this instance is Xavier Niel, owner of the French telephone network Free and also part owner of the daily newspaper *Le Monde*. Niel has a high-flying reputation in French business circles and his intiative destined to help promising start-up companies has attracted a great deal of attention in the press. The facility was installed in a covered hall built in 1927 by the famous engineer Eugène Freyssinet. Listed as a historic monument since 2012, it is 997 feet (304 meters) long and between 236 and 200 feet (72 and 61 meters) wide. Used as a train-truck transfer point for the nearby Austerlitz station, the Halle was redesigned by Wilmotte to reflect the lifestyles and business practices of young digital entrepreneurs. It now features shared, multi-purpose spaces as well as "villages" grouped around services. The southeast end of the covered hall hosts an unusual restaurant, open 24 hours a day. Here the heritage of the past has been evoked by retaining the old loading platforms and rail bed—several restaurant cars have even been included. This bustling, surprising restaurant is linked to the city via a terrace that overlooks a garden. The 365,984-square-foot (34,000-square-meter) building is in pre-stressed concrete, with steel, wood, and glass used by Wilmotte. Jean-Michel Wilmotte states, "Our digital incubator project is a real architectural catalyzer, hosting and drawing together two major creative energies within a unique, innovative and vibrant space that blends the daring brilliance of an engineer born in the 19th century and the raw, unbridled imagination of a new generation." Above all, Jean-Michel Wilmotte shows a real capacity to bring the architecture of the past, be it distant or more recent, into the functioning present. Granted, the Halle Freyssinet with its vast, open design, may have been easier to occupy than some of the old stone buildings that Wilmotte has tackled, but nonetheless, his capacity to link past and present is again in evidence here. Unlike many architects who clearly privilege an exterior envelope or specifically architectural forms, Wilmotte obviously thinks in a multi-faceted way, including the concept of interior designs that blend seamlessly with the exteriors. Objects, lighting fixtures, colors, surfaces, and materials are fully integrated with the architectural design itself in most of his projects. In a reverse sense, his ability to occupy interior spaces and to rethink them in a 21st-century style means that he thinks in a manner that is architectural even when only spaces inside of existing walls are concerned.

Five stars in Paris

Another of his recent projects, the Mandarin Oriental Hotel (Paris, France, 2011) involved making an existing office complex into a five-star hotel. He succeeded not only in this task but also in obtaining an HQE environmental quality label for the finished project. Here, to the contrary of many of Wilmotte's projects, the original architecture of the office buildings was not particularly notable. Instead it is Wilmotte who created luxury and space where there were only desks and hallways before. In another substantial hotel project, which was underway as this book went to press, Jean-Michel Wilmotte was commissioned to entirely renovate and restructure the Lutetia, the only "palace" type hotel on the left bank in Paris. This was not simply a makeover, few of the original interior walls survived the transformation although the façades of the hotel at the corner of the Boulevard Raspail and Rue de Sèvres are classified as being an historic monument. Digging belowgrade to create a spa and swimming pool, opening an existing interior courtyard to make a winter garden, or rearranging the rooms with his trademark lighting and objects, Wilmotte shows the full range of his capacity in the Lutetia project, also calling on specialists to restore historic décor inside the building as required. Those who knew the Lutetia before its transformation will find not only the façade, but a sufficient number of interior elements to remind them of what was, while new visitors will imagine the past glory of the hotel and indulge in its very contemporary feeling. Again, the architect mixes the past and the present in a way that gives a meaning to the word "luxury" in the context of a five-star hotel.

On the banks of the Moskva

As though mastering every dimension from ashtray to office towers were not sufficient, Jean-Michel Wilmotte has also undertaken urban design schemes, such as his Allées Jean-Jaurès (Nîmes, France, 2013) that involves the largest avenue in the southern French city. He imagined kiosks and pergolas adorning a central pedestrian strip of the broad Allées Jean-Jaurès, playing on the motif of the leaves of the age-old nettle trees lining it. Composed of perforated sheet iron back-lit by LEDs, the façades enliven the avenue by providing delicate lighting that evokes Provençal lace. "We wanted to channel the energy of the Jardins de la Fontaine, restoring the original identity to the avenue so that people would feel good there, would go there more willingly," says the architect. Nîmes of course is steeped in history, going back to the time of the Romans, thus interventions here are often fraught with political and aesthetic disputes. Wilmotte again masters these issues much as he does the design aspects, where living links between past and present are woven in a nearly seamless way.

Much more ambitious, his Proposal for Greater Moscow (Russian Federation, 2012) concerned the largest city in Russia. On September 5, 2012, a jury awarded the Franco-Russian team led by urban architect Antoine Grumbach, Jean-Michel Wilmotte, and Sergey Tkachenko the mission of guiding the evolution of the extension of Moscow. Dealing with a project on the scale of this Moscow intervention represents a substantial leap for Jean-Michel Wilmotte, and yet, together with his partners on the project, he has shown his capacity to think of the urban stage much as he does with his own buildings, with an implacable logic and respect for clarity and modernity. One of the guiding principles of the Franco-Russian team's plan is a focus on the Moskva River for the development of both institutional and leisure activities in the greater urban area. Like the Seine in Paris and the Thames in London, the Moskva would thus become a vector of the city's identity. This has not been the case, but the proposal seems to be a "natural" one dictated by the city and its inhabitants. Landscaped development of the river banks, with a constant concern for the quality of life and the valorization of existing heritage, would be accompanied by a redeployment of public transportation (here embodied by a tram line) in order to limit car traffic that today makes the quays inaccessible to pedestrians. For the concept that would potentially have involved 383,013 acres (155,000 hectares) of land, Wilmotte and Grumbach agreed that the key to such an ambitious scheme would be to seize on existing lines of development and to optimize them rather than trying to reverse existing patterns. In this, the Greater Moscow plan is typical of Wilmotte's perception of what exists, of his respect for the past and his open mind for the future.

Jean-Michel Wilmotte is certainly not a proponent of what the Bauhaus and Gropius called the tabula rasa; rather, he seems to immediately identify the strengths and potential of existing systems and to integrate those realities in a modernization that is equally senstitive to the world as it has become. For Wilmotte, it would seem that there is no fundamental conflict between the past and the present. He has never indulged in pastiche nor in a real effort to reconsitute the past, instead, he keeps what is useful and beautiful in the old in order to amplify and confirm the ways of the present. In this he may be nearly unique in the world of contemporary architecture and design. Starting essentially with furniture design, which broadened rapidly into substantial urban schemes like his work on the urban furniture and lighting of the Champs-Elysées in Paris (1994), Wilmotte has in more recent years become one of the top 100 architecture firms in the world, completing major projects ranging from the Allianz Riviera Stadium to private homes. Hotels, corporate headquarters buildings, renovations, wineries, and museums all figure in his list of projects. The fact that he has a base in interior design or furniture and lighting design gives Wilmotte a large degree of flexibilty to also take on interior work when required. In the work of Jean-Michel Wilmotte, there is solidity in the most positive sense of the word, but also a subtle understanding of nature and light. He has, from the first, shown an ability to make otherwise opaque volumes come to life with natural and artificial light: for example, in his renovations of old stone buildings. Above all, Wilmotte is equally at home bringing an 11th-century farmhouse to life, making a 1927 railway facility into a home for cutting-edge technological start-up firms, or creating a building for the legendary Scuderia Ferrari. His success is based in his subtle understanding of architecture and design, in his capacity to reconcile past and present, and finally, in his affable personality, always warm and welcoming.

Philip Jodidio

NEW BUILDINGS

JEAN-MICHEL WILMOTTE

LEE HOUSE

Built with reinforced, in-situ concrete, the Lee House is in Pyeongchang-dong, a residential neighborhood of the South Korean capital, located at the foot of the mountains. The sloped site is part of the wooded mountainside and thus stands apart from the urban sprawl below. A series of terraces and gardens designed with the collaboration of the landscape architects François Neveux and Bernard Rouyer allow the concrete forms to emerge almost mineral-like from the hillside. A cascade pool on the upper terrace runs down along the property line.

The Lee House is set on a generous 20,600-square-foot (1,914-square-meter) site and has a floor area of 3,745 square feet (348 square meters). There are typical Korean ancestral statures in the gardens. Carefully selected pine trees give life to the walls of the house according to changing light. The house is based on a play of cubes, a combination of well-defined simple volumes gridded by black-lacquered aluminum millwork. Glass and concrete surfaces alternate, creating glass voids and concrete solids.

The house provides intimacy for the familylife of the owner, his wife, and their child. The scheme avoids any appearance of complication. The living room, dining room, kitchen and office are on the lower level; three bedrooms, a study and bathrooms on the upper floor. The spaces are simple and generous, with recessed joints underlining the articulation of volumes and materials against a field of rendered and painted concrete. It is, as the architect states, "a white page on which everyday life is written." The house combines Wilmotte's ability to base his architecture on geometric forms, while simultaneously admitting light and nature, elements that soften the frequently straight lines and sharply defined surfaces of his work. Even the placement of ancestral statues in the garden terraces seems very much in harmony with this kind of inclusive modernity.

Location Seoul, South Korea
Completion date 2005
Area 3,745 ft² (348 m²)

SITE PLAN

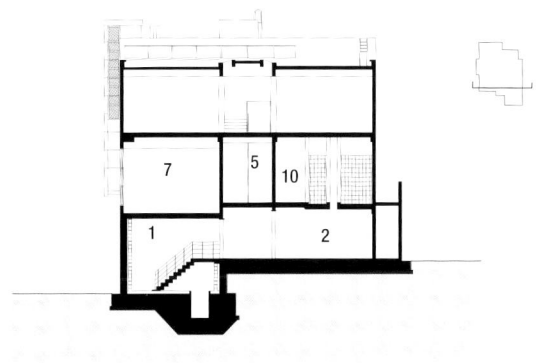

CROSS SECTION

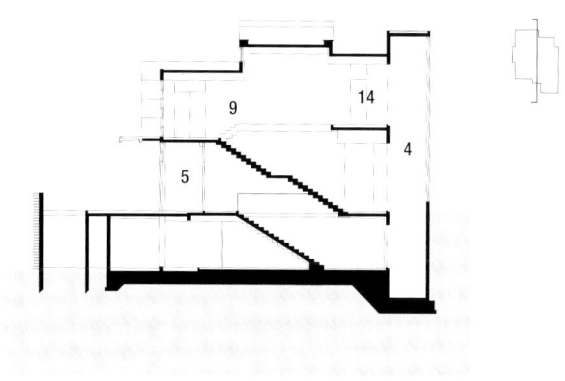

LONG SECTION

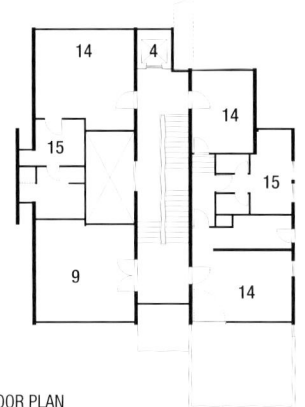

FIRST-FLOOR PLAN

NORTHWEST ELEVATION

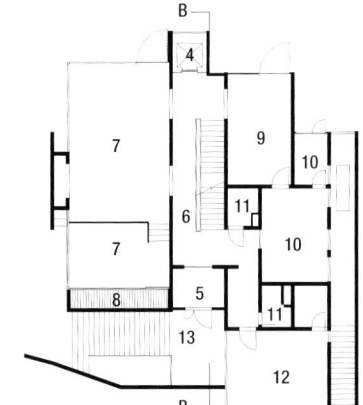

GROUND-FLOOR PLAN

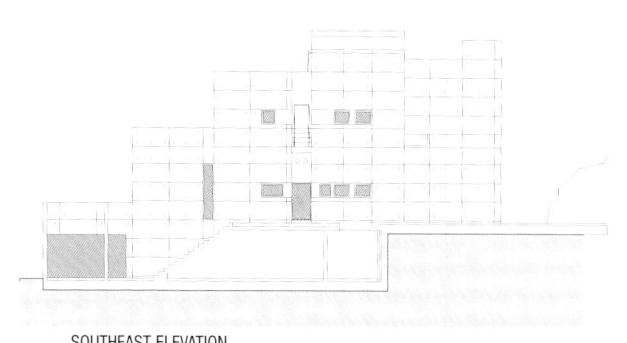

SOUTHEAST ELEVATION

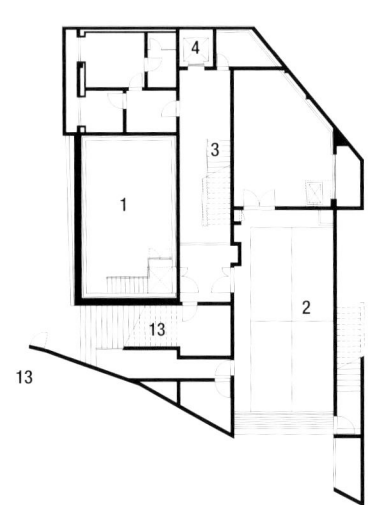

BASEMENT FLOOR PLAN

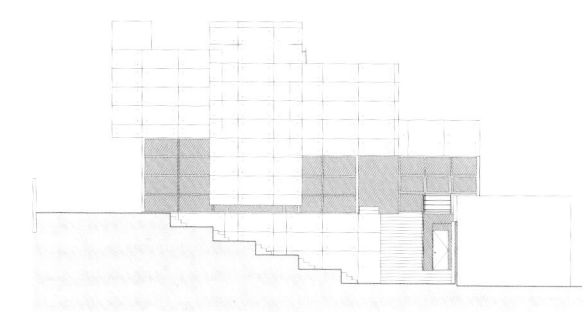

SOUTHWEST ELEVATION

1 Storage
2 Parking
3 Interior staircase
4 Elevator
5 Entrance
6 Hall
7 Living room
8 Loggia
9 Office
10 Kitchen
11 Toilets
12 TV room
13 Pedestrian access
14 Bedroom
15 Bathroom

17

JEAN-MICHEL WILMOTTE LEE HOUSE

JEAN-MICHEL WILMOTTE

PANGYO RESIDENCE

This 104,300-square-foot (9,690-square-meter) luxury apartment complex, set in Kyungkido, which is a southern suburb of the South Korean capital, consists of seven buildings, each with four levels, for a total of 36 apartments, and includes basement garages. The reinforced concrete buildings make use of white Carrara marble and traditional Korean black brick on the ground.

Working again with the landscape architects Neveux-Rouyer, who proposed a sophisticated combination of water and greenery for the 2.5-acre (one-hectare) site, Jean-Michel Wilmotte was associated here with the same entrepreneur who was responsible for the Gana Art Center. The prestige of the French architect's name in South Korea is such that 17 of the apartments were sold to sports personalities, actors, dancers, visual artists, and film producers after a presentation given by Wilmotte prior to construction.

The upscale apartments, each of which has a floor area of approximately 2,150 square feet (200 square meters) have controlled access with a concierge, a fitness center, and shared services. The buildings are scattered on the site, some standing along a main axis, while others are perpendicular to it. The four smallest structures are paired, with one apartment per level. The first pair of buildings near the entrance form a monumental arch in the axis of the composition. The second two are aligned perpendicularly to one side and are serviced by a shared gallery. The three largest buildings initiate and close the alignment, each having two apartments per level, serviced by a shared landing. On both sides of the central alley, clusters of bamboo spring up from the ground, passing through long shafts that bring daylight and natural ventilation into the garage. From automobile to apartment, the itinerary unfolds in several sequences always in contact with plants and landscape. The ascent in the 180-degree glazed lifts begins at a wall of water produced by the overflow of the pool above, in which some of the buildings are set. On each landing, the apartments are accessed via a footbridge-terrace towering above the residence and its landscaped grounds. Each apartment is designed like a villa in a garden, and most of them are open on all sides.

Location Seoul, South Korea
Completion date 2005
Area 104,300 ft² (9,690 m²)

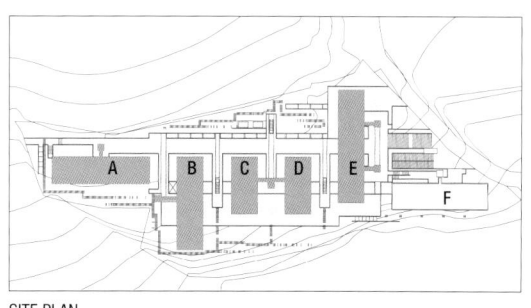

SITE PLAN

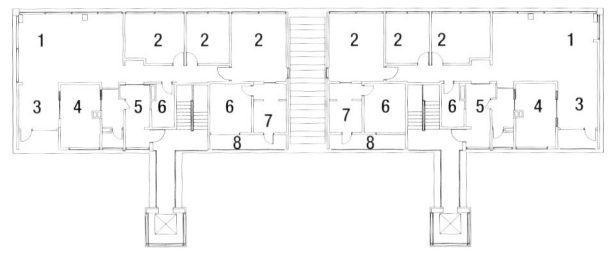
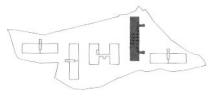

BUILDING D: THIRD-FLOOR PLAN

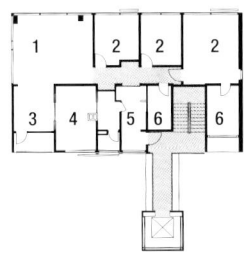
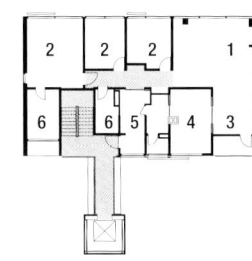
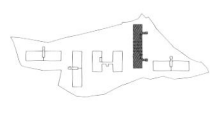

BUILDING D: SECOND-FLOOR PLAN

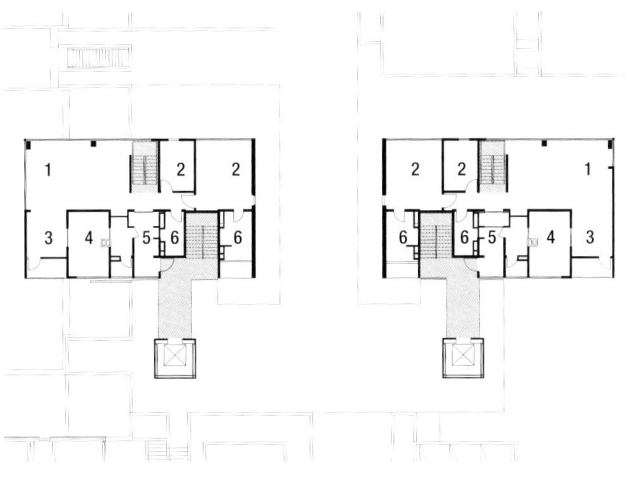

1 Living room
2 Bedroom
3 Dining room
4 Kitchen
5 Entrance
6 Bathroom
7 Dressing room
8 Balcony
9 Fitness center
10 Parking
11 Services

BUILDING D: GROUND-FLOOR PLAN

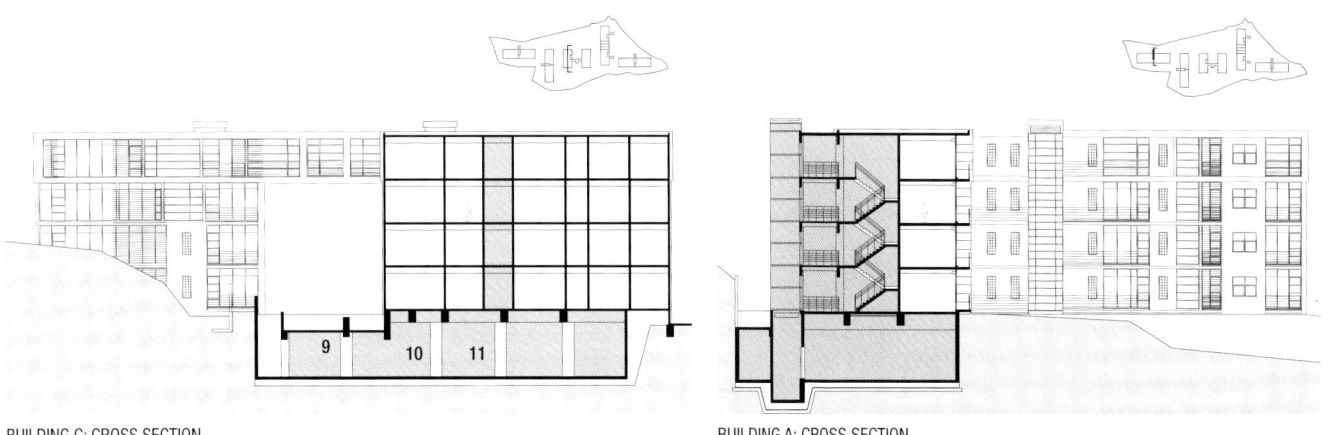

BUILDING C: CROSS SECTION

BUILDING A: CROSS SECTION

23

JEAN-MICHEL WILMOTTE PANGYO RESIDENCE

JEAN-MICHEL WILMOTTE   PANGYO RESIDENCE

JEAN-MICHEL WILMOTTE

SIGNAL TOWER

The Signal Tower was a project for a 930-feet-high (284-meter-high) mixed-use building located in the Défense business area, which is in the axis of the Champs-Elysées in Paris. With a total floor area of 1,237,850 square feet (115,000 square meters), the ecological tower was to include offices (31 floors), apartments (10 floors, 60 apartments), a hotel (24 floors, 230 rooms, and 40 suites), tourist residences (12 stories, 150 residences), shops and public facilities (five floors).

With its base almost entirely (some 80 percent) accessible to the public, the design sought to free up a maximum area at ground level to encourage pedestrians to cross through it. The three independent elements that constitute the tower are placed on a shared hub. They are imagined like glazed pillars, swirling towards the sky, seeking, meeting, and eventually separating without losing sight of each other. The rotation of the tower's plan accentuates the concept of a 'signal' in multiple directions, while the angled aspect of the volumes makes them stand out clearly in an environment where every other tower is straight with the exception of some angled or rounded tops. The result is a strong yet delicate and open architecture, which presents an ambitious solution to contemporary architectural, functional, and ecological needs.

In 2008, the Signal Tower was presented as the first high-rise in the world to use natural ventilation (80 percent), while producing one-third of its own energy. The energy production of the tower would be principally from three sources: geothermal, wind, and photovoltaic panels. Rainwater recycling is also part of the scheme, as is careful calculation based on the triangular footprint to moderate solar gain, while providing maximum natural light. Two-thirds of the site at La Défense was to become the largest green space in the district, or for that matter in any significant urban business district in the world. The Signal Tower was presented as a fully financed operation with existing public transport connections and in a spirit of integration into the heart of the city as a place of exchange and openness.

Location La Défense, Paris, France
Competition date 2008
Area 1,237,850 ft² (115,000 m²)

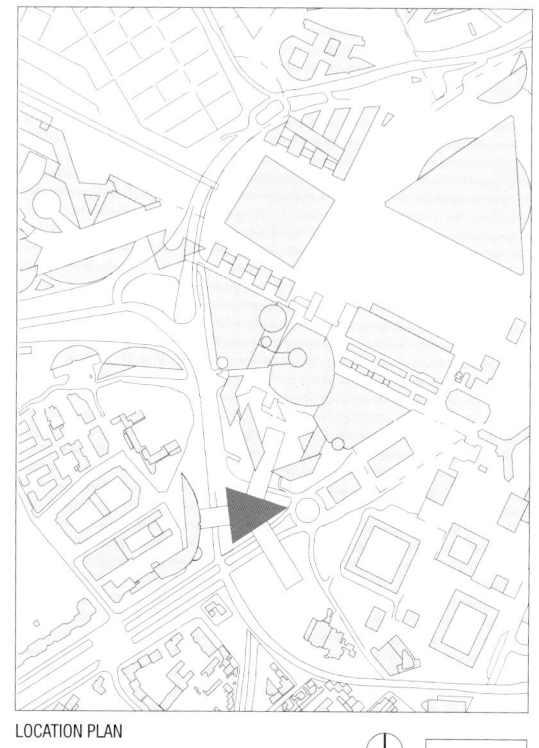

LOCATION PLAN

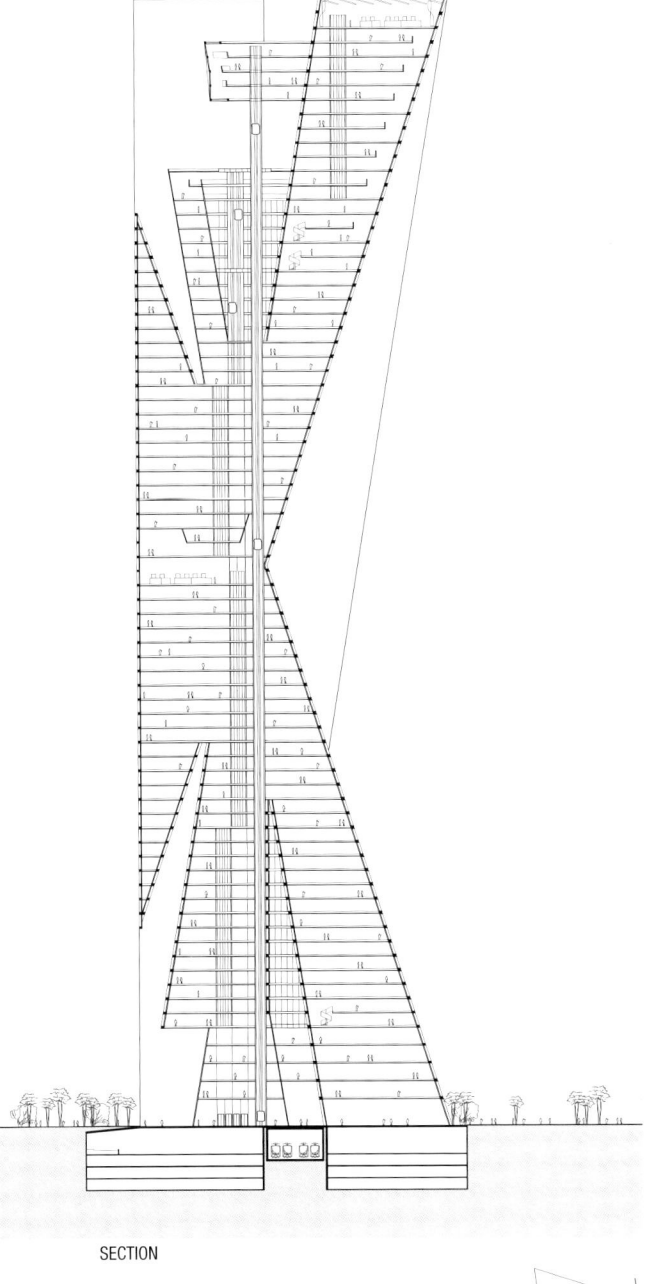

SECTION

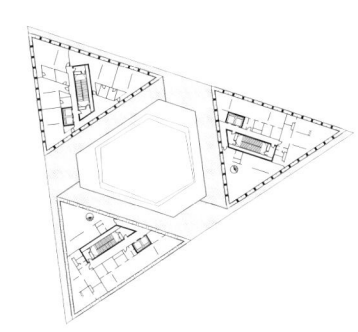

APARTMENTS FLOOR PLAN (LEVEL 74)

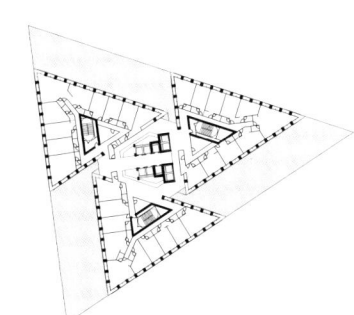

HOTEL FLOOR PLAN (LEVEL 57)

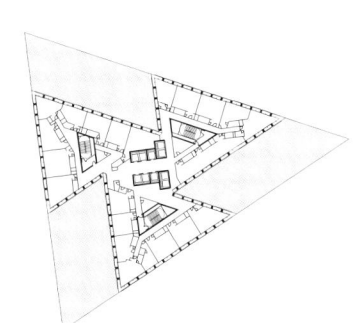

TOURIST RESIDENCE FLOOR PLAN (LEVEL 51)

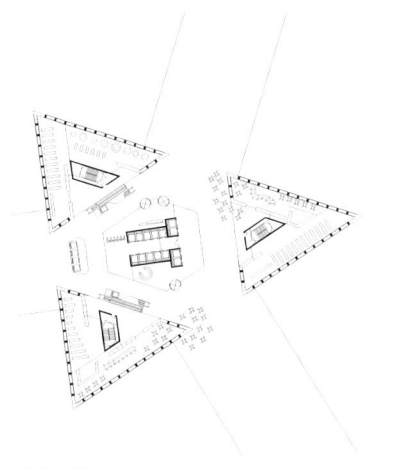

SITE PLAN

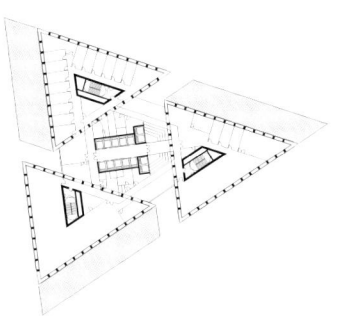

OFFICES FLOOR PLAN (LEVEL 12)

JEAN-MICHEL WILMOTTE

BRAIN AND SPINE INSTITUTE

Located in the 13th arrondissement of Paris in the Pitié-Salpêtrière University Hospital, the Brain and Spine Institute is a center for research and treatment of pathologies of the brain and spinal cord. The 246,495-square-foot (22,900-square-meter) building is a reinforced concrete post-and-beam structure with a gray tinted glass curtain wall. It contains laboratories, patient bedrooms, a human imaging area and offices with half the space devoted to research laboratories. Teaching and training areas include a 180-seat amphitheater.

A major goal of the Institute is to achieve a reduction of the time needed to translate the results of research into clinical applications for patients. It is located close to three buildings housing consultations and hospitalization facilities for the treatment of nervous-system disorders: neurosurgery and neuroradiology, neurology and neuropathology, and psychiatry. The luminous eight-story building with two basement levels provides better flow of communication between floors as well as a flexible infrastructure system adapted to the needs of the research groups. The main entrance is recessed between the two wings of the H-plan building.

The architects deliberately rejected more conventional plans in order to create wide transparent corridors as places to discuss and unwind. The base of the building was designed to allow communication with the future Endocrinology and Nutrition Center planned for the neighboring site. In the past, the different types of research being conducted in different fields (including molecular and cellular biology, neurophysiology, cognitive sciences, and therapy) were too isolated from each other. The multi-disciplinary approach taken by the Institute is a vital innovation in research. The Pitié-Salpêtrière University Hospital offers access to no less than 20,000 healthcare team members, a total of 2,000 beds, and treats more than 100,000 patients suffering from nervous-system disorders every year.

Location Paris, France
Completion date 2010
Area 246,495 ft² (22,900 m²)

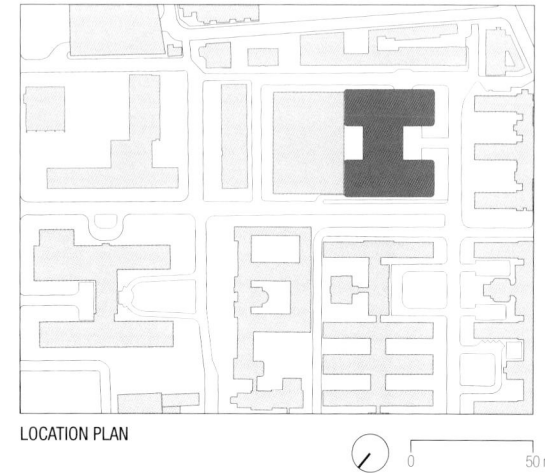

LOCATION PLAN

WEST ELEVATION

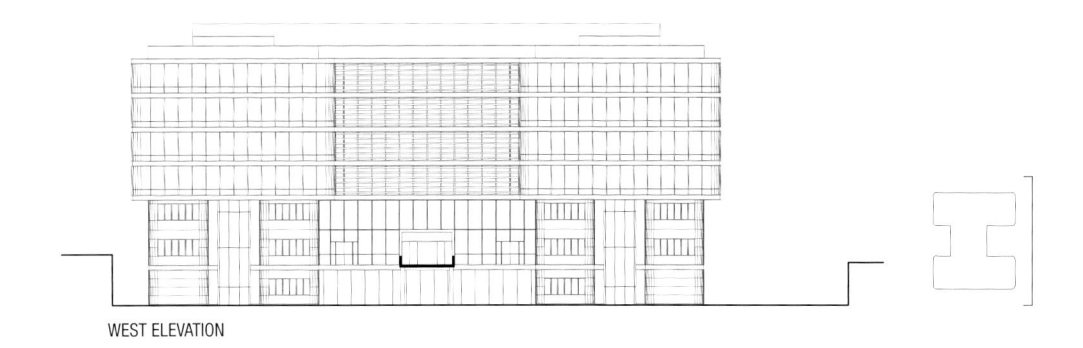

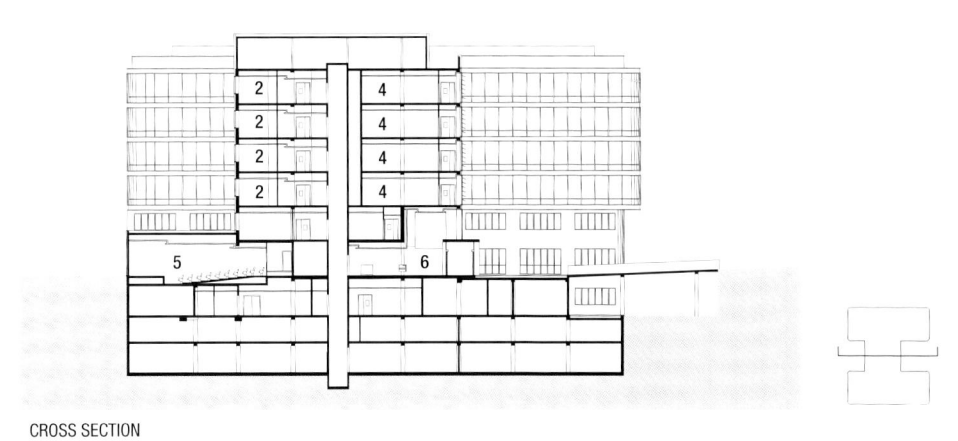

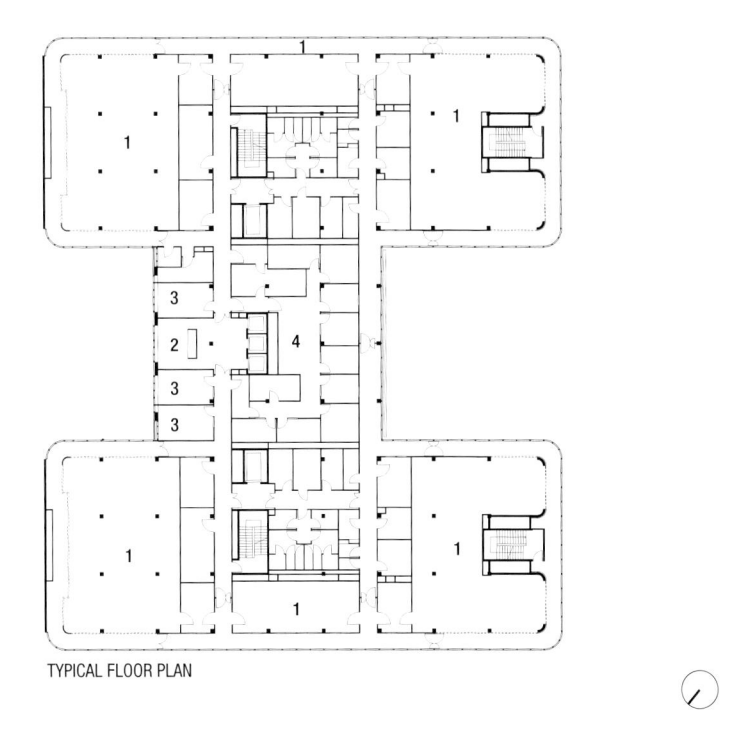

CROSS SECTION

TYPICAL FLOOR PLAN

1 Modular laboratories
2 Staff break room
3 Meeting room
4 Technical platforms
5 Auditorium
6 Reception

0   10 m

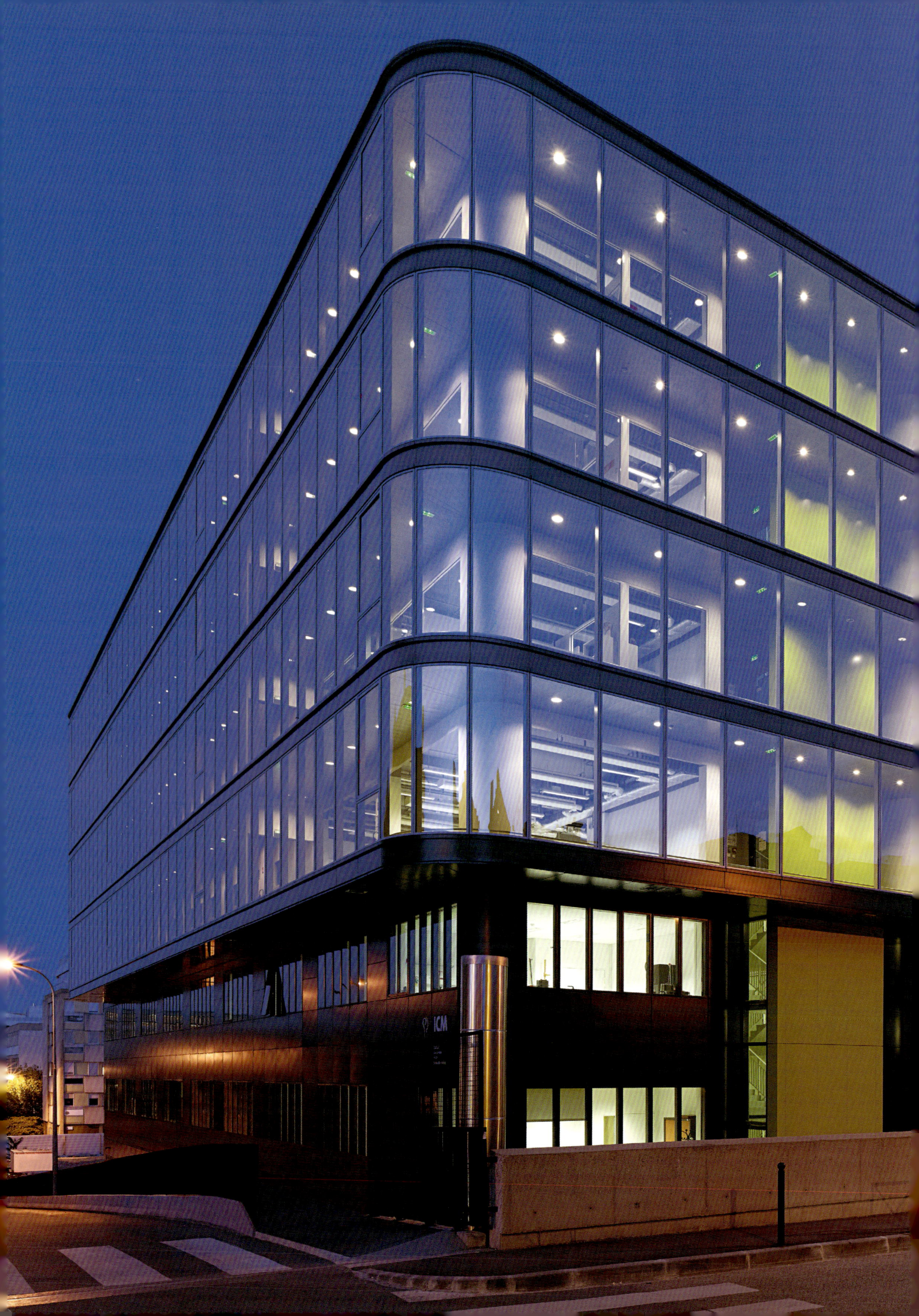
ICM

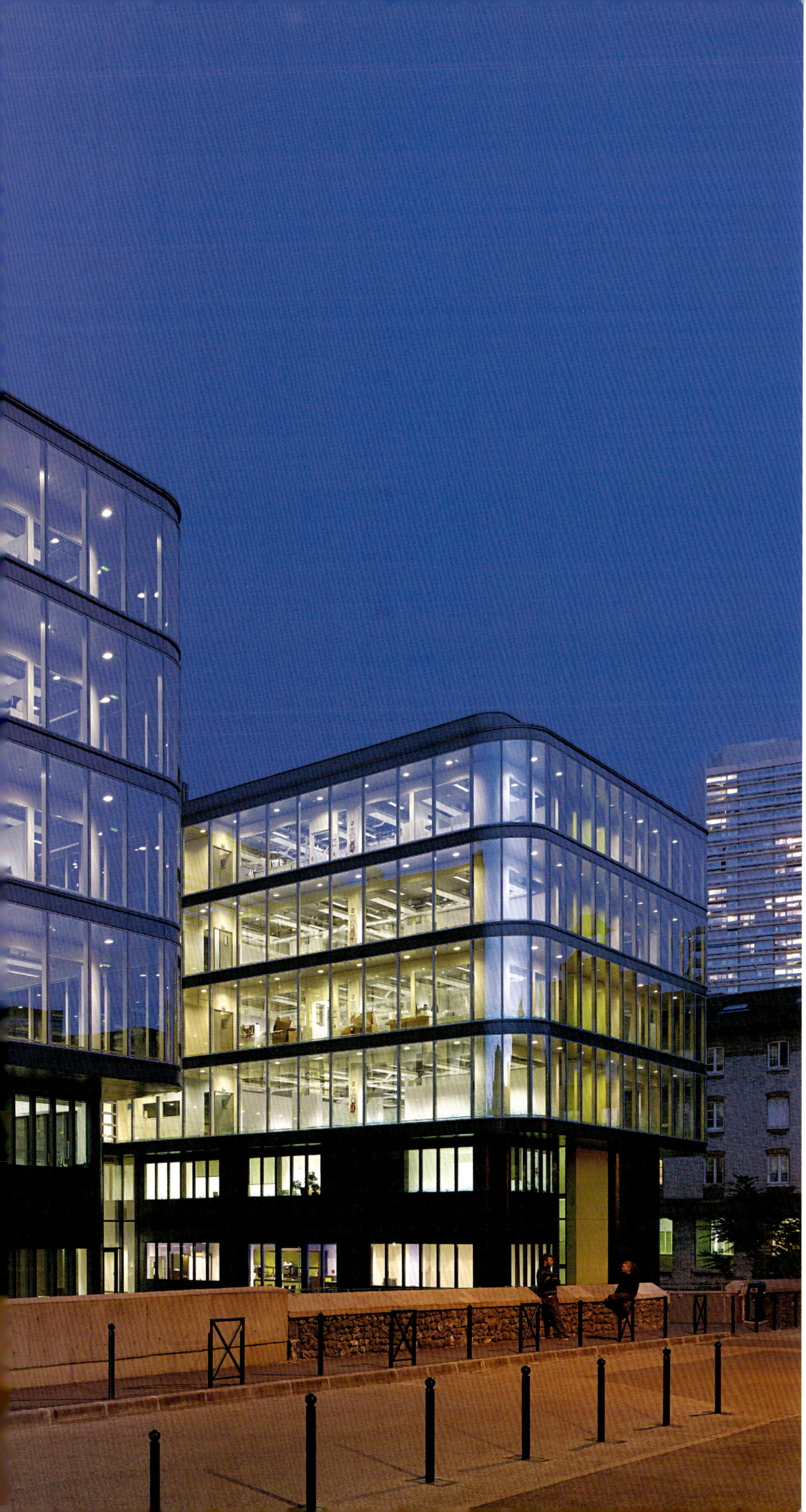

JEAN-MICHEL WILMOTTE BRAIN AND SPINE INSTITUTE

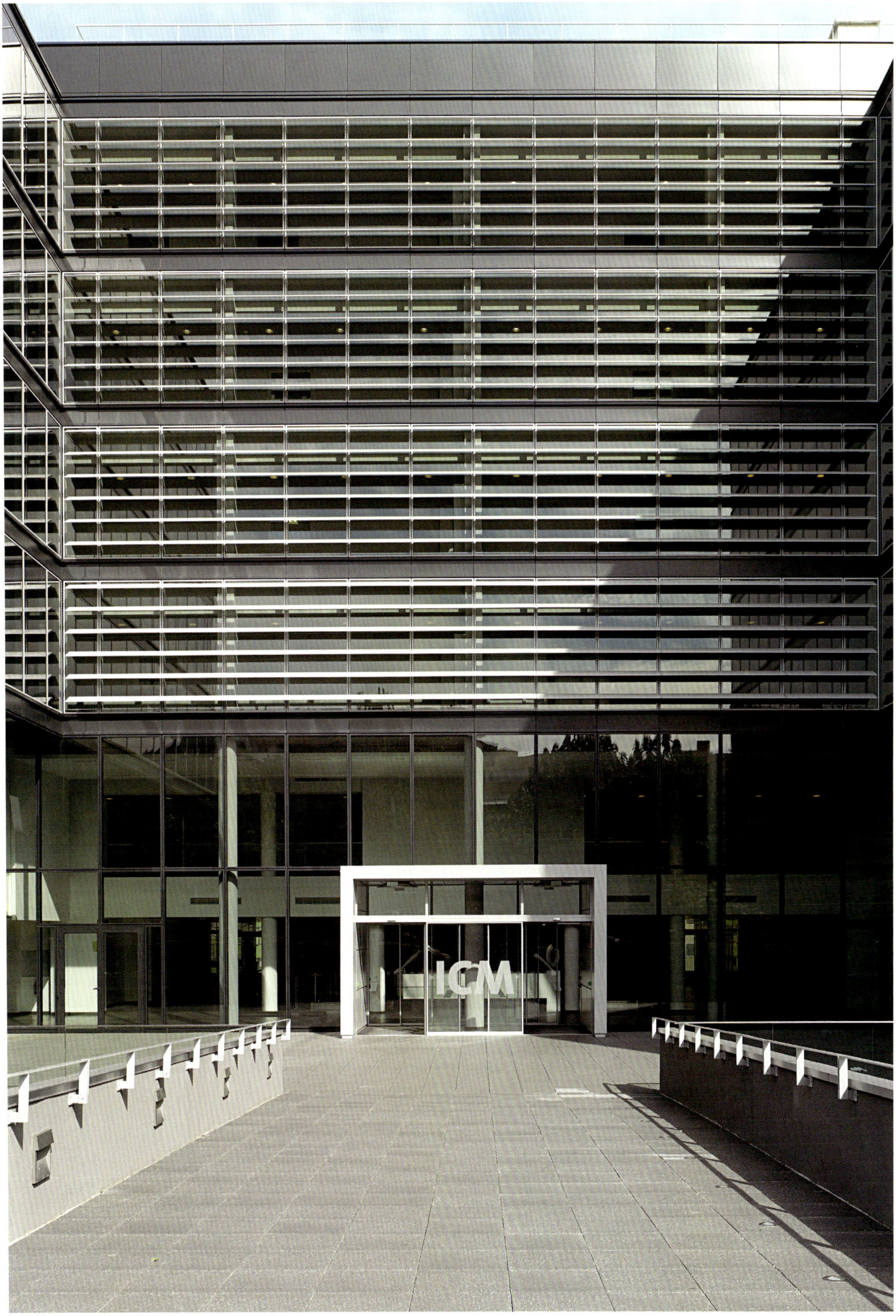
ICM

JEAN-MICHEL WILMOTTE

MONTE CARLO VIEW TOWER

A 20-story high-rise topped by a triplex apartment, the reinforced concrete of this building is clad with aluminum honeycomb composite panels, stainless-steel profiles, and beige Moleanos natural stone. The apartments feature bow windows with glass and metal railings. The top story of the tower features two sweeping windows, which underscore the landmark effect of the architecture as seen from the eastern approach to Monaco, while offering residents of the top floors a magnificent view of 'the Rocks,' the site of the palace of the Prince of Monaco. The design is thus meant to be legible from a distance, while offering a more intimate and personal expression closer in.

There is a six-level, 129-car parking area below the tower, and a retail space at ground level. Located near Monaco's Exotic Garden in a dense neighborhood of highly diverse buildings, Monte Carlo View rises to a height of 200 feet (61 meters), including three floors of office space and 15 floors of apartments, for a total of 107,640 square feet (10,000 square meters) in floor space. The highly contemporary edifice nevertheless respects Monaco's classic building traditions in terms of siting (aligned with the street) and composition (distinct base and attic levels). The structure was designed for the noted local property development company Michel Pastor Groupe.

Location Monaco
Completion date 2012
Area 107,640 ft² (10,000 m²)

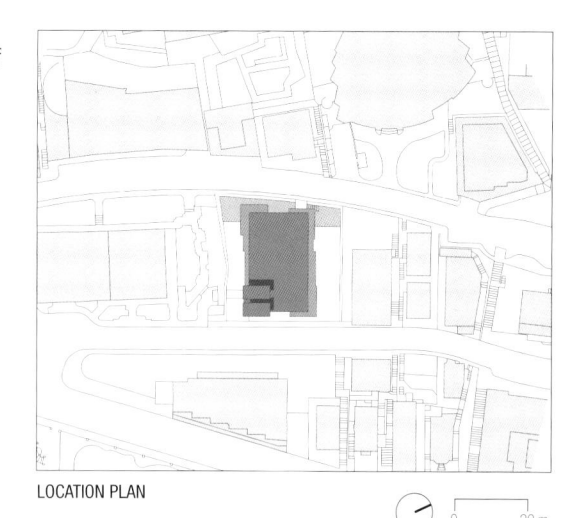

LOCATION PLAN

INSERTION SECTION

1 Entrance hall
2 Office
3 Office reception
4 Services
5 Car-park access
6 Garden
7 Bedroom
8 Living room
9 Dining room
10 Kitchen
11 Infinity-edge pool
12 Solarium
13 Summer kitchen
14 Ceiling space over living room

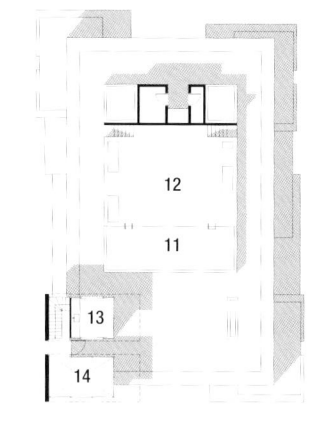

SEASIDE ELEVATION

GROUND-FLOOR PLAN

PENTHOUSE TERRACE FLOOR PLAN (LEVEL 20)

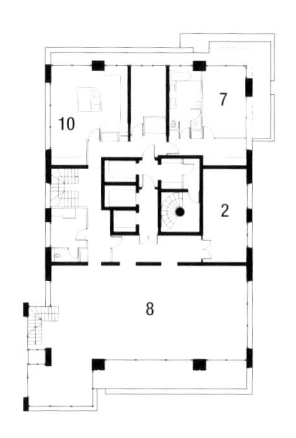

PENTHOUSE FLOOR PLAN (LEVEL 19)

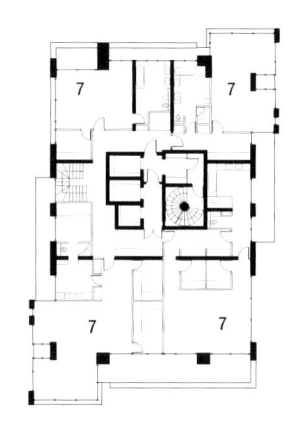

PENTHOUSE FLOOR PLAN (LEVEL 18)

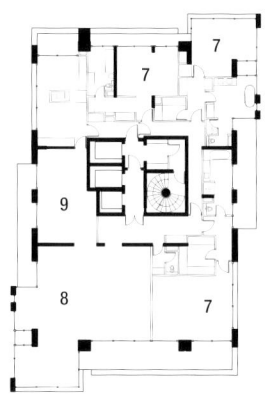

TYPICAL FLOOR PLAN

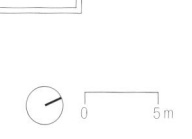

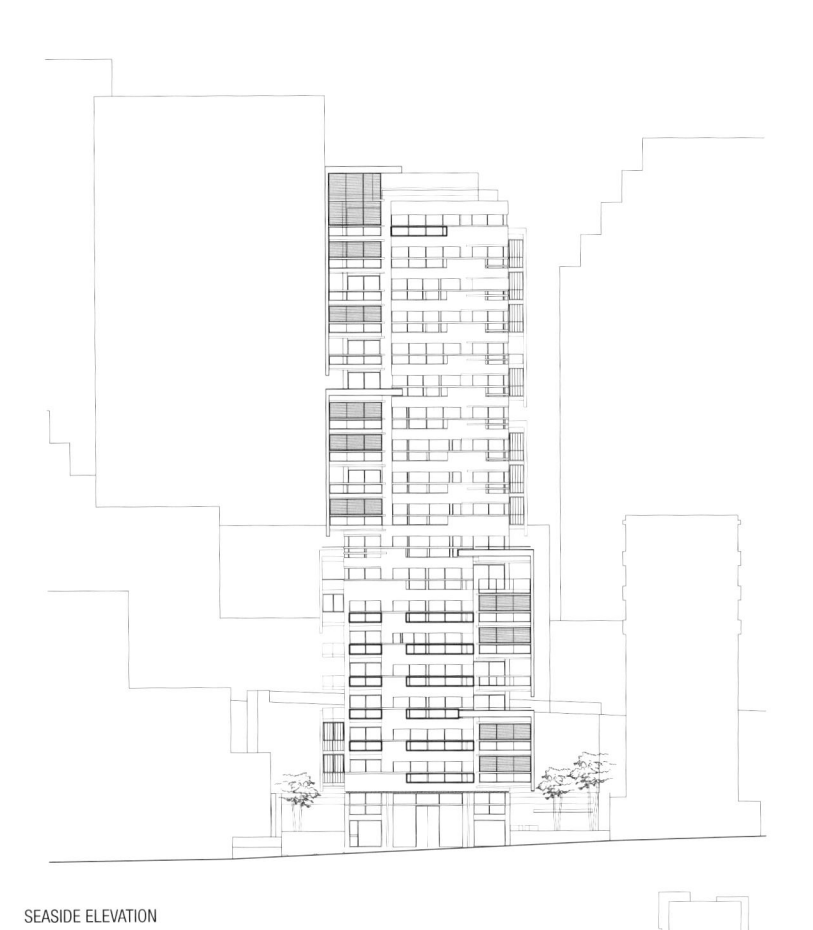

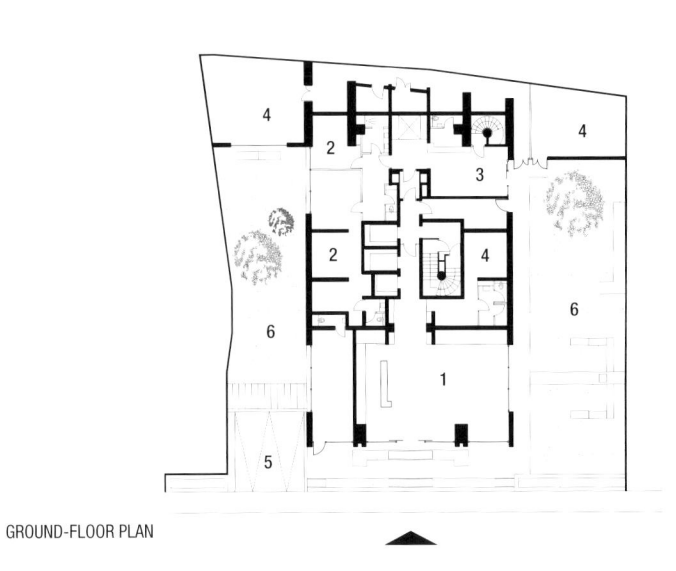

0   5 m

41

JEAN-MICHEL WILMOTTE   MONTE CARLO VIEW TOWER

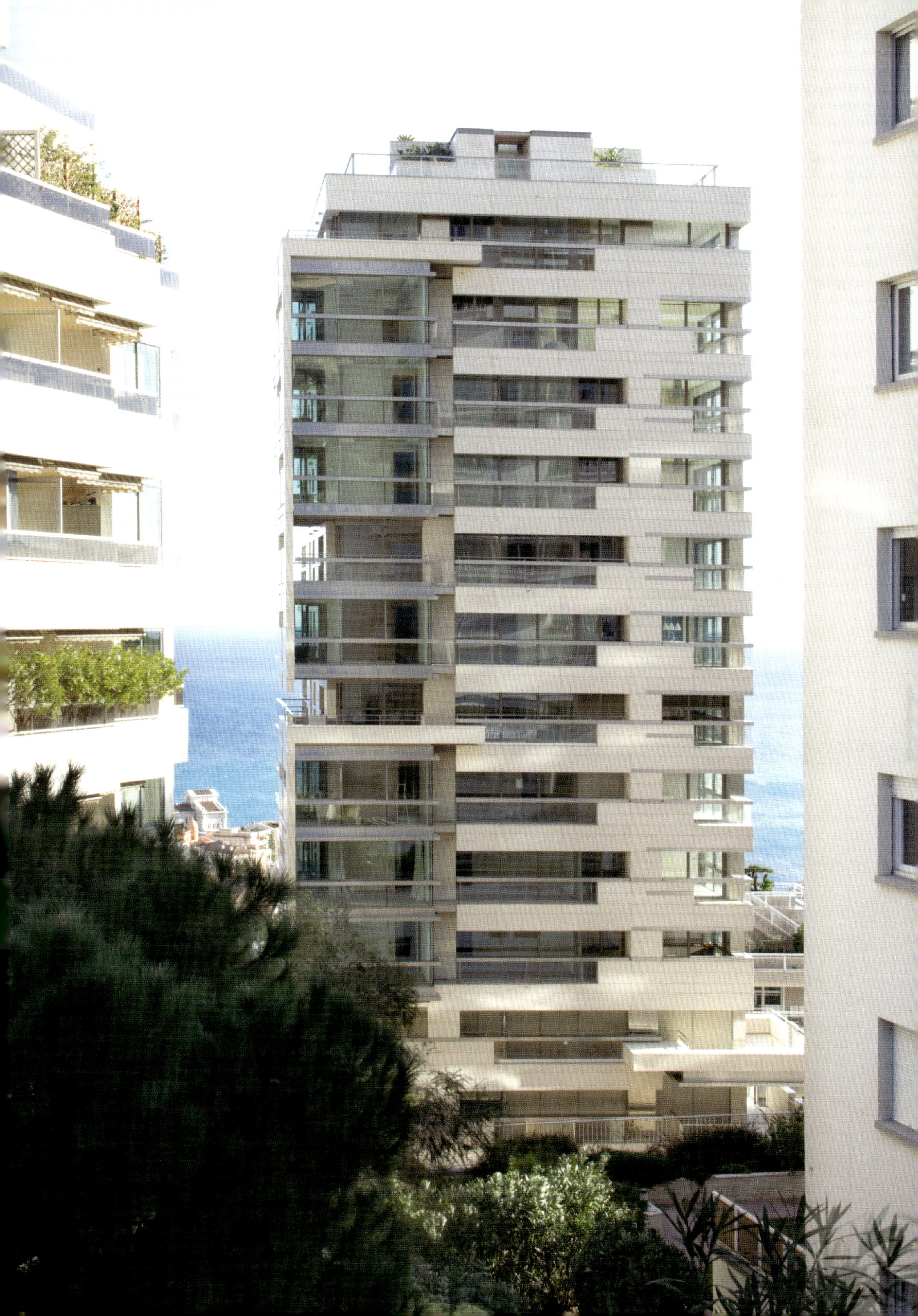

JEAN-MICHEL WILMOTTE

EPADESA CORPORATE HEADQUARTERS

This 161,460-square-feet (15,000-square-meter) low energy office building is located on the Place de la Croisée in Nanterre, near the Défense business district in the west of Paris. The reinforced concrete headquarters for the Défense development authority, EPADESA, has a load-bearing façade finished in aluminum, double-glazed windows with solar control, and wood decking.

The project is in the 'Terrasses of Nanterre' area, which is laid out over 17 similar plateaus developed in sequence, which become areas for leisurely strolls starting at the base of the Grande Arche de La Défense, and descending to the Seine. The office space of the building covers eight floors, with an internal restaurant on the ground floor, and two levels of parking below grade. The complex geometry of the site as well as the varying allowable building heights led to the design of a compact building, which exploits the capacity of the site fully, while respecting the neighboring projects.

The building appears as a metallic monolith, separated from its base by a transparent band of glass running around the entire volume at ground level. This band widens to a height of three floors near the entrance. The building was designed to exacting high-quality environmental standards, receiving the THPE EnR2005 (Very High Energy Performance), and BBC (Low Energy Consumption) rating. The study of the façades was particularly important in the process of obtaining these ratings. They play a primordial role in the environmental impact of the project, bringing a maximum level of light into the interior spaces, while simultaneously allowing light to reach neighboring buildings.

Location Nanterre, France
Completion date 2012
Area 161,460 ft² (15,000 m²)

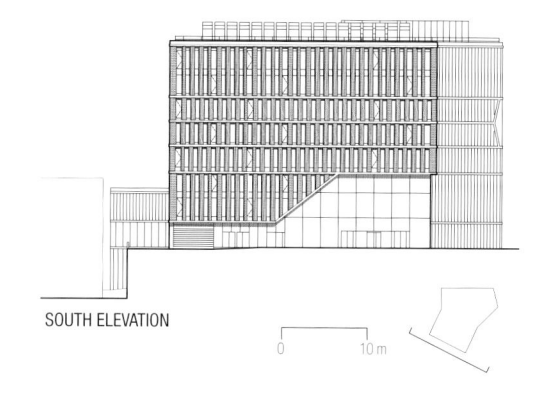

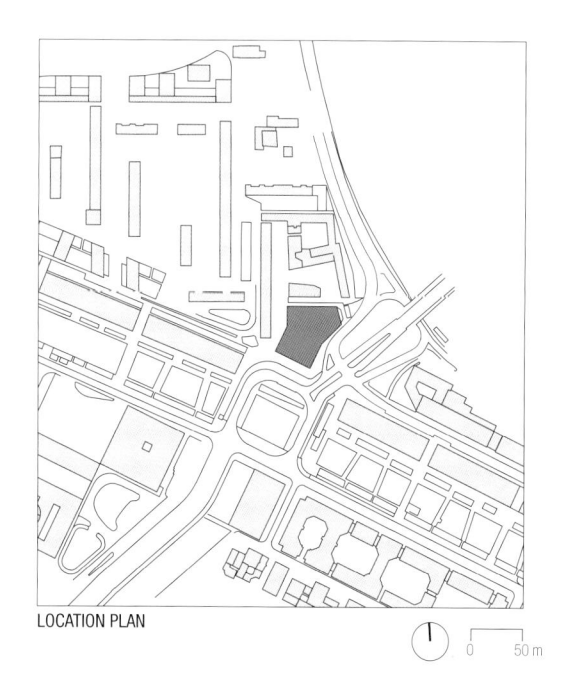

SOUTH ELEVATION

LOCATION PLAN

LONG SECTION

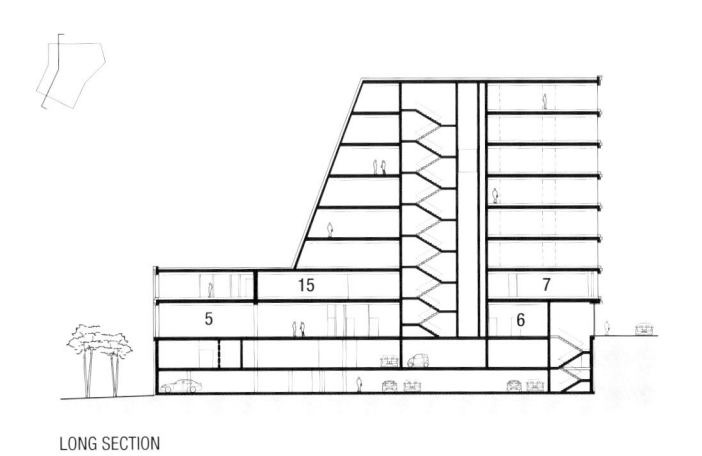

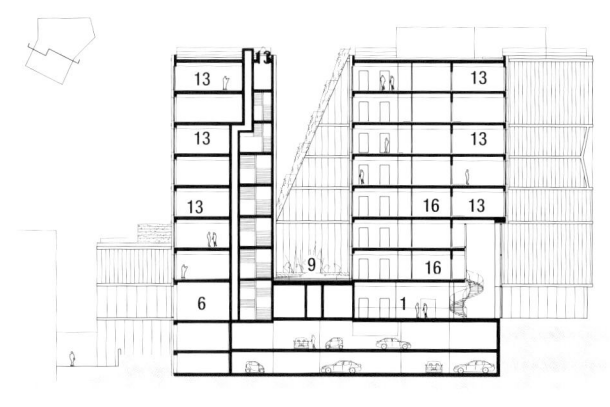

CROSS SECTION

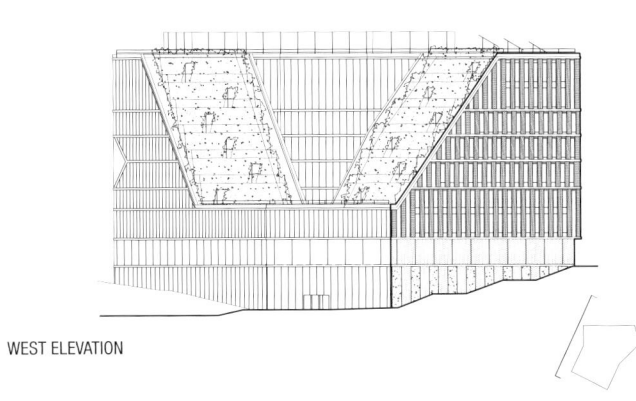

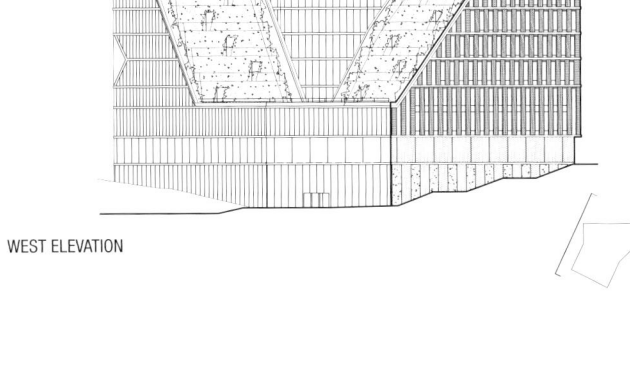

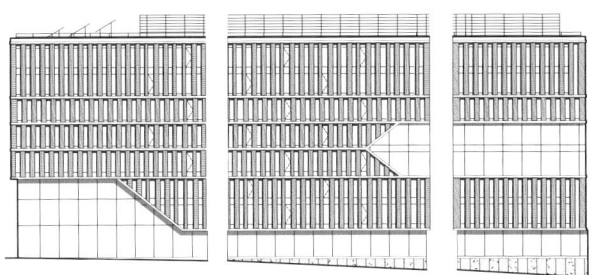

WEST ELEVATION

FIFTH-FLOOR PLAN

EAST ELEVATION

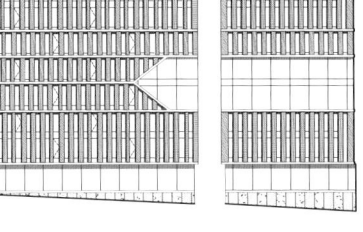

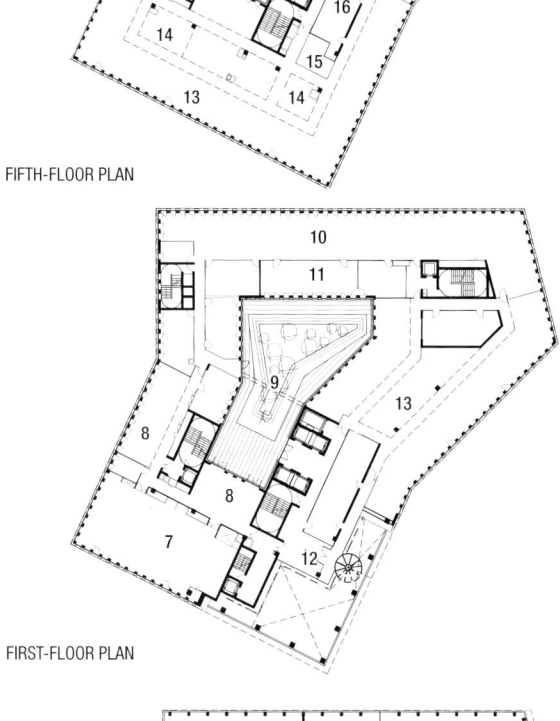

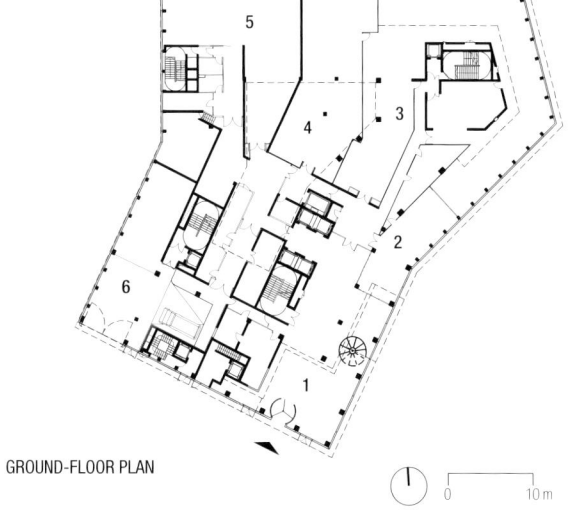

FIRST-FLOOR PLAN

GROUND-FLOOR PLAN

1 Entrance hall
2 Café
3 Restaurant
4 Kitchen
5 Exhibition gallery
6 Car-park access / deliveries
7 Auditorium
8 Foyer
9 Terrace (garden)
10 Business center
11 Executive restaurant
12 Business center access
13 Offices
14 Meeting room
15 Tea room
16 Toilets

0   10 m

JEAN-MICHEL WILMOTTE EPADESA CORPORATE HEADQUARTERS

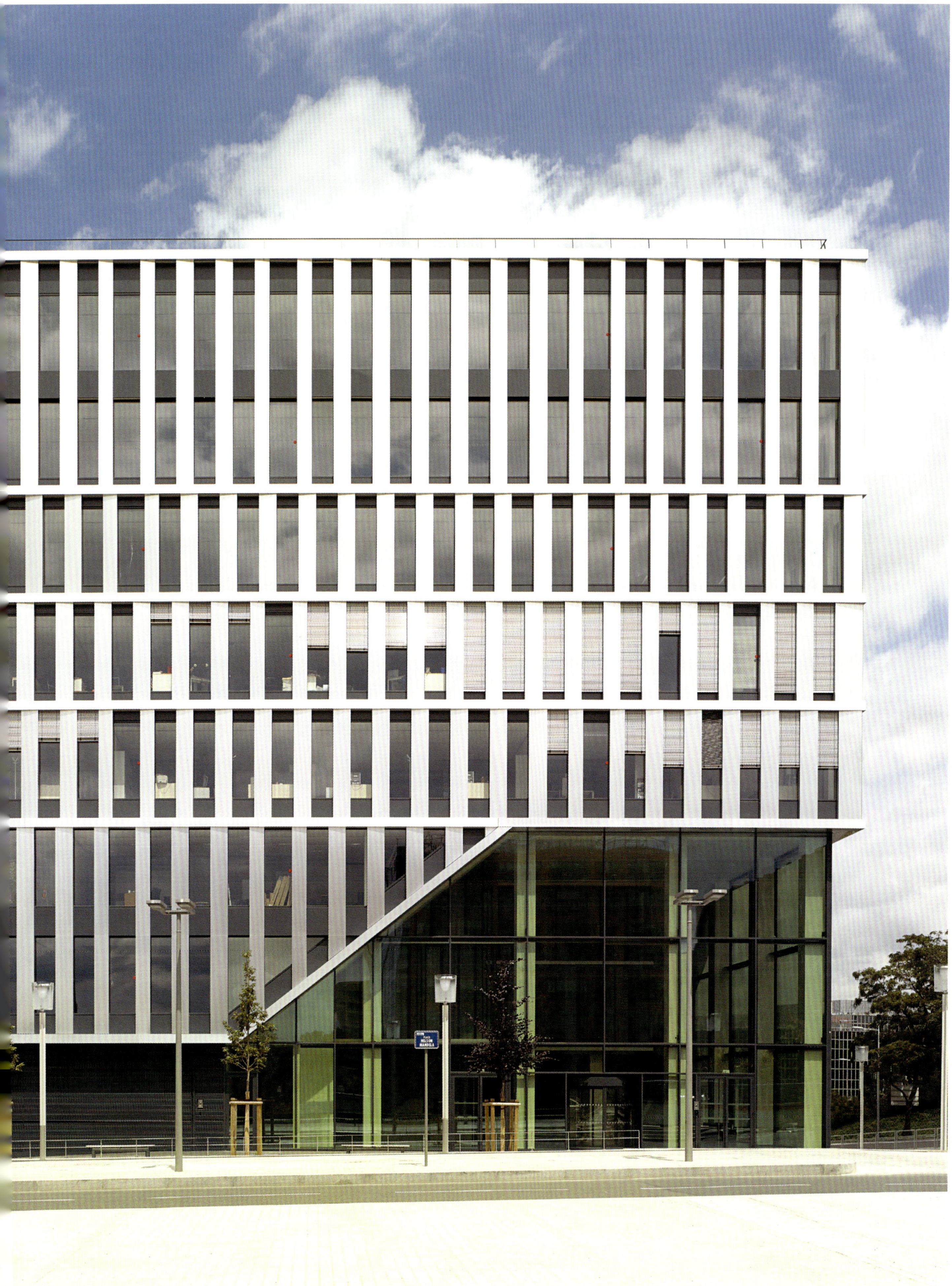

JEAN-MICHEL WILMOTTE

BARRISTERS TRAINING COLLEGE

A competition-winning project, the Barristers Training College for the Paris Court of Appeal (Ecole de Formation Professionnelle des barreaux de la Cour d'Appel de Paris) is intended for the professional training of lawyers for the Paris Court of Appeals. The 94,185-square-foot (8,750-square-meter) building is in stone, wood, glass, steel, aluminum and hammered concrete and was built on a brown-field site. It is 65 feet (20 meters) deep and is set between two corporate-type buildings. It has a central garden that measures 98 feet (30 meters) and a hall/foyer, open to three levels.

The space includes a 360-seat amphitheater and is overlooked by two mezzanines and balconies. The main façade is developed on three sides and is visible from surrounding streets, the RER C train line, tramway, roads along the riverbank, and the Parisian ring road and bypass. The architecture of the building relies on the simplicity of the volume, which results in part from local building regulations. On the upper floors, the façades incorporate wooden slats behind a simple glazing, with double glazing inside.

The visibility of the building is accentuated by the softening of reflections thus obtained. These 'double skin,' triple-glazed frames are developed along 9-foot (2.7-meter) threads enclosing the Epicea (spruce) laminated wood—as high as one story, and with an interval of 11 inches (27 centimeters). The unvarnished wood acts to control humidity in the building, absorbing it when the air is humid and releasing humidity through the single openings at the bottom of each window block in dry conditions. Ultra-violet light slowly turns the wood to a honey color, giving an agreeable patina to the building and confirming the dynamic effects of light and shade.

Location Issy-les-Moulineaux, France
Completion date 2013
Area 94,185 ft^2 (8,750 m^2)

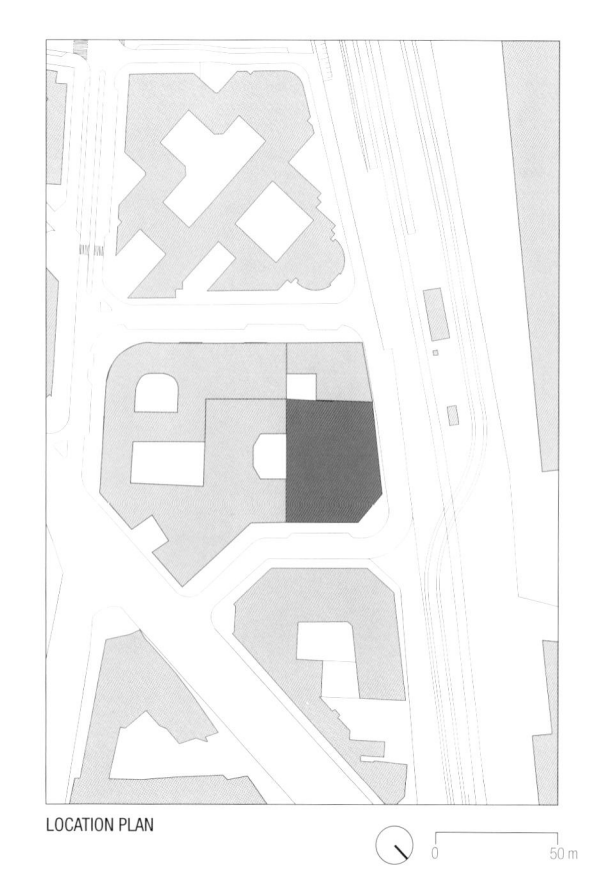

LOCATION PLAN

NORTH ELEVATION

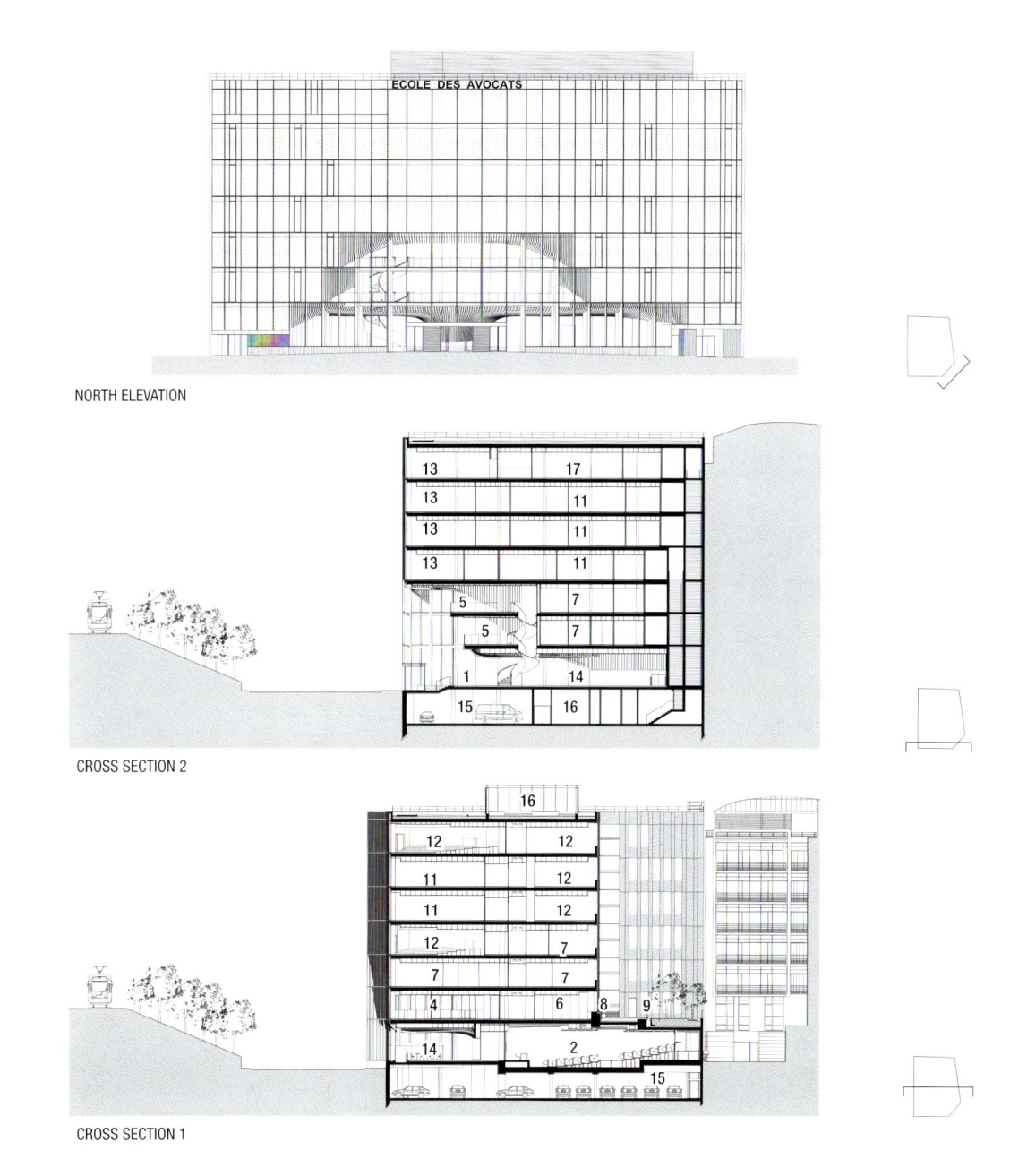

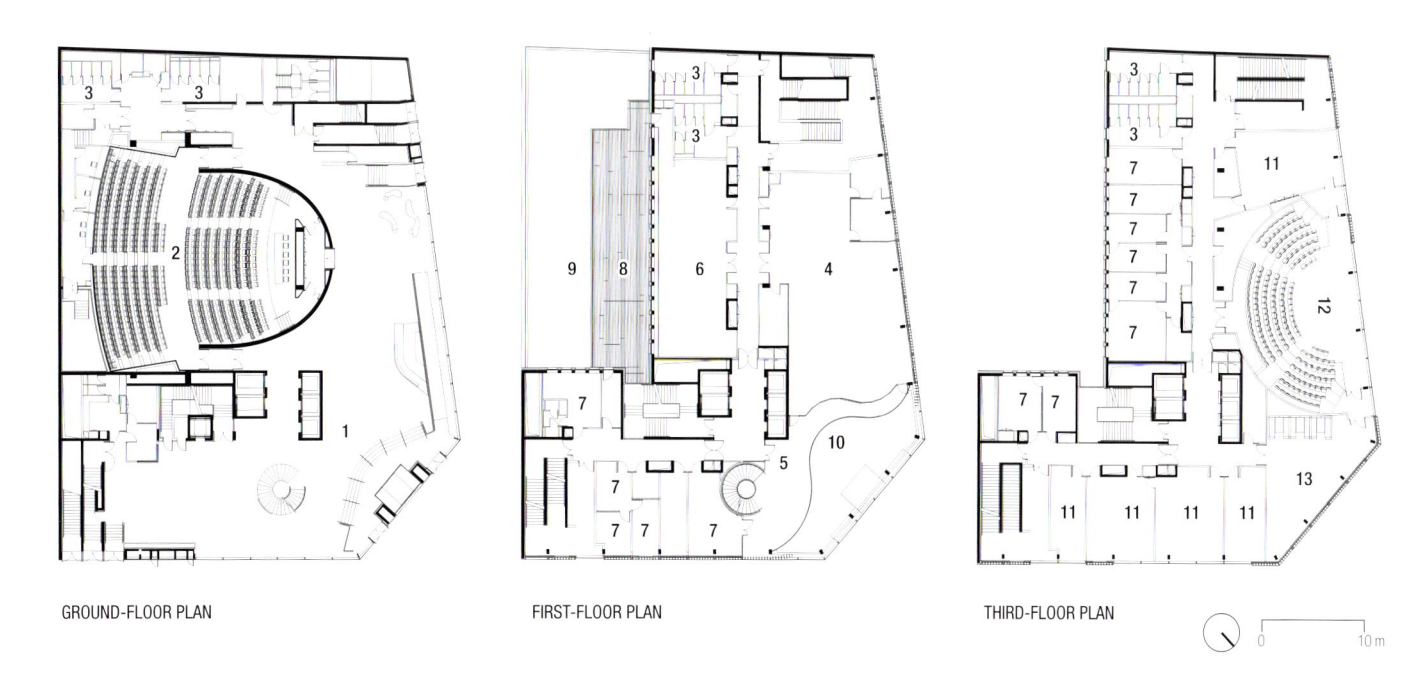

CROSS SECTION 2

CROSS SECTION 1

GROUND-FLOOR PLAN

FIRST-FLOOR PLAN

THIRD-FLOOR PLAN

1 Hall
2 Amphiteatre
3 Toilets
4 Library
5 Mezzanine
6 Café
7 Office
8 Terrace
9 Garden
10 Ceiling space over entrance hall
11 Classroom
12 Hemicycle
13 Break room
14 Reception
15 Parking
16 Services
17 Boardroom

JEAN-MICHEL WILMOTTE   BARRISTERS TRAINING COLLEGE

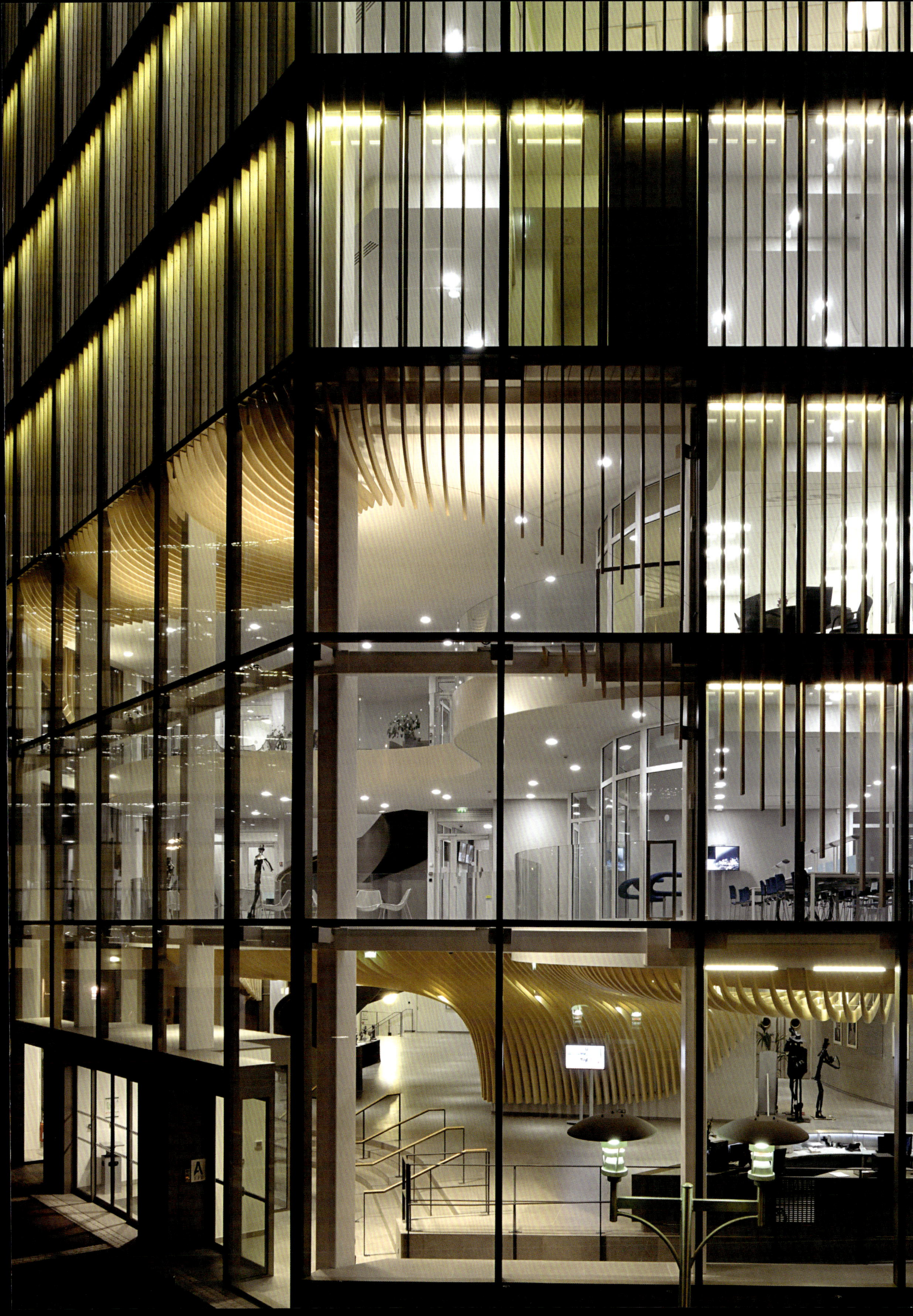

JEAN-MICHEL WILMOTTE BARRISTERS TRAINING COLLEGE

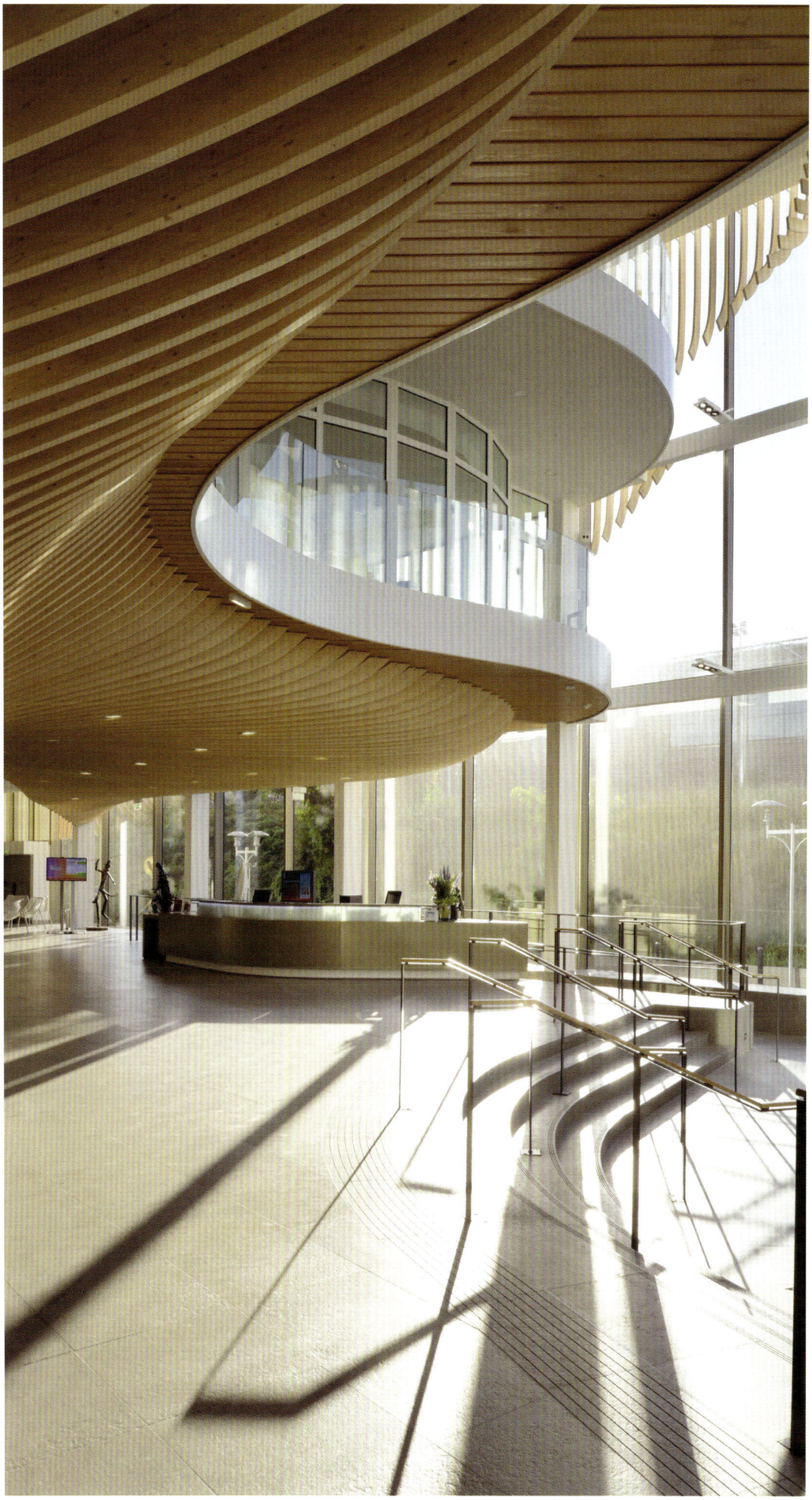

JEAN-MICHEL WILMOTTE

ARTS CENTER, INTERNATIONAL SCHOOL OF GENEVA

The Arts Center includes a multi-use 350-seat auditorium, along with a 200-seat auditorium, exhibition areas intended to be open to the public, dedicated spaces for students to study and meet, modular classrooms, rehearsal rooms, recording and percussion studios, a multimedia center, and conference rooms. The total area of the complex is 50,915 square feet (4,730 square meters). The main construction materials are concrete and Linit U-Profile glass (Lamberts).

The interior design is sober with some materials intentionally left in their natural state. There is little color, a decision made in order to foreground the work of the students. Linear lighting systems in the circulation spaces accentuate the graphic, structured aspect of the spaces. A double-height wall in oak in the foyer marks the presence of the auditorium, where wood is also used.

The project is intended to integrate the school with the cultural and artistic events of the city and the Canton of Geneva. The building was erected at La Grande Boissière near the heart of Geneva and close to the old city. The Art Center project was intended as the final stage of the transformation of the Grande Boissière campus. It plays a role as the component linking all the elements of the academic complex and creates a unified site. The Art Center is connected to the cafeteria, the sports field, and the Greek theater.

The building generates the space and infrastructure necessary to bring together the existing Art, Theater, and Music departments. As is most often the case in his work, Jean-Michel Wilmotte put an emphasis on transparency, lightness, conviviality, and nature, which are combined here as a metaphor for the creativity and innovative spirit of the students.

Location Geneva, Switzerland
Completion date 2014
Area 50,915 ft² (4,730 m²)

LOCATION PLAN

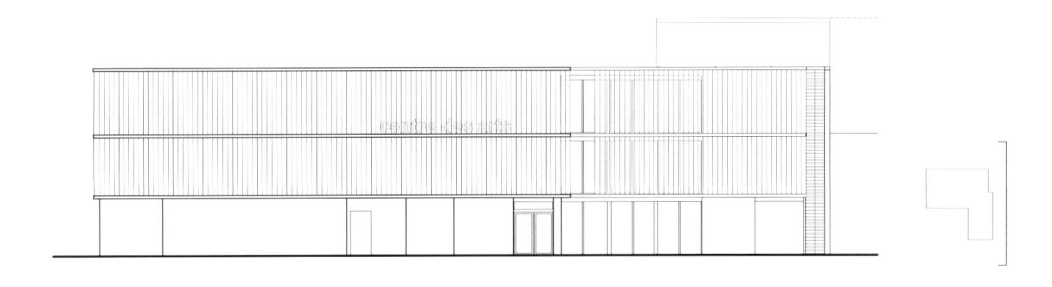

EAST ELEVATION

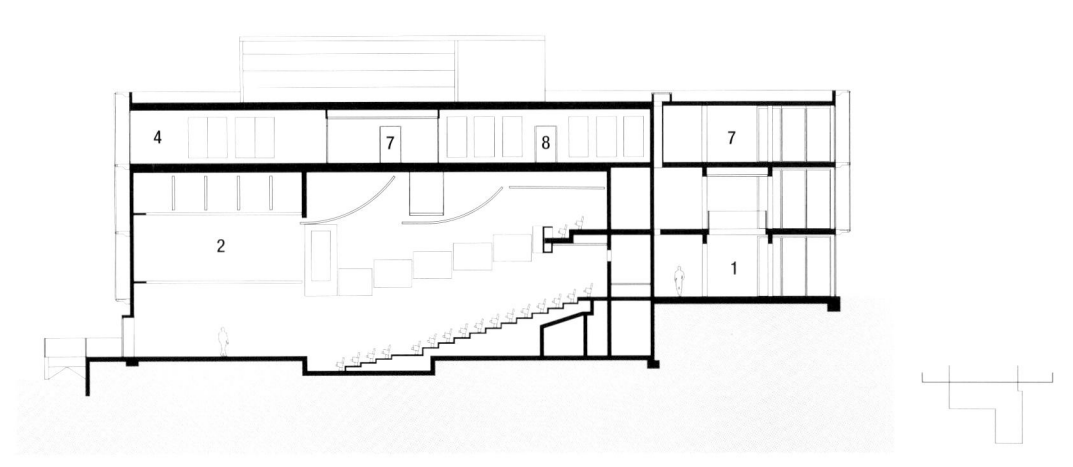

LONG SECTION

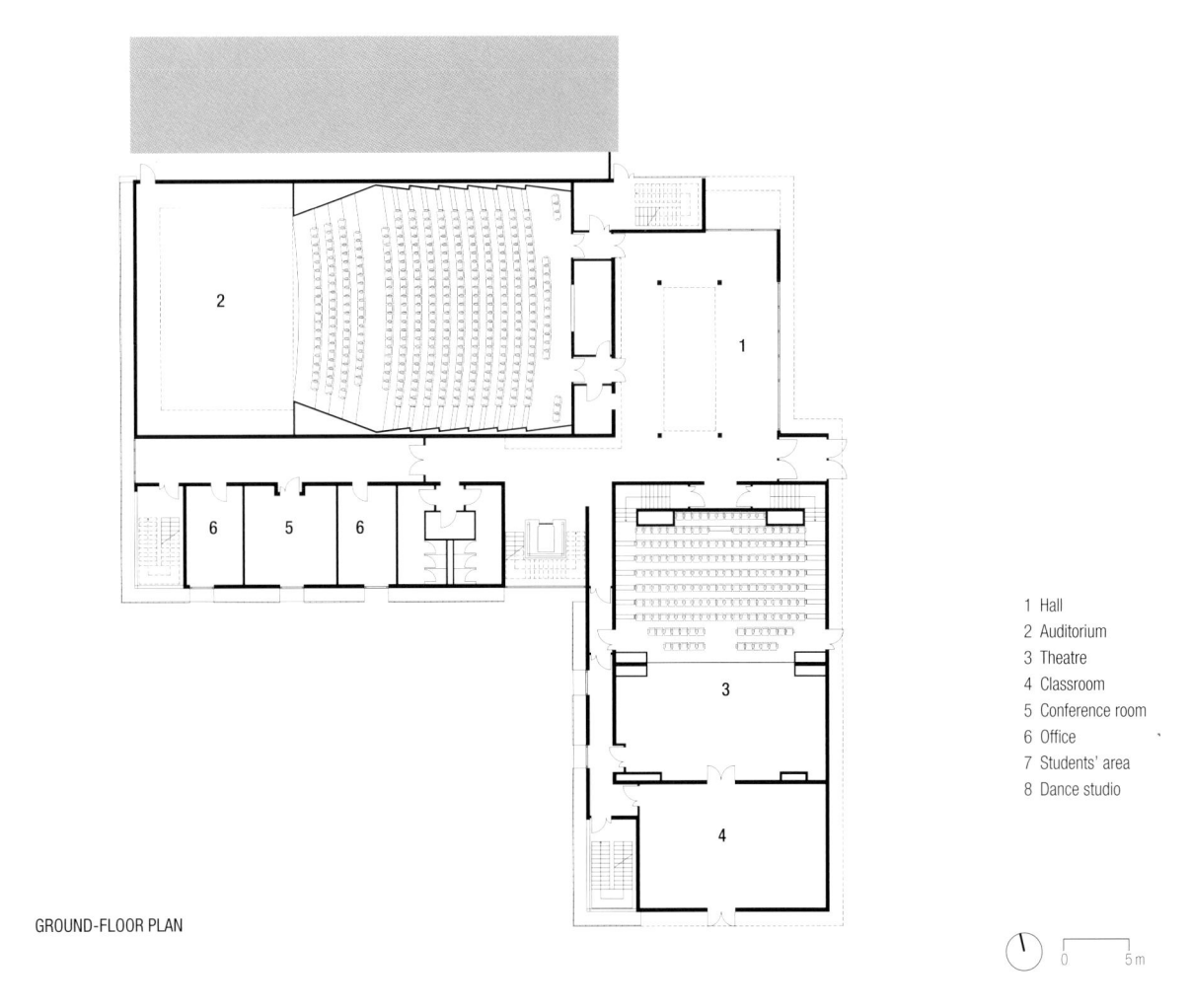

GROUND-FLOOR PLAN

1 Hall
2 Auditorium
3 Theatre
4 Classroom
5 Conference room
6 Office
7 Students' area
8 Dance studio

0 5 m

JEAN-MICHEL WILMOTTE   ARTS CENTER, INTERNATIONAL SCHOOL OF GENEVA

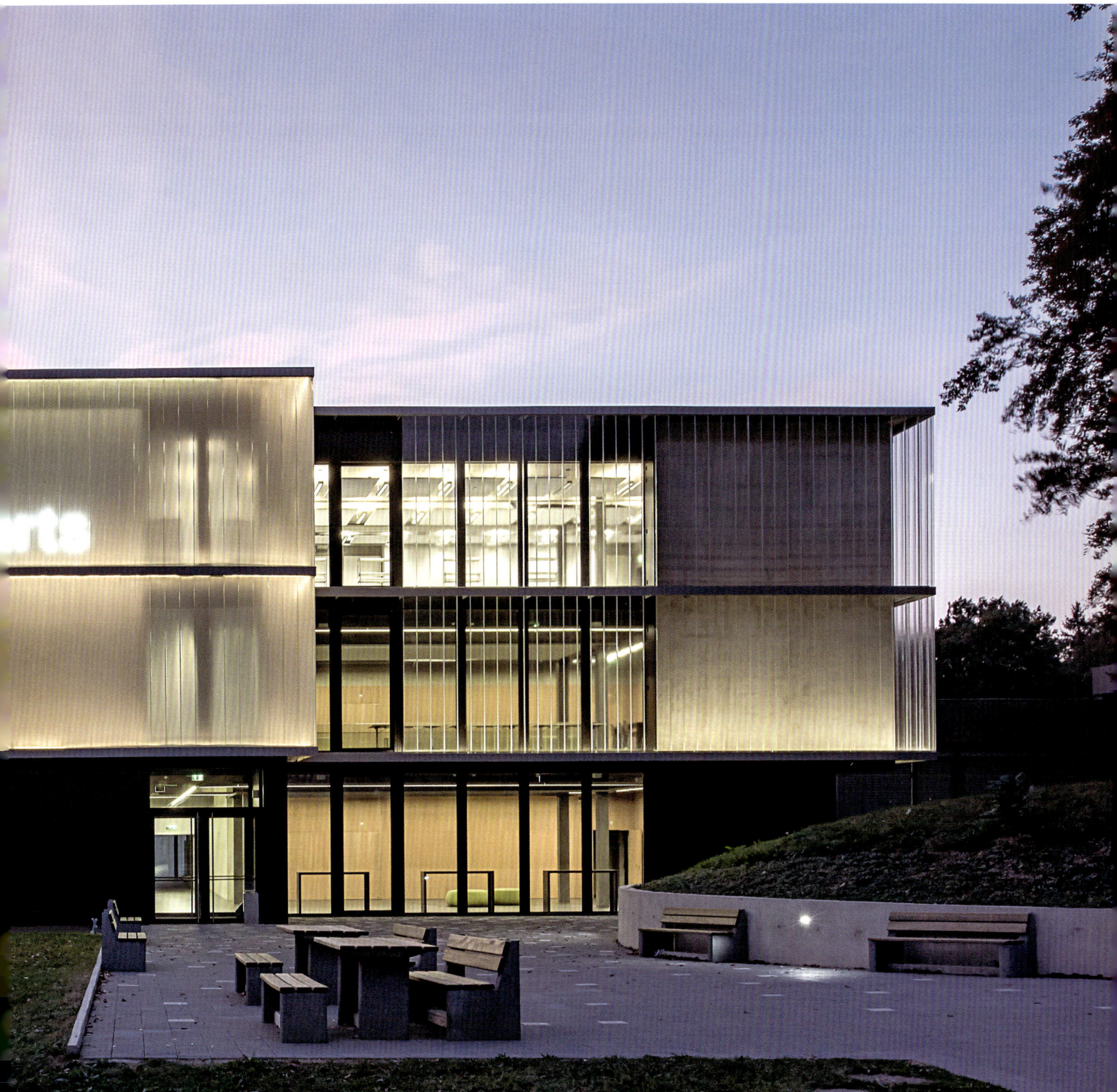

JEAN-MICHEL WILMOTTE

ALLIANZ RIVIERA STADIUM

The stadium is located in the Plaine du Var Eco-District of Nice. The project included a development plan based on retail, leisure, and food services. The plan was designed to work symbiotically with the stadium to create a coherent complex able to generate urban synergy, use, and energy. Set on a 35-acre (14-hectare) site, more than two-fifths of which was designated for residential construction, the construction cost of the 36,180-seat stadium was €217 million. Jean-Michel Wilmotte and his team won the 2010 competition and began construction in August 2011.

The complex uses more than 4,800 laminated timber sections and 6,000 laminated wood braces for a total of 141,260 cubic feet (4,000 cubic meters) of spruce wood. Lightness and transparency were key concepts that guided its design. No large structural elements interrupt the stadium's central oculus, which is open to the sky above. The enveloping translucent skin of the façade reveals an ethereal skeletal structure underneath, which creates a play of light and shadow along its surface. Despite its location in a seismic activity area, the stadium includes a 150-foot (46-meter) cantilever. During the day, the stadium is filled with diffused natural light, while at night it glows from within. Its undulating EFTE membrane seems to float, acting like a protective veil that lifts to welcome spectators.

Inside, the stadium is comfortable and inviting, with light-filled spaces, expansive views of the surrounding landscape, and generously scaled walkways. The stadium was designed to accommodate numerous event configurations, including sport, concerts, and other large public events.

Its 430-by-240-foot (131-by-73-meter) pitch can accommodate soccer, rugby, tennis, boxing, and motor racing, among other sports. Despite its large scale, the cauldron shape of the stadium creates a surprising sense of intimacy within, with 80,730 square feet (7,500 square meters) of lounges and reception areas reserved for private use. Allianz Riviera is one of the first energy-positive stadiums to be built. Roof-mounted photovoltaic modules cover 80,730 square feet (7,500 square meters), providing a significant proportion of the building's electrical needs. Rainwater is collected on the roof and used for pitch irrigation and lavatories. Ventilation stacks harness prevailing winds to provide natural ventilation to the interior spaces.

Location Nice, France
Completion date 2013
Site area 35 acres (14 hectares)
Stadim 581,256 ft² (54,000 m²), 36,180 seats

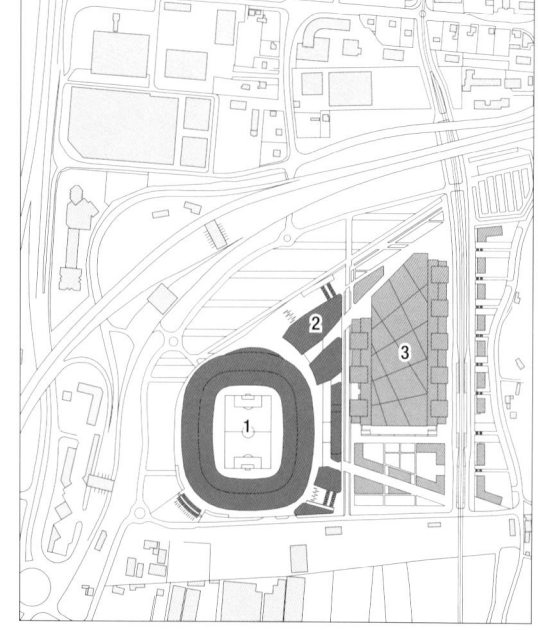

LOCATION PLAN

1 Stadium
2 Real-estate development office
3 Eco-friendly site linked to the stadium

FORECOURT FLOOR PLAN

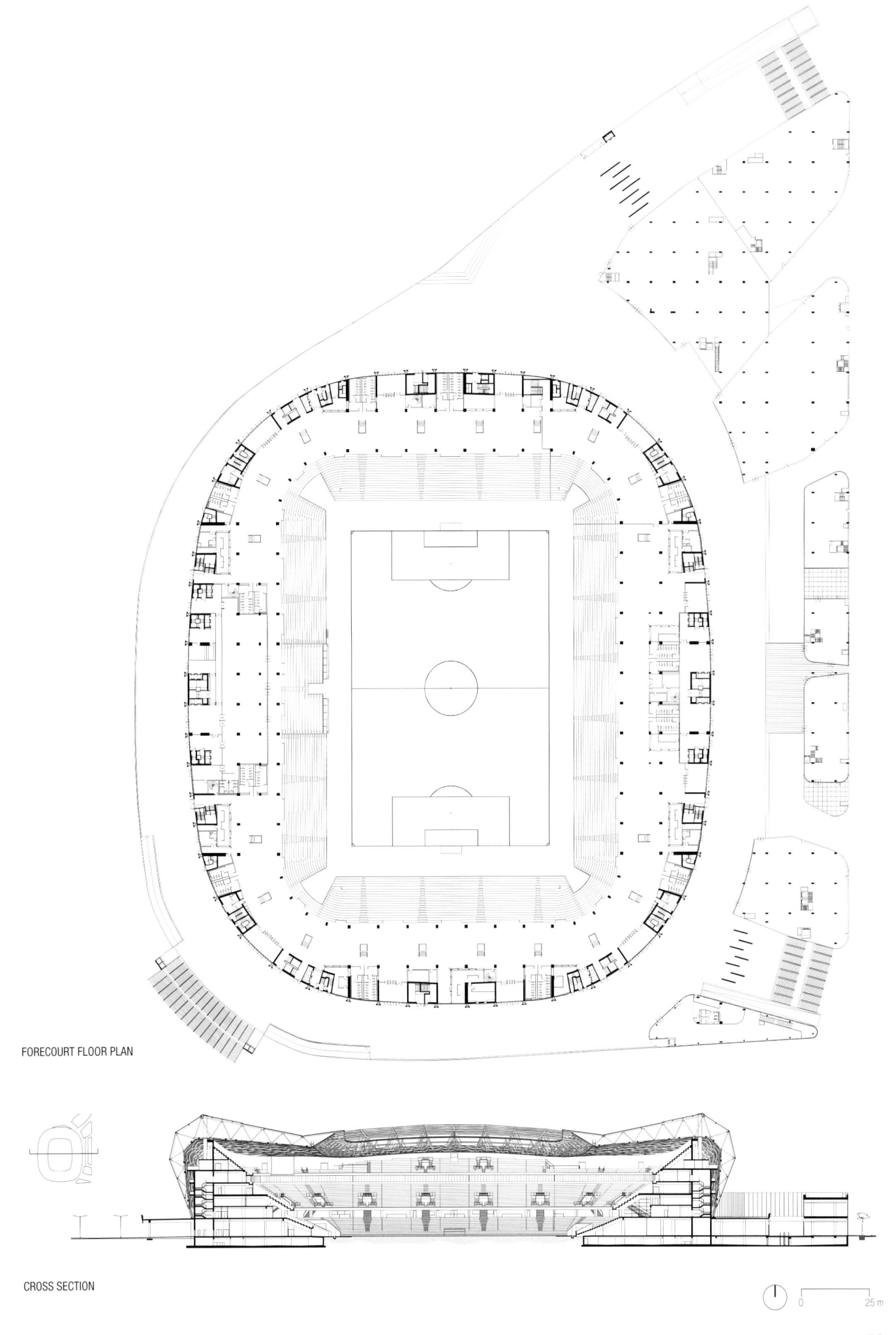

CROSS SECTION

0　25 m

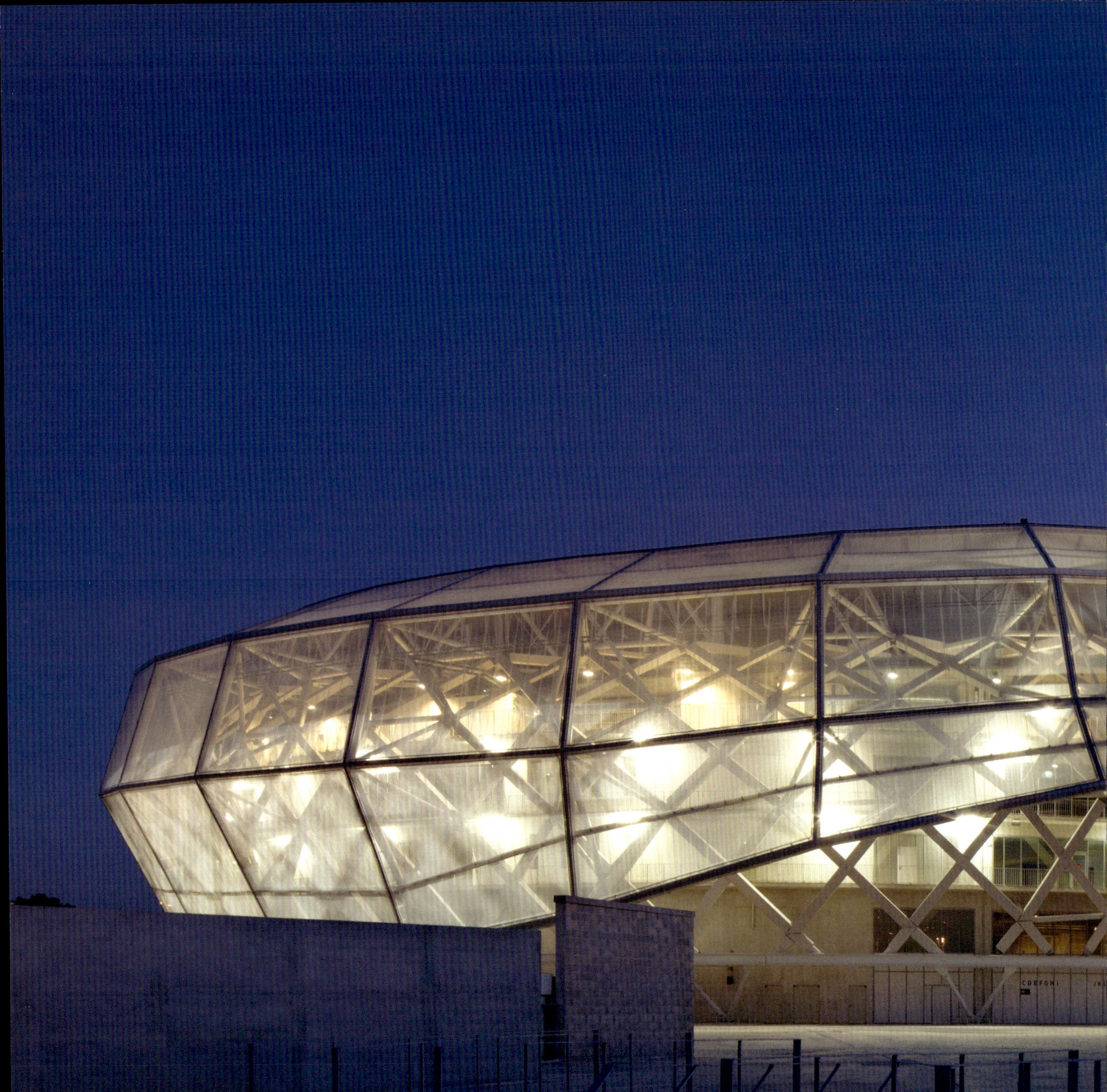

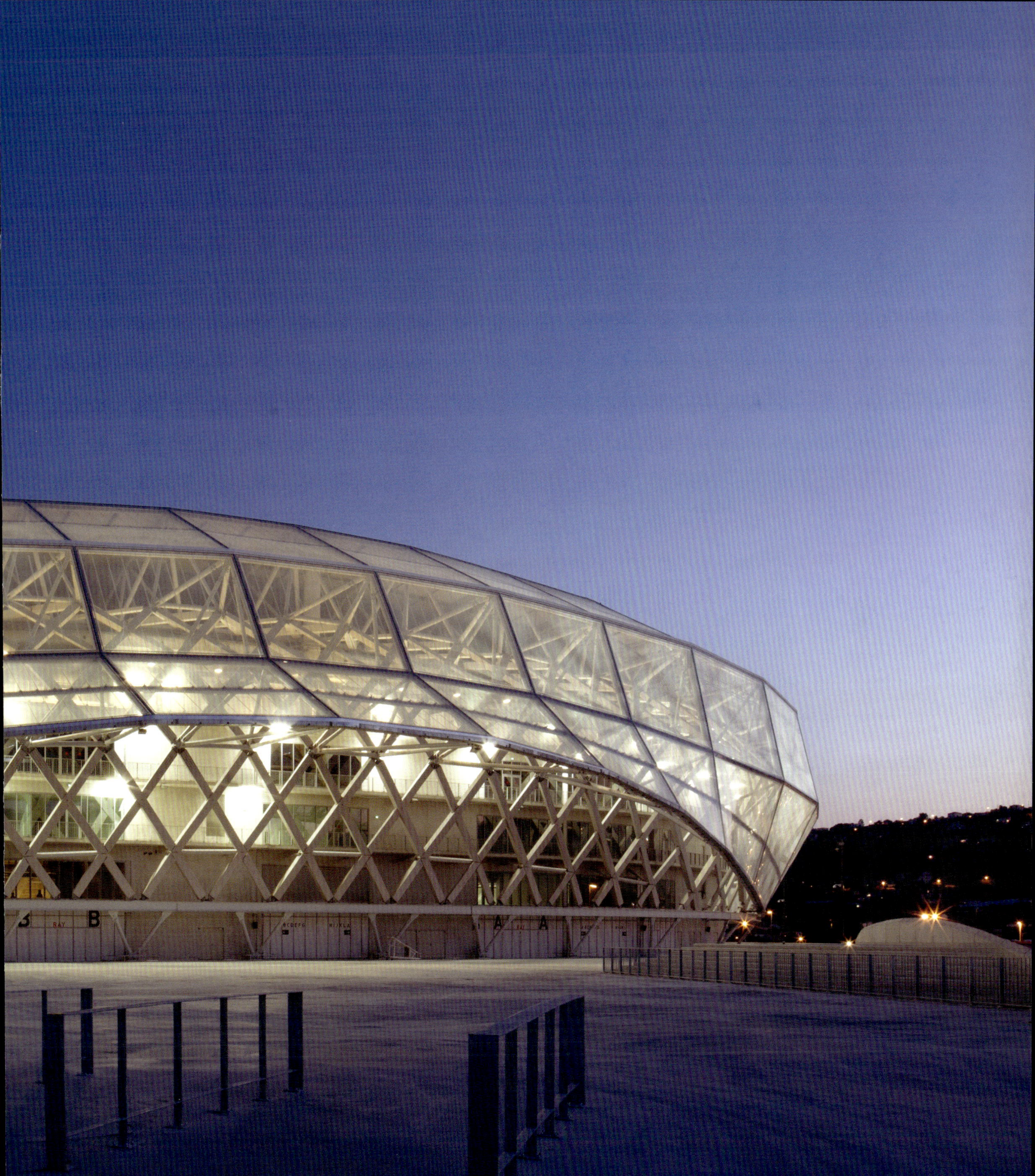

JEAN-MICHEL WILMOTTE ALLIANZ RIVIERA STADIUM

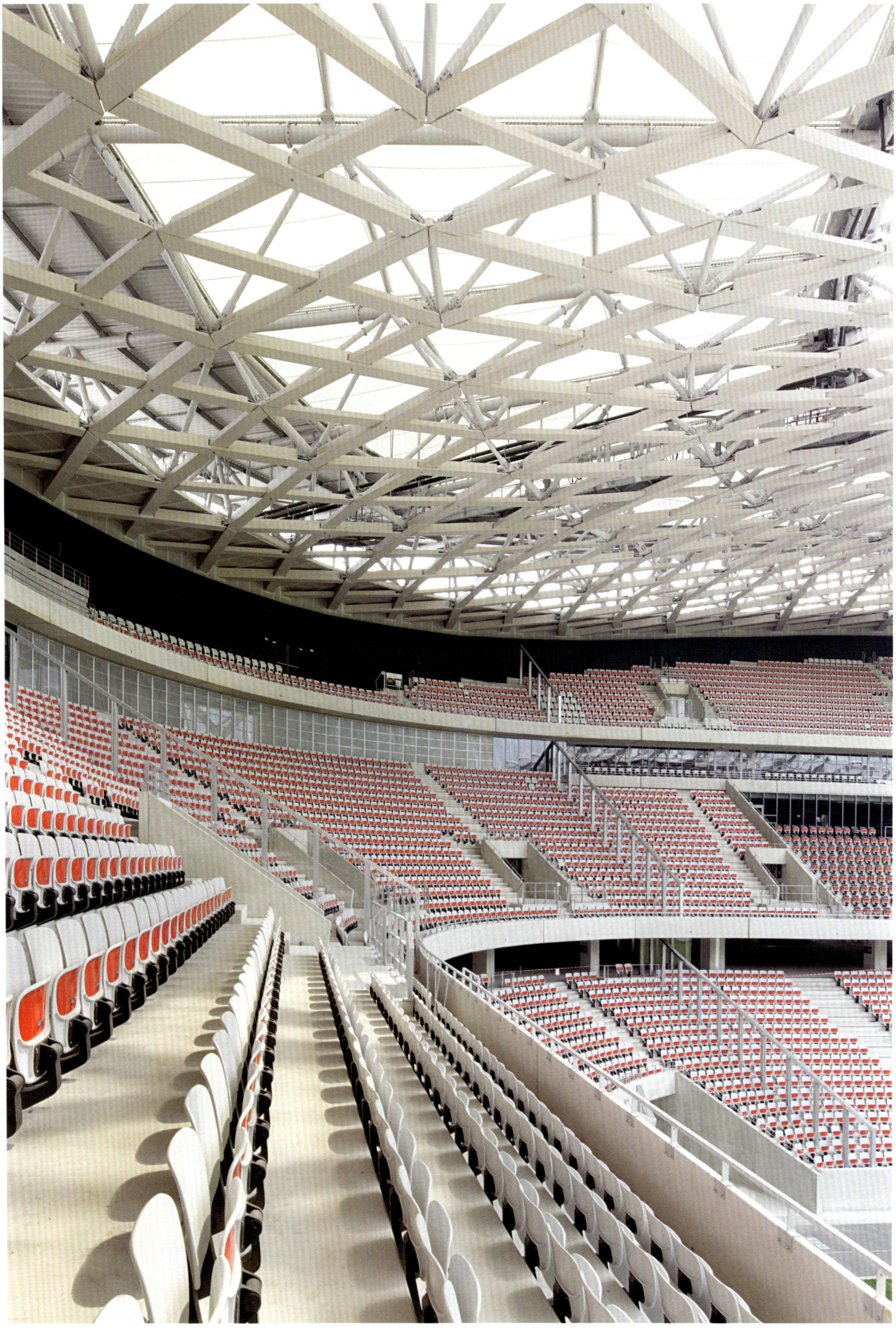

JEAN-MICHEL WILMOTTE ALLIANZ RIVIERA STADIUM

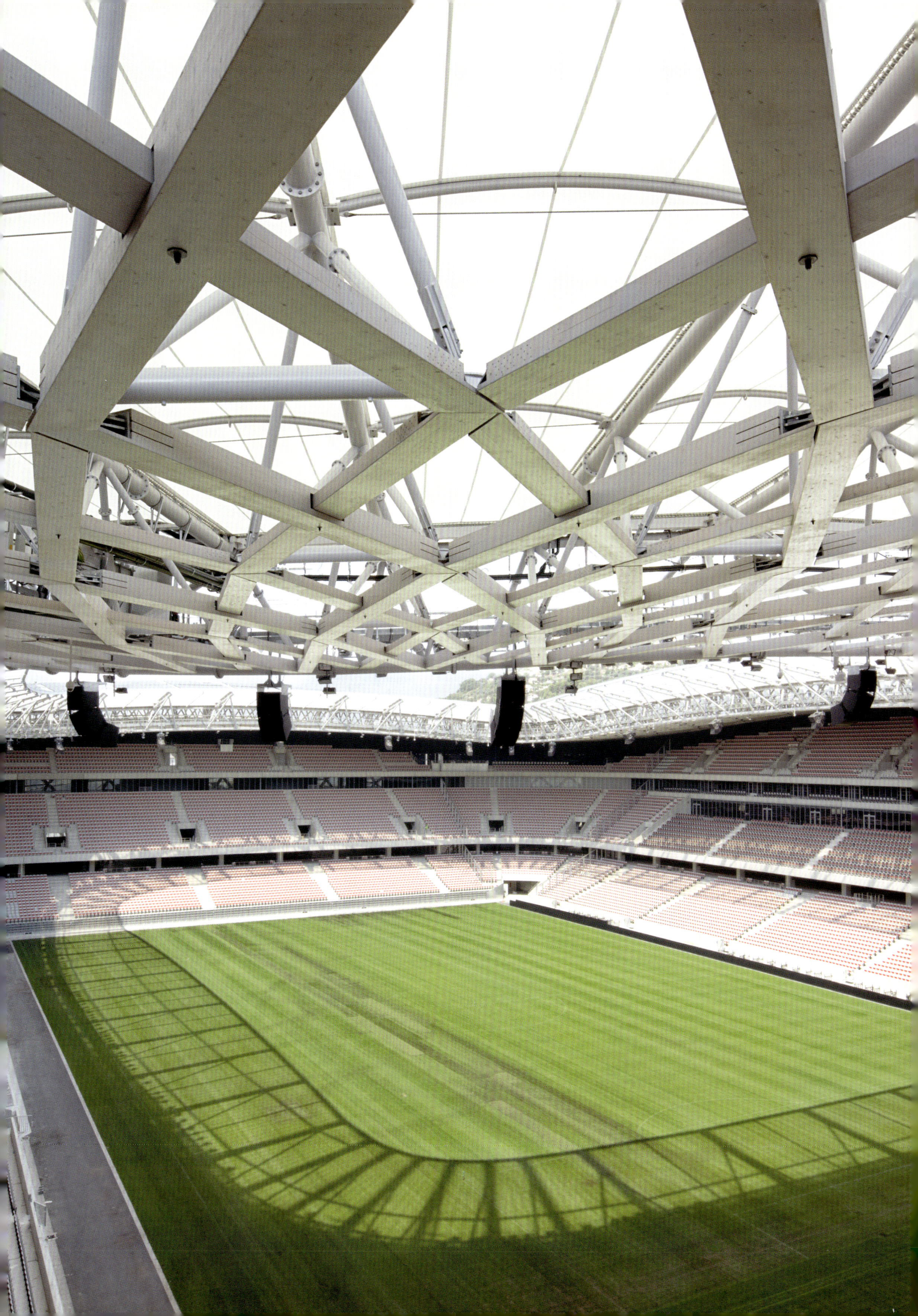

JEAN-MICHEL WILMOTTE

QUADRANS BUILDINGS

In the spring of 2018 Jean-Michel Wilmotte delivered the last two of the four buildings for the Quadrans service campus on the site of the new French Ministry of Defense. The overall site area, near the Seine, has long been occupied by the French military, and the Air Force and the Navy formerly had buildings here. Contrary to a frequent approach of the military, this complex was designed to be open to the city, and not enclosed like a fort. The approach taken is characteristic of traditional Parisian buildings such as large, rectangular townhouses with interior courtyards.

The office buildings occupy 992,440 square feet (92,200 square meters) on half of the 7-acre (2.8-hectare) plot, the other half being allocated to a landscape garden. "Flat, variously angled trumeaus orchestrate the façades and office spaces," explains Wilmotte. "We chose three dominant color and material ranges—silvery aluminum, bronze, and manganese—for the sundial-like façades that move and come to life in the daylight."

The overall project comprises four seven-story buildings and the landscaped park. They are reinforced concrete buildings with post-and-beam structures. The main materials used are concrete, stone, stainless steel, Corten steel, composite panels, thermo-coated aluminum frame curtain walls, and terraces in Ipe wood. Double-height entrance halls, and fully glazed upper floors contribute to an overall strategy linked to the presence of natural light.

Terraces and rooftops are generously planted, and 4,735 square feet (440 square meters) of solar panels provide a significant part of the energy needs of the structures. Offices can be modulated in size, providing maximum interior flexibility.

Location Paris, France
Completion date 2015 & 2018
Area 992,440 ft² (92,200 m²)

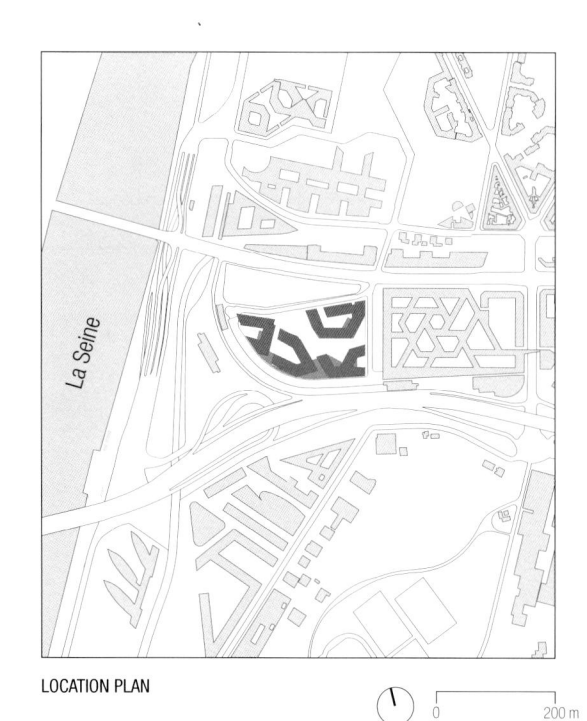

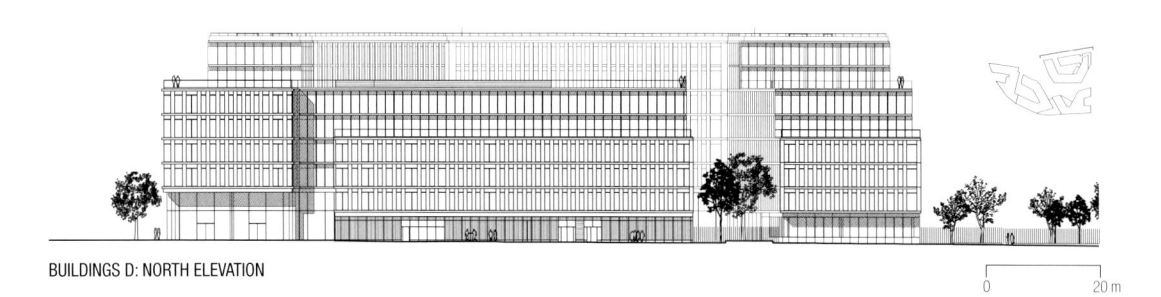

LOCATION PLAN

BUILDINGS D: NORTH ELEVATION

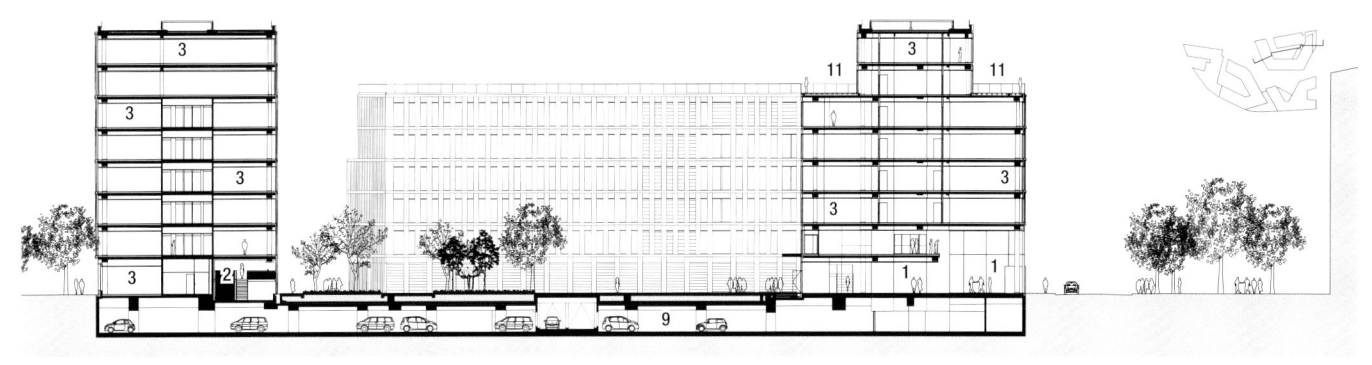

BUILDINGS D: CROSS SECTION

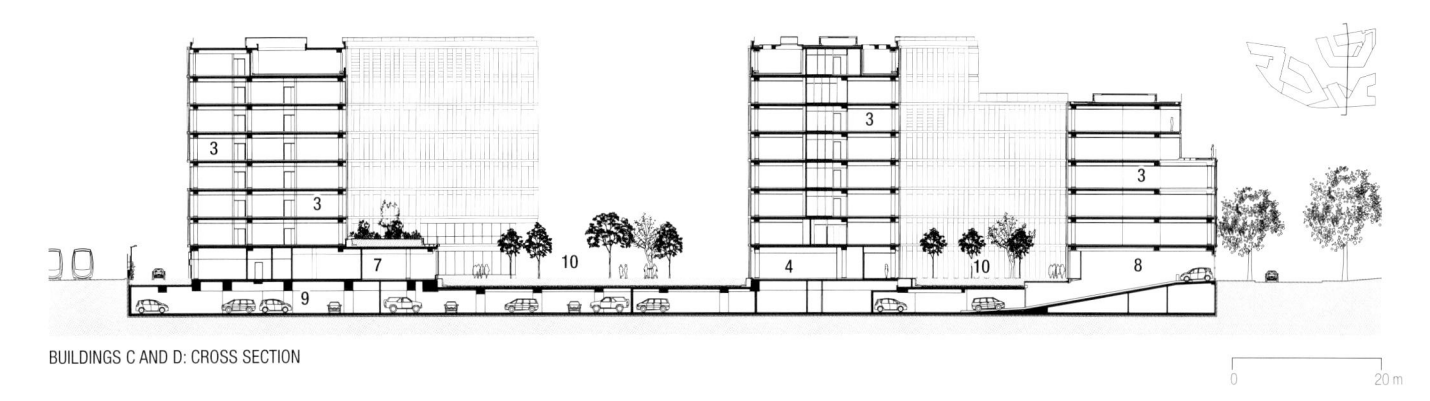

BUILDINGS C AND D: CROSS SECTION

1 Entrance hall
2 Bicycle room
3 Offices
4 Meeting room
5 Café
6 Shop
7 Restaurant
8 Car-park access
9 Parking
10 Garden
11 Terrace

SITE PLAN

JEAN-MICHEL WILMOTTE   QUADRANS BUILDINGS

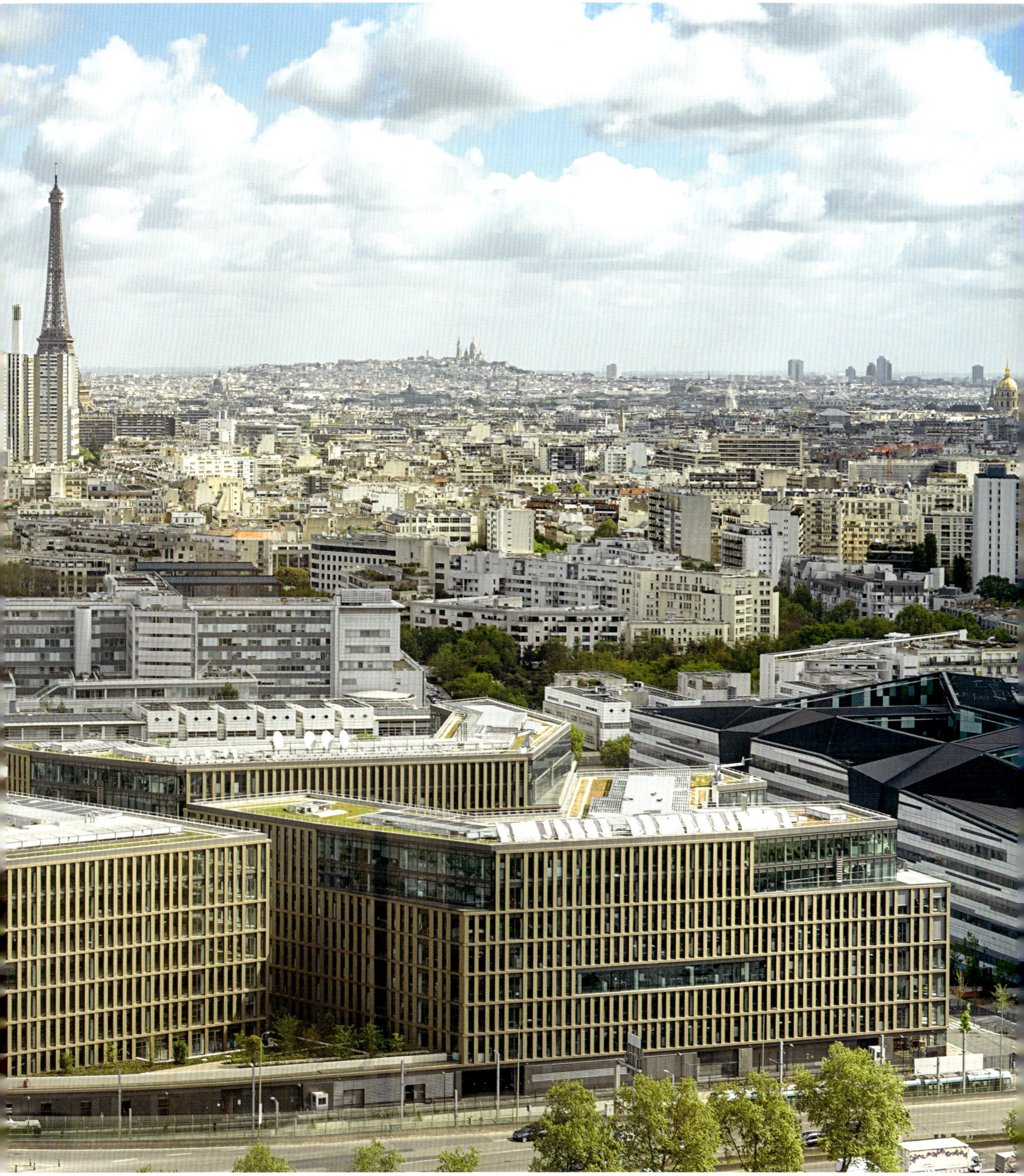

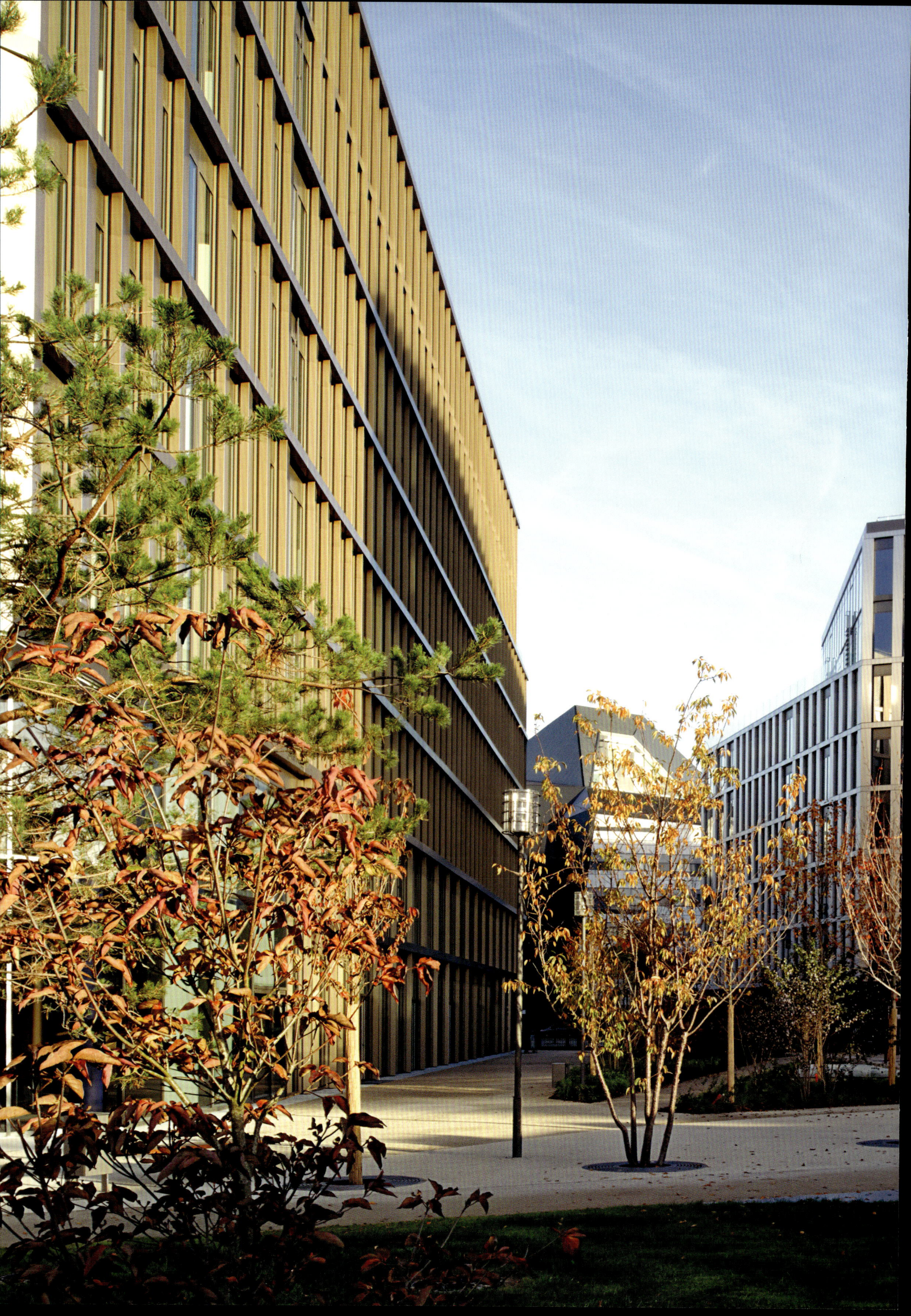

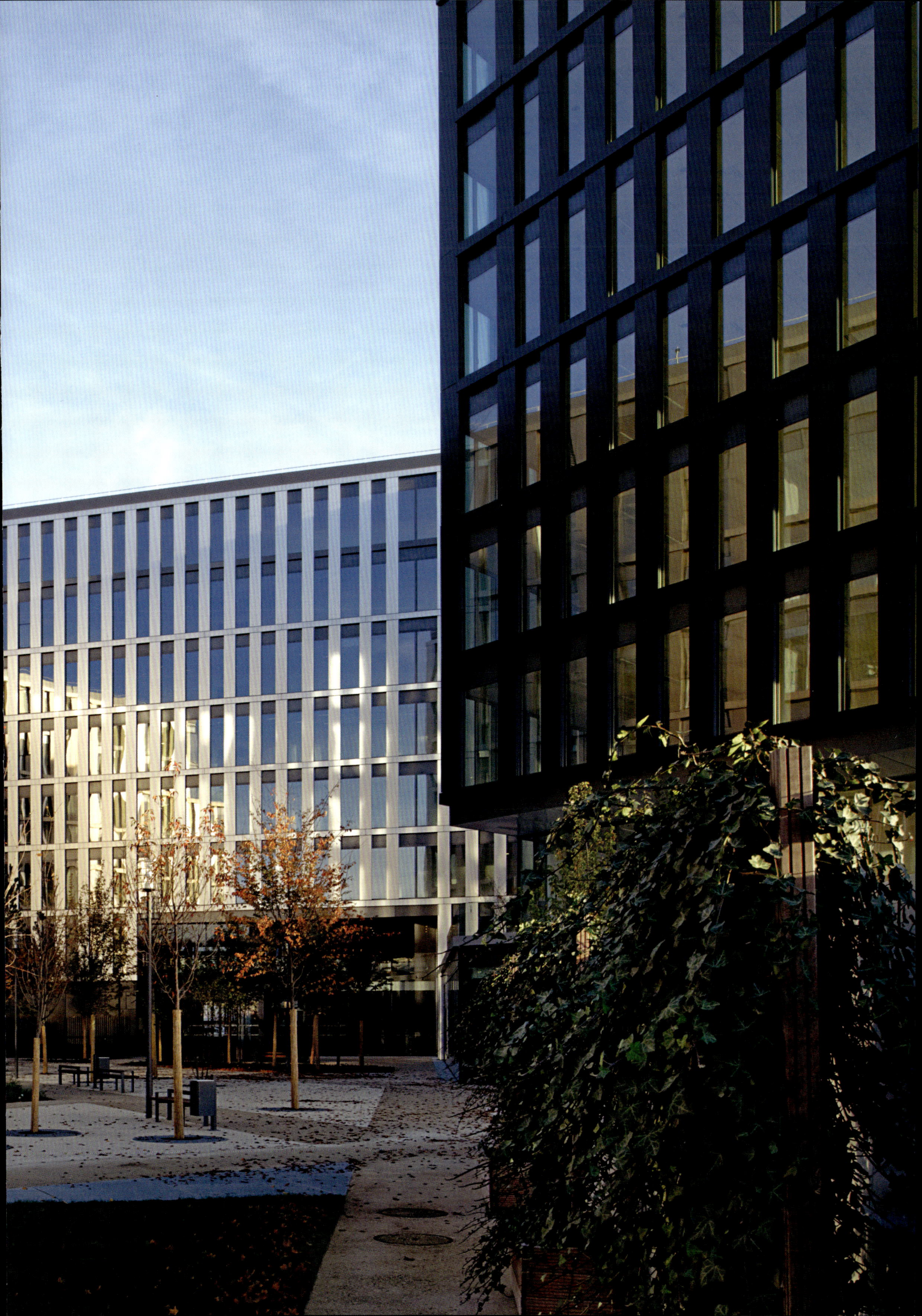

JEAN-MICHEL WILMOTTE

6 PANCRAS SQUARE, GOOGLE HEADQUARTERS

Located opposite St Pancras International railway station, built for BNP Paribas Real Estate, this mixed-use energy efficient office building is one of six structures forming Development Zone 5 in the southern part of the so-called KXC site and, as such, fits into an overall master plan. The building is currently being assessed under BREEAM 2008 'New Construction assessment' and is expected to achieve an 'Excellent' rating. It is a 531,740-square-foot (49,400-square-meter) reinforced concrete (basements and ground floor) and steel structure (with metal decks for the upper levels). The main materials used are terracotta, anodized aluminum, concrete, and glass. Jean-Michel Wilmotte was also in charge of the design of the interior public areas of the building.

The project lies within the King's Cross Conservation Area, alongside the Grade I–listed structures of King's Cross and St Pancras stations, the Grade II–listed German Gymnasium and the Stanley Building South. The surrounding buildings are robust and simple. The choice of materials and the detailing of the façades were informed by the heritage and character of these buildings. The façades are constructed in steel framework with terracotta piers that create a rich and dynamic contrast to the glazed areas. The curtain wall system is a re-interpretation of the load-bearing masonry seen nearby, with its interwoven metal frames and terracotta infills.

The concept development was based on the creation of a volume with a central atrium flanked by two cores, which structurally liberate both the internal floor plates of the structure and the façade from internal constraints. The composition is based on a horizontal and vertical hierarchy. The lower two levels are scaled to provide a strong base for the building, responding more efficiently and directly to the public realm. Above this, the middle and crown are formed by an expression of function and performance with a 10-foot-wide (3-meter-wide) grid system. Sustainability was an integral part of the concept development from the inception. The project incorporates passive design features, highly efficient building services, and a low-carbon energy supply.

Location King's Cross Central, London, United Kingdom
Completion date 2015
Area 531,740 ft² (49,400 m²)

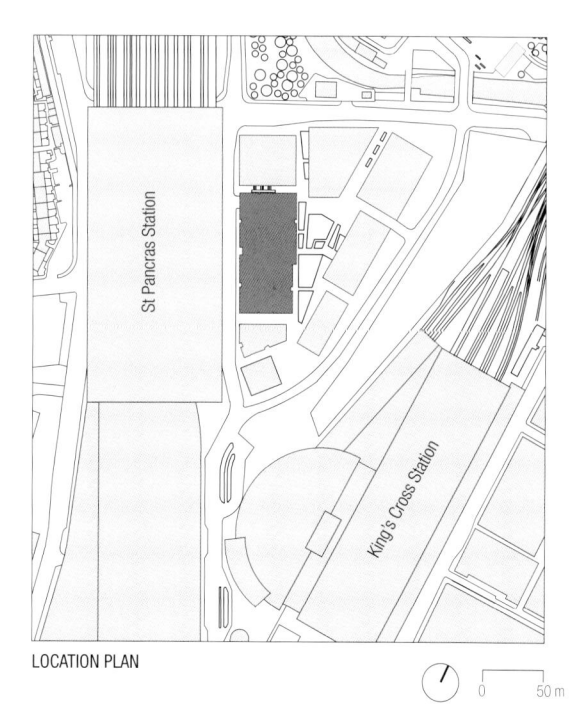

LOCATION PLAN

1 Main entrance
2 Atrium
3 Offices
4 Retail
5 Café
6 Toilets
7 Ramp to basement
8 Terrace
9 Services

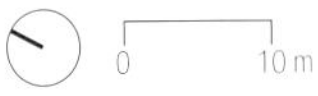

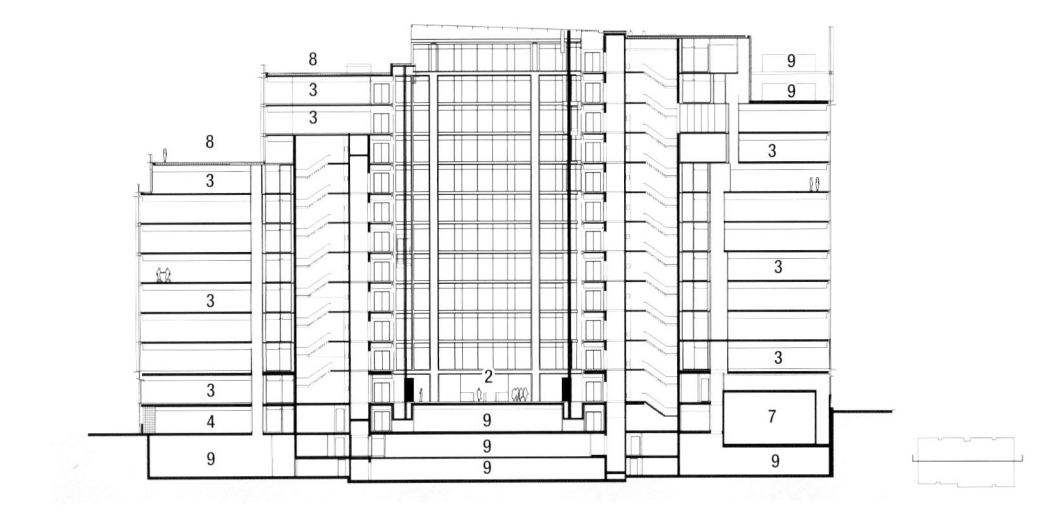

LONG SECTION

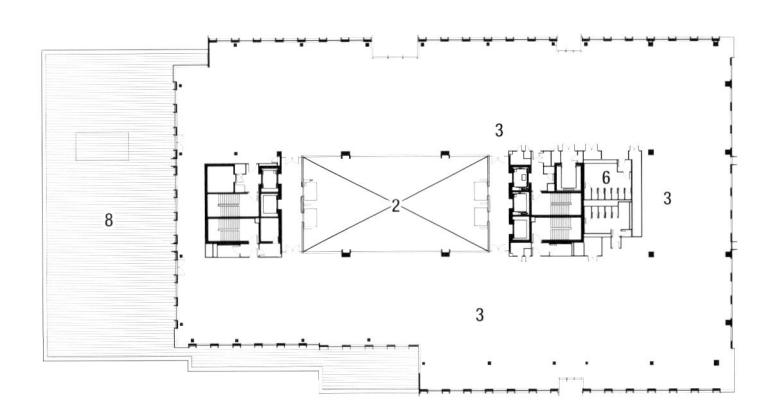

EIGHTH-FLOOR PLAN

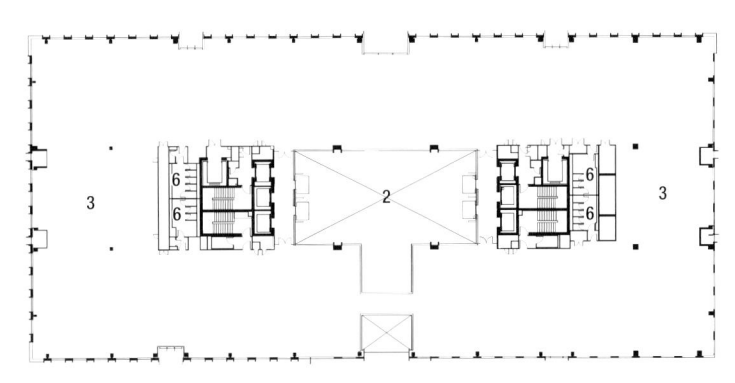

FIRST-FLOOR PLAN

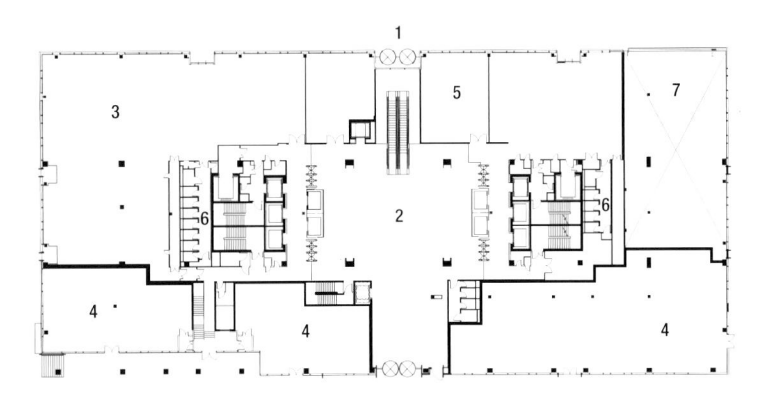

GROUND-FLOOR PLAN

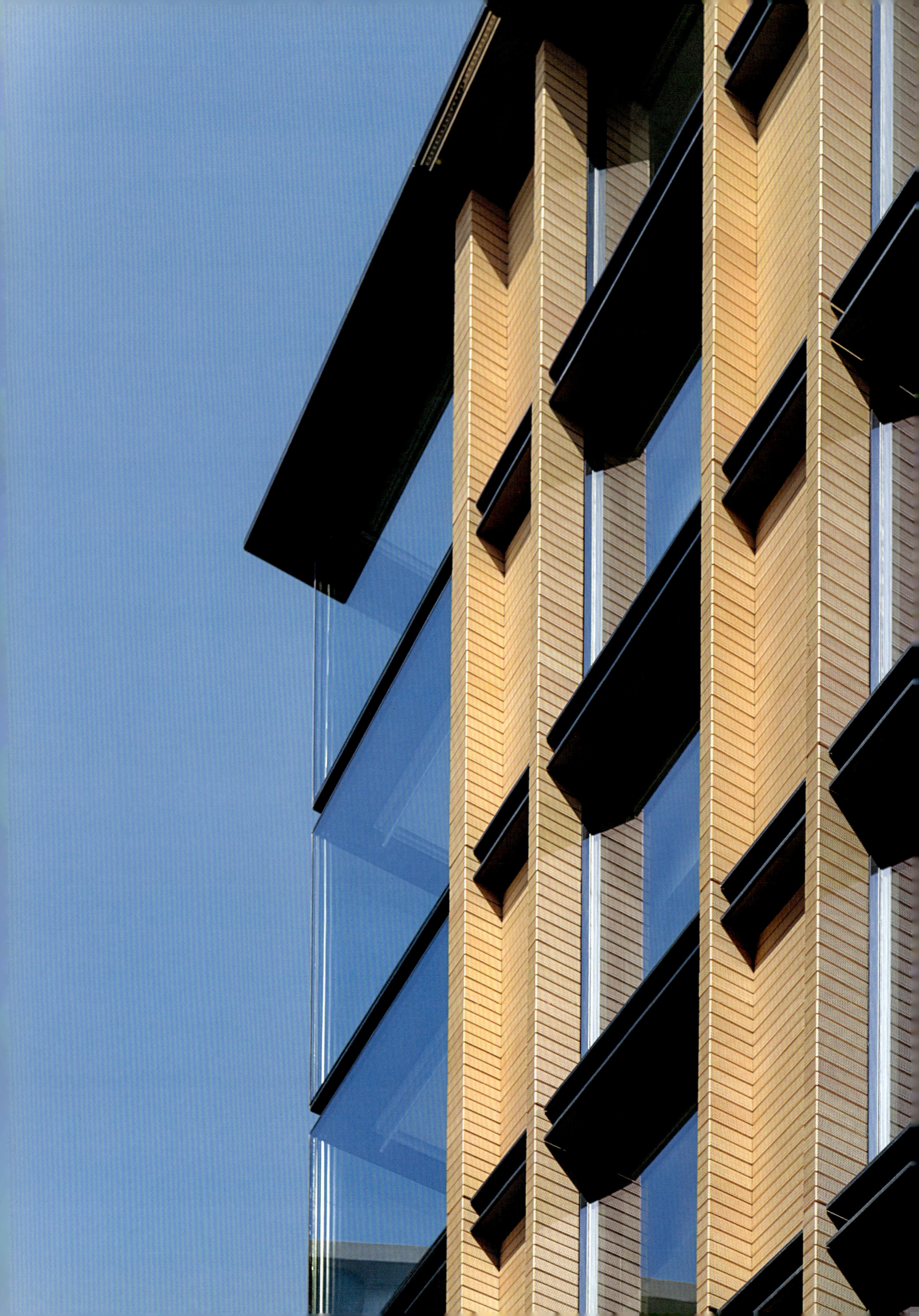

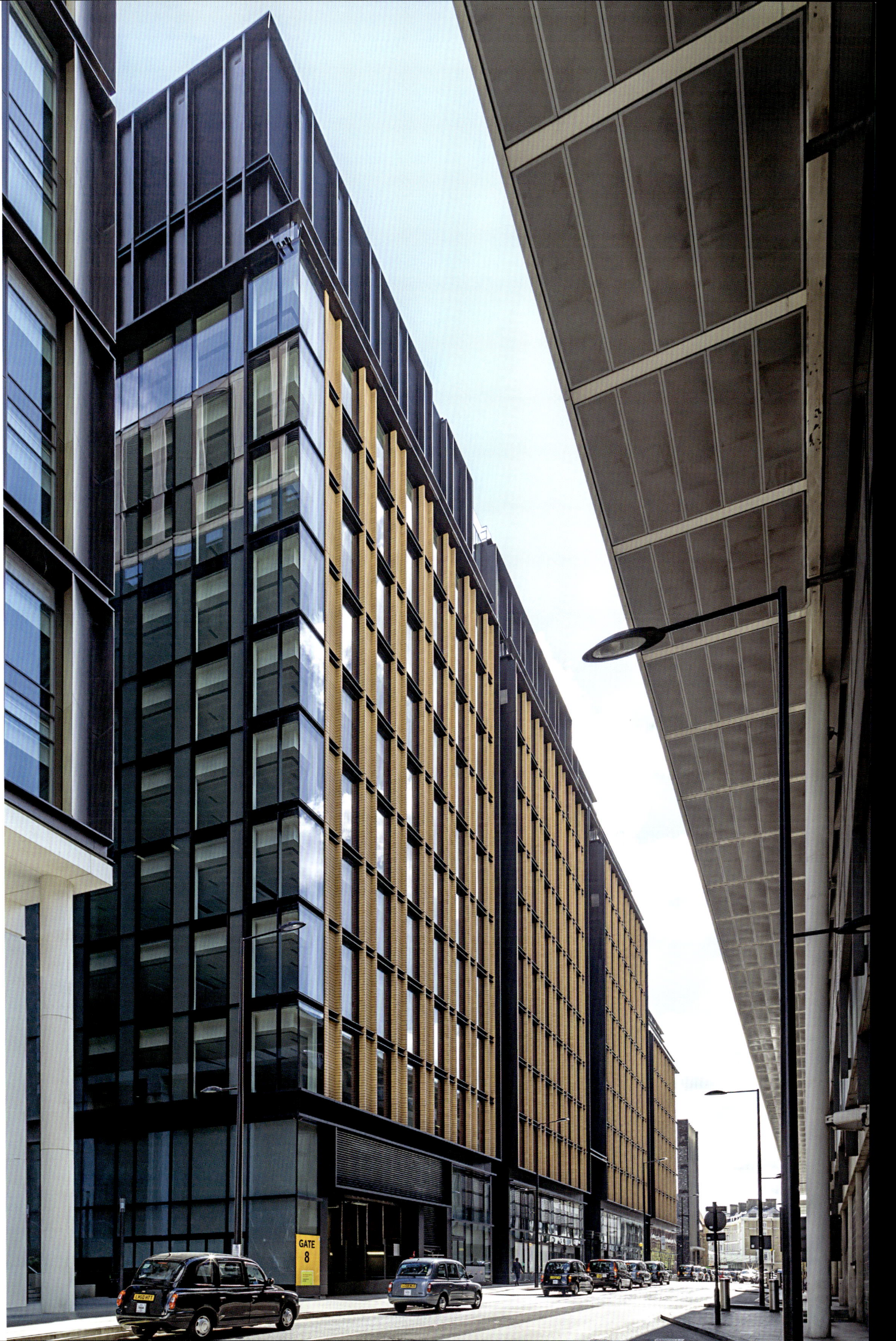
GATE
8

JEAN-MICHEL WILMOTTE 6 PANCRAS SQUARE, GOOGLE HEADQUARTERS

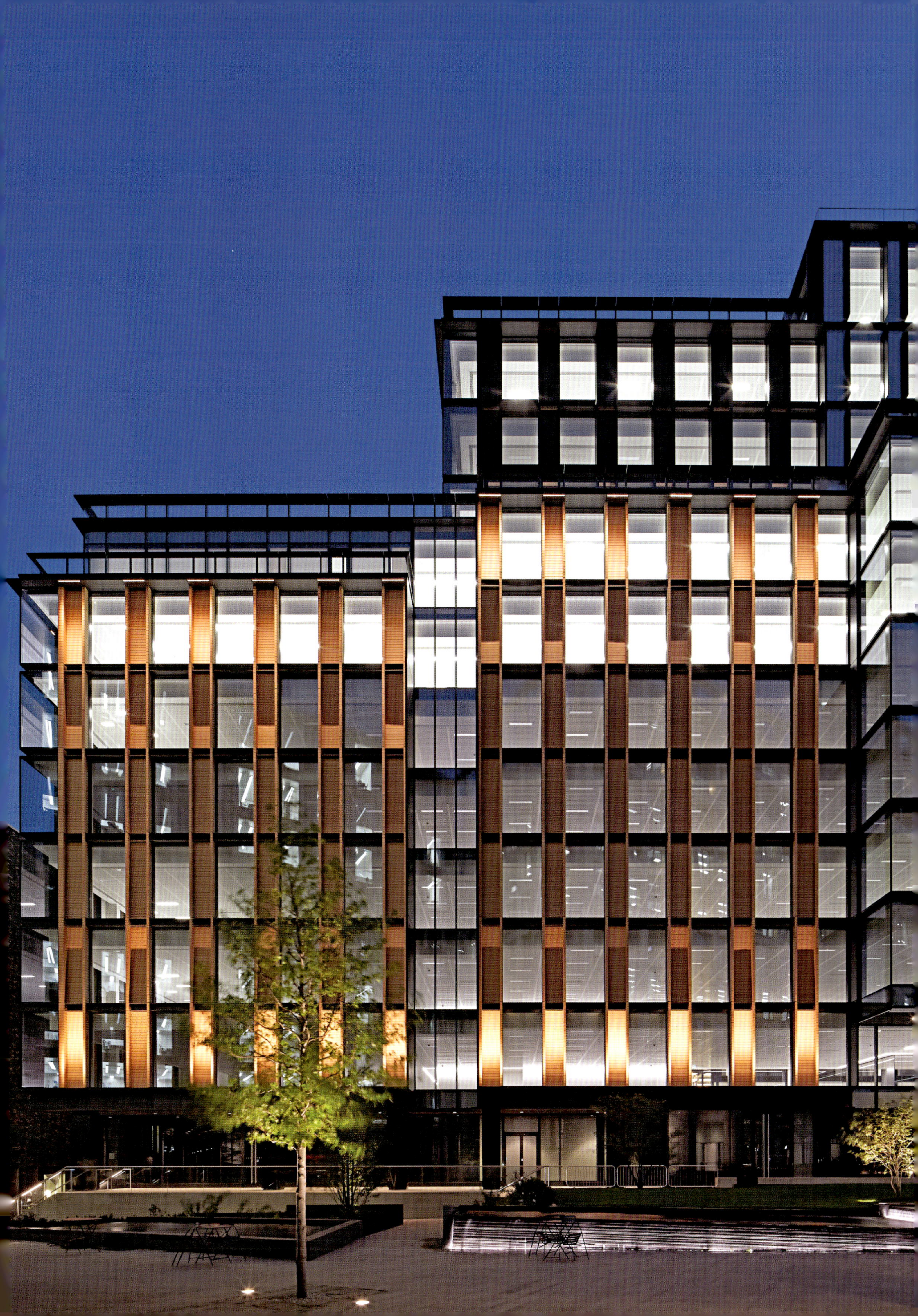

JEAN-MICHEL WILMOTTE

DAEJEON CULTURAL CENTER

Located on a triangular site in the heart of the city of Daejeon, the Cultural Center is a 98,275-square-foot (9,130-square-meter) circular reinforced concrete structure clad with aluminum panels and glass. It includes a 350-seat theater, an exhibition hall, a music studio, office, and a 79-space parking lot. Each floor of the building is dedicated to one element of the program, moving upwards from the most public level to the most private level.

The elliptic multi-function theater is the heart of the Cultural Center. The exhibition area on level 3 is linked to the main hall by the two monumental stairs and is designed around an exterior sculpture garden. The program associated with the studios is distributed throughout the volume, with a principal natural-lit circulation along the interior façade, with views of the sculpture garden. Offices are on level 5 with a rooftop garden above. A large studio space is located in the 'point' of the east façade.

Visible from three sides despite the urban development around it, the Center stands out as a physical landmark, a cultural sign marking the importance of the project within the limits of the city, and the events to be staged within its walls. To the east, the volume stretches forward towards the view, like a flower bending to capture the sunlight, creating an animated and monumental entry façade visible from a distance.

The placement of the building within the site creates two differently scaled public spaces: a large triangular plaza accessed by a continuous stair, generous and scaled to the city, and a more intimate space to the west niched in between a forest of bamboo, and the west façade of the Center. The glass façade allows objects on display to be viewed from the exterior, while also bringing light into the structure during the day, as required.

Location Daejeon, South Korea
Completion date 2015
Area 98,275 ft^2 (9,130 m^2)

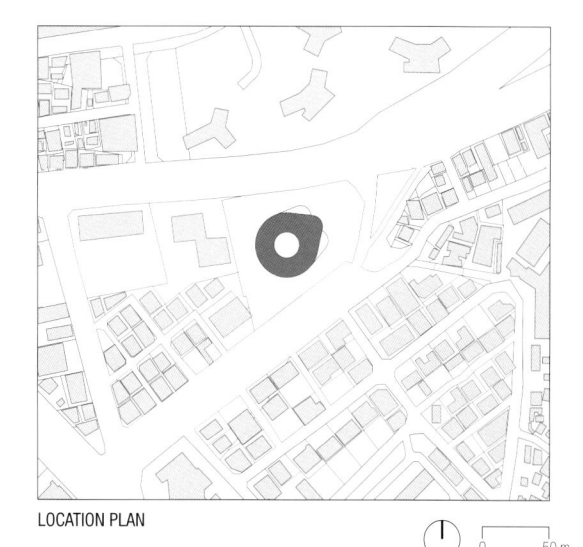

LOCATION PLAN

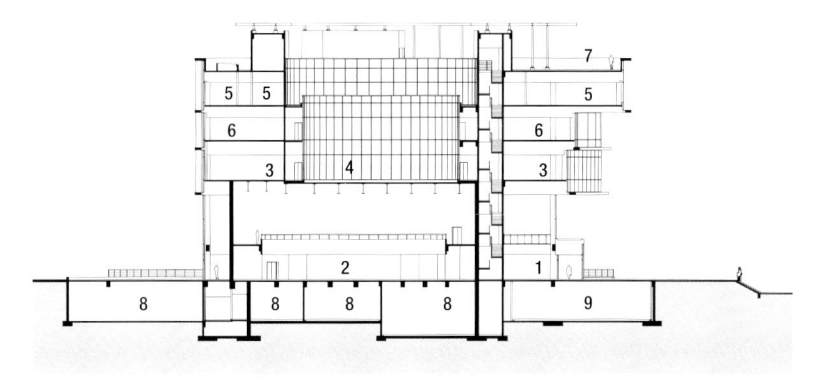

LONG SECTION

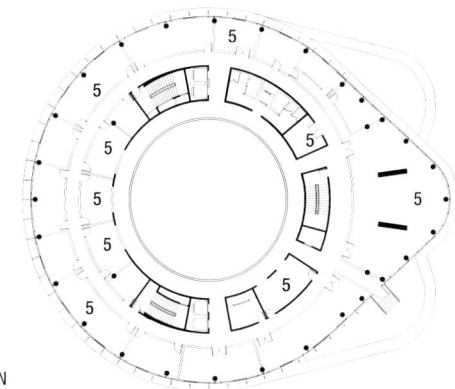

FIFTH-FLOOR PLAN

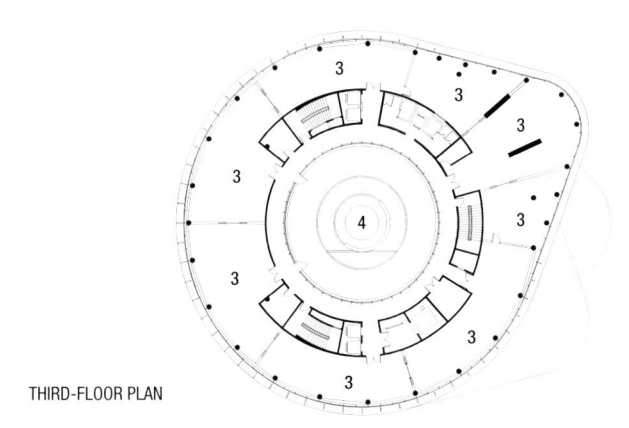

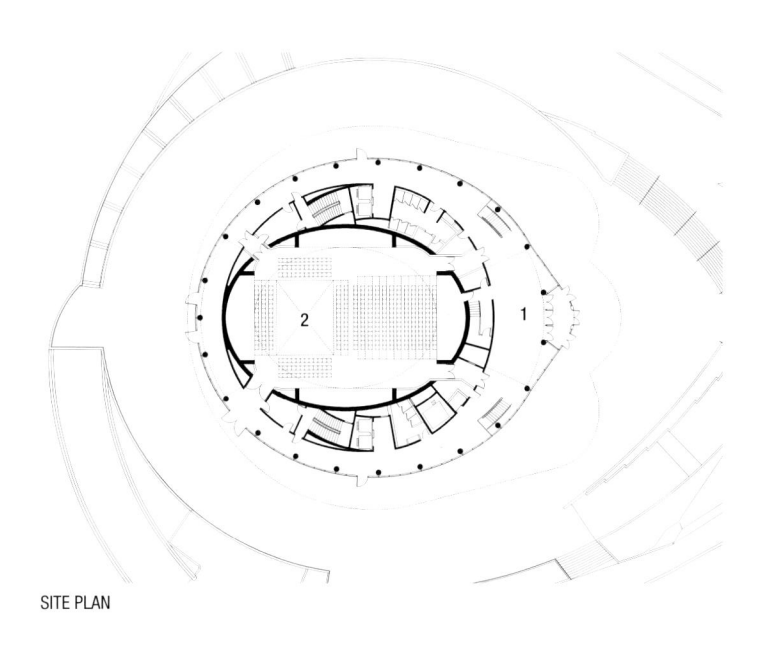

THIRD-FLOOR PLAN

SITE PLAN

1 Entrance hall
2 Multi-purpose room
3 Exhibition gallery
4 Patio
5 Offices
6 Workshop
7 Accessible roof
8 Services
9 Parking

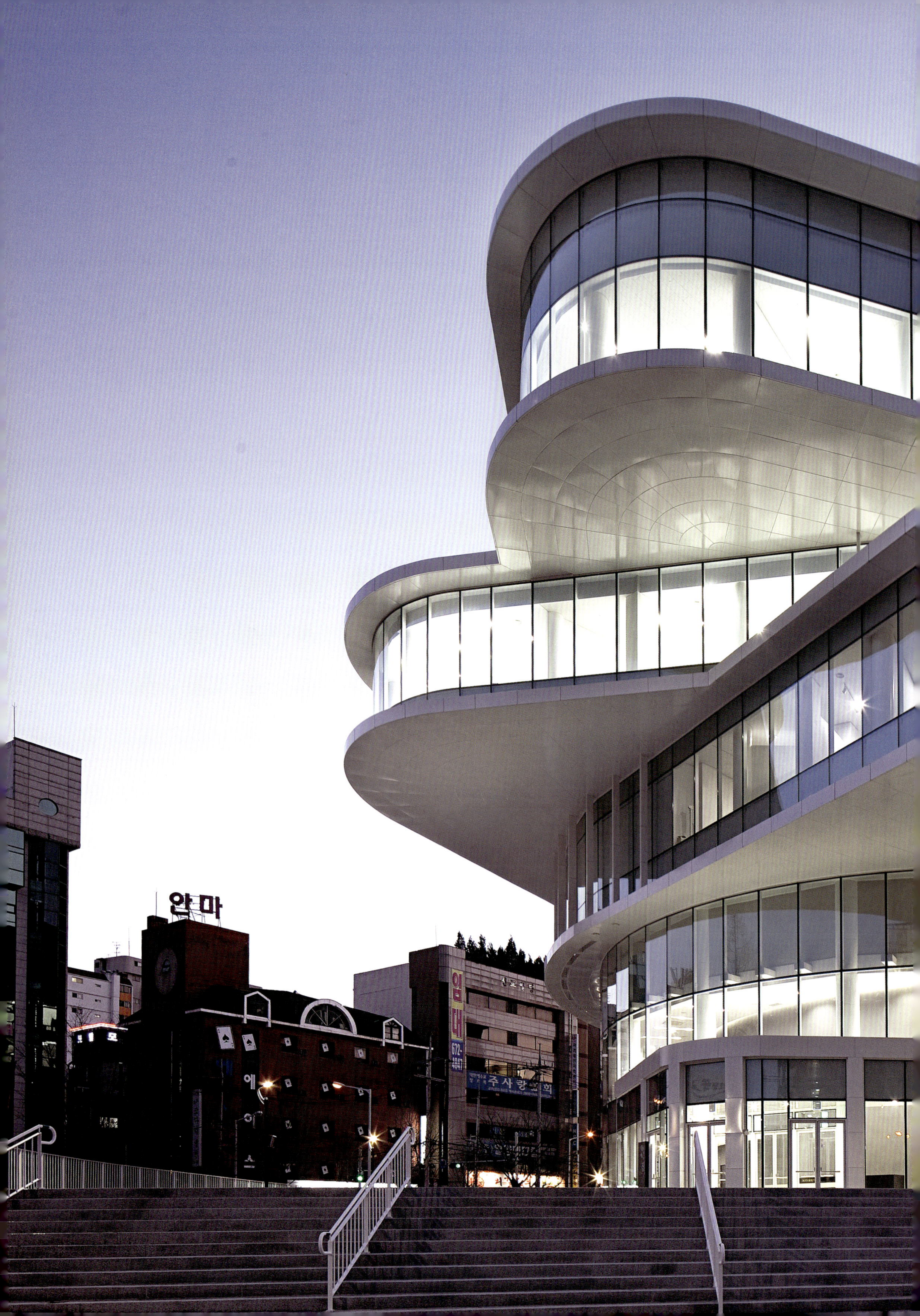
안마
임대
672-

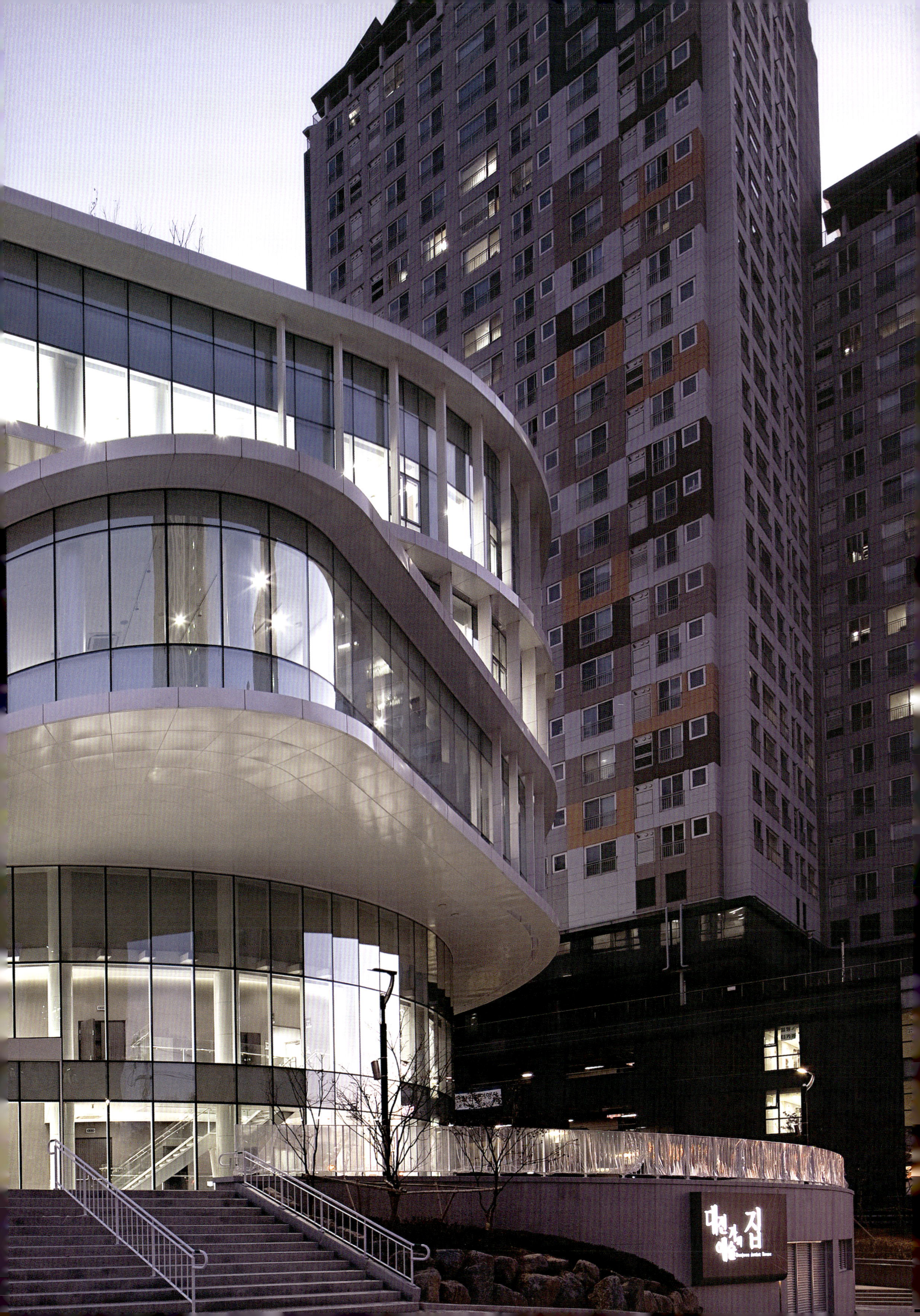
집

JEAN-MICHEL WILMOTTE DAEJEON CULTURAL CENTER

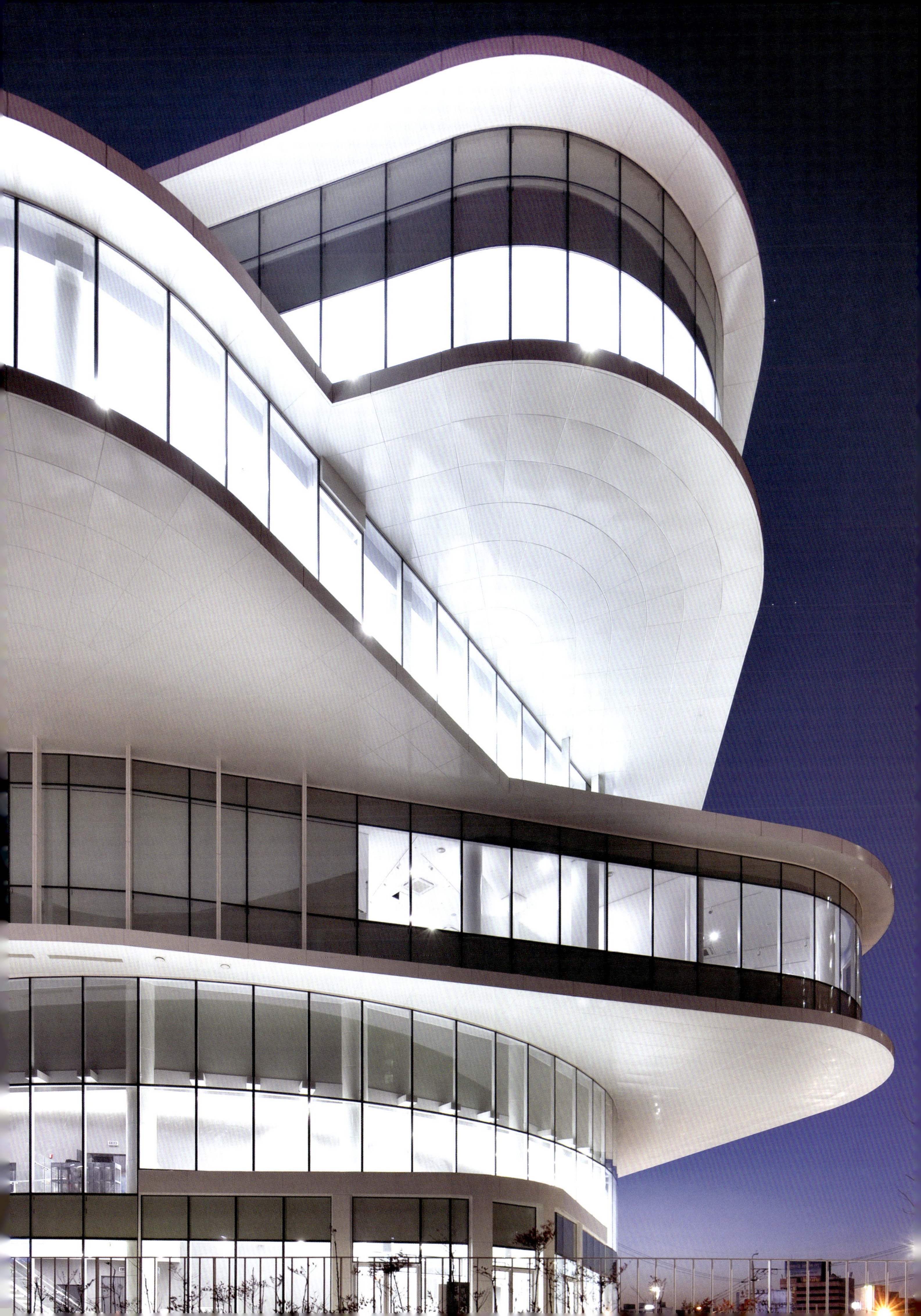

JEAN-MICHEL WILMOTTE

FERRARI SPORTING MANAGEMENT CENTER

Devoted to the design and assembly of Ferrari Formula 1 racing cars, the Sporting Management Center is a 258,335-square-foot (24,000-square-meter) reinforced concrete structure. The façades are in silk-screened glass panels (ground floor) and double-skin glass on the upper floors. The architectural choices were made with the desire to conceive an iconic building, with a strong visual identity, which could and will evolve with the Scuderia in the years to come.

The interior design, on three levels, includes spaces for designers, technical offices, research and development, communication, and management zones. Three main streams coexist in this space: the GeS (sport management) employees, external visitors, and the materials and products. One of the key challenges of this project was to organize them by designing efficient and harmonious floor plan layouts.

Ferrari's signature red, black, and metal, as well as the winding shape of the envelope, contribute to creating the building's strength and character and the impression of momentum that it generates. Conveying ideas of speed, performance, and acceleration, which are intrinsic to the brand's identity, into a graphic and spatial interpretation, results in the transformation of the building into a glass clad vessel, with façades that allow the control of natural light, while effectively limiting views from the exterior into the private areas where confidentiality is a fundamental condition.

The use of rooftop solar panels, both thermal and photovoltaic, a water recuperation system produced by compressors, and the design of the gardens from the greenery to the landscaping all allow the building to blend intelligently into the site and to achieve an environmentally friendly and sustainable level of performance.

Location Maranello, Italy
Completion date 2015
Area 258,335 ft^2 (24,000 m^2)

LOCATION PLAN

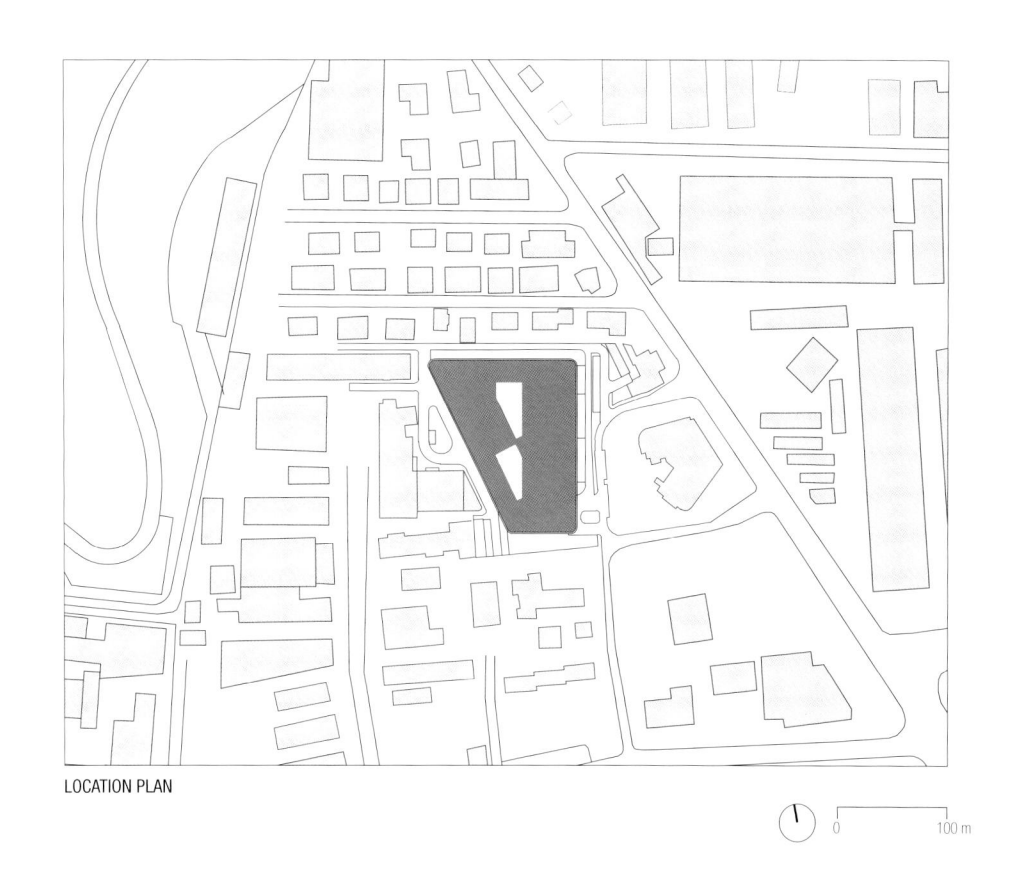

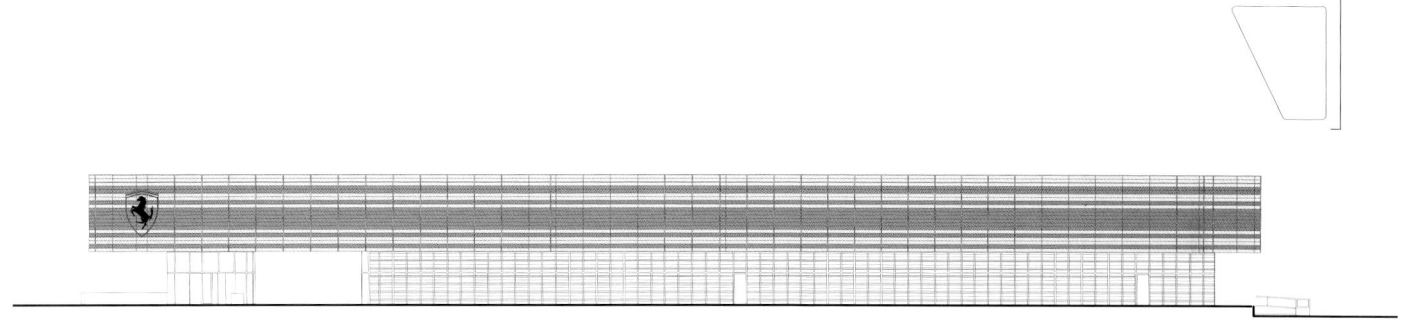

EAST ELEVATION

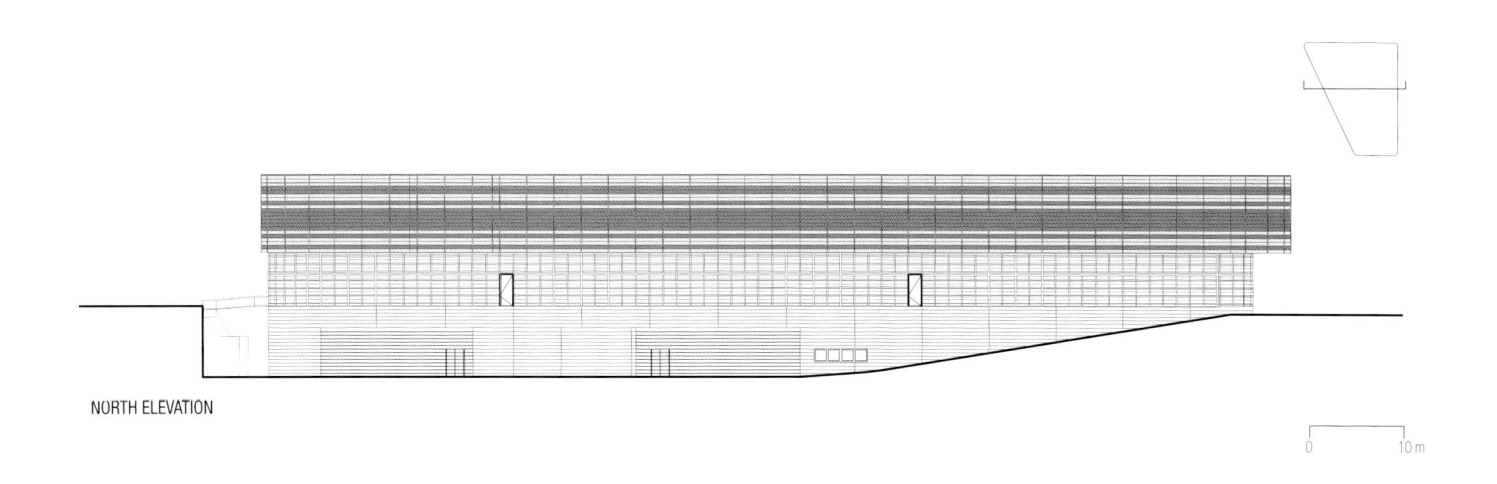

NORTH ELEVATION

85

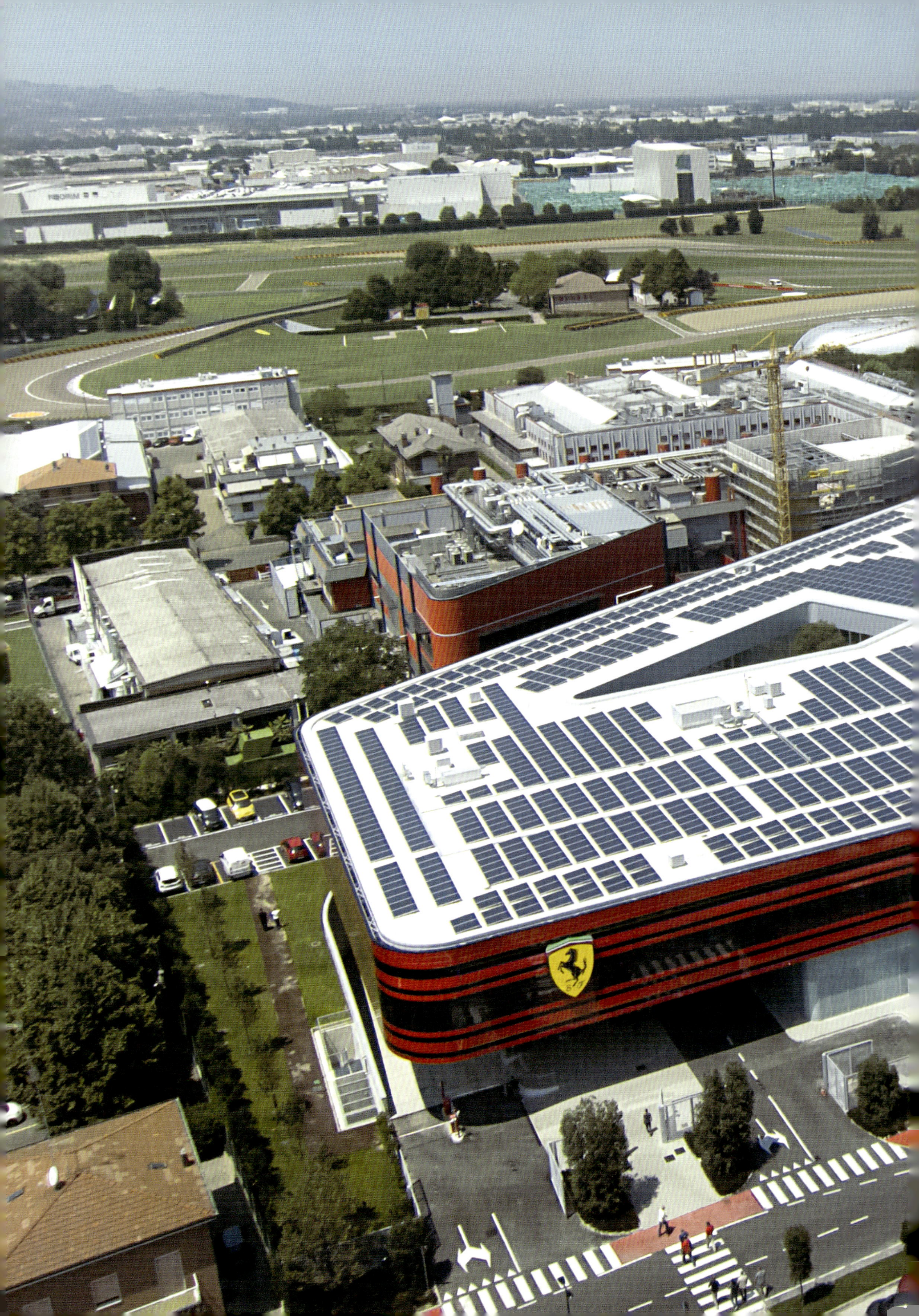

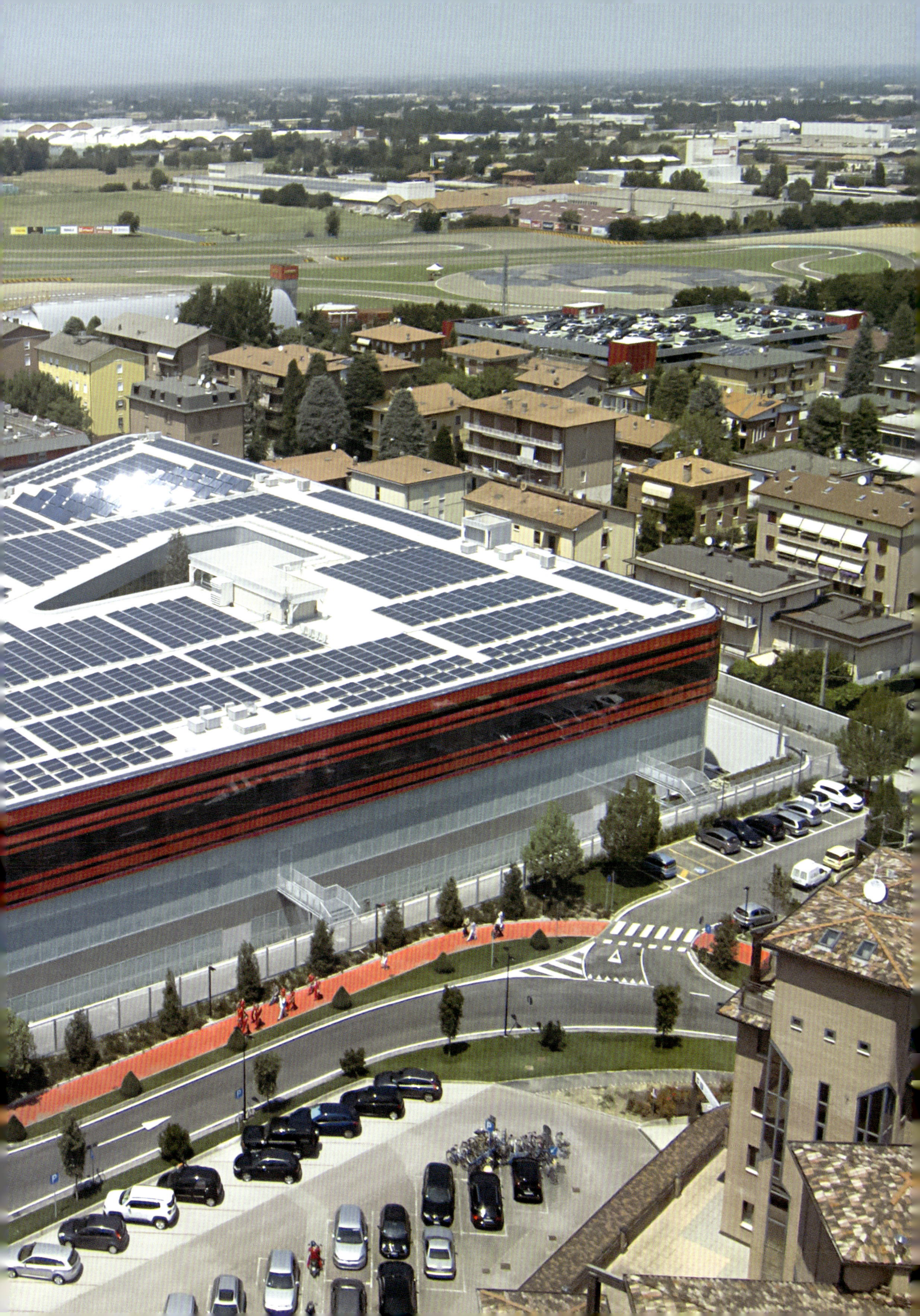

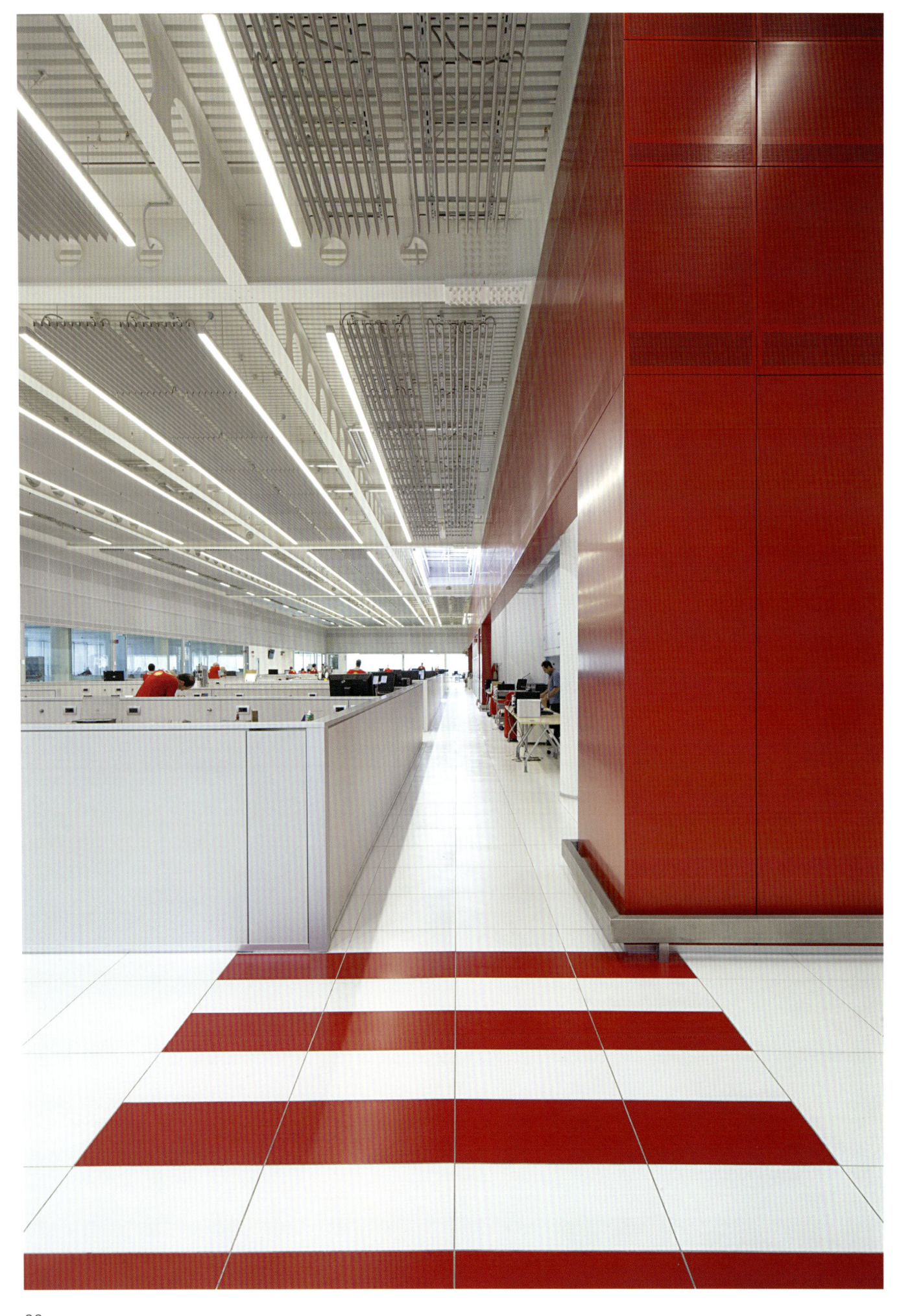

JEAN-MICHEL WILMOTTE FERRARI SPORTING MANAGEMENT CENTER

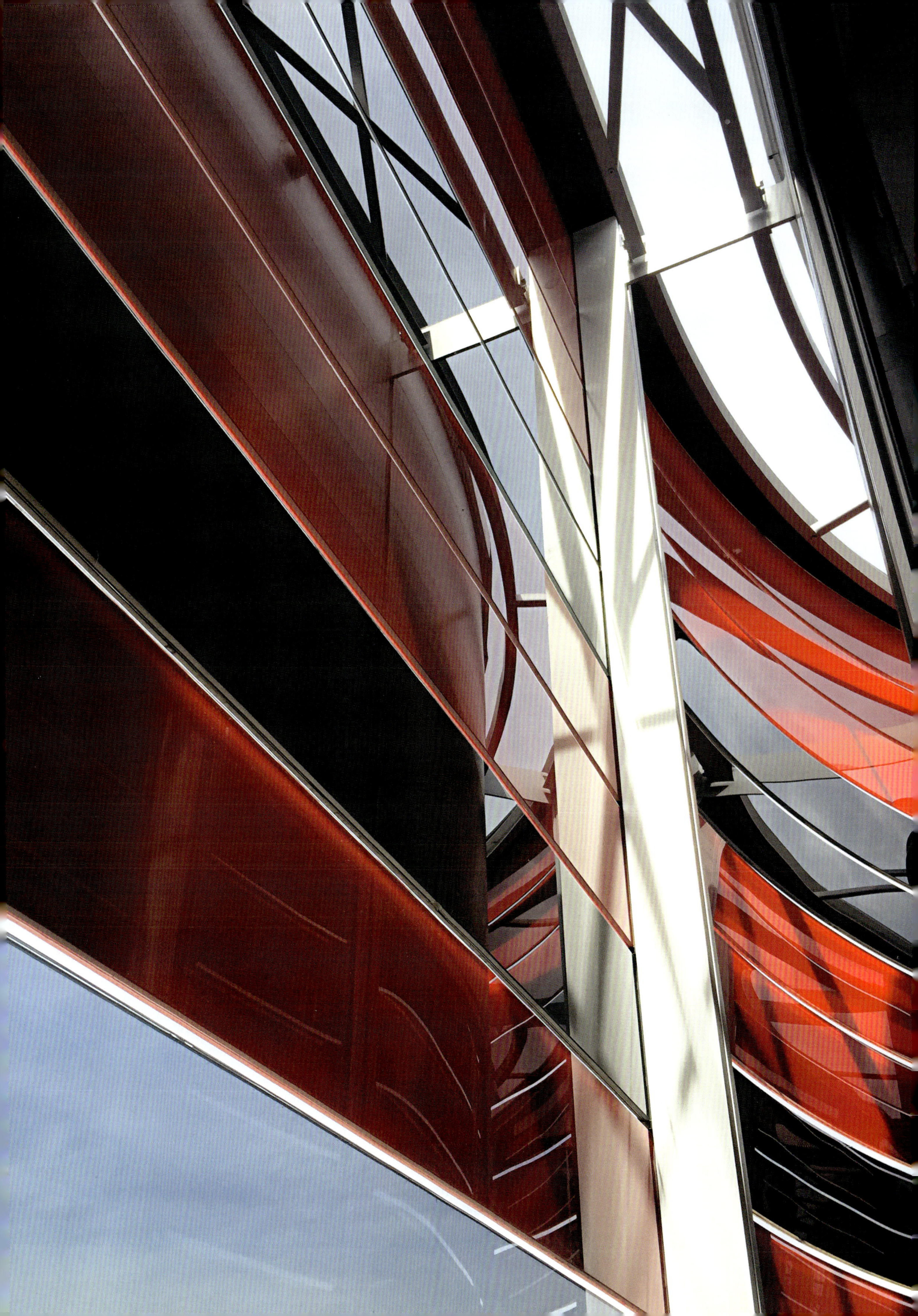

JEAN-MICHEL WILMOTTE

RUSSIAN ORTHODOX SPIRITUAL AND CULTURAL CENTER

The Russian Orthodox Spiritual and Cultural Center in Paris is clearly visible along the Seine, not far from the Pont de l'Alma and the Quai Branly Jacques Chirac Museum. It was built on the site of the former French national meteorological services building, close to the banks of the Seine.

There are in fact four distinct buildings in the complex, an Orthodox church, a parish hall and religious center, a school, and a cultural center. The church itself is capped with five traditionally shaped gold domes, peaked with Russian Orthodox crosses. These domes intentionally emerge as a landmark in the distinct skyline of the Left Bank quarter of Paris.

In designing this complex, the architects followed three main principles: respect for the canons of the Russian Orthodox Church, the incorporation of the center into a quintessentially Parisian, densely built neighborhood, and the desire to nonetheless create a very contemporary building. Inspired by medieval Orthodox churches, known for their sobriety, the architects adopted a minimalist approach and chose the same stone used at the nearby Trocadéro palace and the area at the base of the Eiffel Tower. Faceted and orchestrated horizontally, this stone clads the simple volumes, whose height was carefully calculated. The church, identifiable by its five gilt domes, occupies the center of the composition.

The 50,105-square-foot (4,655-square-meter) edifice, built for the government of the Russian Federation, is a reinforced concrete structure, which makes use of Massangis natural stone, glass, and gold leaf.

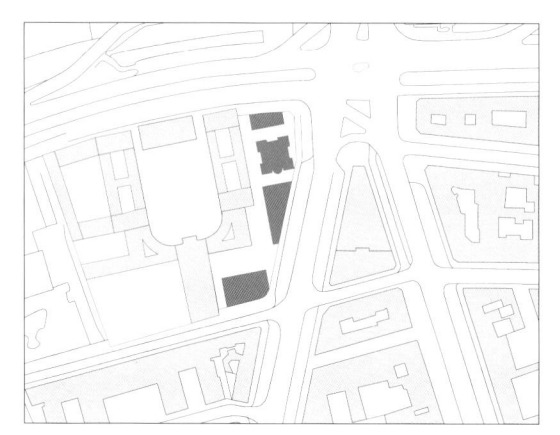

Location Paris, France
Completion date 2016
Area 50,105 ft^2 (4,655 m^2)

LOCATION PLAN

EXPLORATORY SKETCH OF ELEVATION

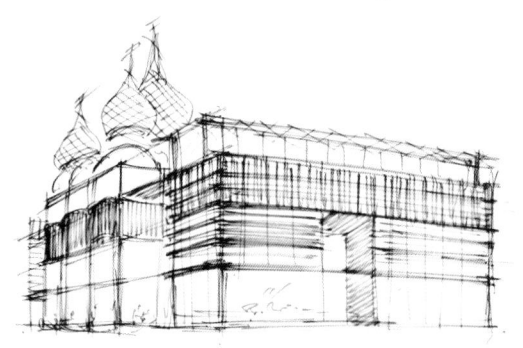

EXPLORATORY SKETCHES OF NORTH ELEVATION

CROSS SECTION

CHURCH ENTRANCE ELEVATION

LONG SECTION

SITE PLAN

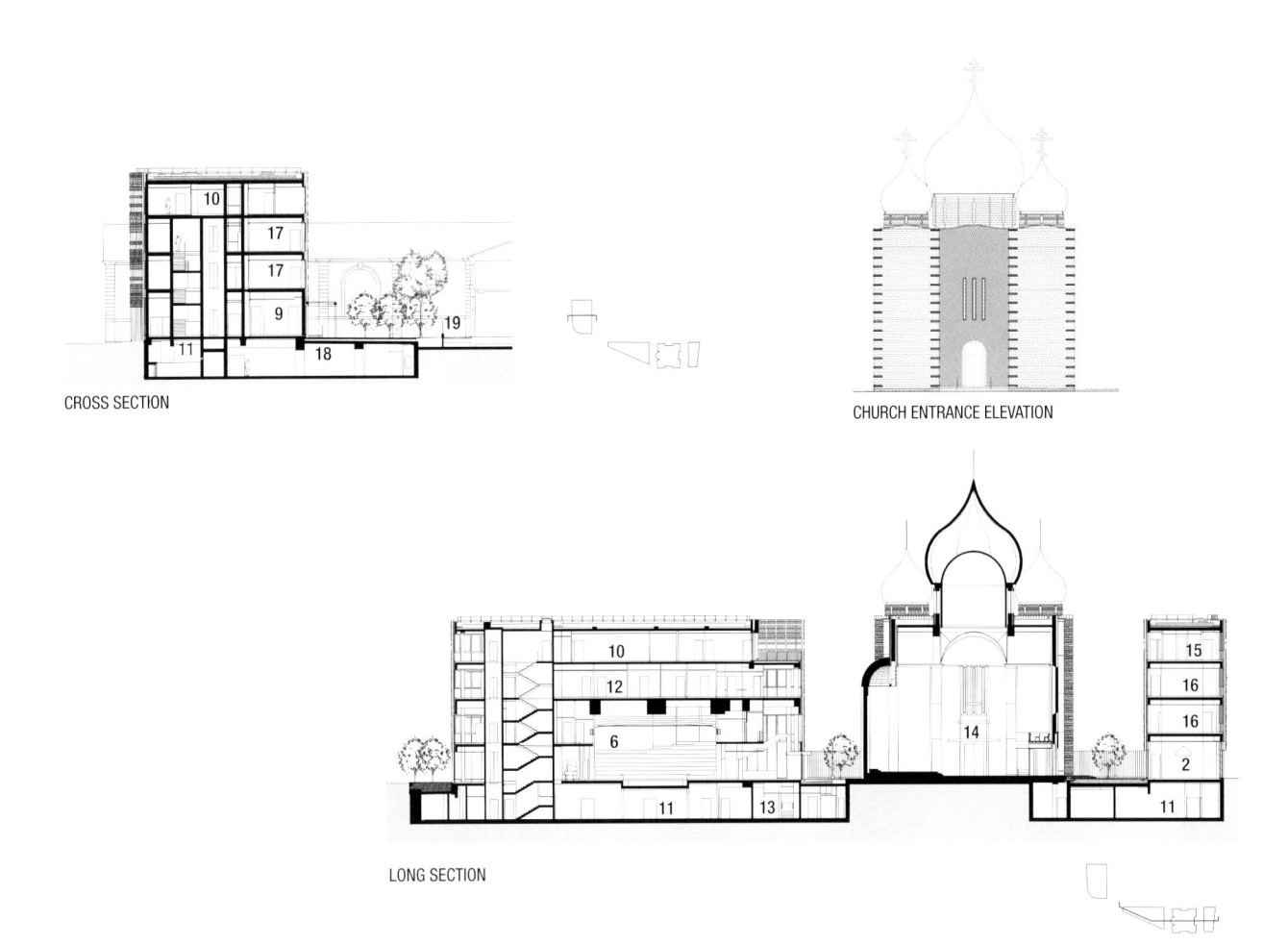

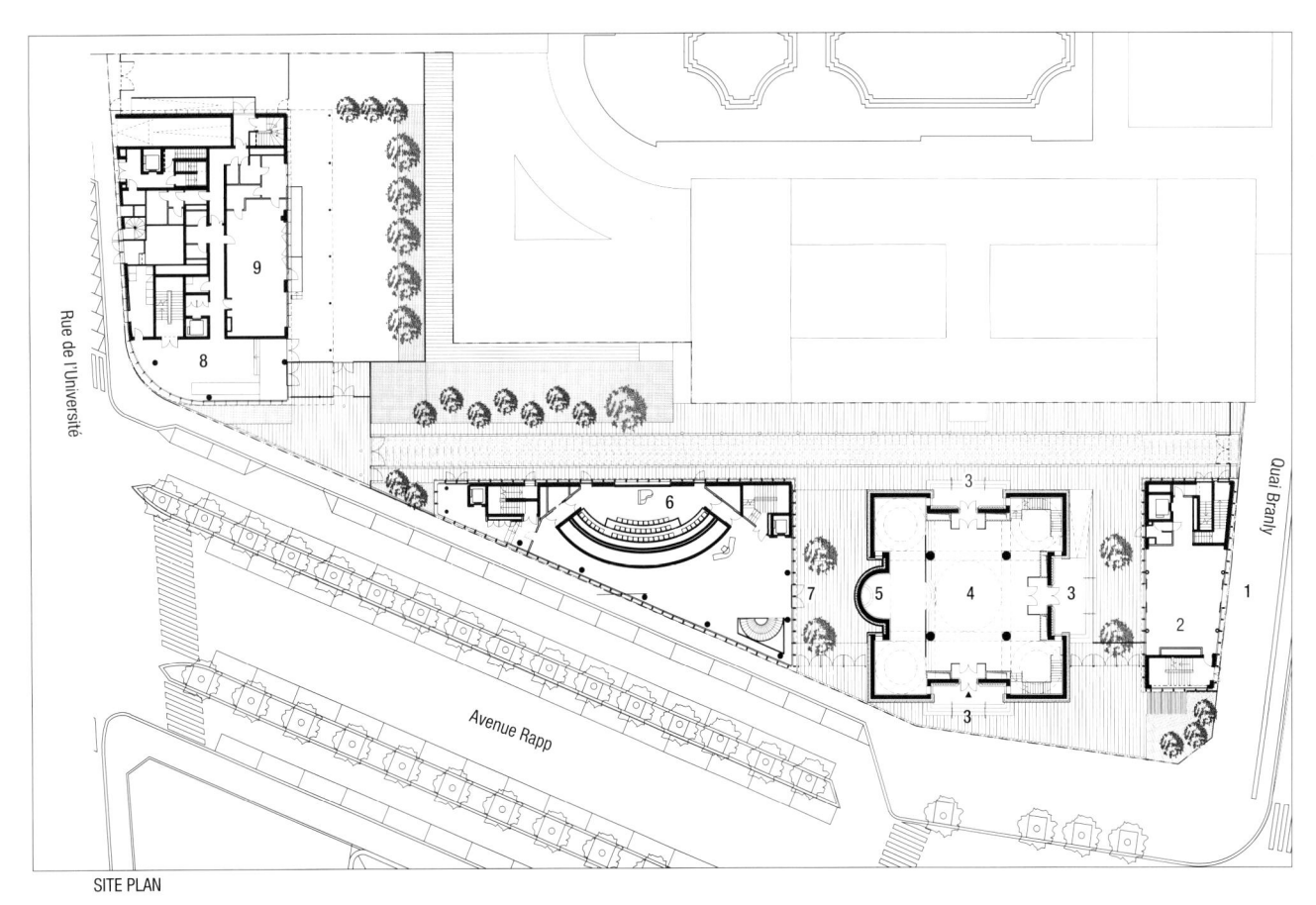

1. Quai Branly building entrance
2. Bookshop
3. Church entrance
4. Church choir
5. Altar
6. Auditorium
7. Avenue Rapp building entrance
8. Rue de l'Université building hall
9. Refectory
10. Apartment
11. Services
12. Parish center
13. Cloakroom
14. Church
15. Café
16. Exhibition hall
17. Classroom
18. Parking
19. Playground

0   10 m

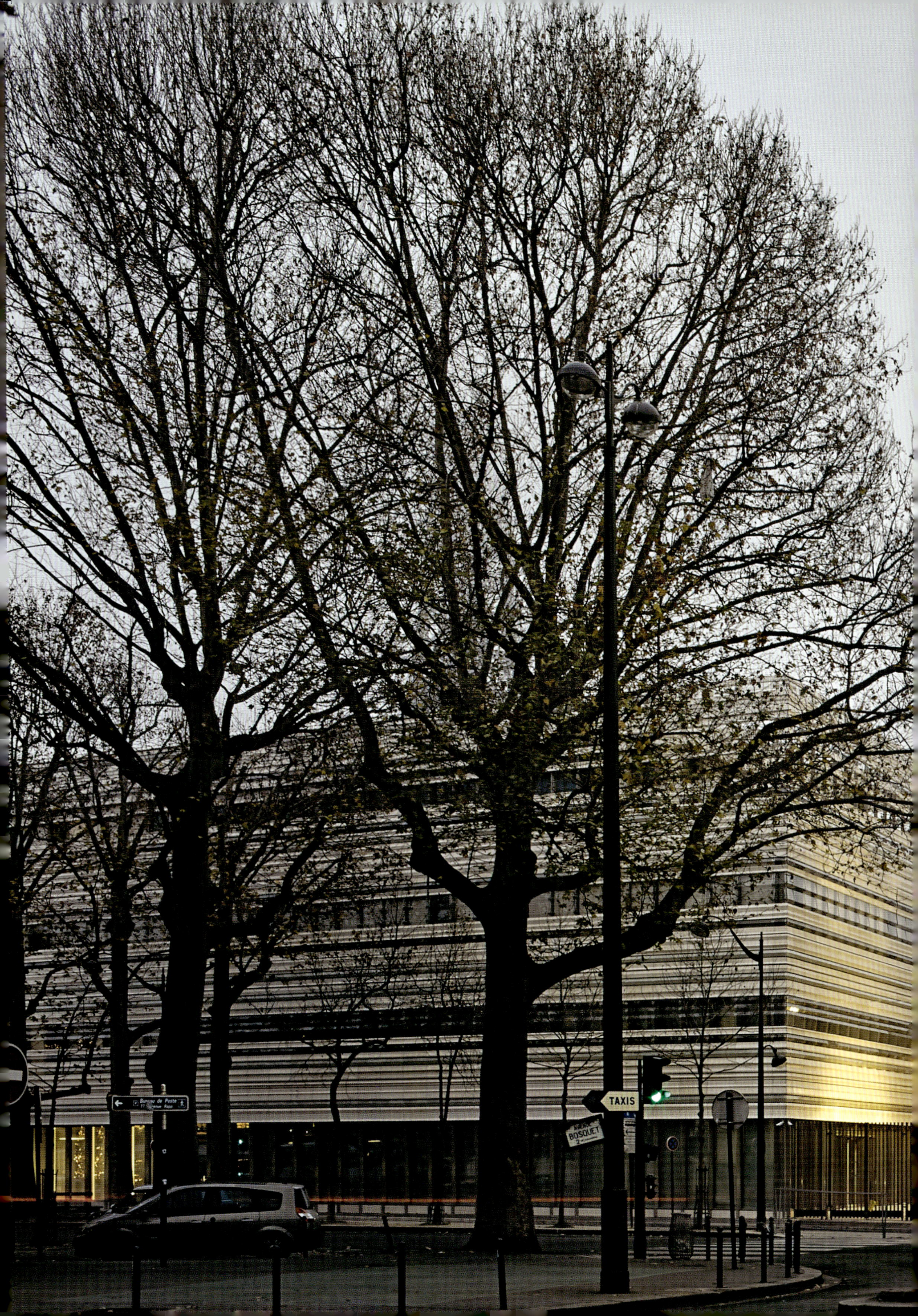
TAXIS
BOSQUET

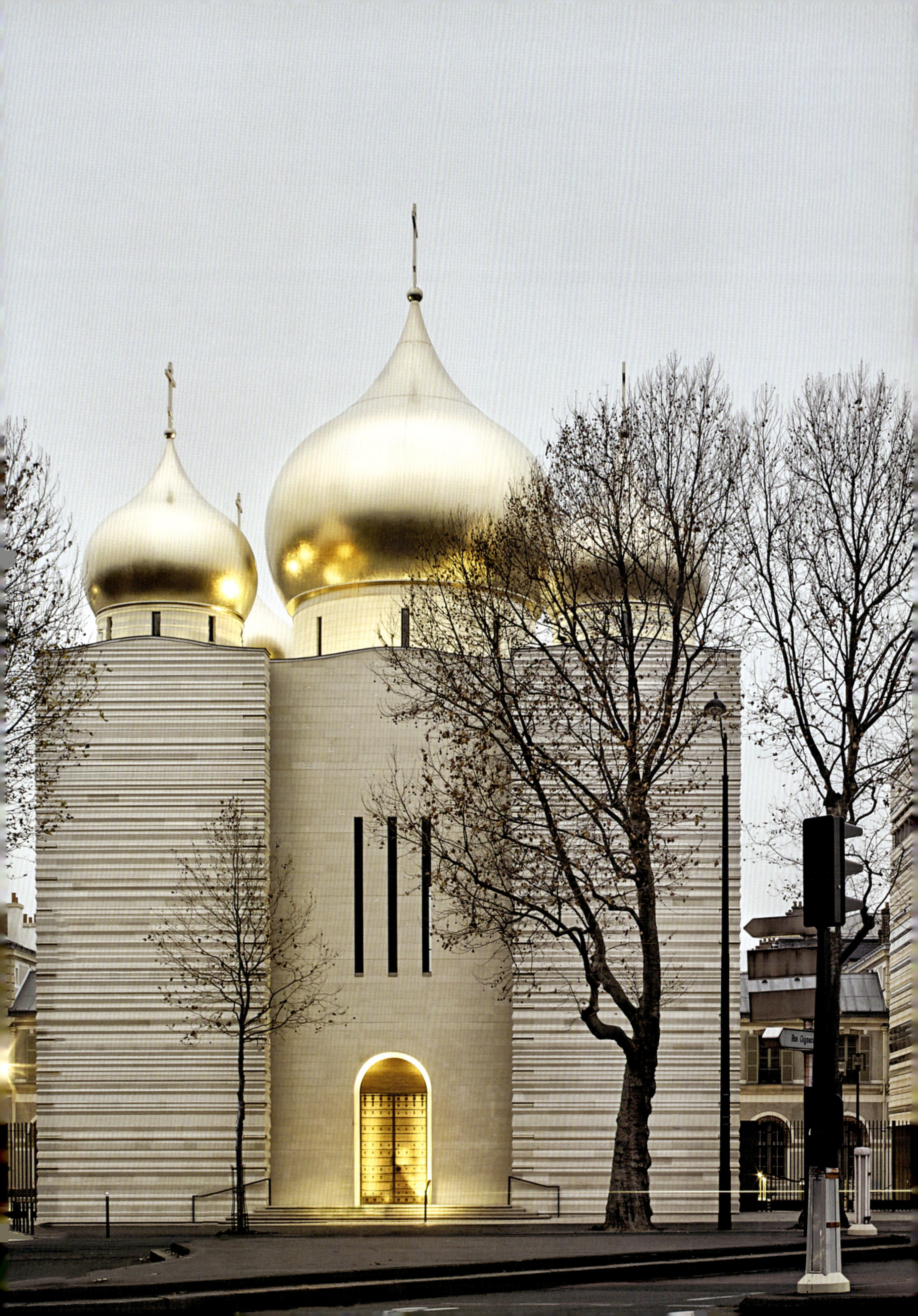

JEAN-MICHEL WILMOTTE RUSSIAN ORTHODOX SPIRITUAL AND CULTURAL CENTER

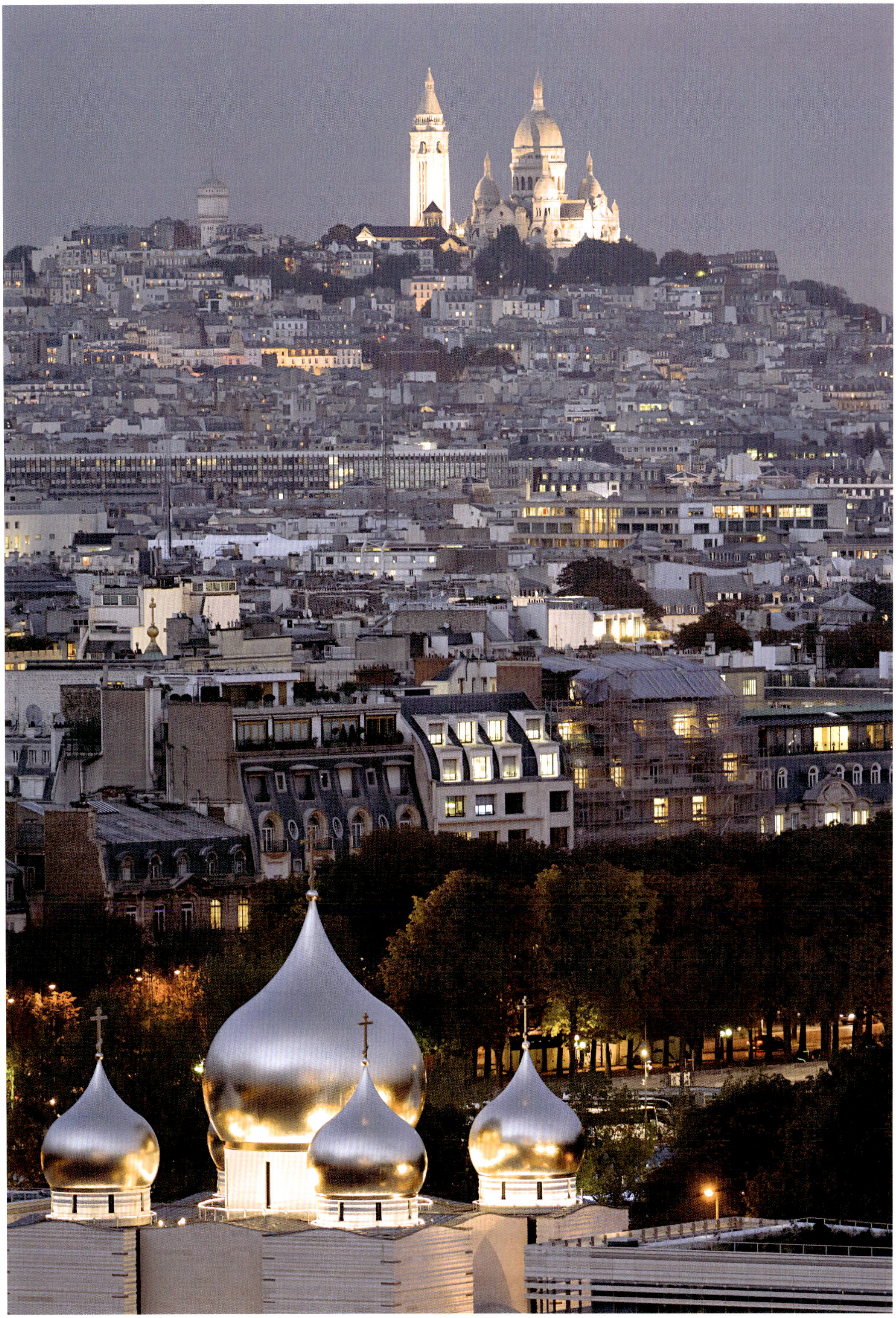

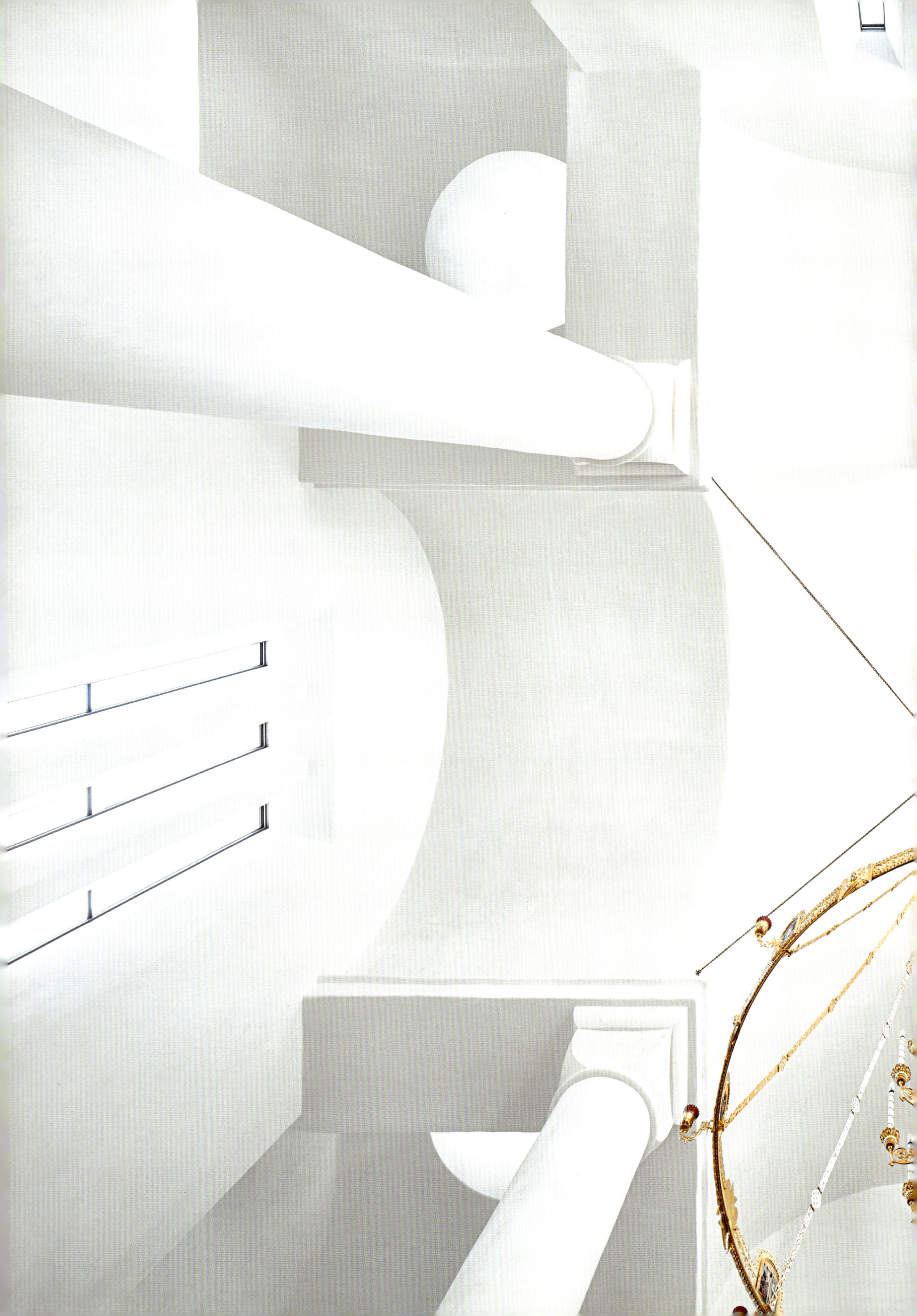

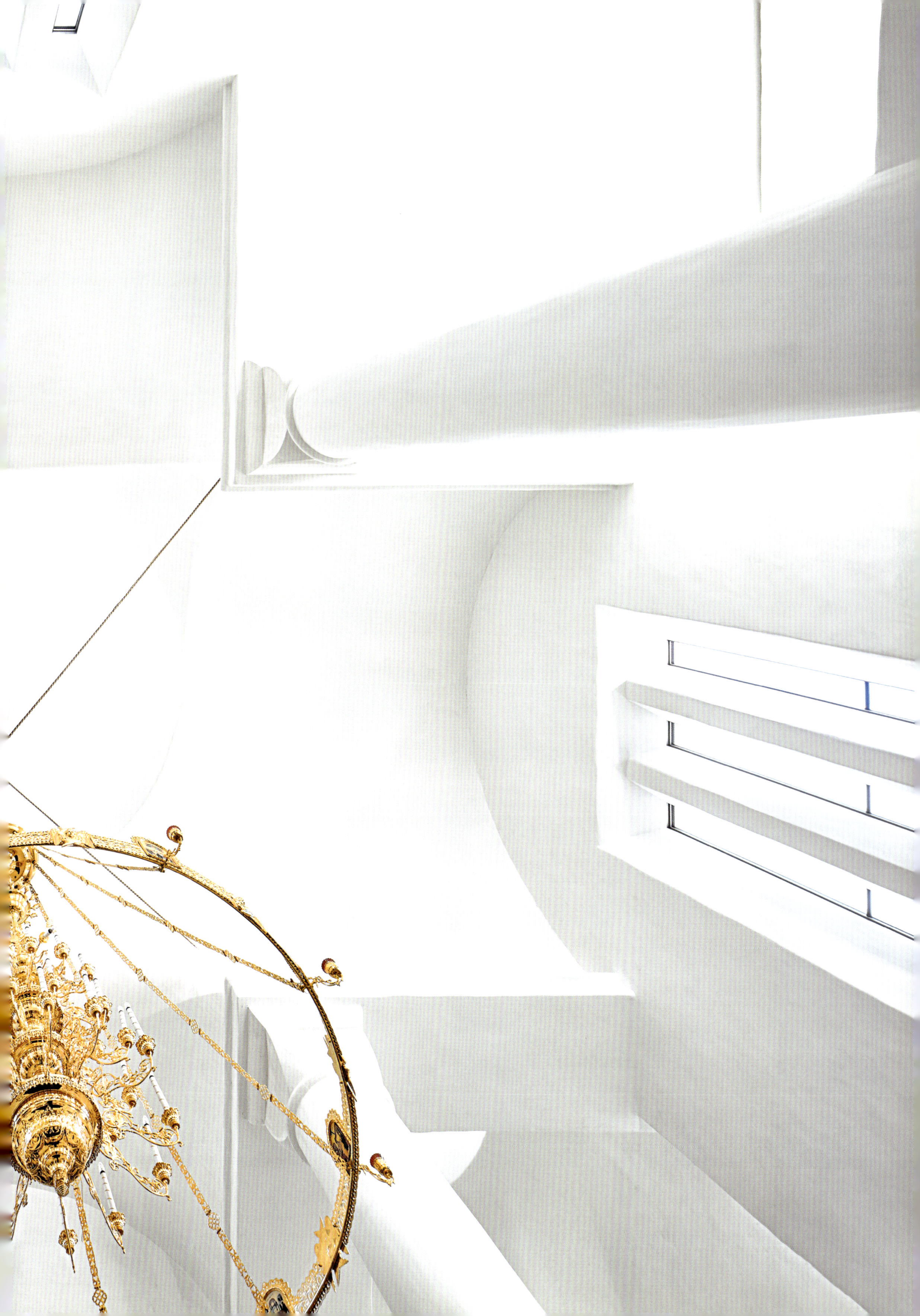

JEAN-MICHEL WILMOTTE

PRIVATE CHALET

This 6,460-square-foot (600-square-meter) chalet for a private client relies on a reinterpretation of local vernacular architecture. Built with reinforced concrete and a wood frame, the house also has surfaces in textured stained oak, Portuguese slate, and sheet metal. The Portuguese slate was chosen for the ample dimensions of each piece, used for the base of the house and for the roof. Fixtures used for the exteriors are in anthracite black metal.

"For thirty years farmhouses were dismantled for their wood, which gave a country feel to new chalets. It was nothing more nor less than transposition… pastiche. So what is a contemporary chalet? Finding an answer to that question is a fascinating challenge," states Jean-Michel Wilmotte. By reinterpreting practices, revisiting materials, acknowledging the past while asserting modernity, the design of this house represents an effort to ask what is most significant in mountain architecture, while attempting to avoid the pitfalls that frequent construction of luxury residences in the Alps have encountered.

For this project, the office carefully researched the kinds of wood finishes used in the Alps, seeking to refer to mountain architecture, while remaining resolutely modern. The south-facing terraces and pool penetrate into the chalet itself. The spa has stone walls and flooring, which are similar to the slate used outside. The same kind of continuity between exterior and interior occurs on the upper level, with full height openings.

Location Mont Blanc region, France
Completion date 2016
Area 6,460 ft² (600 m²)

LOCATION MAP

WEST ELEVATION

SOUTH ELEVATION

NORTH ELEVATION

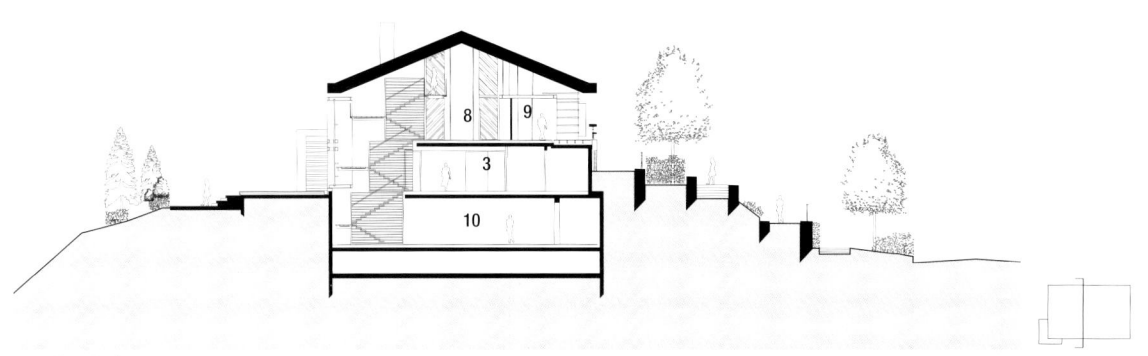

CROSS SECTION

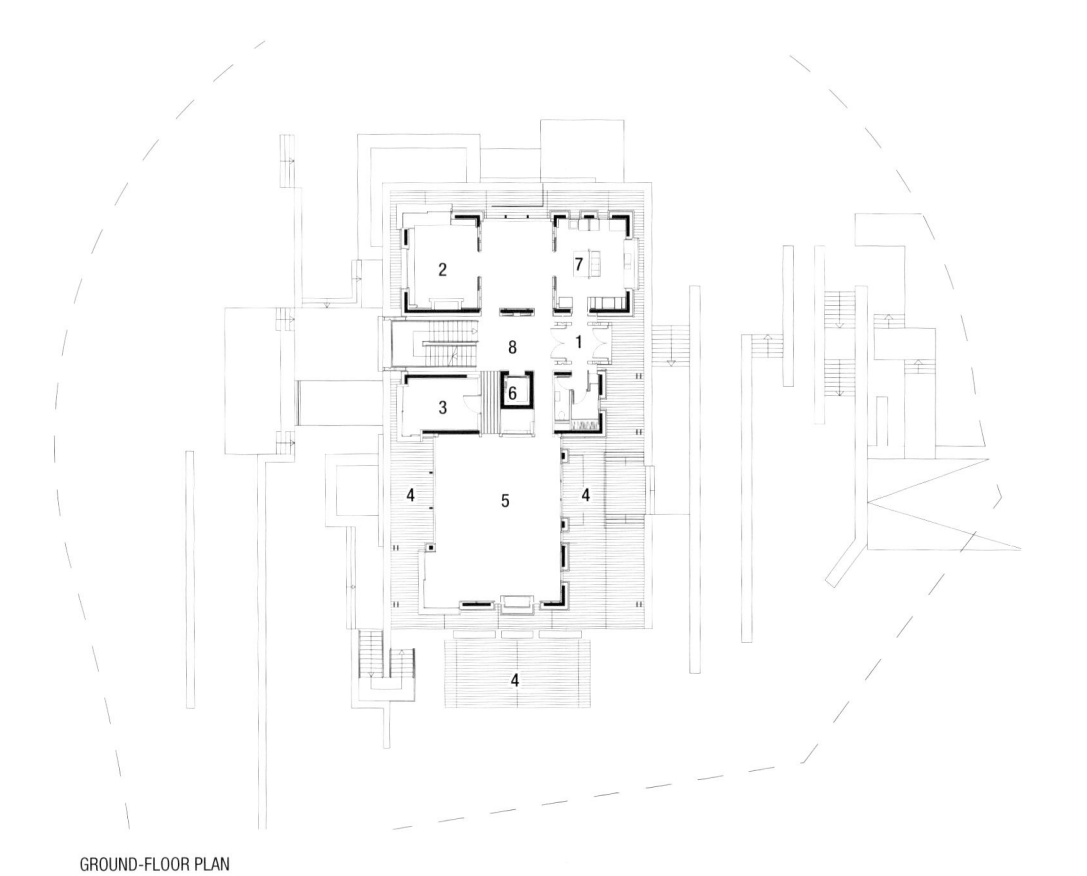

GROUND-FLOOR PLAN

1 Entrance
2 Small lounge
3 Bedroom
4 Terrace
5 Living room
6 Elevator
7 Kitchen
8 Entrance hall
9 Hall
10 Parking

0 10 m

99

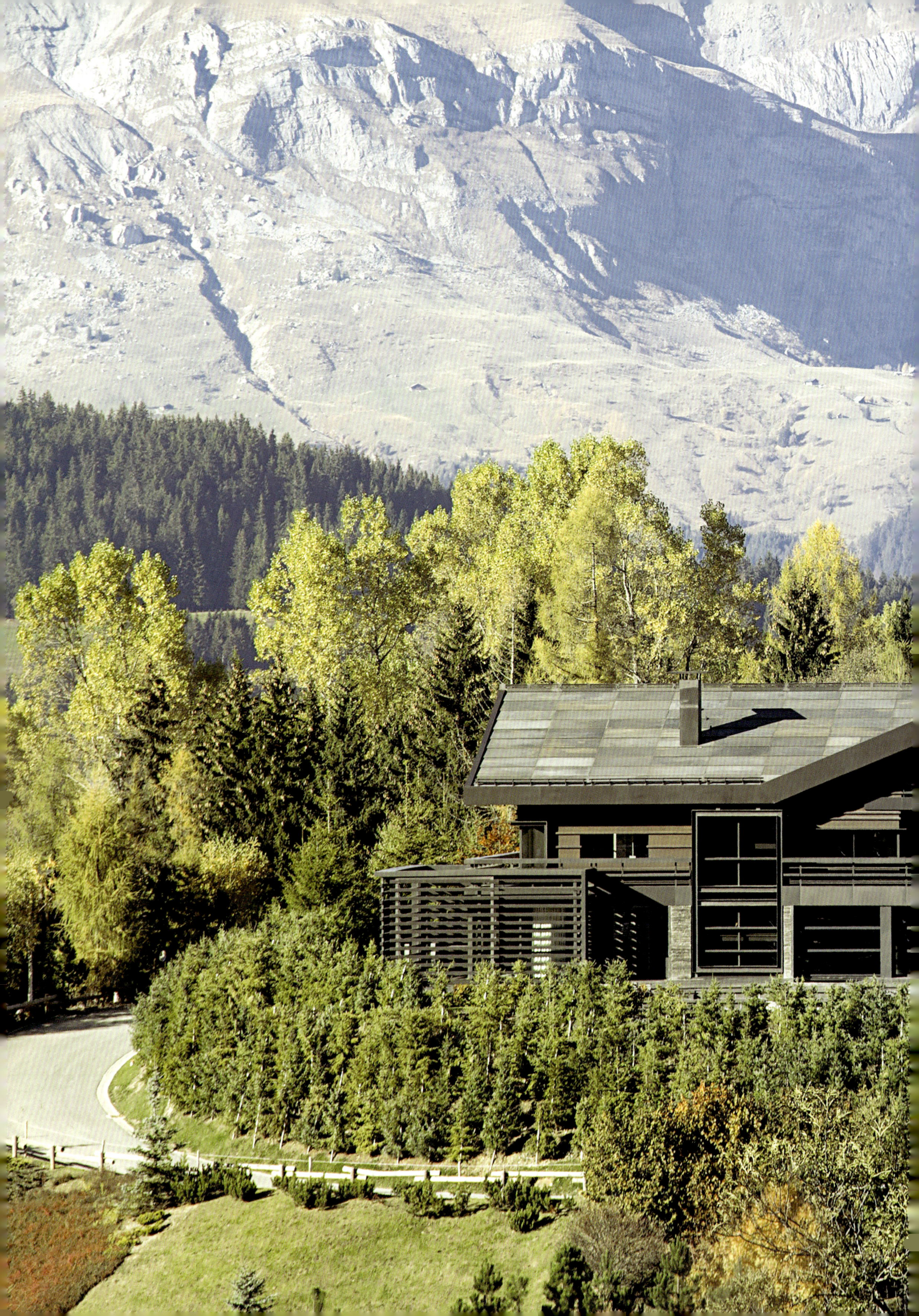

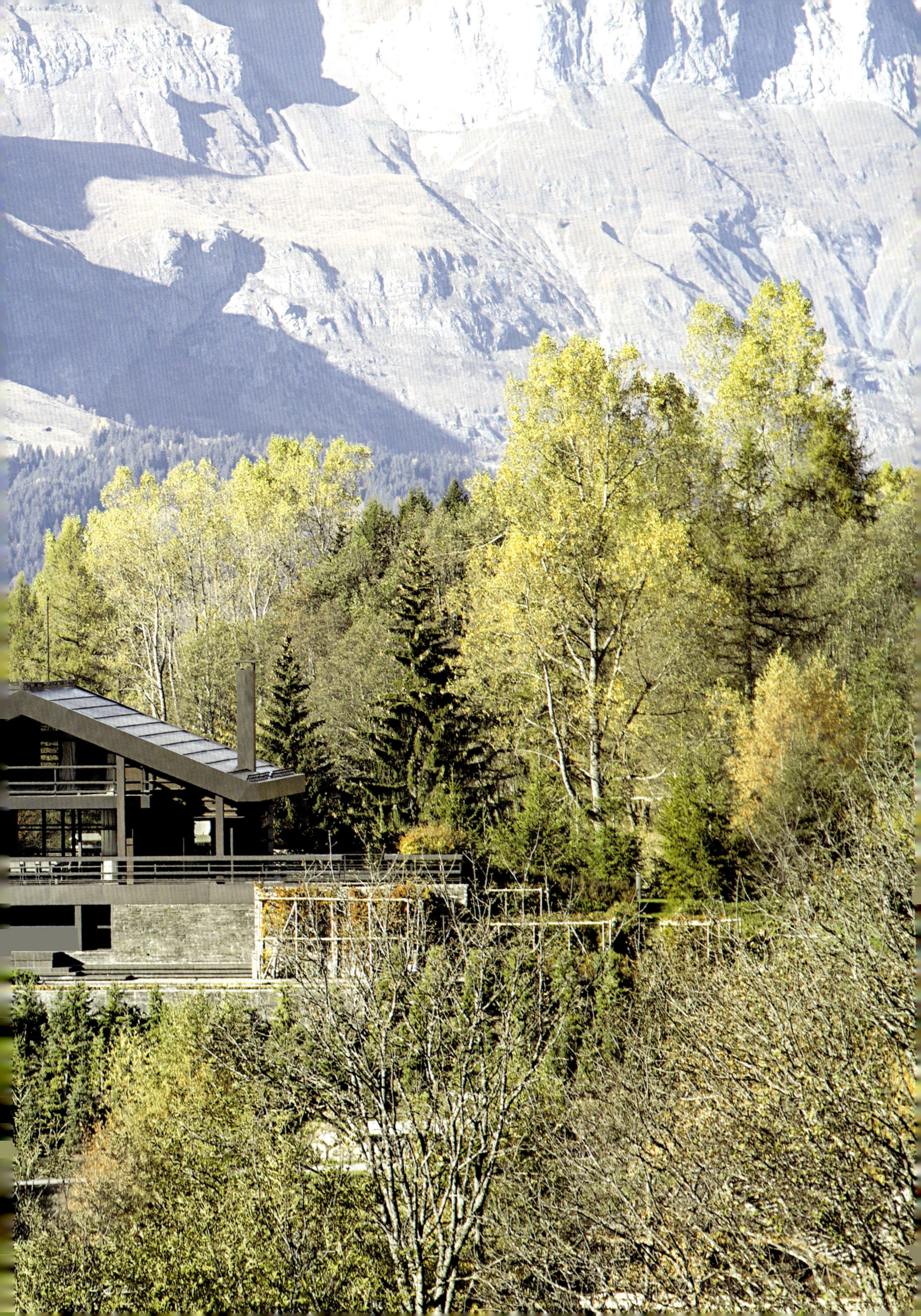

JEAN-MICHEL WILMOTTE   PRIVATE CHALET

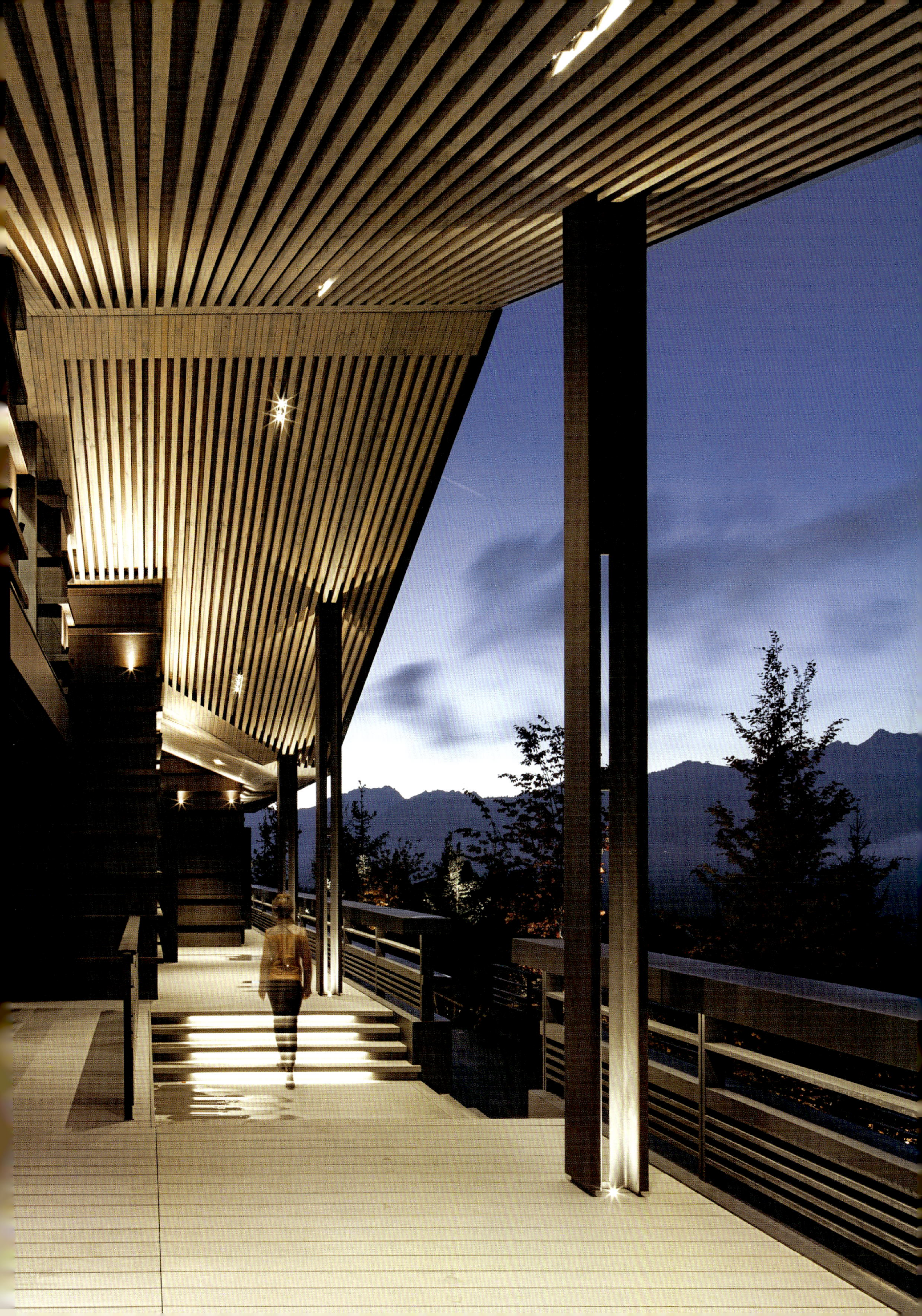

JEAN-MICHEL WILMOTTE

EIFFAGE CORPORATE HEADQUARTERS

The 258,335-square-foot (24,000-square-meter) building offers corporate headquarter offices, an exhibition hall, library, company cafeteria, and car park. It is a concrete structure with a steel frame clad in aluminum and a ventilated curtain wall. Built on the historic site of Eiffage, the French civil engineering company, which is the corporate heir of the firm founded by Gustave Eiffel, designer of the Eiffel Tower, the new building is made up of three distinct volumes. It is intended for 1,200 to 1,600 employees.

The new building is linked to the existing building by a 'bridge' composing part of the Pierre Berger Campus, which unites all the company's businesses. Sober and functional, the building emphasizes steel and concrete, two areas of expertise mastered by this construction-industry firm. The façades of two of the three volumes are composed of gray aluminum punctuated with projecting, prismatic windows. The highly polished aluminum window frames create a regular pattern that orchestrates the geometric façade. A majestic steel spiral staircase in the main hall leads to the garden level below, which hosts the building's public zones—cafeteria and corporate restaurant. The staircase is a veritable piece of sculpture, sanded and lacquered on site. A light fixture of fluorescent tubes mimics the spiraling progress of the stair, step by step.

The 6,030-square-foot (560-square-meter), light-filled main hall runs from north to south. Designed as an exhibition space, it showcases Eiffage's expertise—mobile display units, designed to hold large models, were devised specially for the hall and its temporary exhibits. The hall is not showy, but reflects functional esthetics: raw concrete poured in-situ, glazed stone tile flooring, a sound-insulated double ceiling, black metal doors and window frames. From every point in the hall visitors have a view of the garden just below, forming a natural bowl around the building.

Location Vélizy-Villacoublay, France
Completion date 2015
Area 258,335 ft² (24,000 m²)

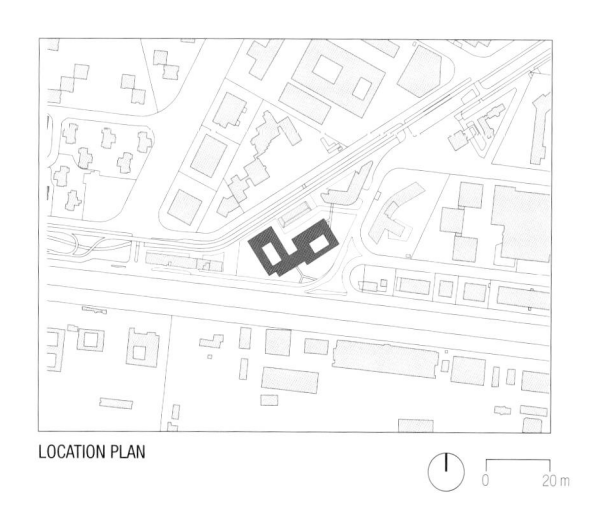

LOCATION PLAN

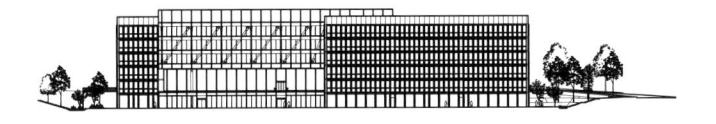

SOUTH ELEVATION

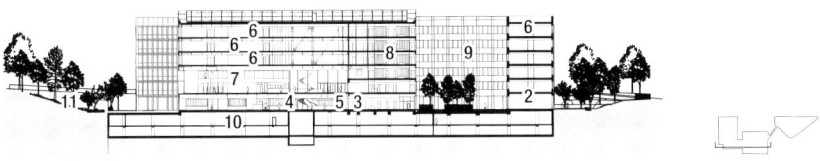

LONG SECTION

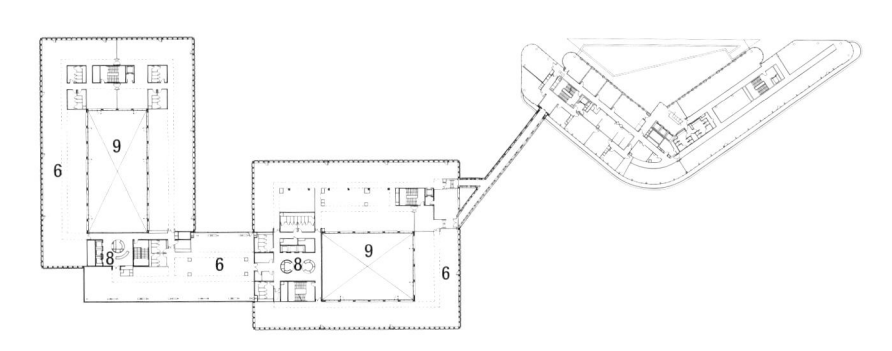

FOURTH-FLOOR PLAN

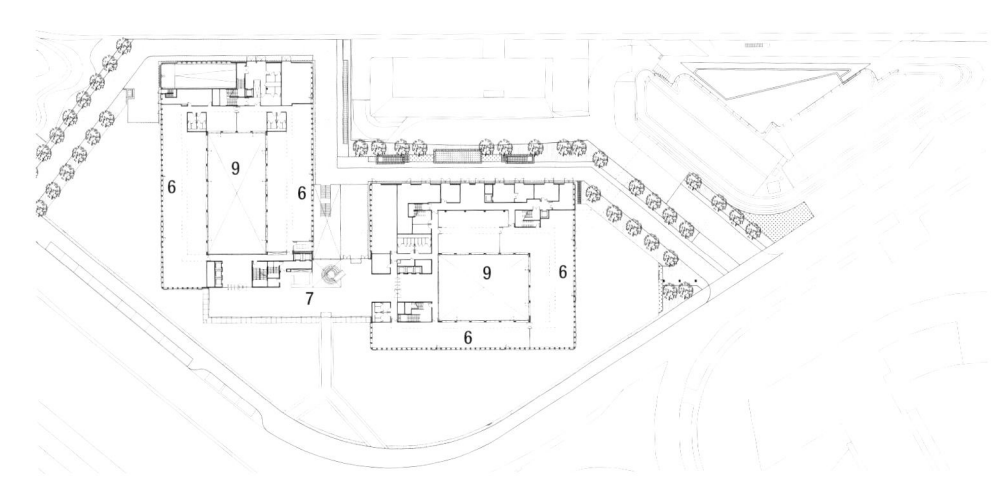

GROUND-FLOOR PLAN

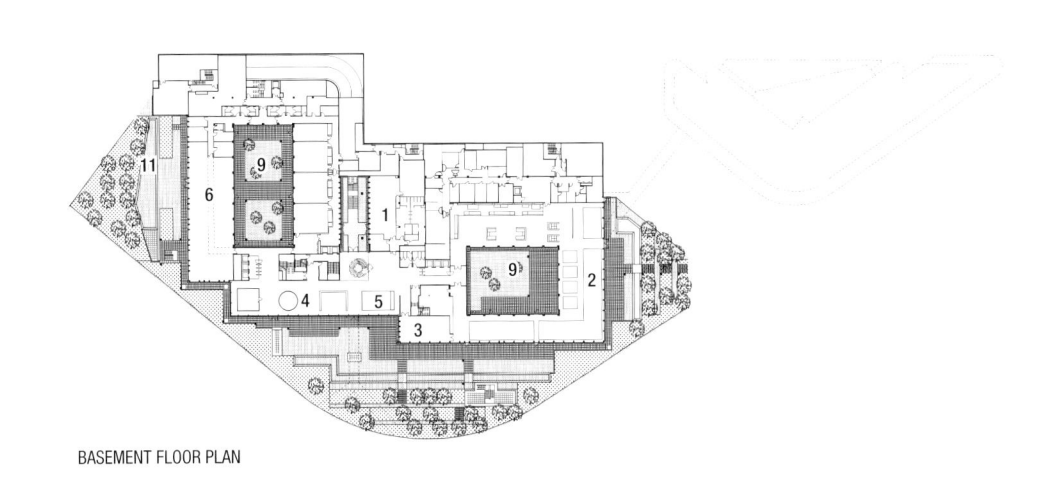

BASEMENT FLOOR PLAN

1 Fitness room
2 Restaurant
3 Library
4 Recreation room
5 Café
6 Offices
7 Hall
8 Lobby
9 Patio
10 Parking
11 Garden

0   20 m

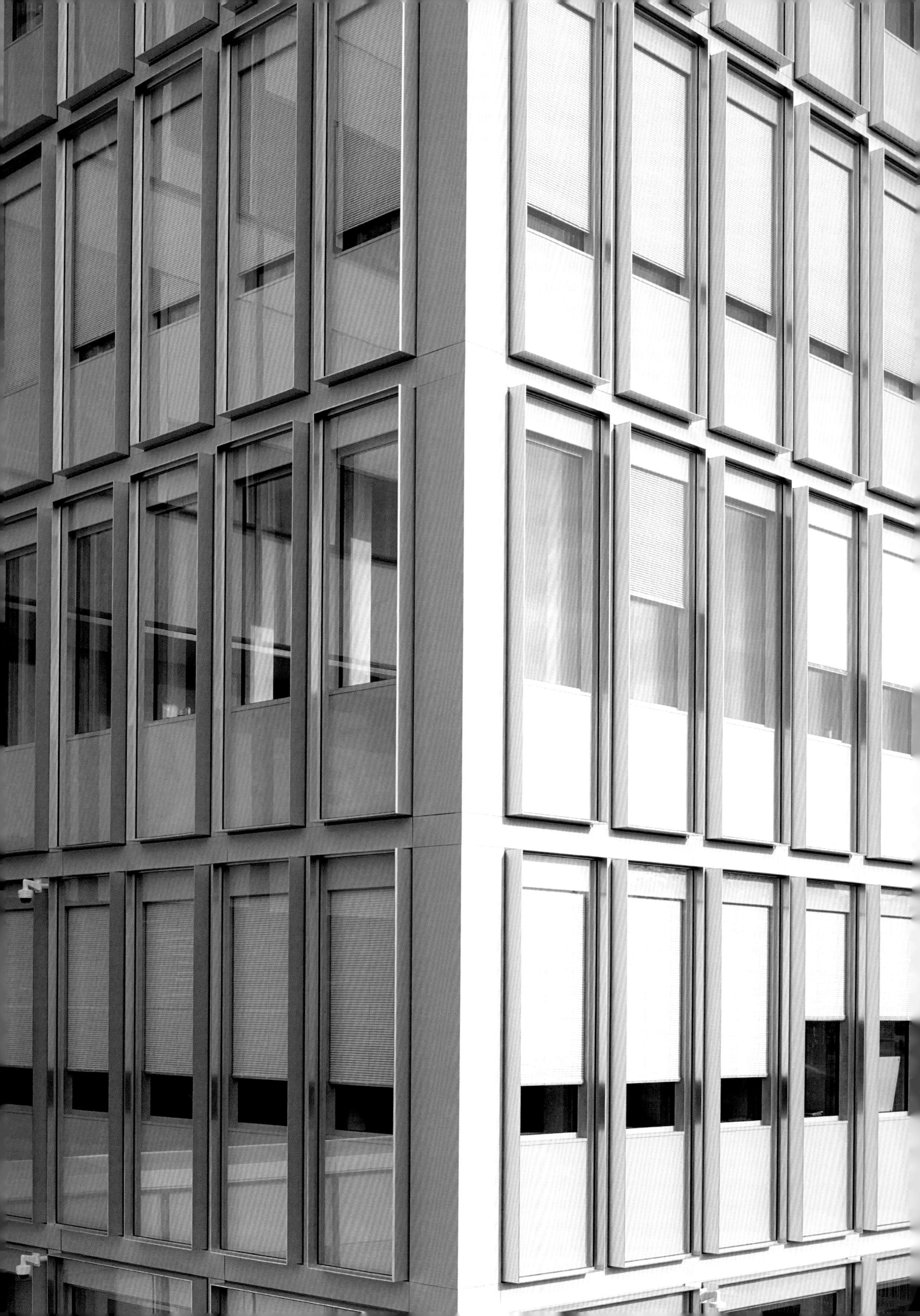

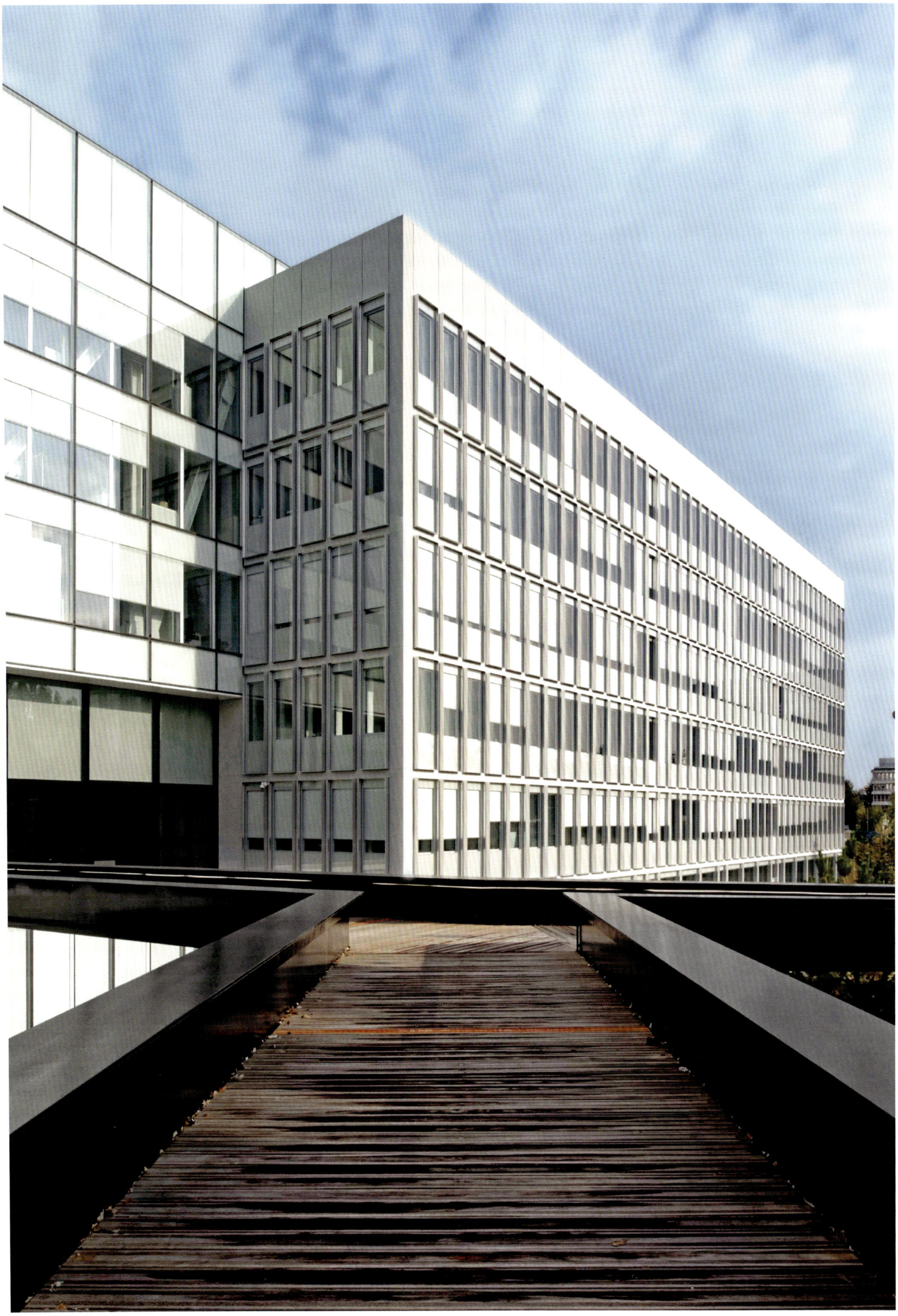

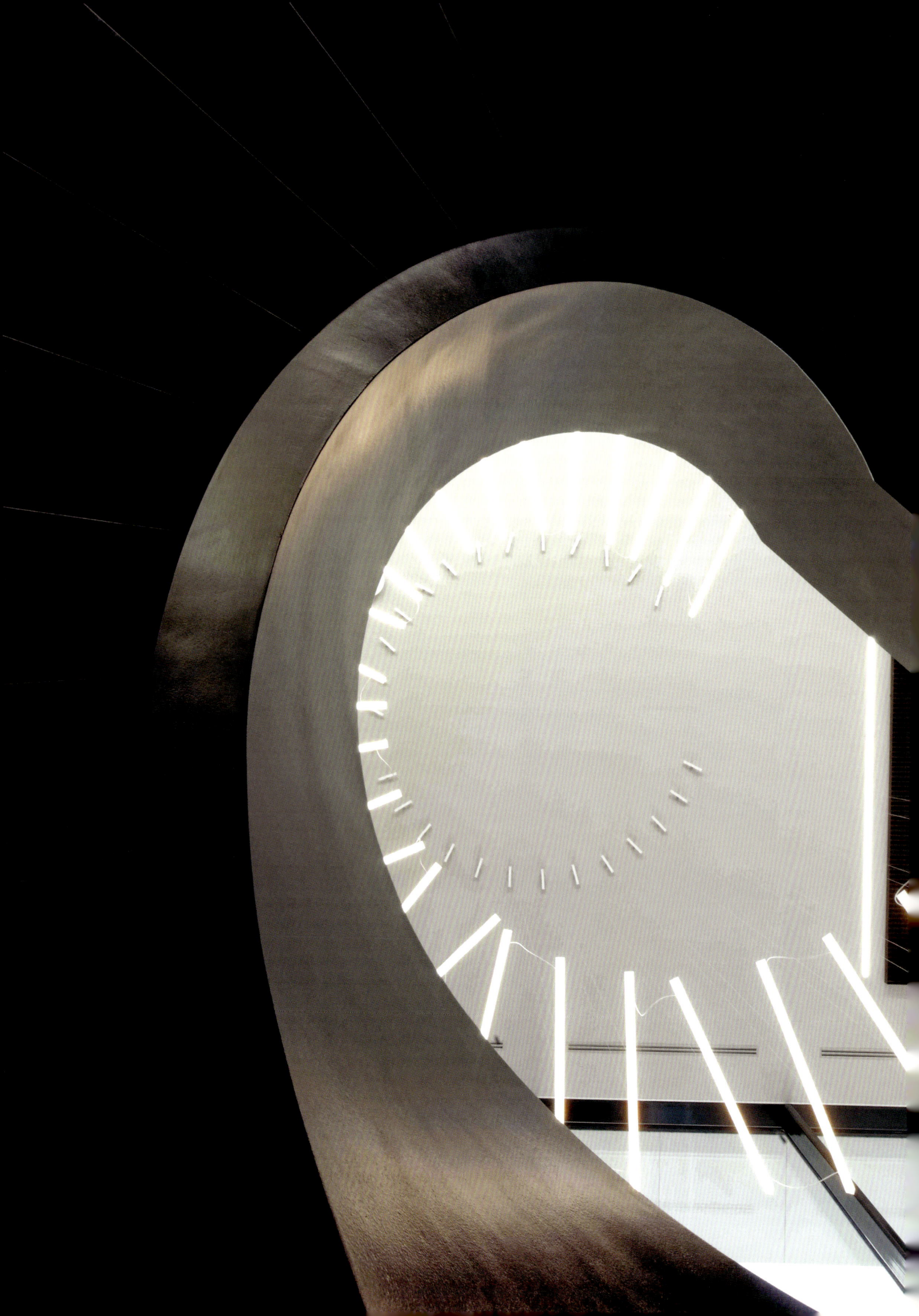

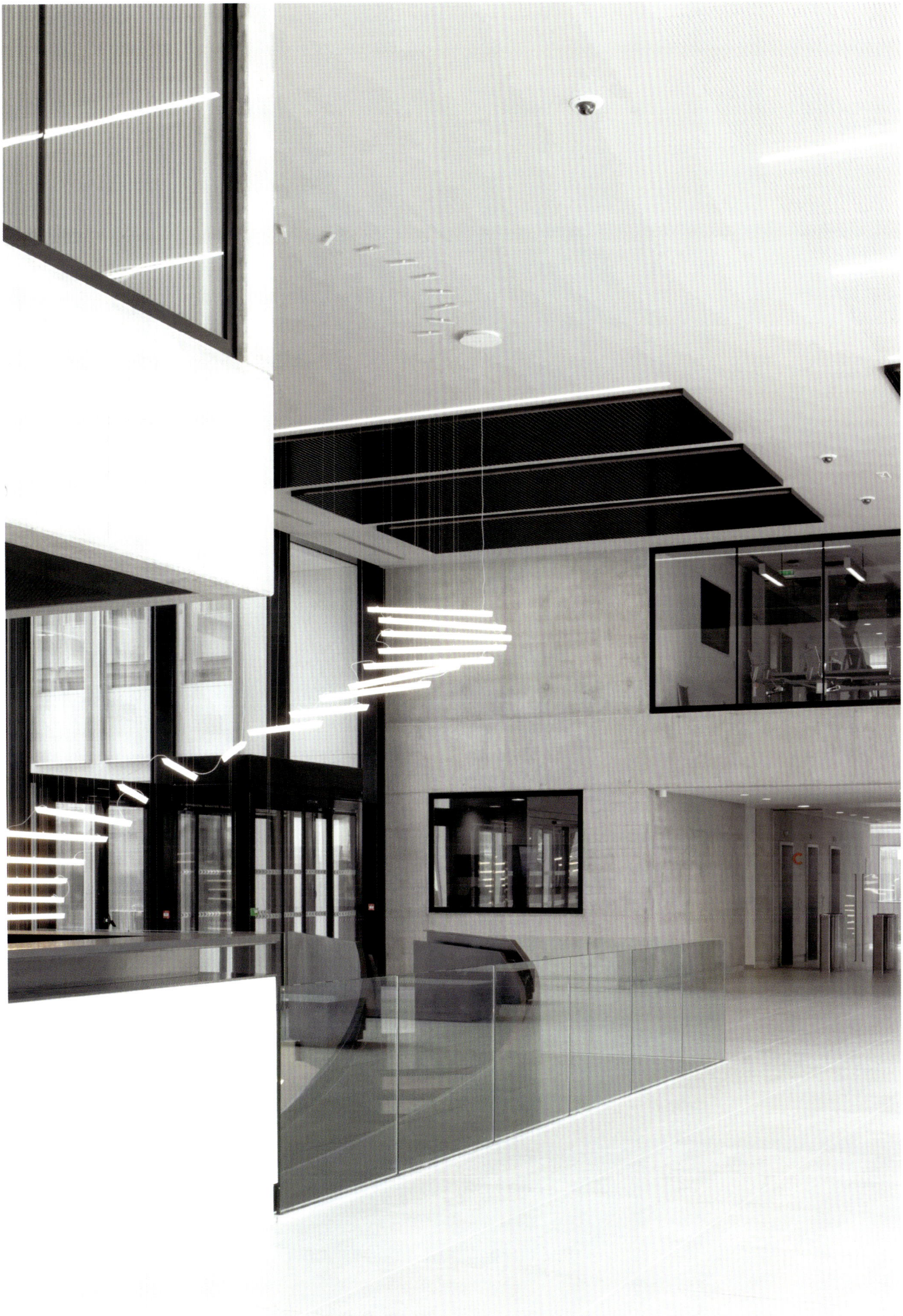

JEAN-MICHEL WILMOTTE

BLEU CIEL RESIDENTIAL TOWER

Located in Harwood's 17-city block district, 'Harwood Village' will be the latest addition to the Uptown area of Dallas. The site is a rectangular block sandwiched between McKinnon Street to the north, North Harwood Street to the south, and Wolf Street to the east. Setting a benchmark in urban living, the ambition of the project is to bring new life to the city's urban sprawl.

The planned project will include Bleu Ciel, a 31-story residential tower, Seven, a 27-story office building and The Square, comprising a landscaped public plaza with shops and restaurants. Bleu Ciel will rise to a height of 370 feet (113 meters) and is imagined as a 'gateway' to the Harwood District. The development will add more than 49,515 square feet (4,600 square meters) of retail and restaurant space, over 299,235 square feet (27,800 square meters) of office space, as well as 230 apartment homes. Apartments in Bleu Ciel range from one-bedroom units to two-bedroom study units, all with a large private terrace catering to the needs of contemporary living.

Bleu Ciel proposes a typology where the city does not stop at the front door, but extends into and enlivens the home. Sculptural in form and curvilinear in plan, the tower is driven by a number of physical influences, the most important one being the context of the site itself. The curvilinear terraces with frosted glass railings give the tall tower a soft appearance, a counterpoint to neighboring rectilinear structures. To prevent the tower from overpowering its neighbors, the design steps back the forms—a gesture that also allows it to better withstand wind forces.

Location Dallas, Texas, United States
Completion date 2018
Area 461,000 ft² (42,800 m²)

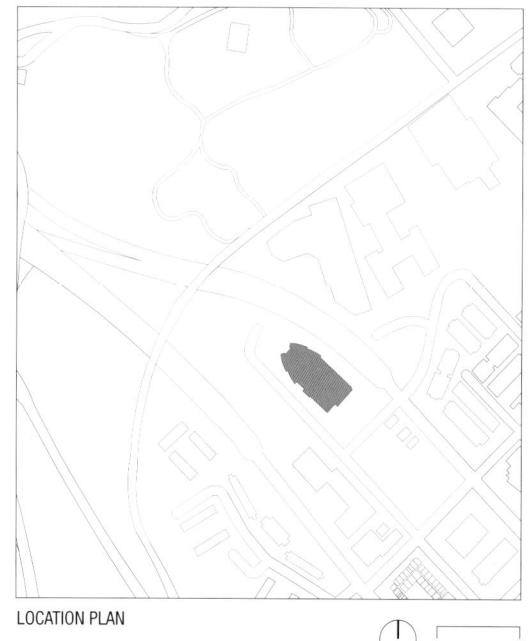

LOCATION PLAN

DUPLEX APARTMENTS TERRACES FLOOR PLAN

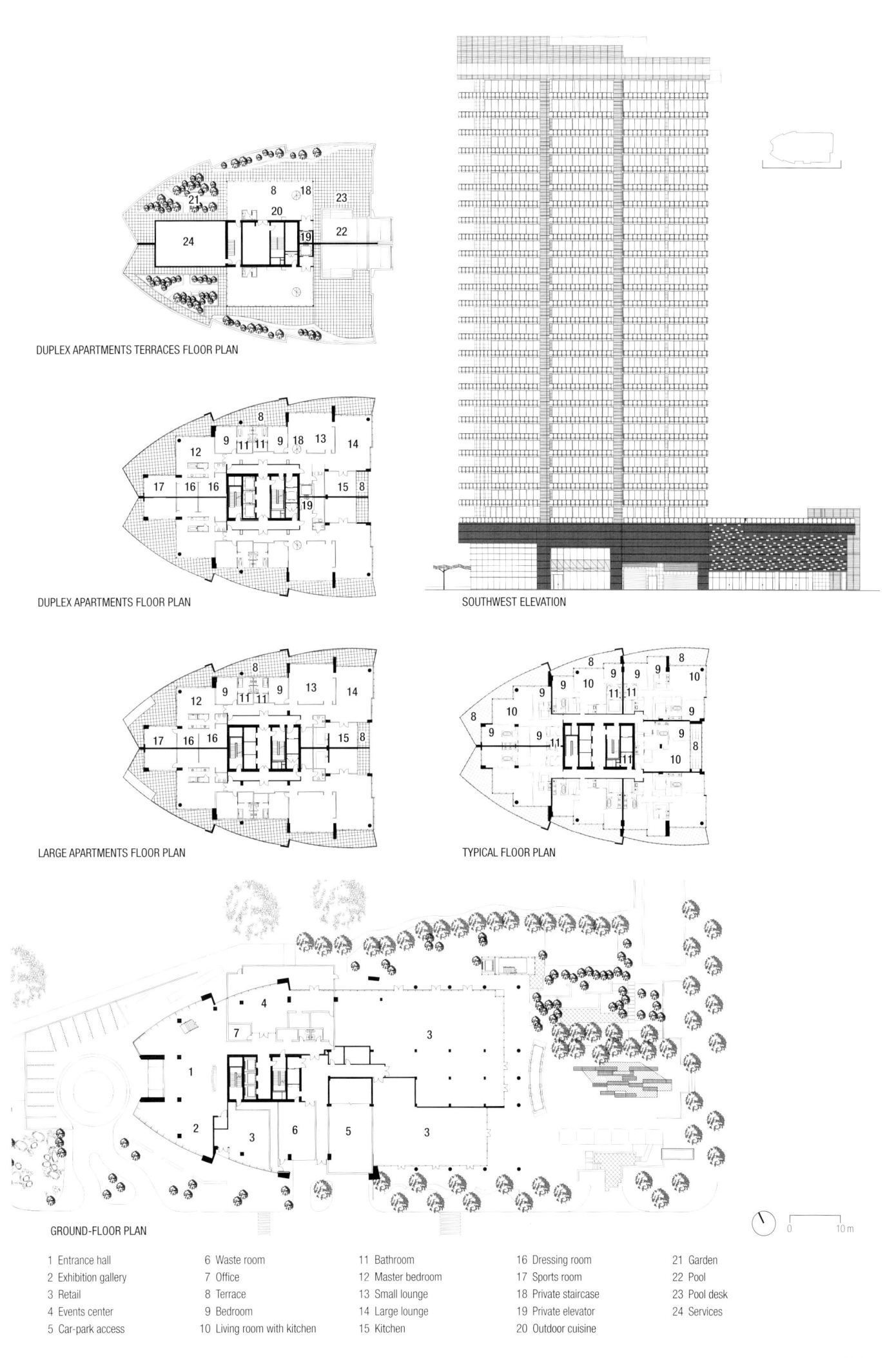

DUPLEX APARTMENTS FLOOR PLAN

SOUTHWEST ELEVATION

LARGE APARTMENTS FLOOR PLAN

TYPICAL FLOOR PLAN

GROUND-FLOOR PLAN

1 Entrance hall
2 Exhibition gallery
3 Retail
4 Events center
5 Car-park access
6 Waste room
7 Office
8 Terrace
9 Bedroom
10 Living room with kitchen
11 Bathroom
12 Master bedroom
13 Small lounge
14 Large lounge
15 Kitchen
16 Dressing room
17 Sports room
18 Private staircase
19 Private elevator
20 Outdoor cuisine
21 Garden
22 Pool
23 Pool desk
24 Services

JEAN-MICHEL WILMOTTE   BLEU CIEL RESIDENTIAL TOWER

113

JEAN-MICHEL WILMOTTE

GIROFLÉES TOWER

The Giroflées Tower will be a 22-story, 425-foot (130-meter) residential tower built on the eastern side of Monaco in the Saint-Roman district. It is located between the Rue des Giroflées and the Boulevard du Tenao and will have 73 luxury apartments. There will also be a family center, a spa, retail space, and three pools, including two private ones on the roof.

The reinforced concrete structure with six subterranean parking levels was carefully designed to maximize views of the Mediterranean to the south. Stainless steel, stone, and glass were used for cladding, with an eye to reducing energy consumption as much as possible. Sliding panels function as solar screens and the broad terraces provide efficient shading.

When completed, the highly efficient Giroflées Tower will undoubtedly earn an environment-friendly certification (BREEAM Very Good). Water usage, heating, and cooling areas all carefully controlled to reduce the carbon footprint of the tower. The landscape design is by Jean Mus, who is based not far away in the village of Cabris, while interior décor is by Ora Ito. The building was imagined as though it emerges from the center of gardens and terraces near ground level, leaving a green space around it, but also within its walls. The actual building occupies 28 percent of the site, leaving ample space for greenery. The client for the project is the Michel Pastor Group.

Location Monaco
Completion date 2020
Area 226,040 ft² (21,000 m²)

LOCATION PLAN

SOUTH ELEVATION

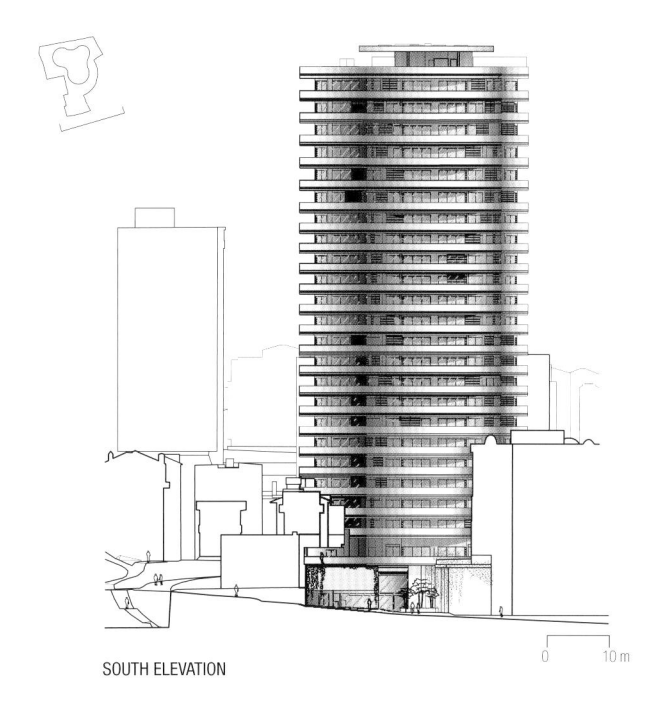

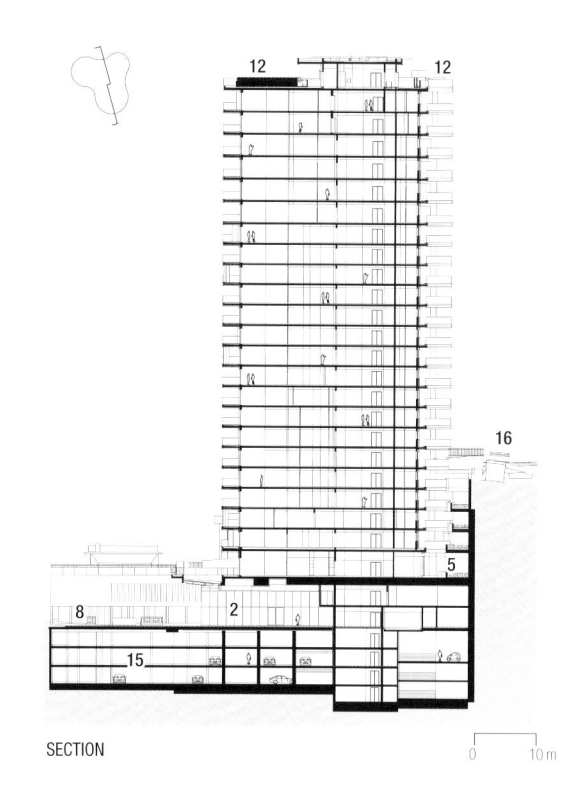

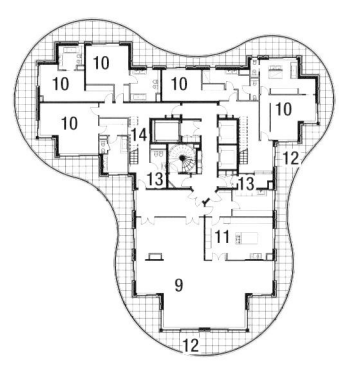

SECTION

TWO TRIPLEX APARTMENTS FLOOR PLAN (LEVEL 21)

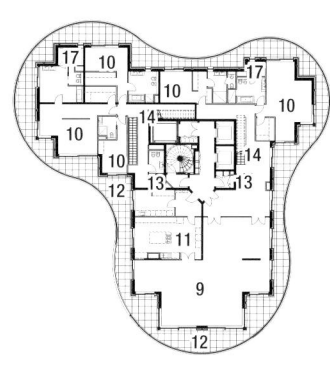

TWO TRIPLEX APARTMENTS FLOOR PLAN (LEVEL 22)

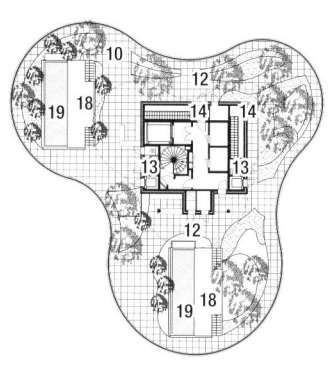

TWO TRIPLEX APARTMENTS FLOOR PLAN (LEVEL 23)

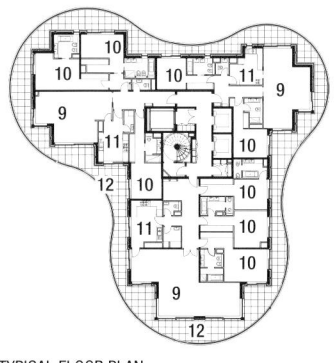

TYPICAL FLOOR PLAN

1. Reception hall
2. Retail
3. Security control room
4. Bicycle parking
5. Motorbike parking
6. Waste room
7. Services
8. Car-park access
9. Living room
10. Bedroom
11. Kitchen
12. Terrace
13. Private elevator
14. Private staircase
15. Parking
16. Access road from the north at level 5
17. Sauna
18. Deck
19. Swimming pool

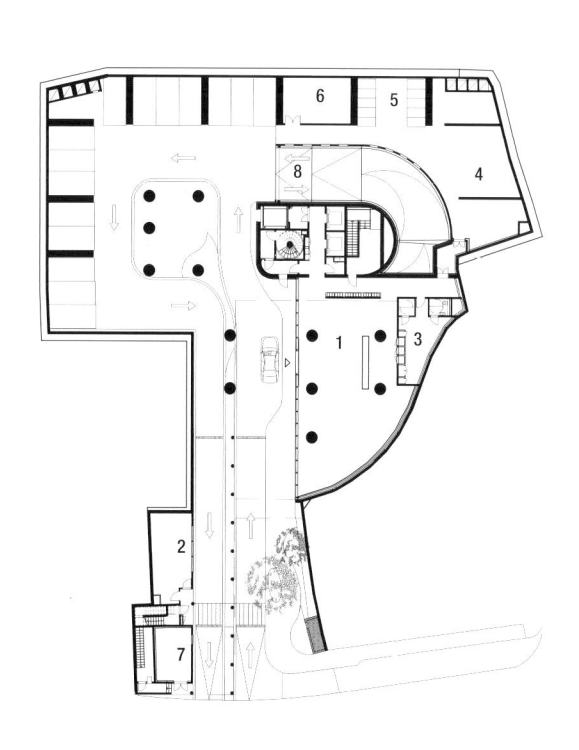

LOWER ENTRANCE FLOOR PLAN

115

JEAN-MICHEL WILMOTTE   GIROFLÉES TOWER

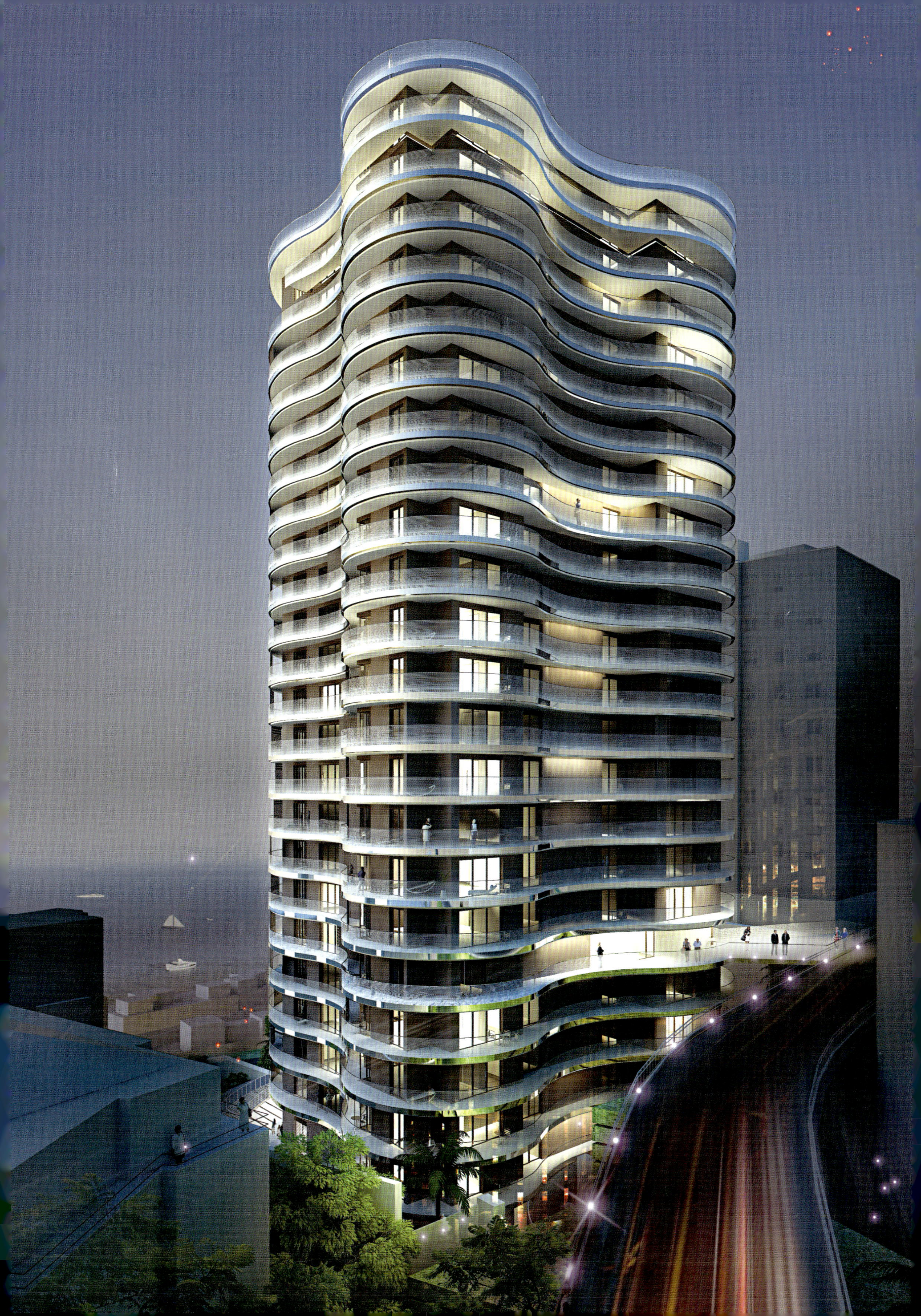

RENOVATION PROJECTS

JEAN-MICHEL WILMOTTE

LA RÉSERVE HOTEL, RAMATUELLE

Jean-Michel Wilmotte was called on to redesign this 1970s building making it into a five-star hotel with a 10,765-square-foot (1,000-square-meter) spa. The total floor area of the project is 89,340 square feet (8,300 square meters) and it has a 96,875-square-foot (9,000-square-meter) site. There are 12 rental villas near the sea on the property as well. The seven rooms and 16 suites in the complex range in size from 540 to 1,080 square feet (50 to 100 square meters), each with a private terrace or garden.

The reinforced concrete structure is coated in concrete, and clad in dry stone, natural stone (flooring), and wood decking outside. The hotel is located on a hill planted with holm oaks and stone pines with views of the Mediterranean, the Baie de Bonporteau and Cap Taillat.

The shell and the plaster and brick façades of the original building were recovered. The indoor pool, with its overflowing edge, also plunges toward the sea. The ground in front was lowered so that terrace activities did not interrupt the swimmers' view. "The vegetation and the view of the sea are my paintings," says Wilmotte. The project won a 2011 Wallpaper Design Award as 'Best New Hotel.'

Location Ramatuelle, France
Completion date 2009
Area 89,340 ft² (8,300 m²)

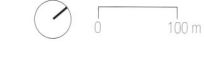

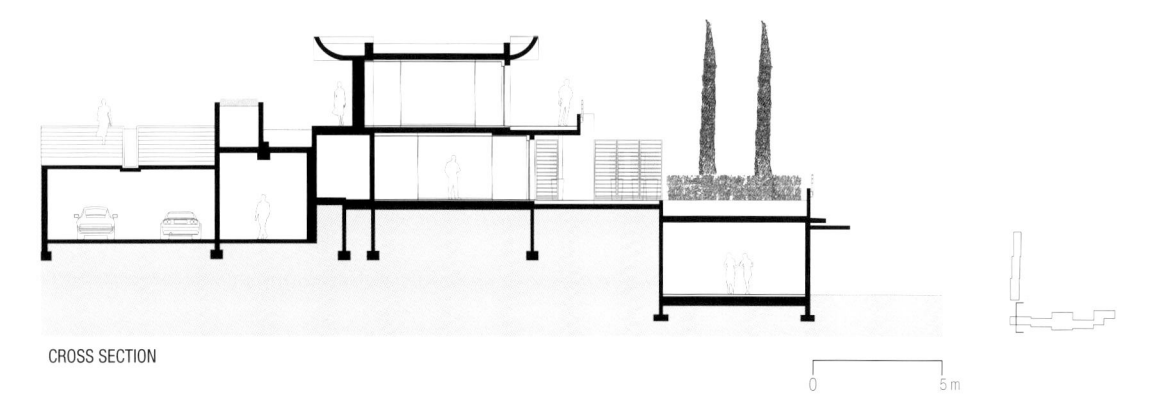

LOCATION PLAN

CROSS SECTION

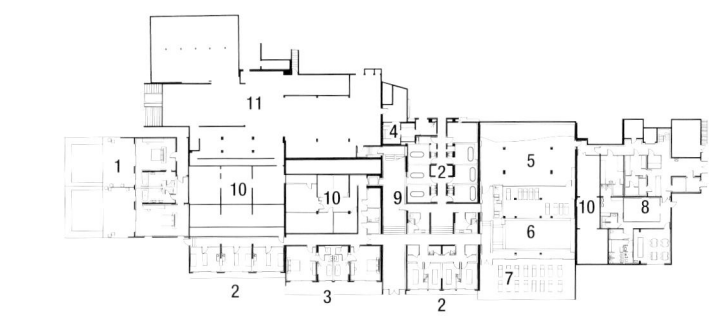

SECOND-FLOOR PLAN

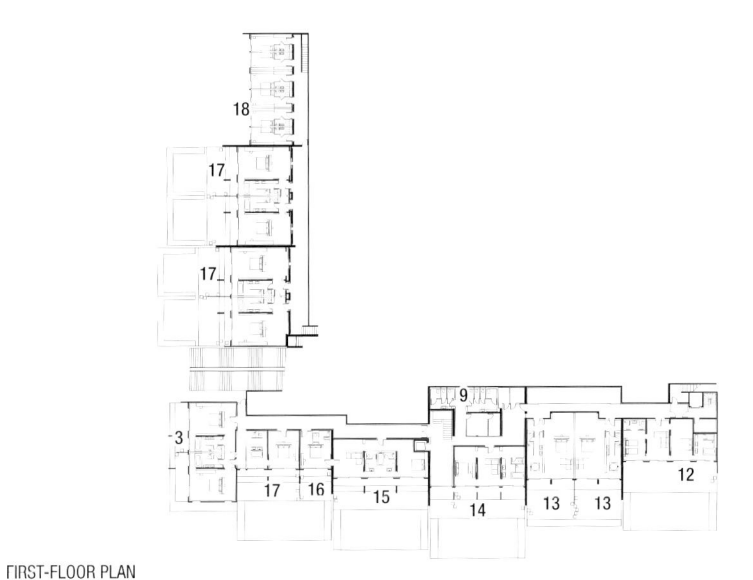

FIRST-FLOOR PLAN

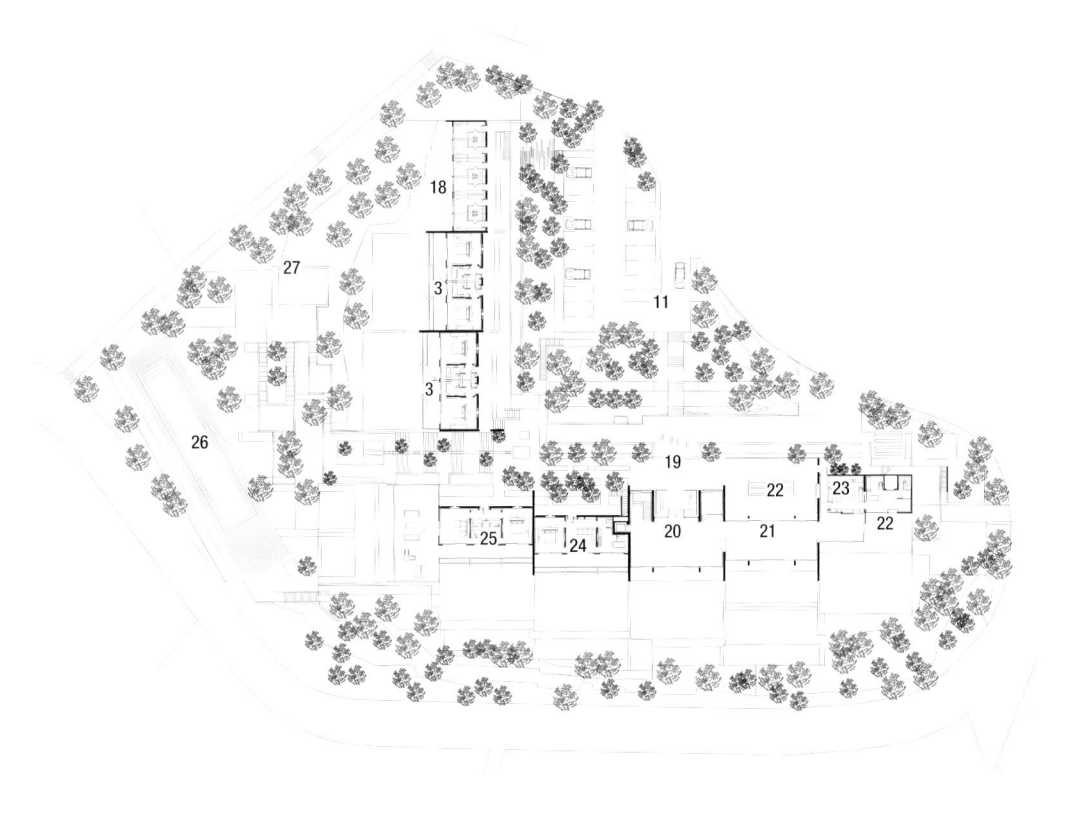

GROUND-FLOOR PLAN

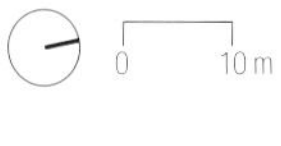

1 Deluxe rooms with garden
2 Wellness rooms
3 Deluxe rooms
4 Hammam
5 Fitness room
6 Indoor swimming pool
7 Swimming pool terrace
8 Services
9 Sanitary facilites
10 Technical premises
11 Parking
12 Camarat Suite with double and twin beds
13 Deluxe junior suite with garden
14 Prestige suite with garden
15 Premier suite with garden
16 Superior room with garden
17 Deluxe rooms with garden
18 Staff rooms
19 Entrance
20 Lounge
21 Dining room
22 Restaurant terrace
23 Kitchen
24 Prestige suite
25 Taillat Suite with private terrace
26 Swimming pool
27 Pool house

JEAN-MICHEL WILMOTTE LA RÉSERVE HOTEL, RAMATUELLE

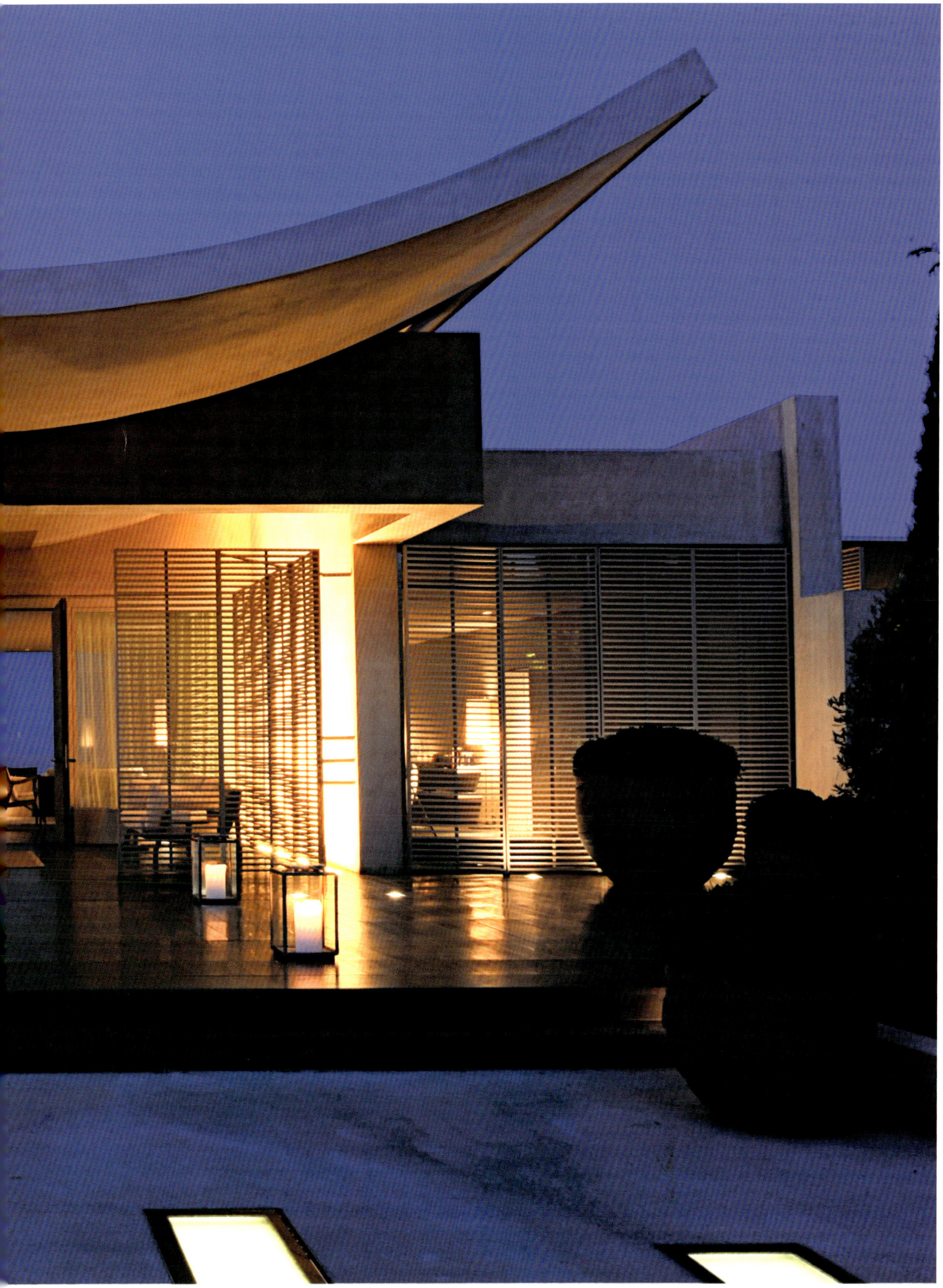

JEAN-MICHEL WILMOTTE   LA RÉSERVE HOTEL, RAMATUELLE

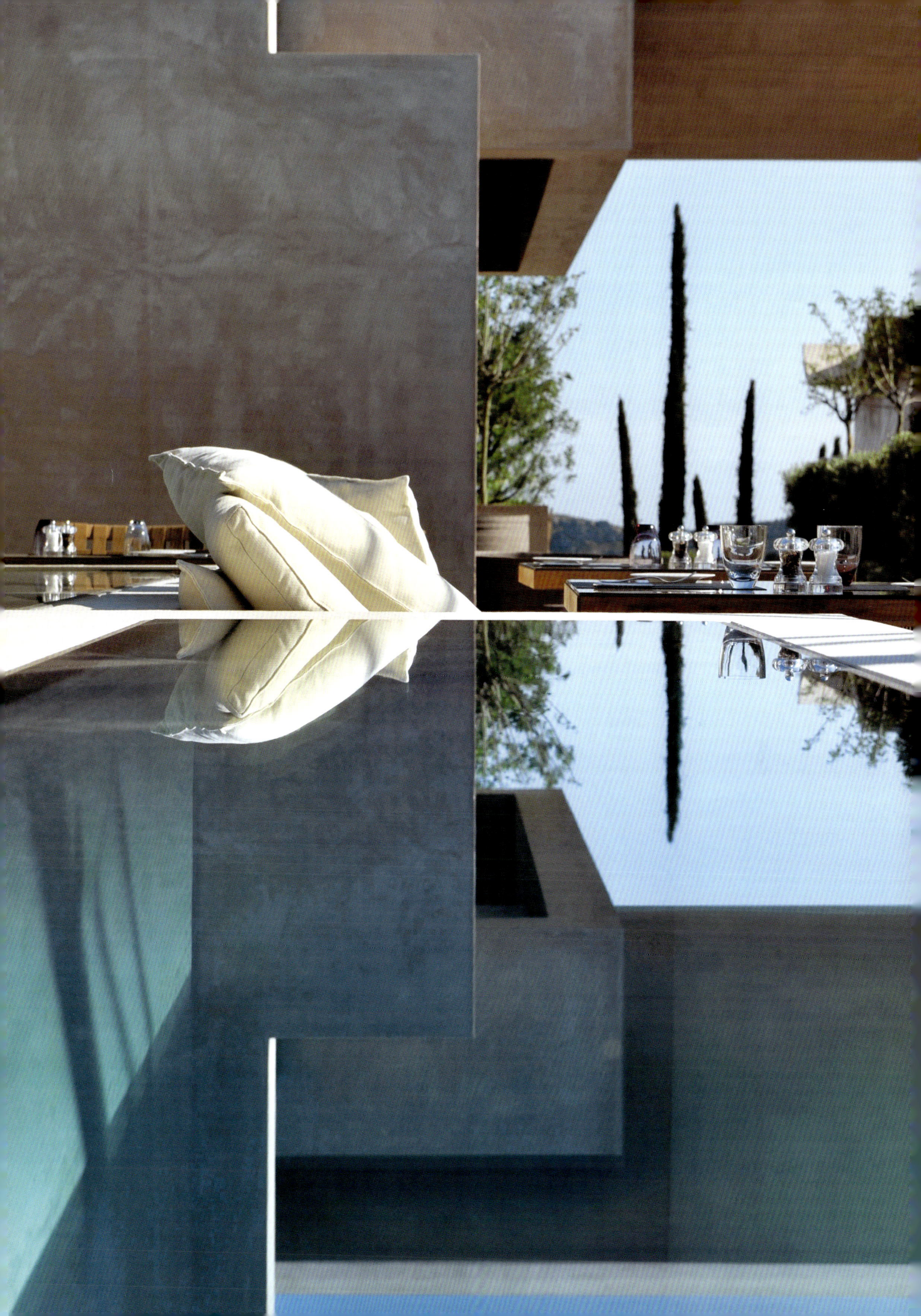

JEAN-MICHEL WILMOTTE LA RÉSERVE HOTEL, RAMATUELLE

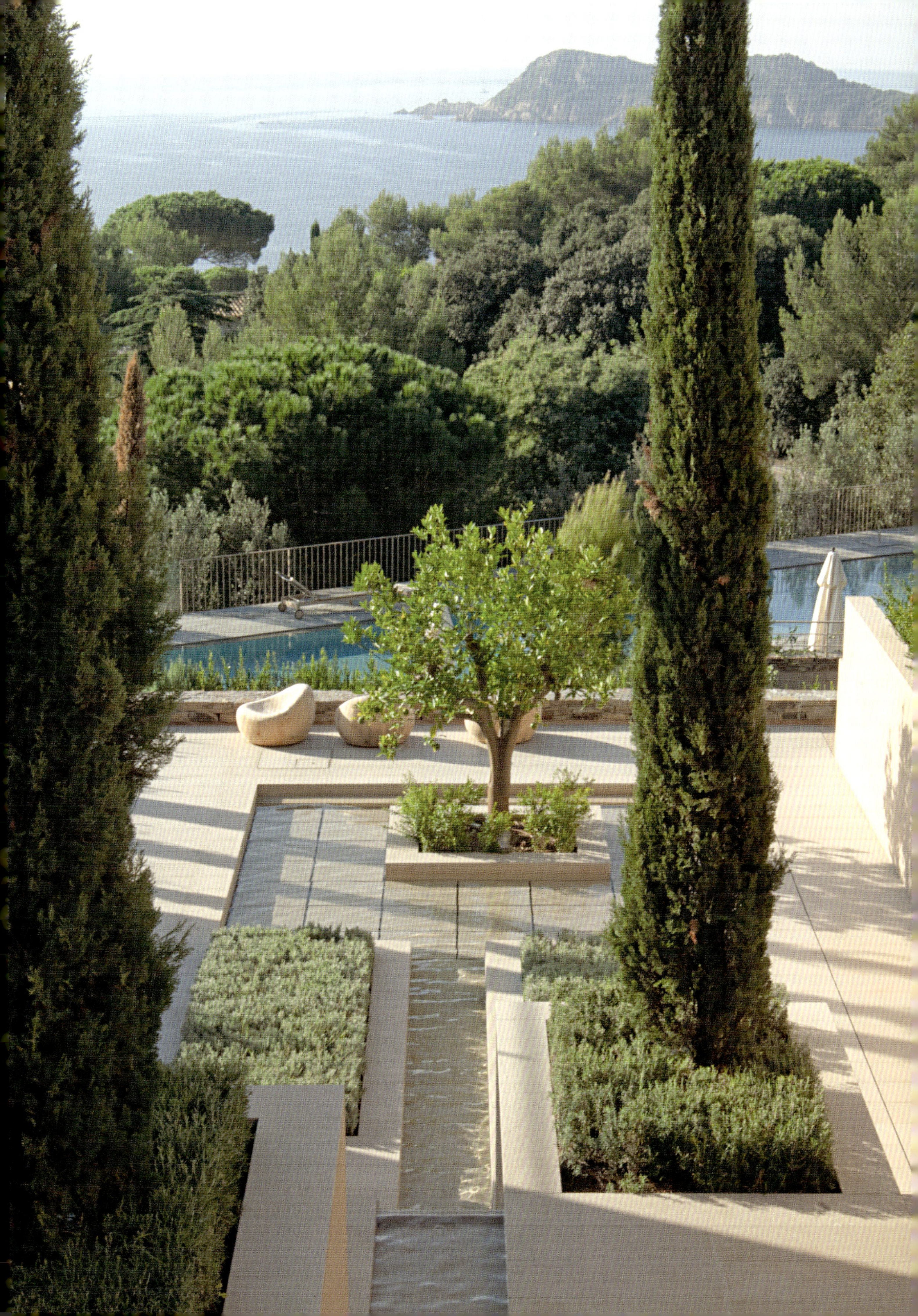

JEAN-MICHEL WILMOTTE

JEAN PIERRE RAYNAUD STUDIO

The owner of this house, who collaborated actively on the design with the architect Jean-Michel Wilmotte, is the noted French artist Jean Pierre Raynaud. Raynaud bought an existing Norman-style house called the Clos d'Hortense in the town of Barbizon, not far from Paris. Barbizon is of course known for the artists' school of the same name that included such figures as Jean-François Millet and Théodore Rousseau in the mid-19th century. This artistic reference was not a matter of indifference for Raynaud, even though his own work does not have much to do with the figurative paintings of the Barbizon School.

The architect removed 1960s extensions to the house and added a large glazed interior space and also developed 5,110 square feet (475 square meters) of exterior terraces. A 680-square-foot (63-square-meter) 100-year-old Nordic-style pavilion that was located on the grounds, and was part of the Universal Exposition of 1889 was painted black at the request of the artist, who used the property to display his own works. Although he called the house his studio, Jean Pierre Raynaud does not create works in a traditional studio environment, and used the main 2,585-square-foot (240-square-meter) house mainly for display of completed pieces such as the large gilded 'Flower Pot,' which is emblematic of his work and sat in the ornamental pool that extends from the studio space.

The landscape design is by Neveux Rouyer. Jean Pierre Raynaud and his wife Daphné have since sold this property. Raynaud has consistently built (or demolished) his own houses as part of his artistic process, as his earlier houses in La Celle Saint-Cloud and La Garenne-Colombes, both also near Paris, demonstrated.

Location Barbizon, France
Completion date 2010
Area 2,585 ft² (240 m²)

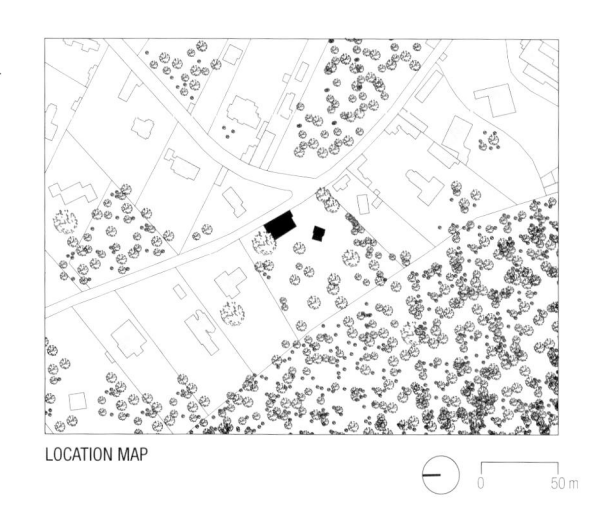

LOCATION MAP

SECOND-FLOOR PLAN

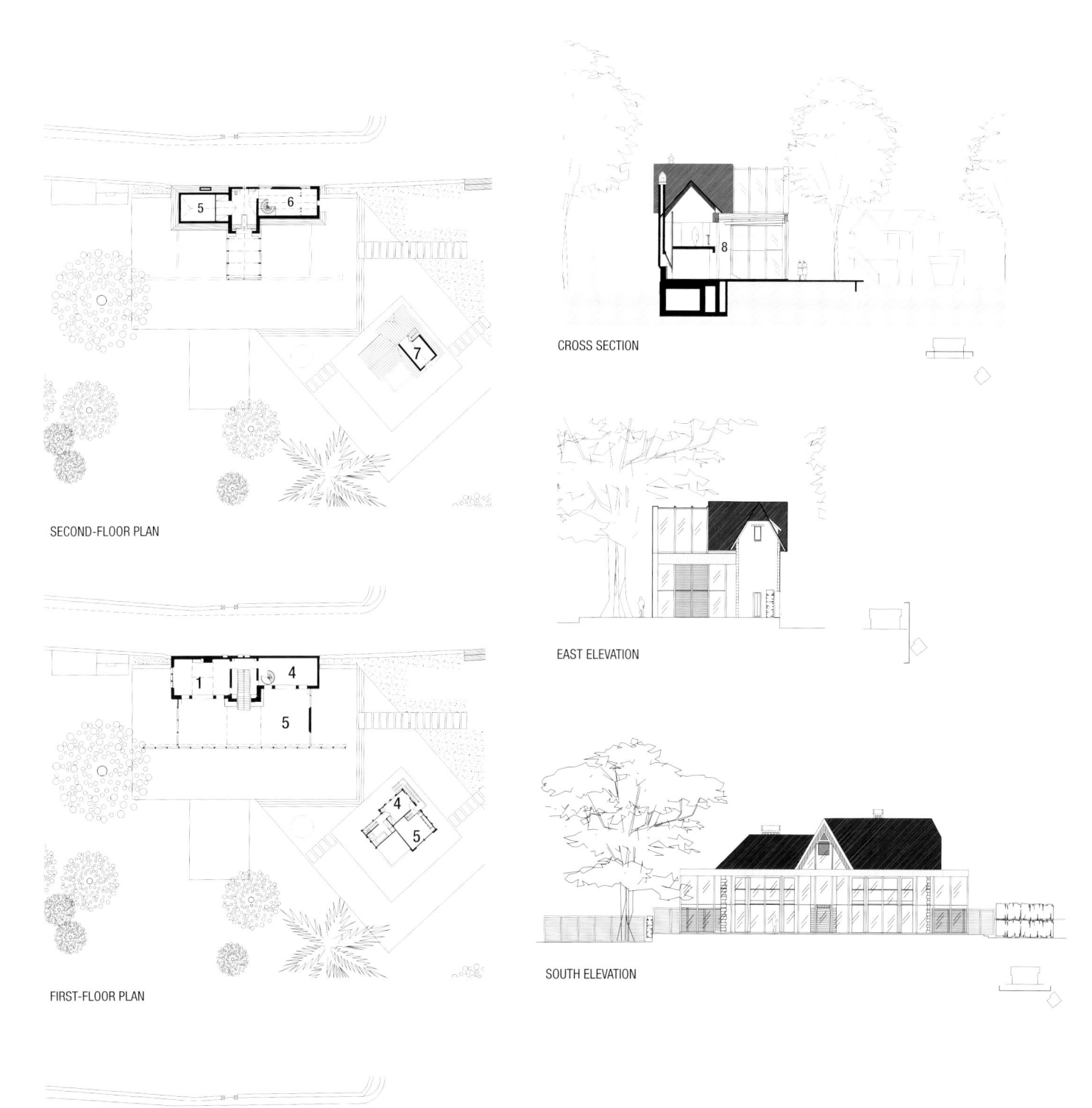

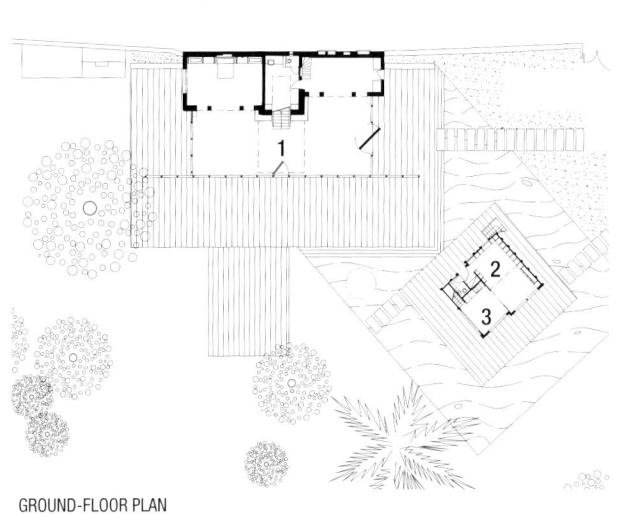

FIRST-FLOOR PLAN

GROUND-FLOOR PLAN

CROSS SECTION

EAST ELEVATION

SOUTH ELEVATION

1 Workshop
2 Reception
3 Living room
4 Office
5 Double level
6 Meditation space
7 Bedroom
8 Workshop double level

0　　5 m

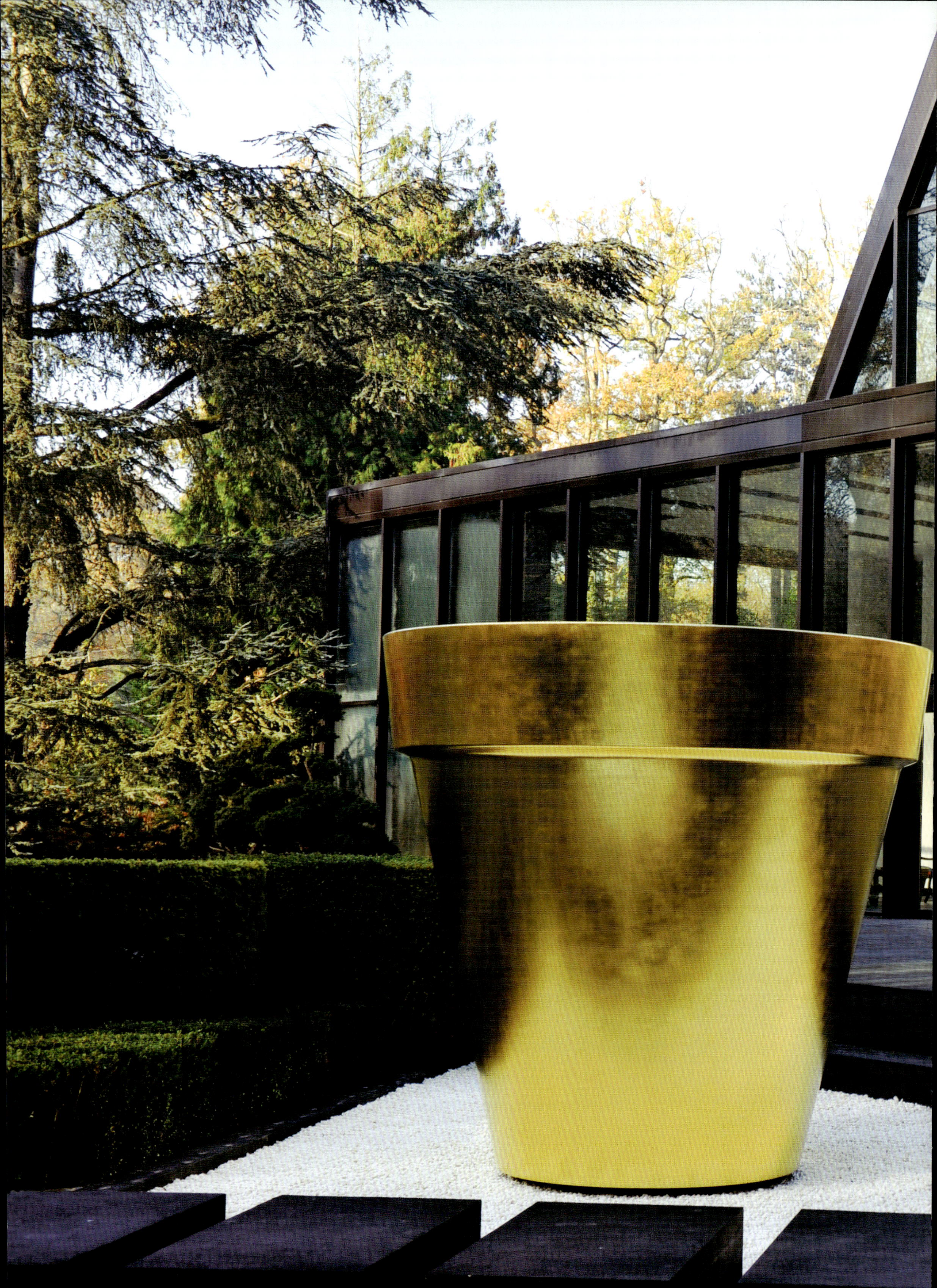

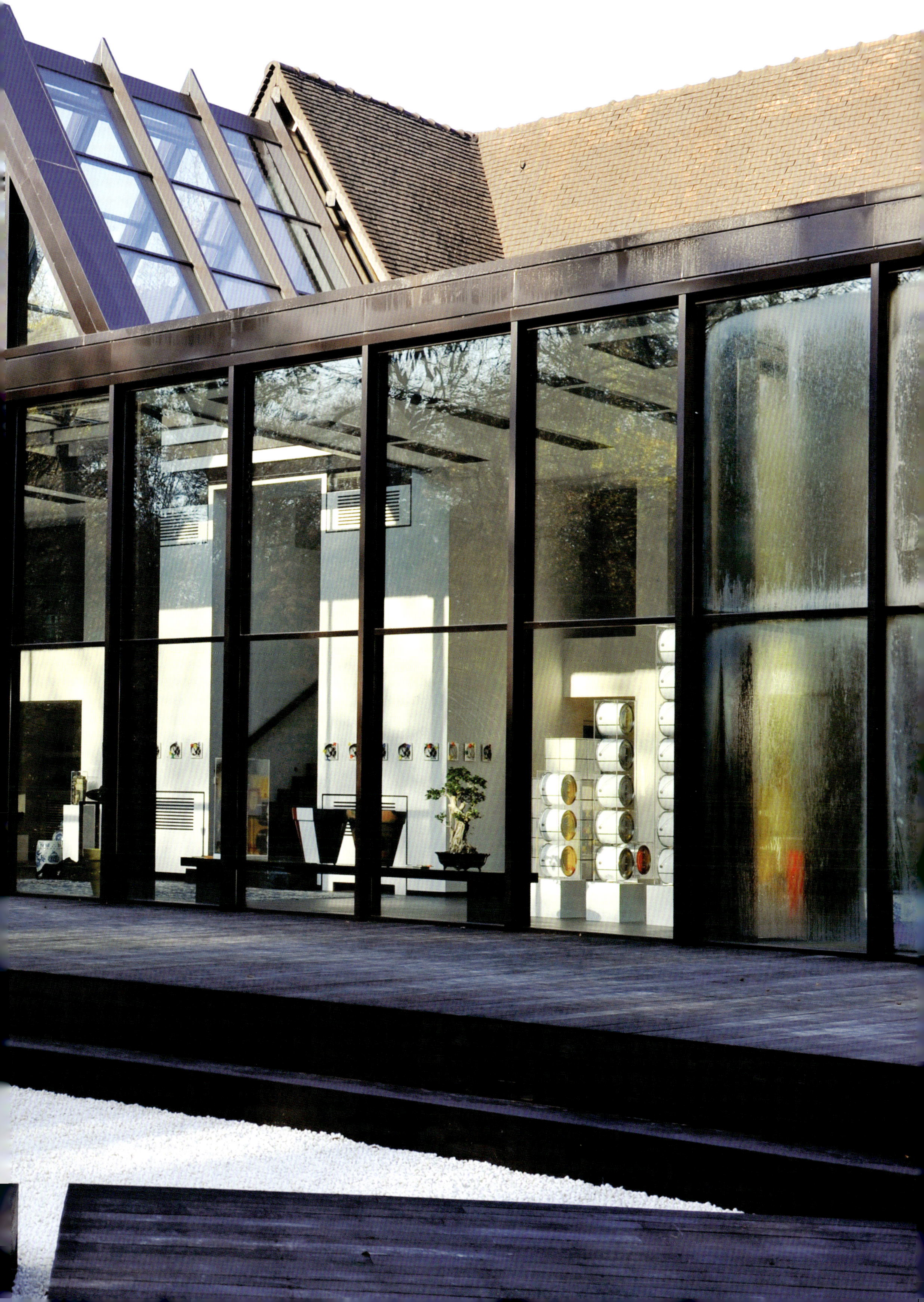

JEAN-MICHEL WILMOTTE JEAN PIERRE RAYNAUD STUDIO

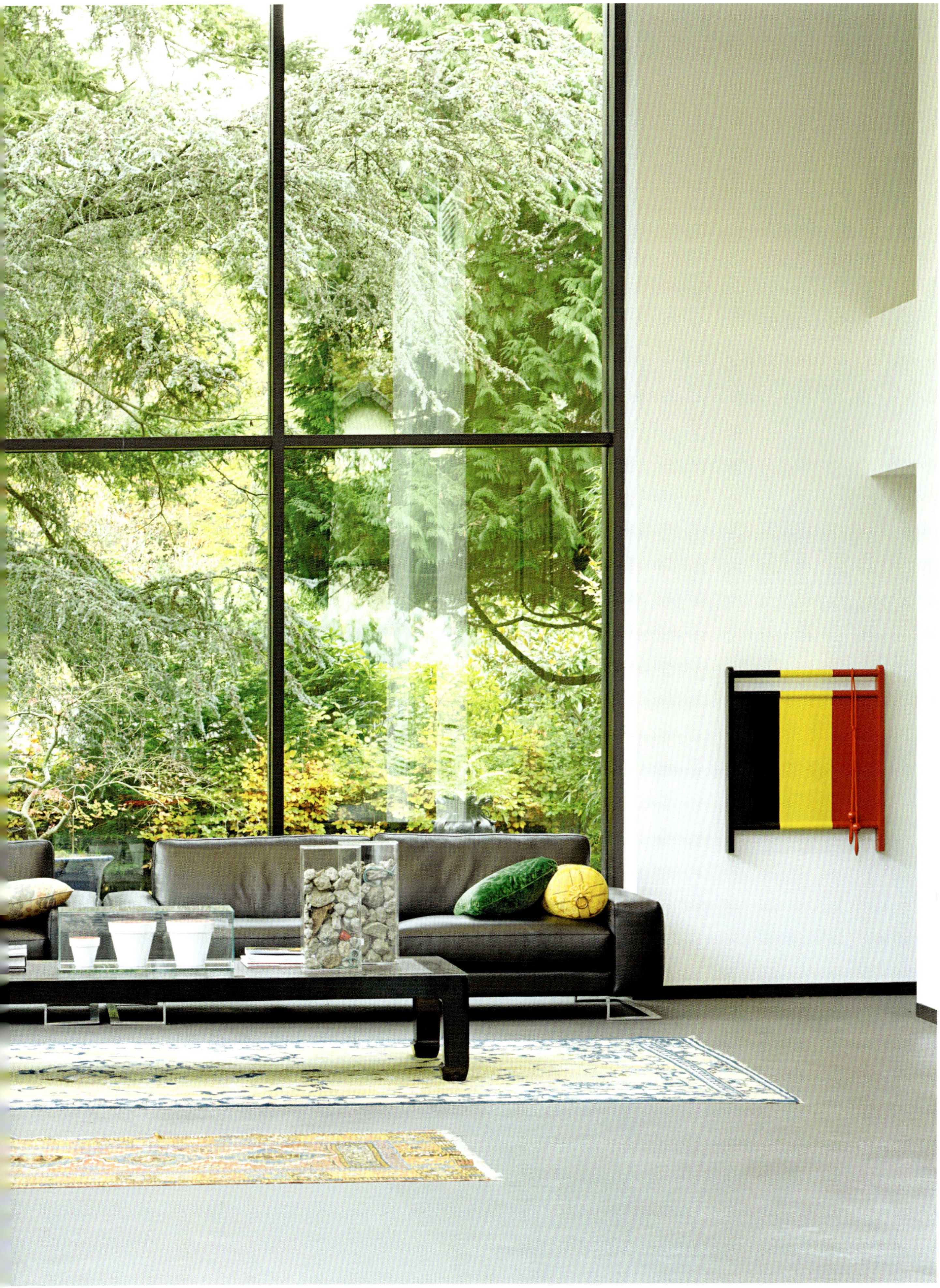

JEAN-MICHEL WILMOTTE

MANDARIN ORIENTAL HOTEL

At the request of the Mandarin Oriental Group, Jean-Michel Wilmotte undertook the restructuring of an existing office complex, turning it into a five-star hotel including 99 rooms and 32 suites. It was the first luxury hotel to receive the HQE environmental quality label in France. The main materials employed are concrete, natural stone for the street façade, and natural stone and lime plaster for the façade overlooking the garden. The landscape architects were Neveux-Rouyer, who often work with the architect.

The Mandarin Oriental Hotel is located on a deep 32,290-square-foot (3,000-square-meter) plot located between Rue Saint-Honoré and Rue du Mont-Tabor. Composed of three buildings and two inner courtyards, this complex had only one street façade, on the Rue Saint-Honoré. The architects decided to demolish the building between the two courtyards in order to endow the future hotel with a generous central garden that measures 69 by 72 feet (21 by 22 meters). The double-height spa of the hotel is set beneath the central courtyard. Around it four façades were entirely revamped in a reinterpretation based on the monumental doorways and windows on the street façade. The interior decoration of the hotel was done by Sybille de Margerie. The five-star Mandarin Oriental Hotel has received the exclusive 'Distinction Palace' rating.

Location Paris, France
Completion date 2011
Area 236,805 ft² (22,000 m²)

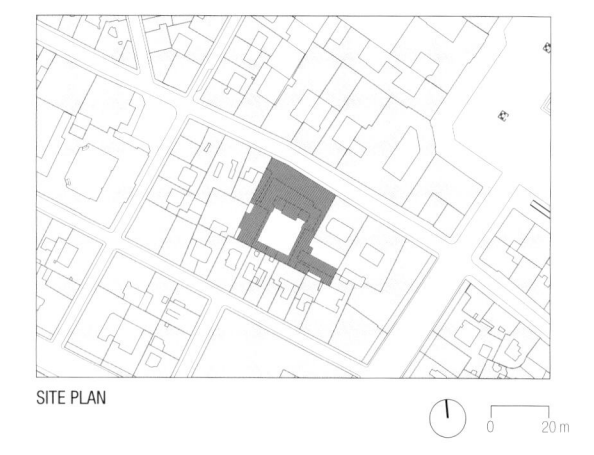

SITE PLAN

STREET ELEVATION

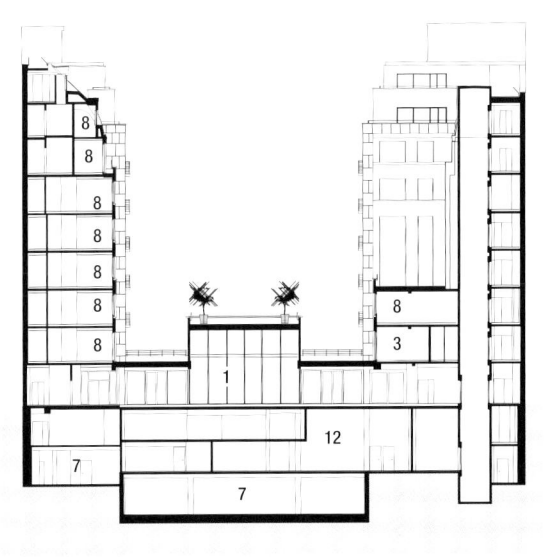

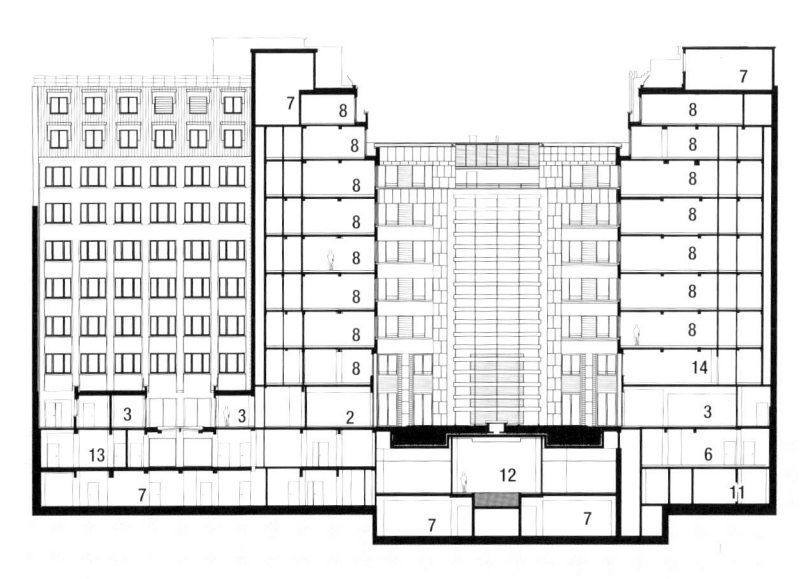

CROSS SECTION 1

CROSS SECTION 2

SIXTH-FLOOR PLAN

1 Reception hall
2 Bar
3 Restaurant
4 Shops
5 Garden
6 Kitchen
7 Services
8 Bedroom/suite
9 Terrace
10 Private terrace
11 Storage
12 Spa
13 Cloakroom
14 Meeting room

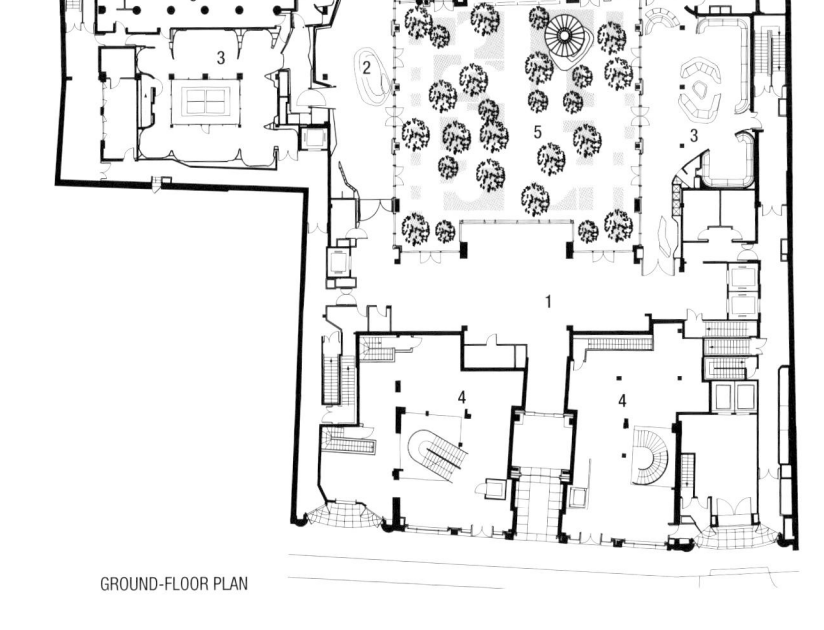

GROUND-FLOOR PLAN

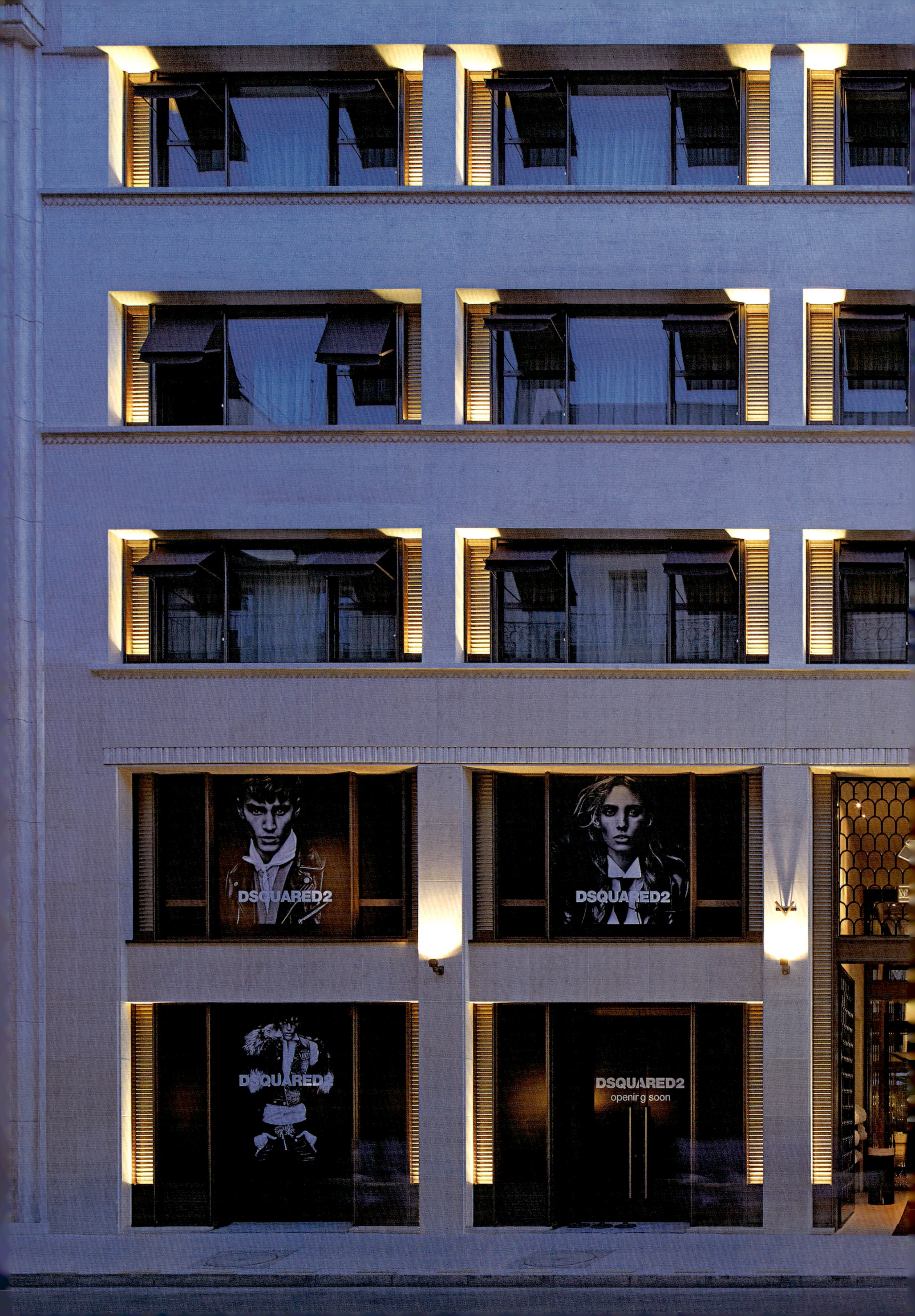
DSQUARED2
DSQUARED2
DSQUARED2
DSQUARED2
opening soon

ORIENTAL
PORTS
1961
PORTS
1961
PORTS
PORTS
PORTS
1961
COMING FALL

JEAN-MICHEL WILMOTTE   MANDARIN ORIENTAL HOTEL

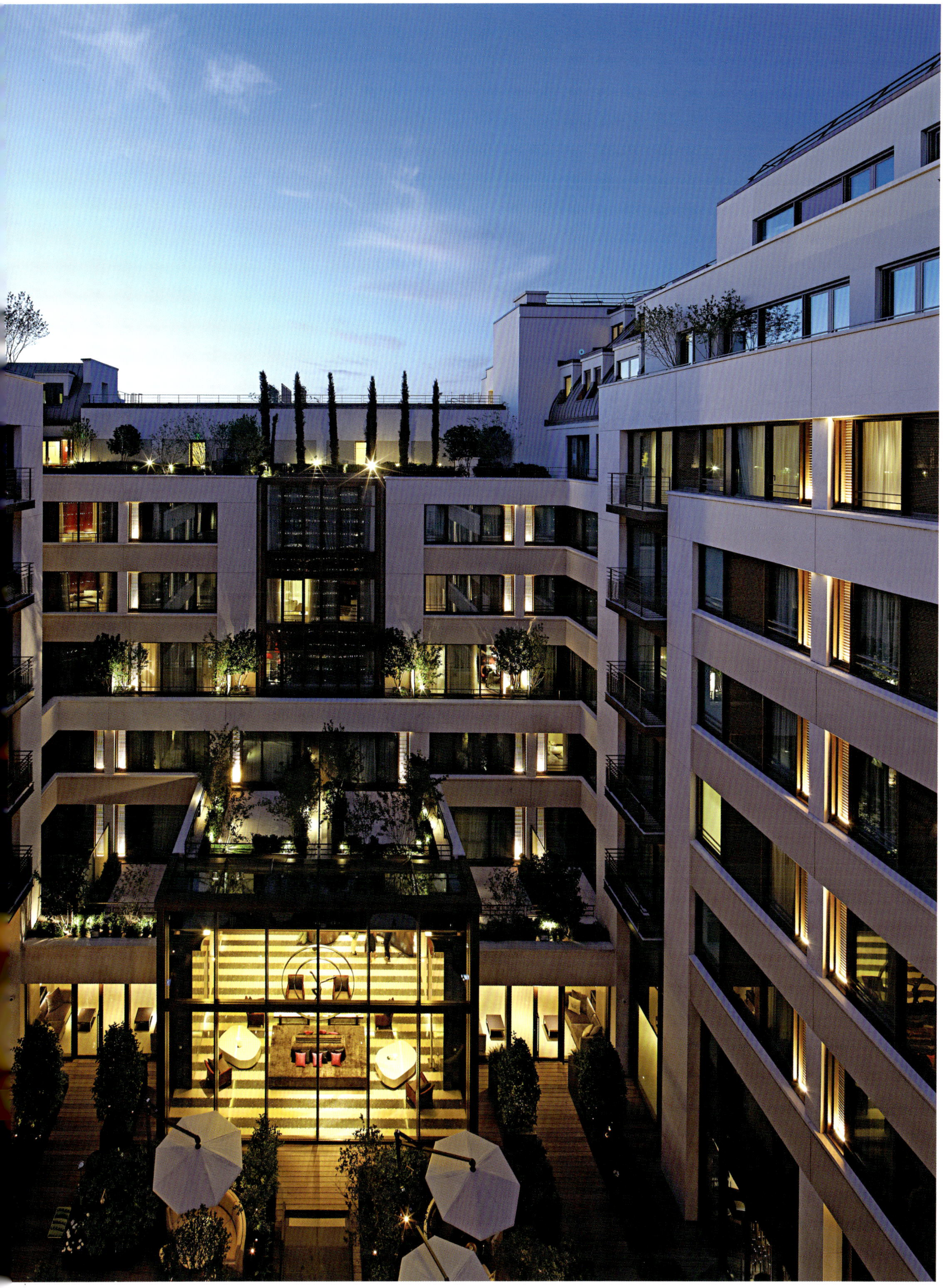

JEAN-MICHEL WILMOTTE

CHÂTEAU PÉDESCLAUX WINERY

Château Pédesclaux, the fifth winery in the Pauillac region to have obtained the Grand Cru Classé ranking, began restructuring its vineyard in 2009 and asked Wilmotte & Associés Architectes to design the new technical facilities, notably a gravity-driven winemaking process. Wine is in fact no longer pumped, but is transported in large stainless steel vat-elevators, which rise from the basement to the second floor of the building. The technical facilities also provide a stage for dramatic lighting.

The restructuring of the estate included renovation of the Château. Existing buildings were demolished, to be replaced by a central facility that combines the vat room, wine cellars, and bottling room in a cuboid building with an area of 20,020 square feet (1,860 square meters). The château, meanwhile, was enlarged with a lateral extension of glass—it now hosts a tasting room and business offices. The tasting room offers a view of the vineyards to the south; its furnishings were specially designed by Victoria Wilmotte. Transparency is the shared theme that unites the two buildings. The solid brown façade of the vat room seems to rest directly on the 116 stainless-steel vats, theatrically arranged and lit from behind the glass wall at the base of the building.

"I'm one of those people who defend and promote the idea that a sense of aesthetics, proportion, refinement, and comfort automatically generate a feeling of well-being," says Jean-Michel Wilmotte. The barrel warehouse is built with white reinforced concrete in the basement, while a bronze metallic structure is deployed in the vat room on the ground and first floors.

Located in the Haut Médoc region near Bordeaux, Paulliac includes such prestigious wines as Château Latour, Lafite Rothschild, and Mouton Rothschild. The 82,880-square-foot (7,700-square-meter) winery designed by Wilmotte makes use of black quartz concrete, bronze anodized aluminum strips for the vat façade, a glazed front with large dimension glass panels, white concrete slabs, and an American walnut floor inside.

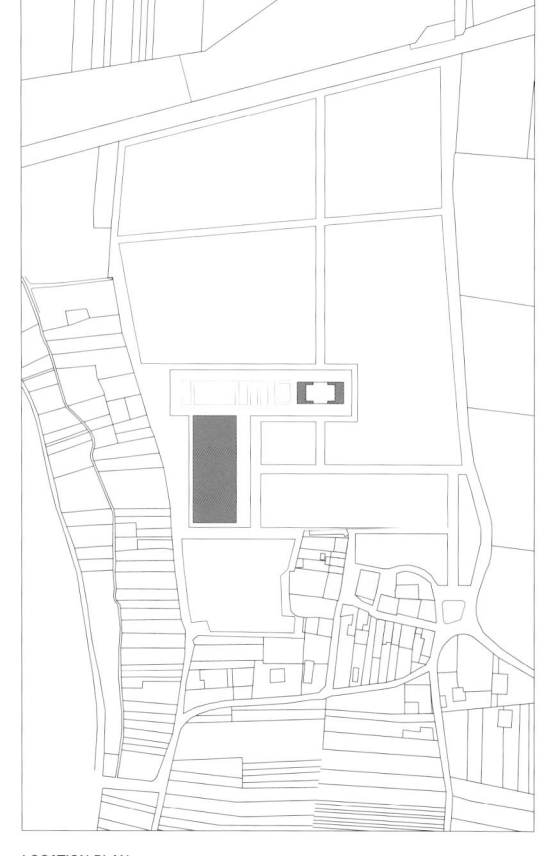

Location Pauillac, France
Completion date 2015
Area 82,880 ft² (7,700 m²)

LOCATION PLAN

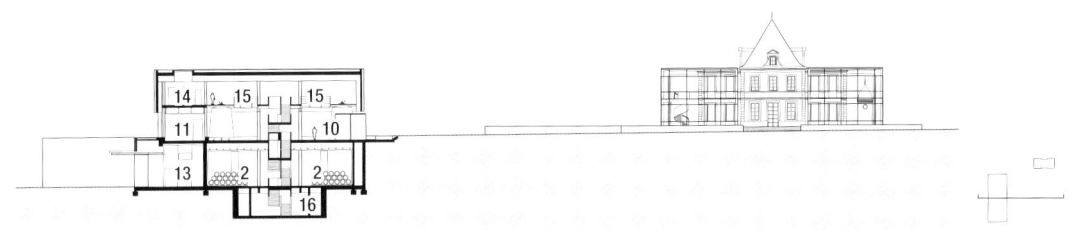

CROSS SECTION OF WINERY AND WEST ELEVATION OF CHÂTEAU

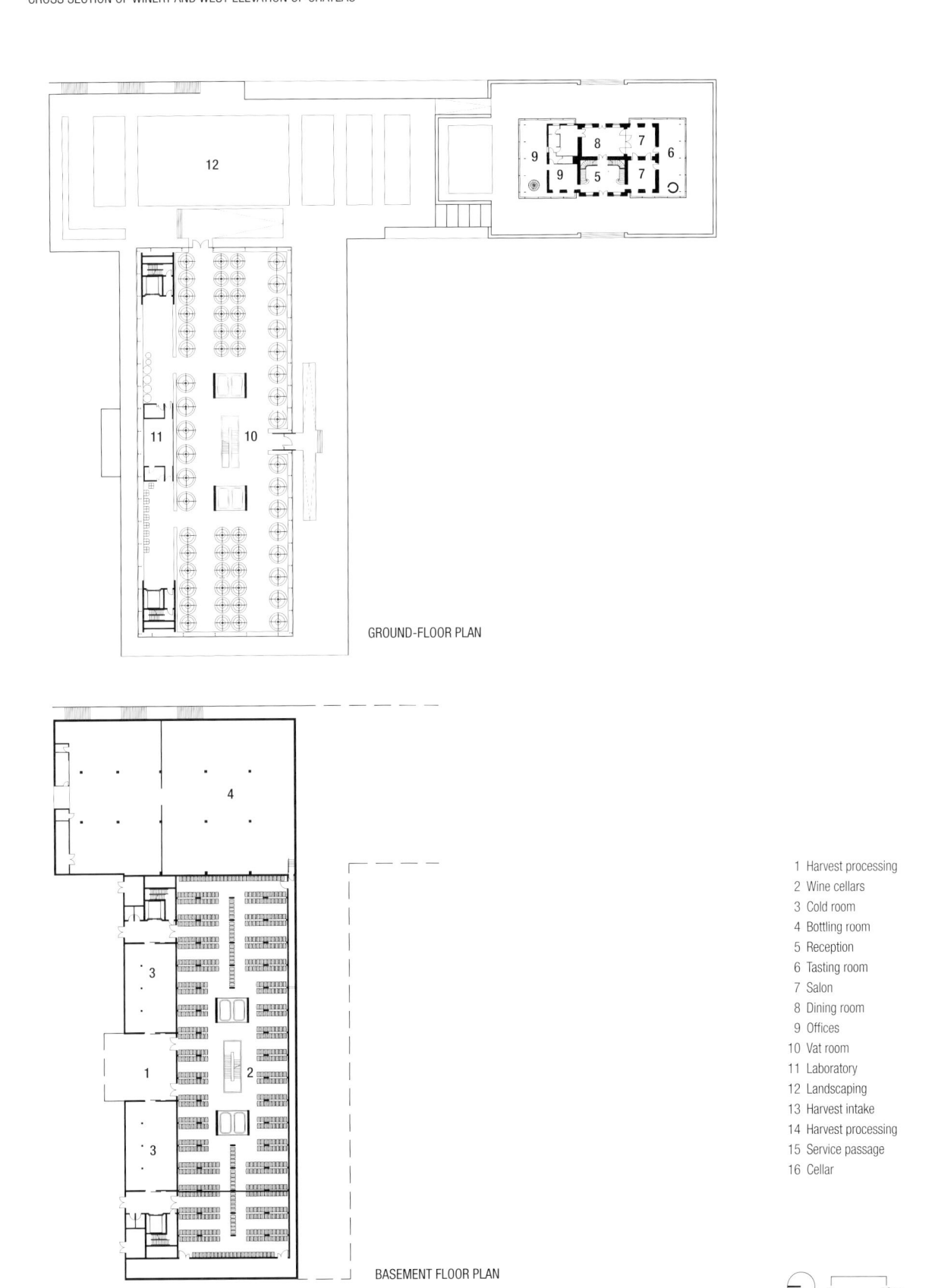

GROUND-FLOOR PLAN

BASEMENT FLOOR PLAN

1 Harvest processing
2 Wine cellars
3 Cold room
4 Bottling room
5 Reception
6 Tasting room
7 Salon
8 Dining room
9 Offices
10 Vat room
11 Laboratory
12 Landscaping
13 Harvest intake
14 Harvest processing
15 Service passage
16 Cellar

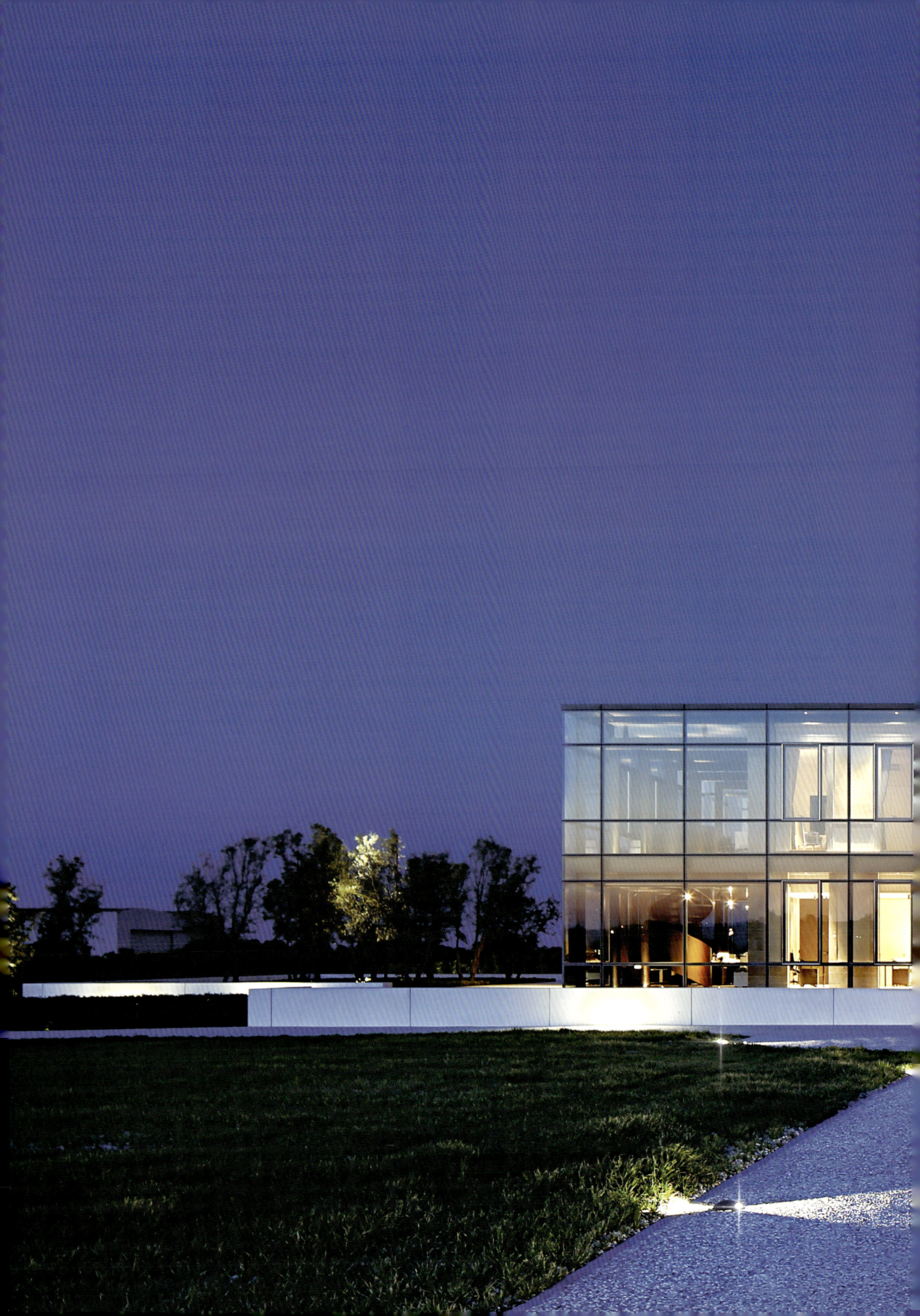

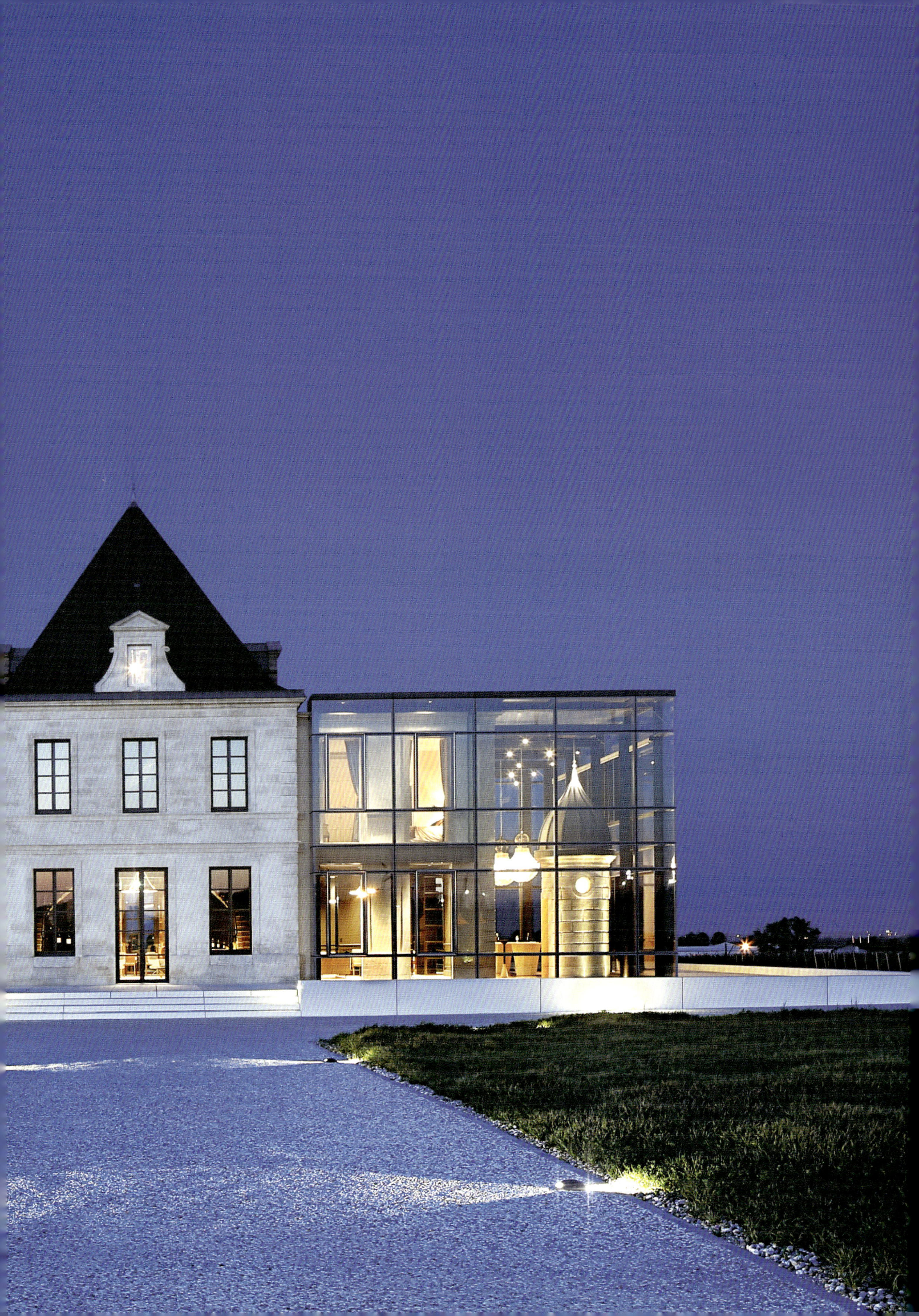

JEAN-MICHEL WILMOTTE   CHÂTEAU PÉDESCLAUX WINERY

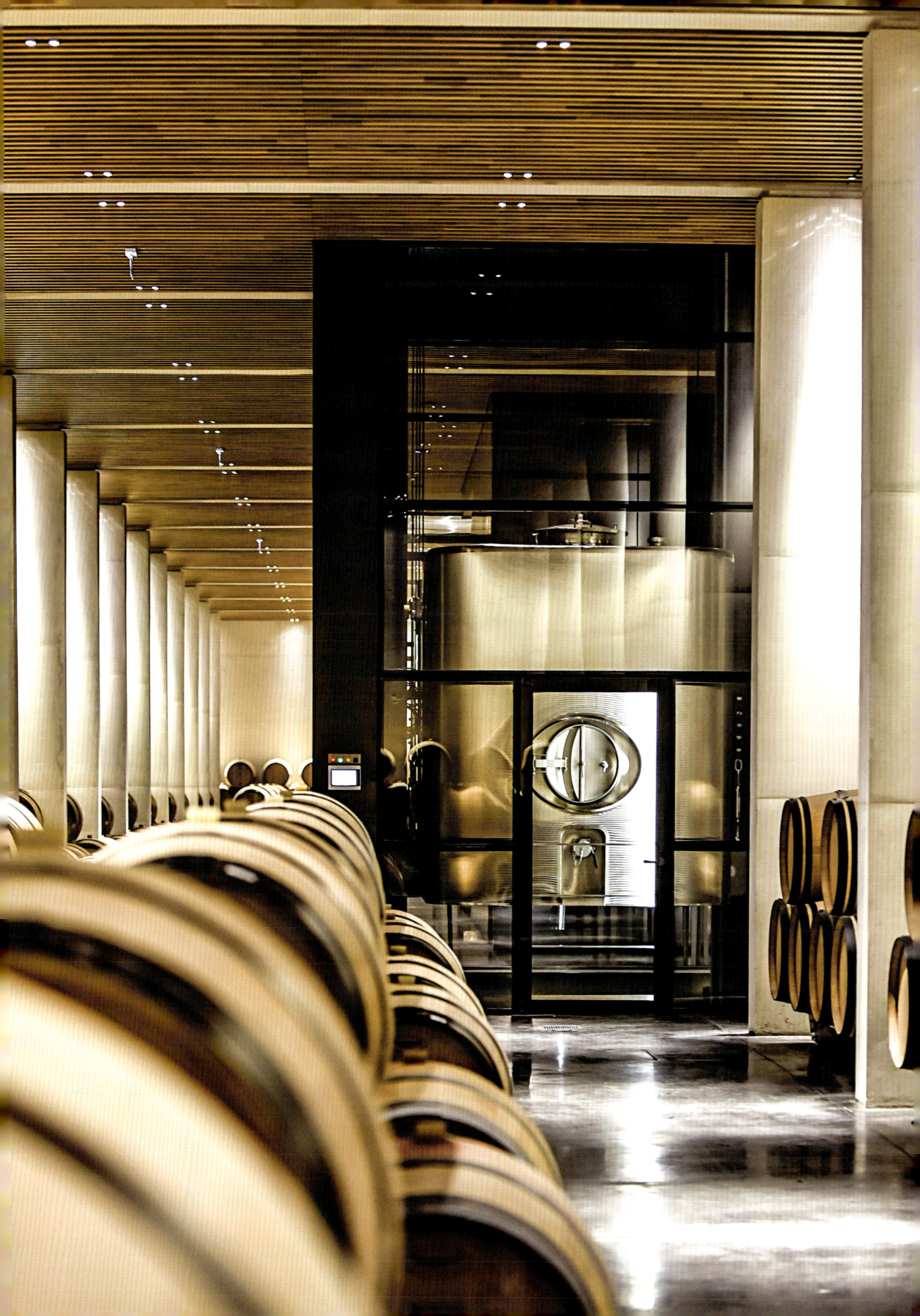

JEAN-MICHEL WILMOTTE

SUMMIT HOUSE, JCDECAUX UK HEADQUARTERS

JCDecaux, the global outdoor advertising and street furniture company, has its new headquarters, covering 69,965 square feet (6,500 square meters), in the Paddington area of central London, close to Edgware Road and the Paddington Basin, between the Bayswater & Paddington conservation area to the south and the Paddington Opportunity Area to the north. The existing site had two separate office buildings built in 1968 and 1970, a pub, residential apartments, and retail space.

The scheme by Wilmotte & Associés Architectes included the complete refurbishment of both buildings to the highest specifications, following the guide of the British Council for Offices, the extension of the reception area into the plot formerly occupied by the pub, demolition and extension of the sixth floor to simplify the massing, and the unification of the internal arrangement of the two buildings. This creates a significant improvement to views along Praed Street through the appropriate use of materials and generates a suitable transition to the conservation area.

The existing fabric of the buildings was completely stripped out, except for the façades of the residential units facing the conservation area. To provide a larger reception area, it was required to carry out structural modifications by removing six concrete columns, which were replaced by large trusses. The main façade was rebuilt using a curtain wall system, with anodized aluminum fins emphasizing the verticality of Praed Street.

The ground floor was rebuilt in black Indian granite, which creates the podium for retail and reception areas. Due to the low ceiling levels of the existing buildings, it was decided to conceal the majority of the services in a central spine running the length of the office. Soffits and exposed ductwork were then painted black, making them 'disappear', and giving the impression of a higher floor to ceiling. Acoustic panels were instated and lighting was meticulously designed in order to mitigate potential problems with low ceiling heights.

The project was designed to BREEAM 2011 Very Good standards. The extension, refurbishment, interior design, and recladding project involved existing concrete structures and alterations in steel. The visible materials are rendered concrete, aluminum, and glass.

Location Paddington, London, UK
Completion date 2016
Area 69,965 ft^2 (6,500m^2)

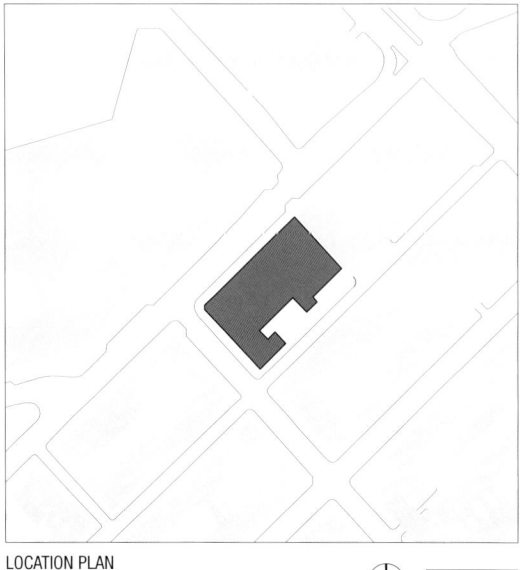

LOCATION PLAN

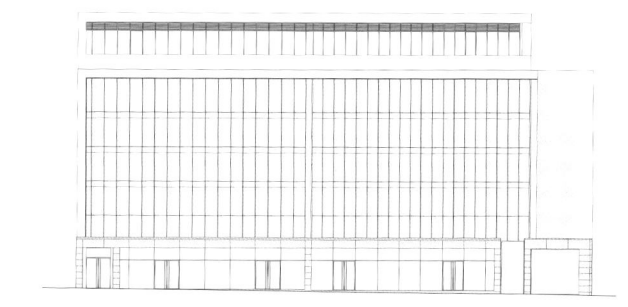

NORTH ELEVATION

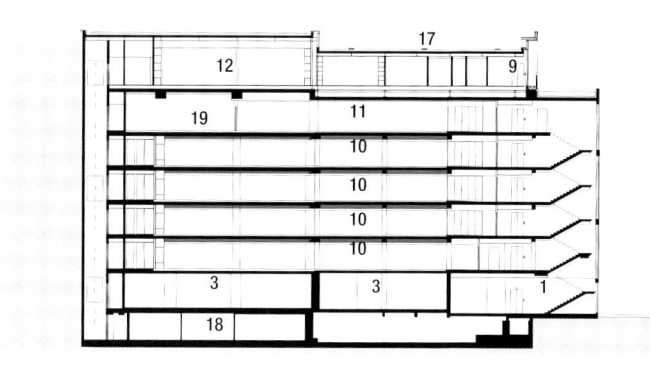

CROSS SECTION

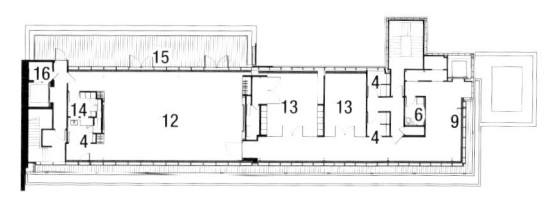

SIXTH-FLOOR PLAN

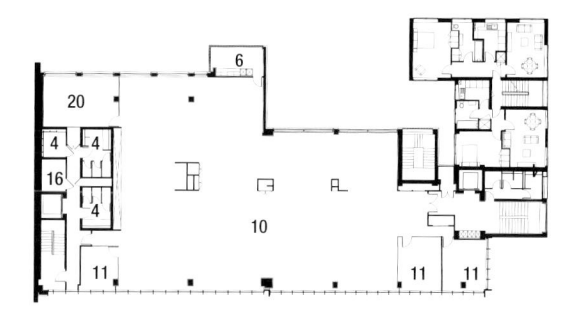

SECOND-FLOOR PLAN

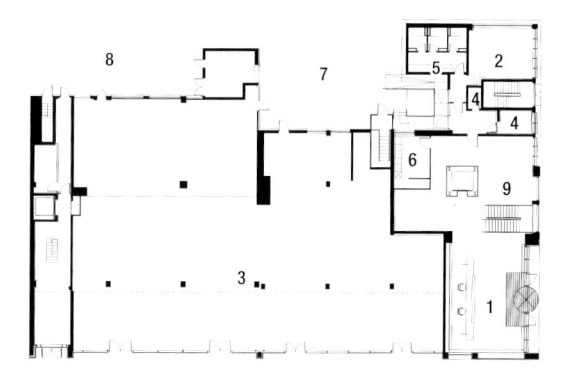

GROUND-FLOOR PLAN

1 Reception
2 Gymnasium
3 Retail
4 Toilets
5 Showers
6 Kitchenette
7 Car park—directors
8 Car park—staff
9 Lounge
10 Offices
11 Meeting room
12 President office
13 PA office
14 Library
15 Terrace
16 Storage
17 Plants
18 Archives
19 Café
20 Director's office

147

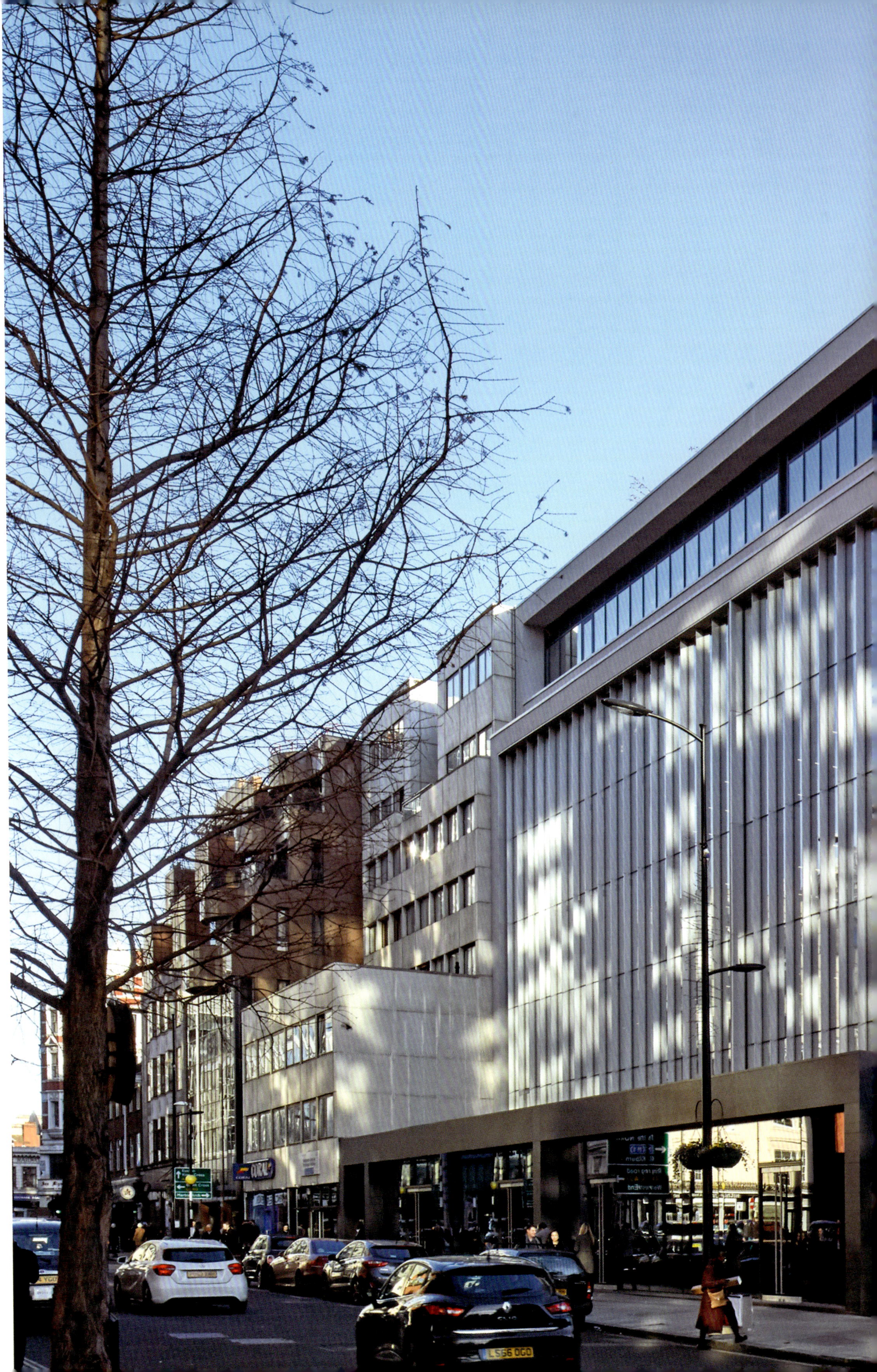
LS66 OGO

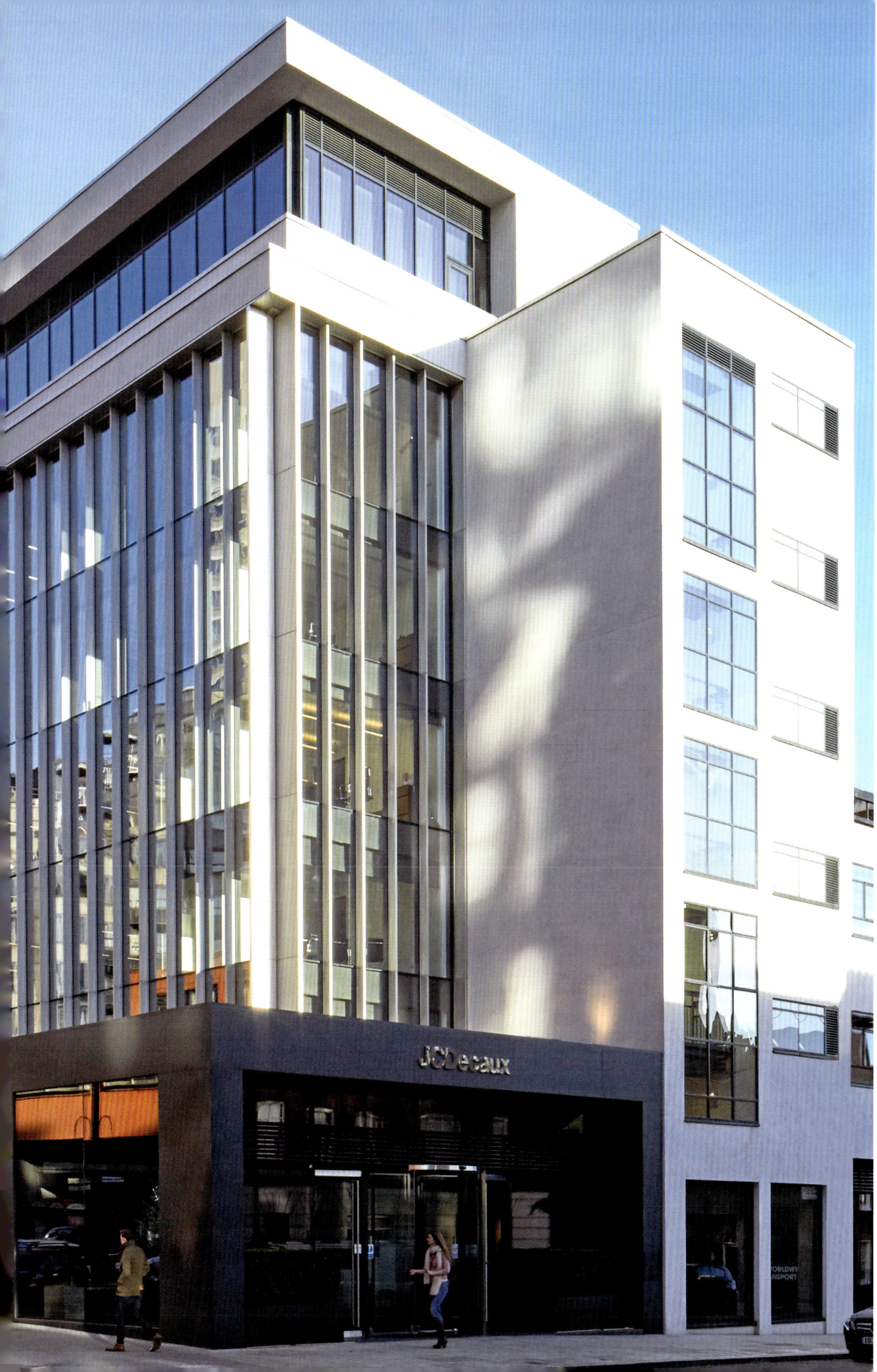
JCDecaux

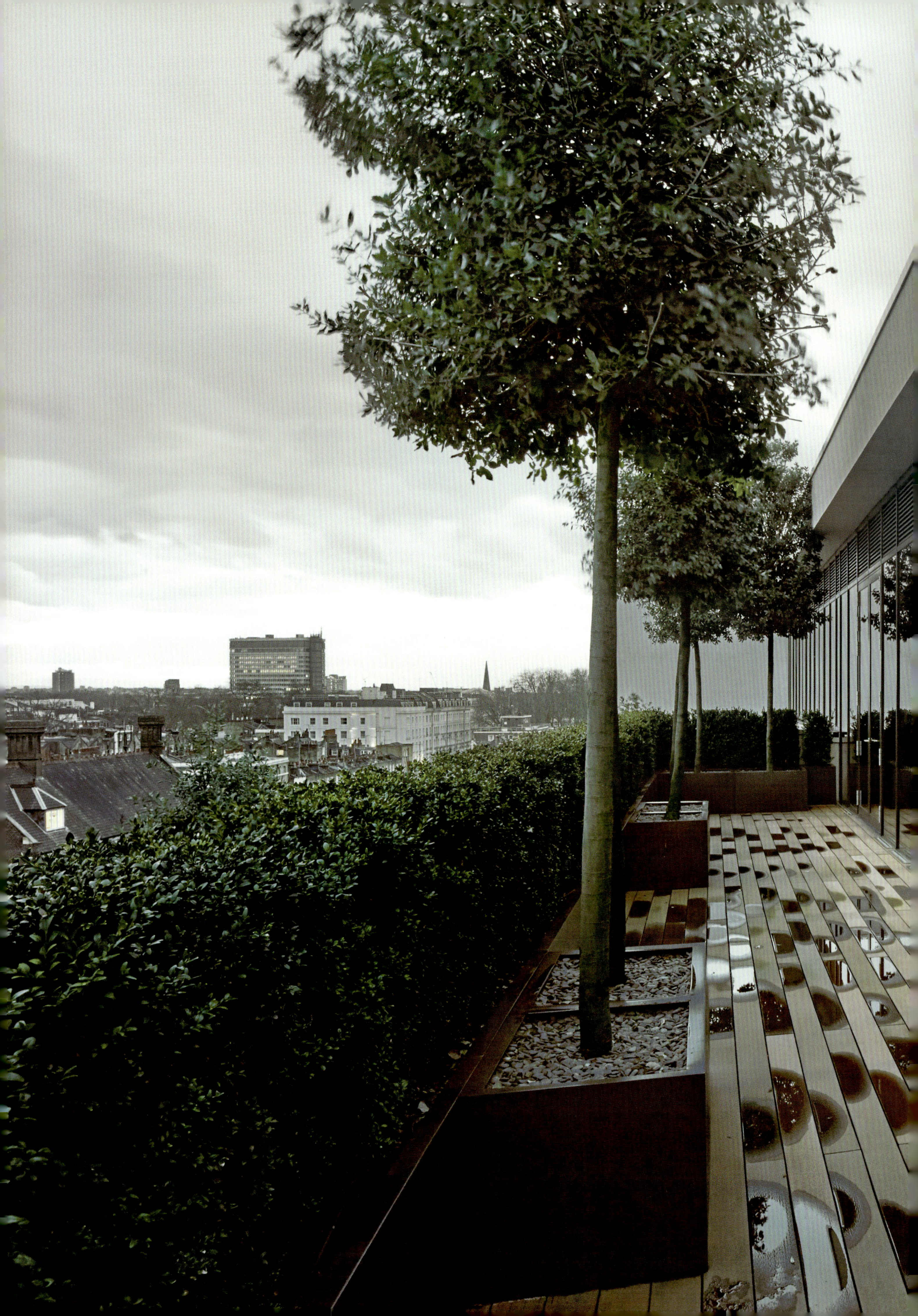

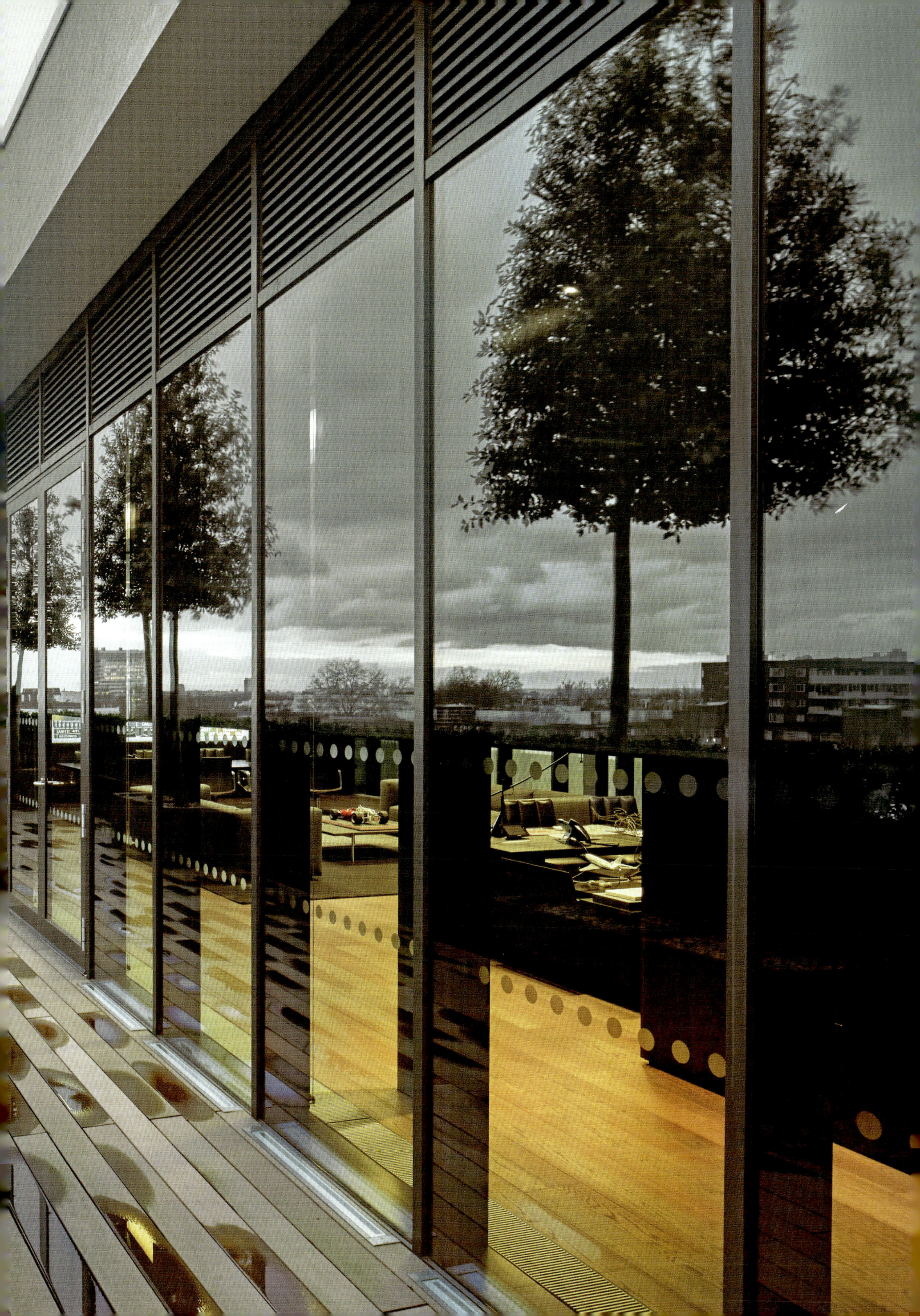

JEAN-MICHEL WILMOTTE

STATION F START-UP CAMPUS

Xavier Niel is a well-known French businessman who has been involved with the telephone network Free and Le Monde daily newspaper, among other projects. Together with Jean-Michel Wilmotte, he has created space for an initiative destined to help promising start-up companies. They took over a covered hall built in 1927 by the engineer Eugène Freyssinet, which has an exceptionally light load-bearing structure. In 2012 it was listed as an historic monument. It is 995 feet (304 meters) long and is between 200 and 235 feet (61 and 72 meters) wide.

Long used as a train-truck transfer point for the nearby Austerlitz railway station, the Halle was redesigned to reflect the new lifestyles and business practices of young digital entrepreneurs. It now features shared, multi-purpose spaces, as well as 'villages' grouped around services. The southeast end of the covered hall hosts an unusual restaurant, open 24 hours a day. Here the heritage of the past has been evoked by retaining the old loading platforms and rail bed—several restaurant cars have even been included. The bustling, surprising restaurant is linked to the city via a terrace that overlooks a terraced garden. The project will add life to the Paris-Rive Gauche industrial-renovation development.

Visually open, the central bay of the covered hall is the main axis of circulation. It is organized around shared, multi-purpose facilities, where the floor makes way to provide entry to an underground auditorium automatically. The main areas are crossed by two covered urban passageways intended to act as digital window displays, enabling local residents to feel close to this creative melting pot, while discovering the facilities brought to their neighborhood to encourage digital innovation. Above and beyond encouraging discussion and exchange, the passageways are aimed at forging a strong urban link between two districts currently cut off from one another by railway lines.

The 365,975-square-foot (34,000-square-meter) building is in pre-stressed concrete, with steel, wood, and glass.

Location Paris, France
Completion date 2017
Area 365,975 ft^2 (34,000 m^2)

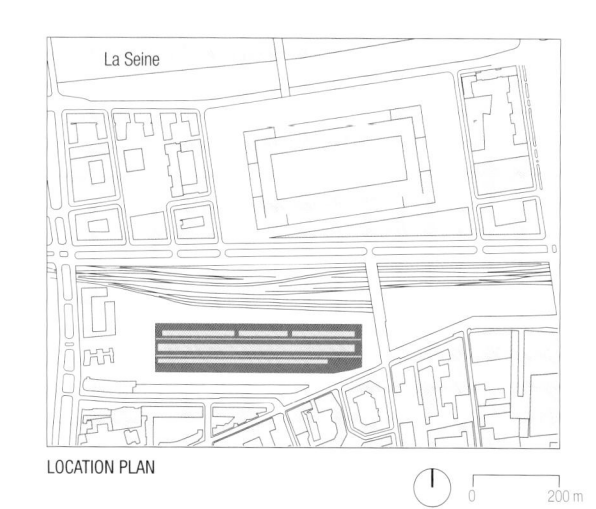

LOCATION PLAN

CROSS SECTION

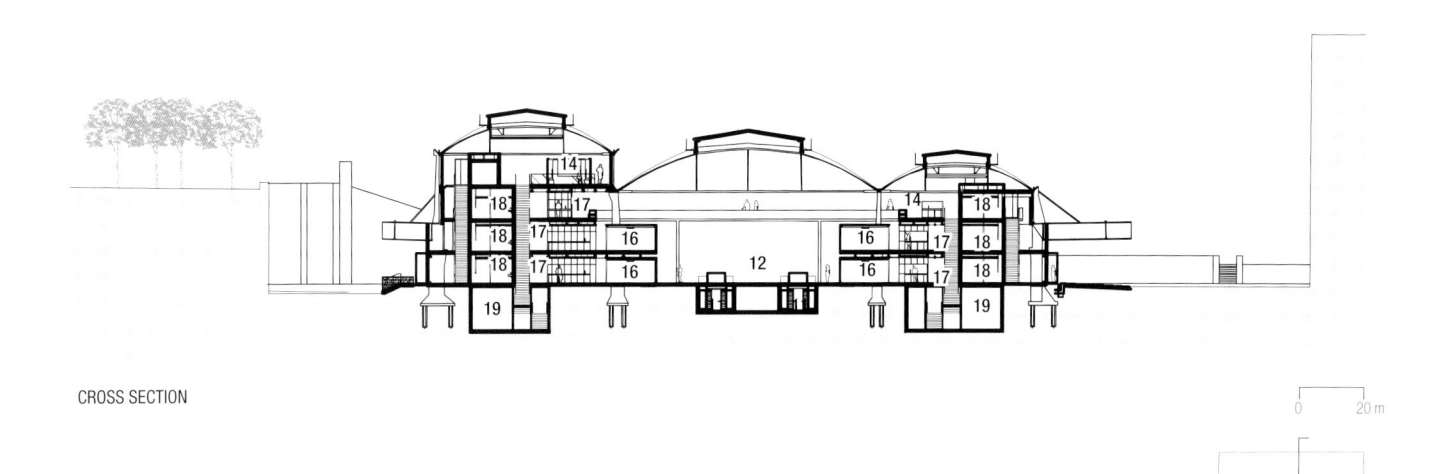

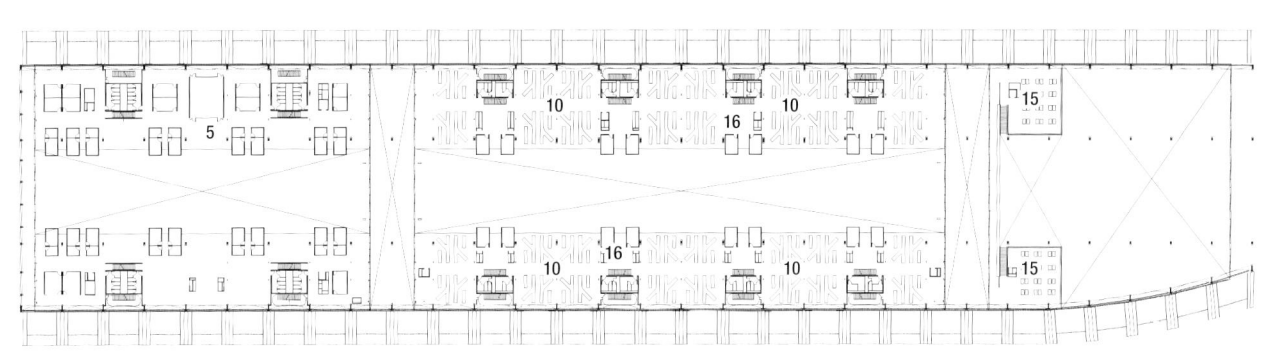

FIRST-FLOOR PLAN

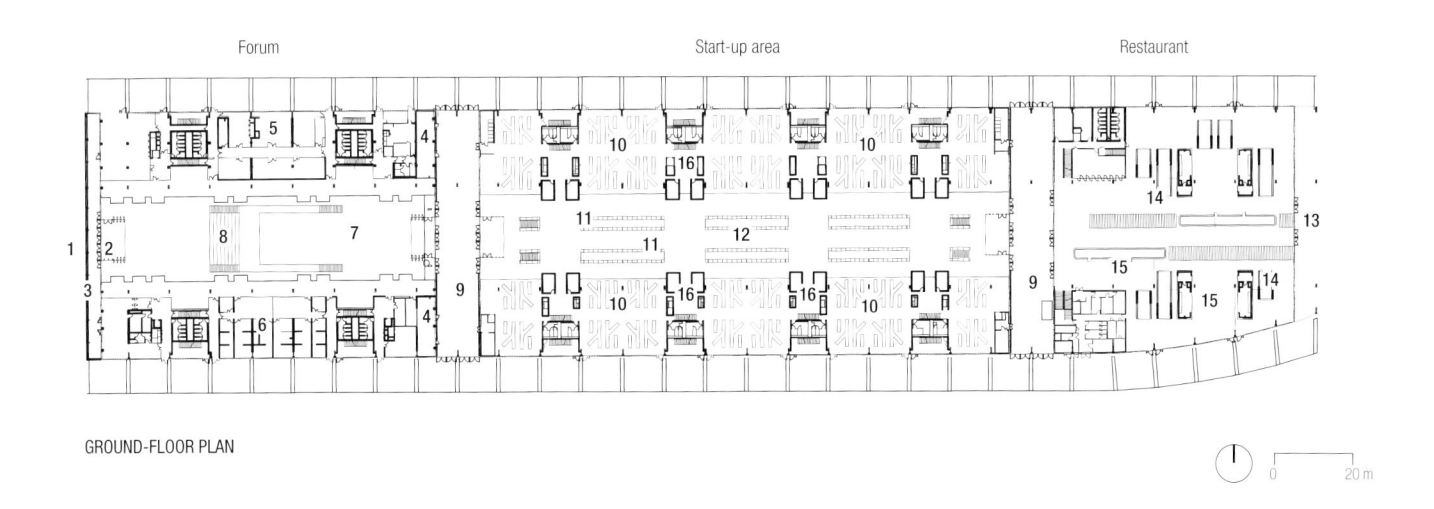

Forum — Start-up area — Restaurant

GROUND-FLOOR PLAN

1 West entrance
2 Reception
3 Peristyle
4 Shop
5 Fablab
6 Public services zones
7 Multi-purpose space
8 360-seat auditorium
9 Public walkway
10 Co-working space
11 Cloakrooms
12 Central mail and multi-purpose space
13 East entrance
14 Kitchen
15 Restaurants
16 Shared meeting rooms
17 Informal meeting rooms
18 Toilets
19 Services

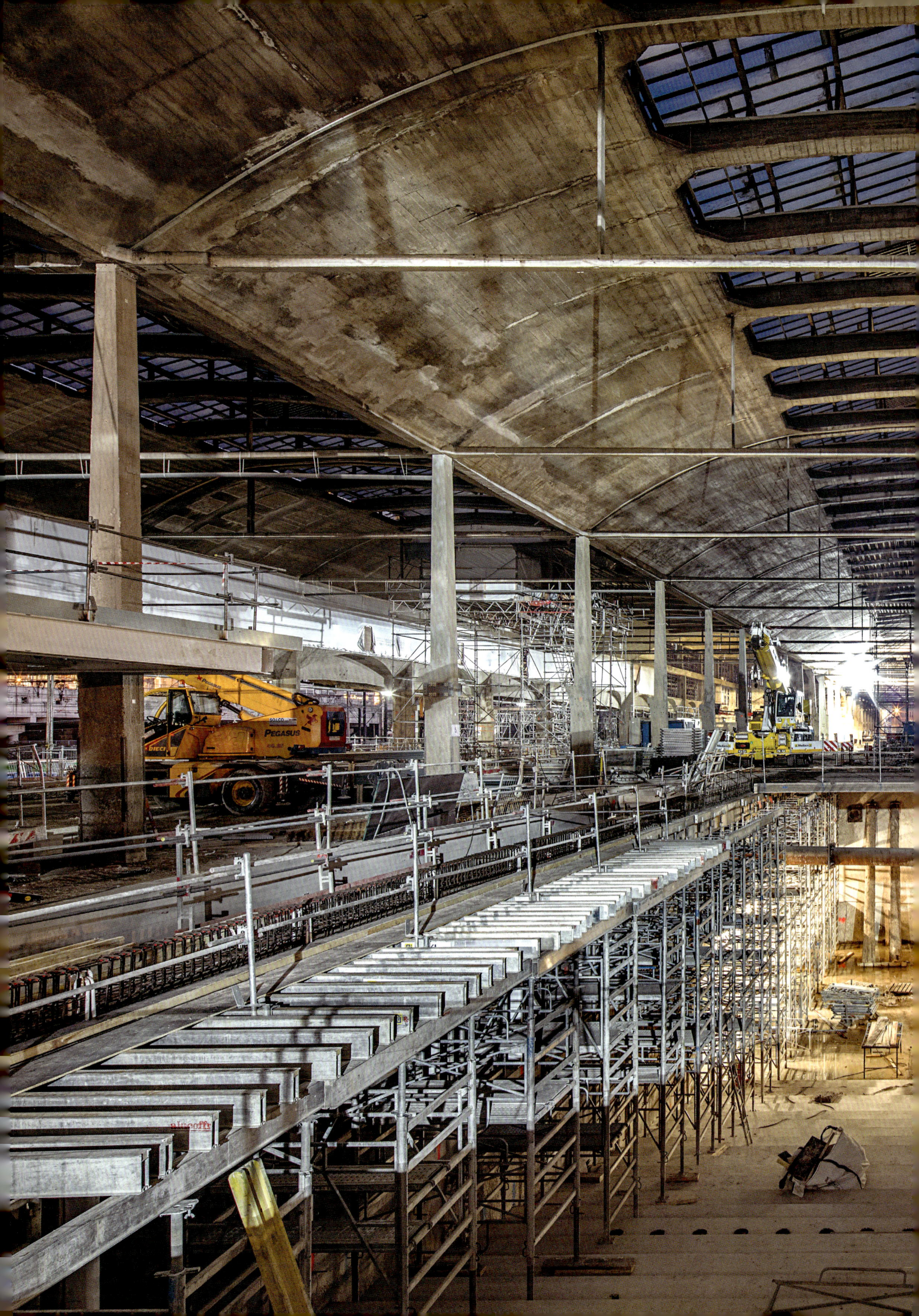
PEGASUS

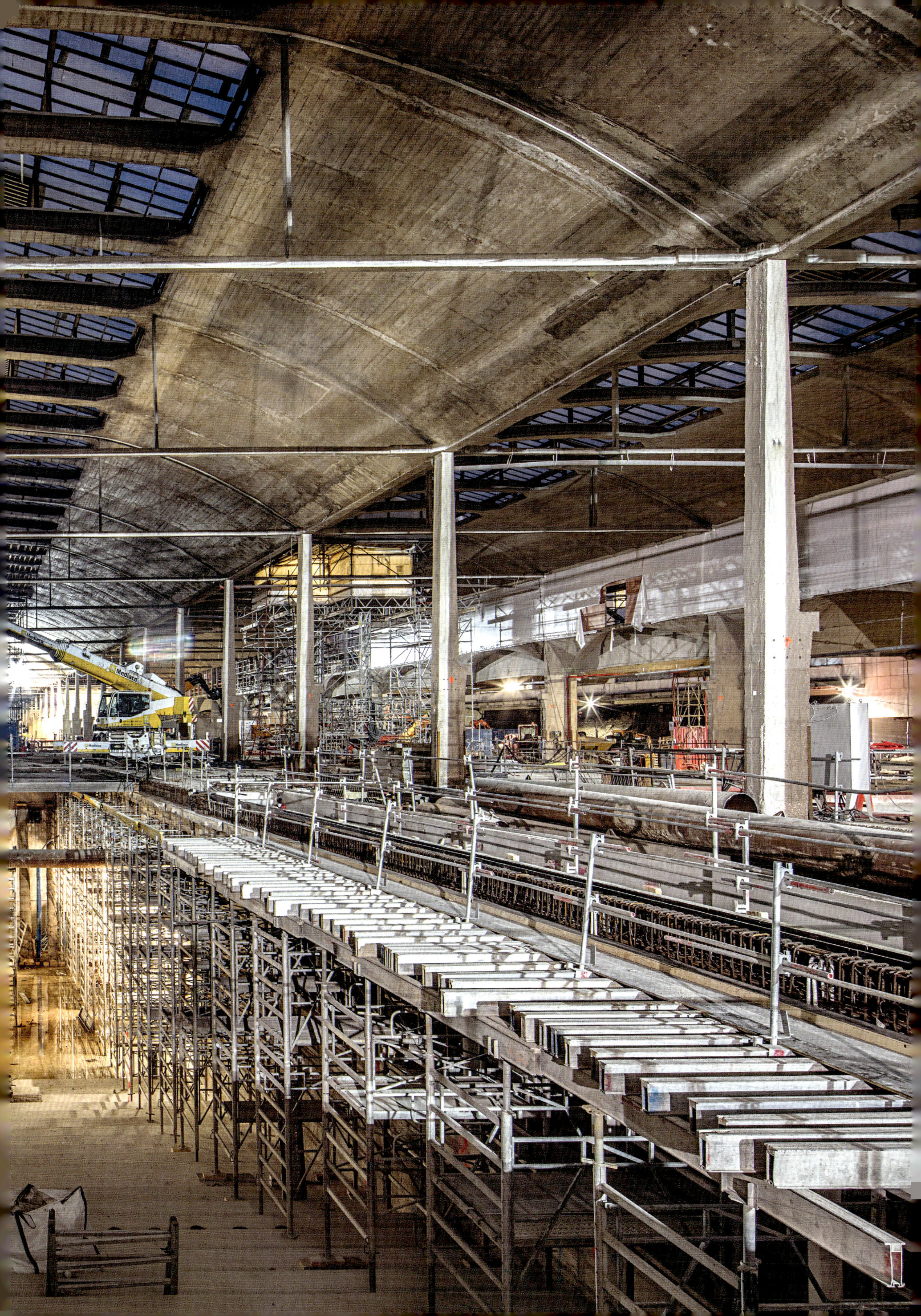

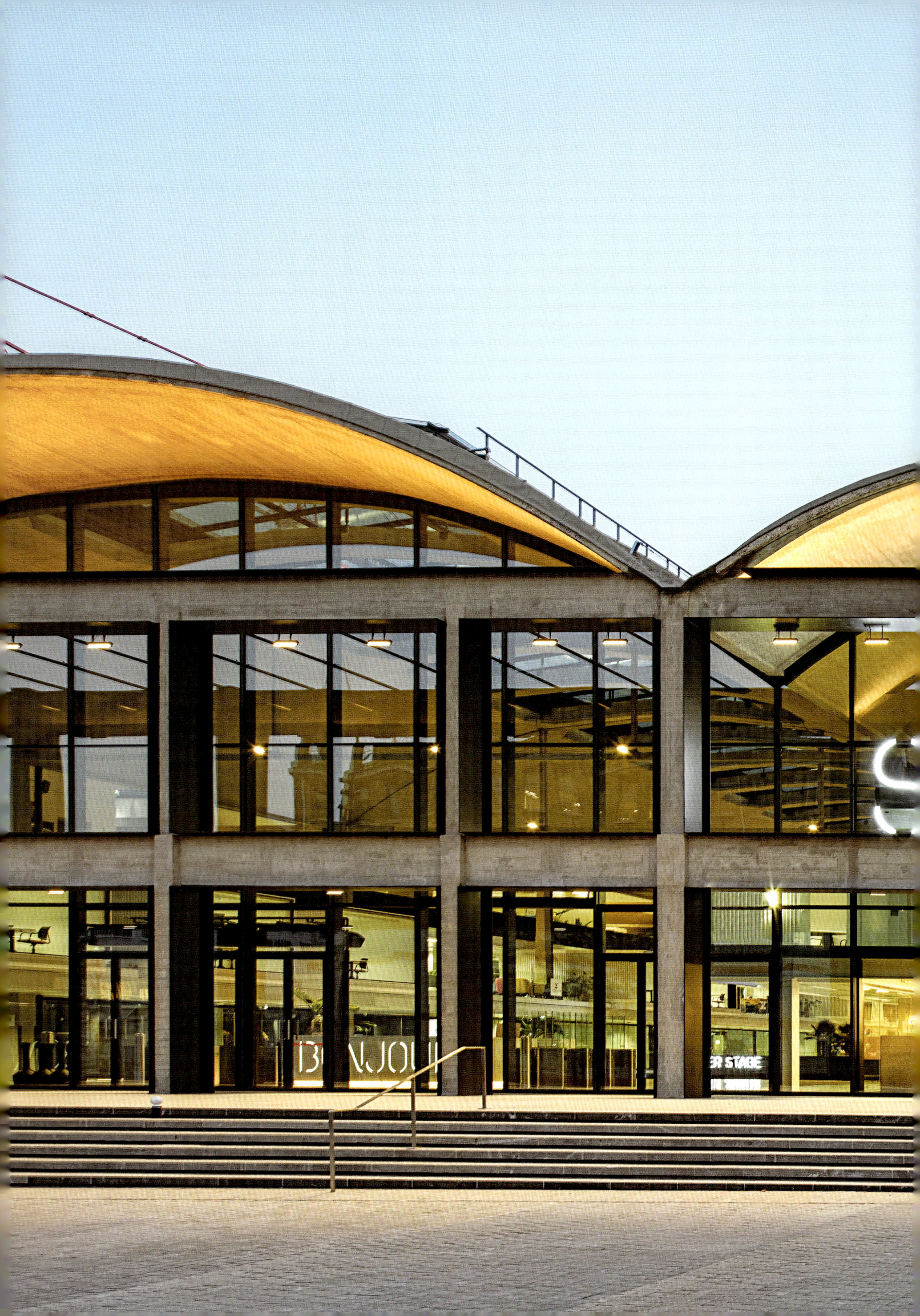

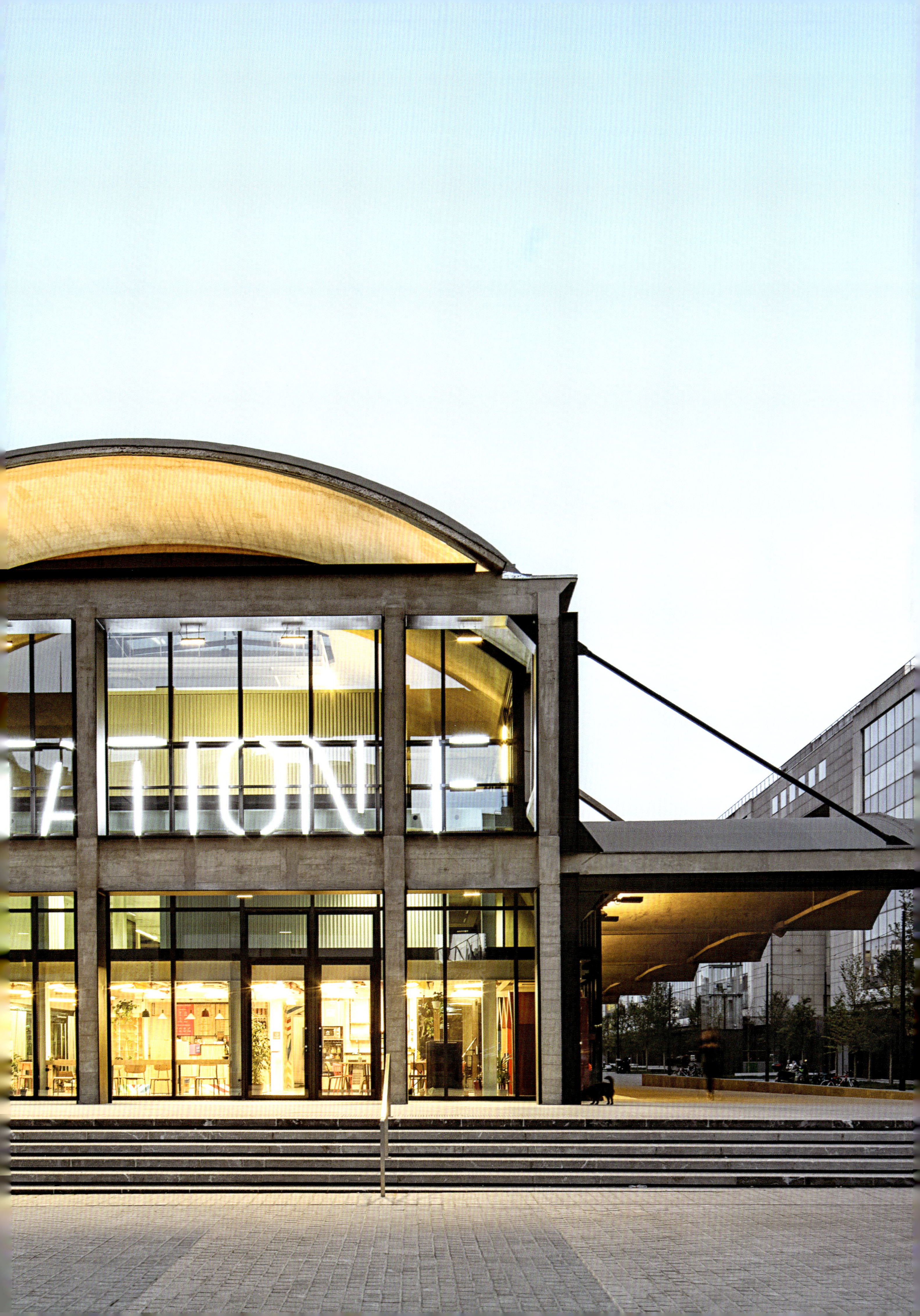

JEAN-MICHEL WILMOTTE STATION F START-UP CAMPUS

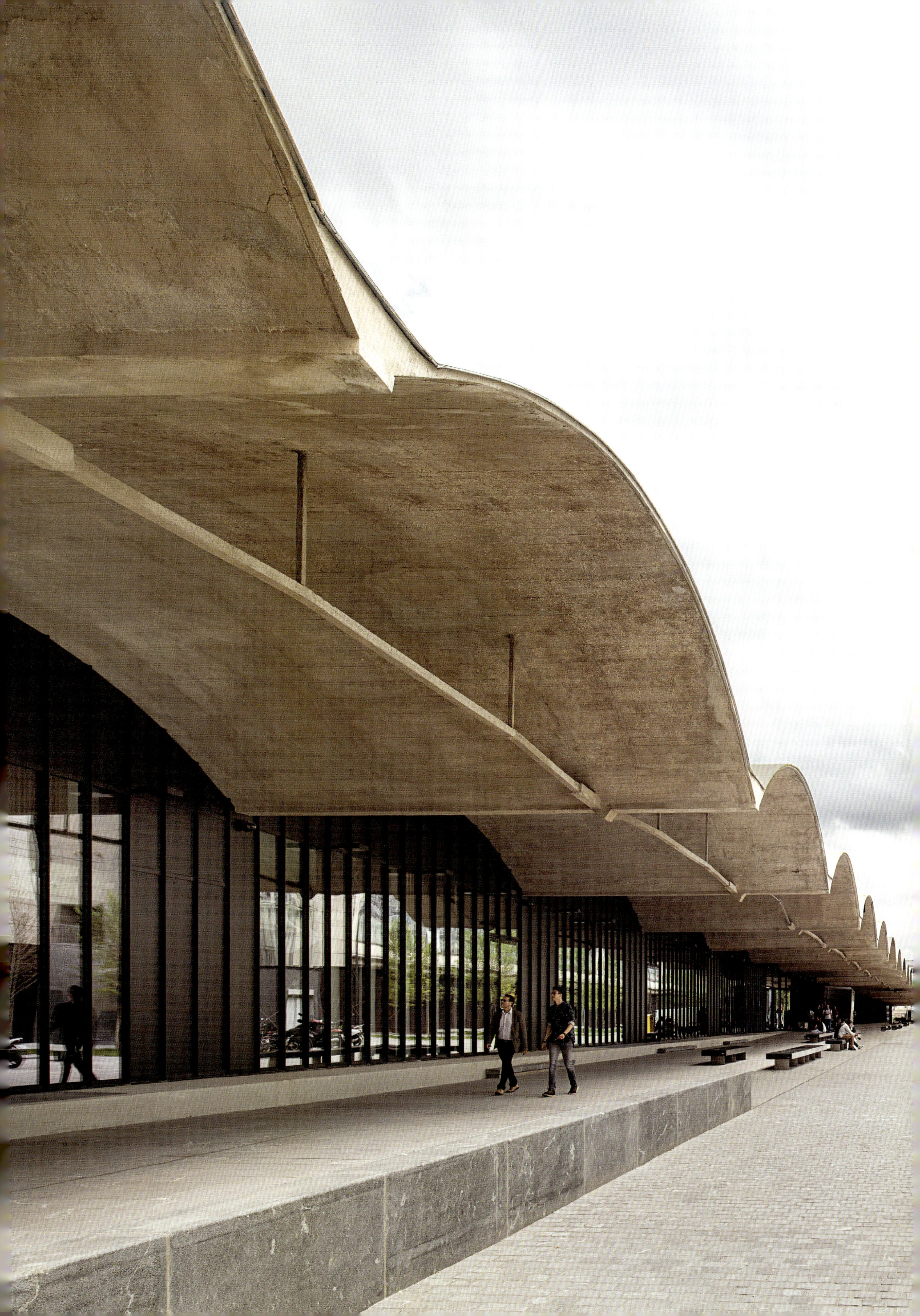

JEAN-MICHEL WILMOTTE   STATION F START-UP CAMPUS

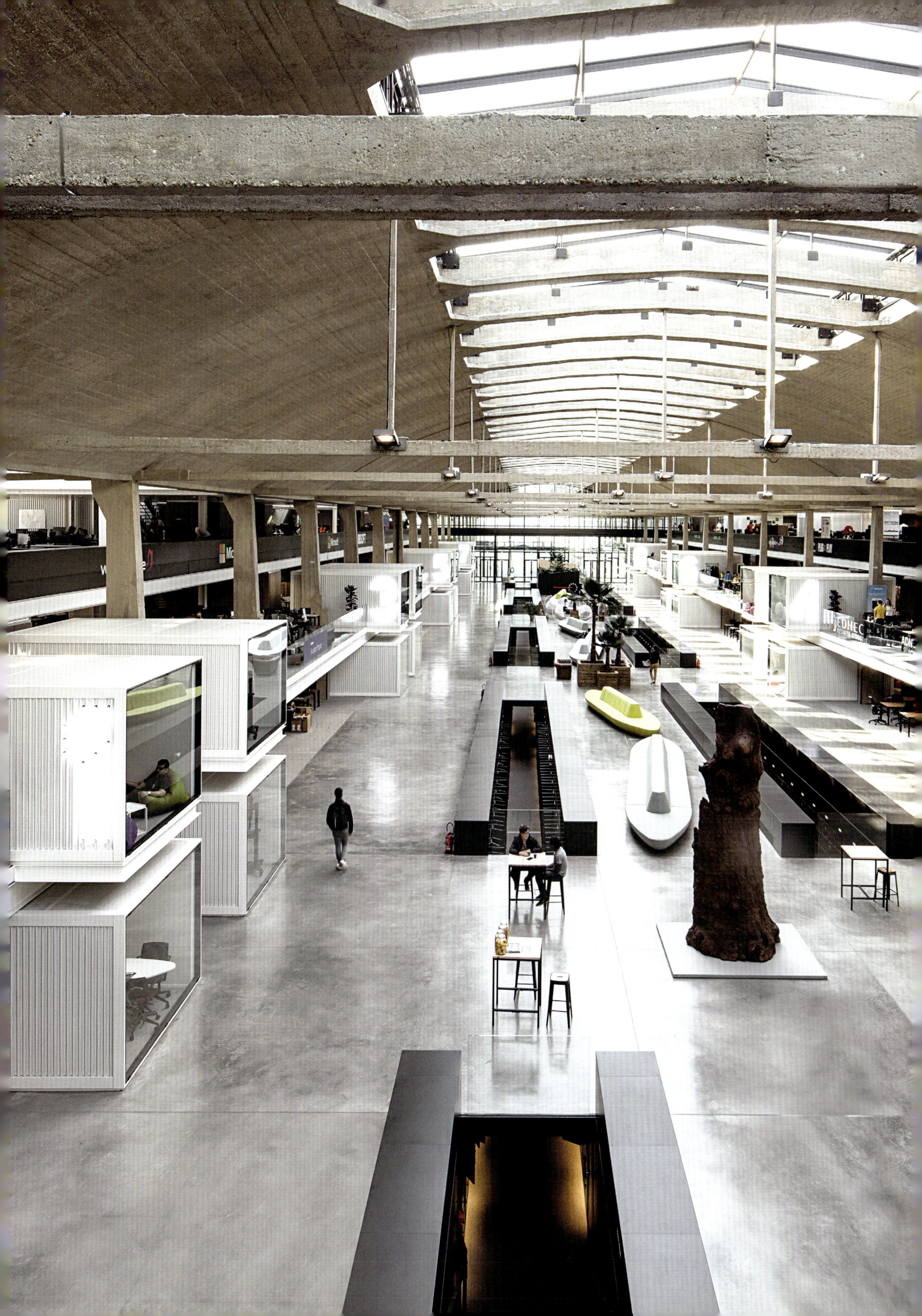
EDHEC

JEAN-MICHEL WILMOTTE

COLLÈGE DES BERNARDINS

This ambitious project involved the renovation of 53,820 square feet (5,000 square meters) of stone buildings that date from the 13th and 15th centuries. The architect added a new roof with specially made terracotta tiles and a steel frame that supports two upper floors. A total of 300 underground concrete micropiles were added to stabilize the complex.

The Collège des Bernardins dates from 1247, making it contemporary with the Sainte-Chapelle, which is also in Paris. It is the largest surviving non-religious medieval building in the city, and was a major center of Western thought. Stripped of its educational function during the French Revolution, the building was altered: its refectory, a three-aisled hall of 17 bays, was partitioned, and was ultimately abandoned in 1970 by the firefighters then stationed there.

Wilmotte's renovation of the college (done jointly with Hervé Baptiste, a senior architect at the Monuments Historiques, and under the aegis of the Diocesan Association of Paris) resuscitated this refined Gothic structure, enlivened by a play of light and shadow. The chapterhouse, a handsome, unbroken 225-foot-long (68-meter-long) space, today hosts reception and exhibition areas, as well as a bookstore.

Usable floorspace had to be created beneath the steeply sloping roof structure, and the load transmitted to the ground floor had to be strictly limited. The response of the architect was to make use of paired portal truss frames, which doubled as enclosures for services, thus leaving substantial interior space. It now houses two auditoriums, which could not have existed otherwise. This solution also allowed the ceiling of the lower floor to hang from the structure's metal tie-beams, reducing the load on the thin columns of the chapterhouse. The project won the 2010 European Union Prize for Cultural Heritage.

Location Paris, France
Completion date 2008
Area 53,820 ft² (5,000 m²)

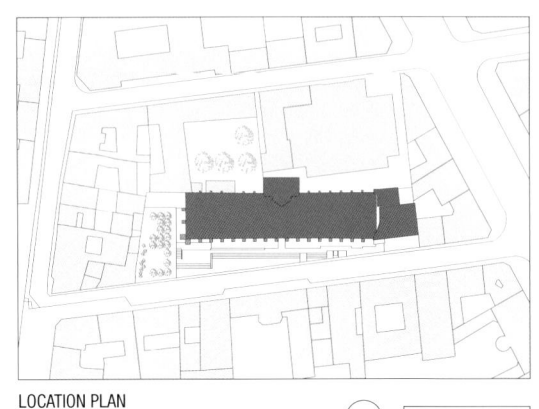

LOCATION PLAN

SOUTH ELEVATION

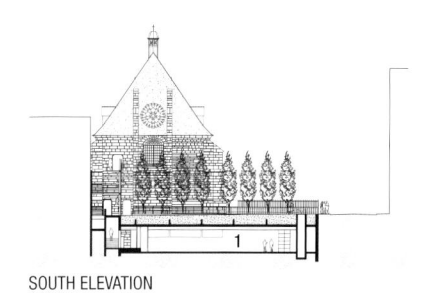

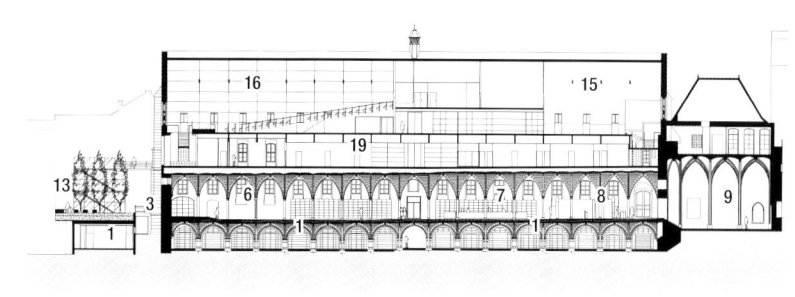

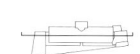

EAST ELEVATION

CROSS SECTION

LONG SECTION

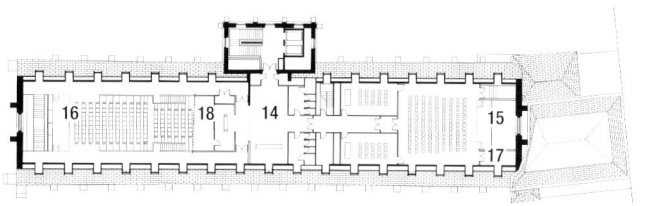

SECOND-FLOOR PLAN

GROUND-FLOOR PLAN

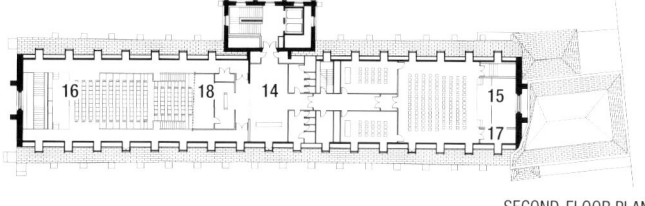

BASEMENT FLOOR PLAN

1 Classroom
2 Deambulatory
3 Drainage channels
4 Library
5 Entrance
6 Exhibition gallery
7 Reception
8 Bookshop
9 Music room
10 Prayer room
11 Upper forecourt
12 Lower forecourt
13 Garden
14 Hall
15 Small auditorium
16 Large auditorium
17 Archives
18 Services space beneath seating
19 Offices

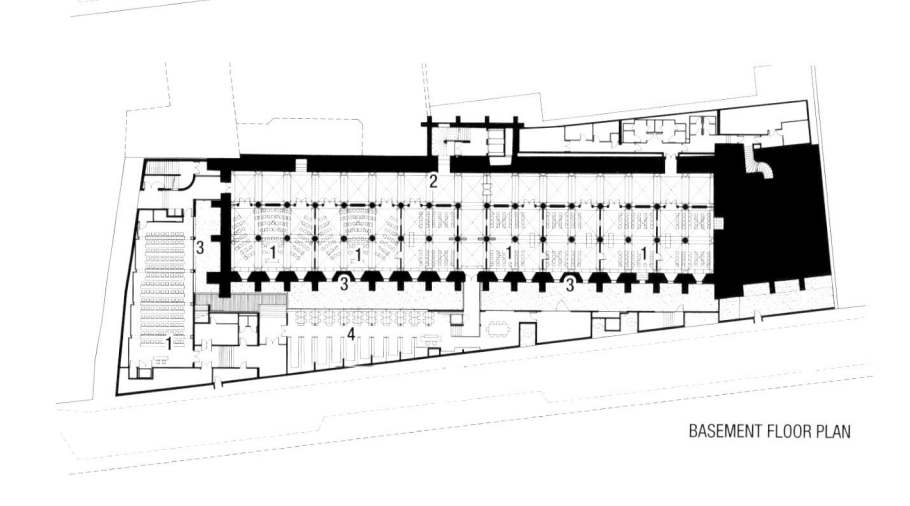

JEAN-MICHEL WILMOTTE   COLLÈGE DES BERNARDINS

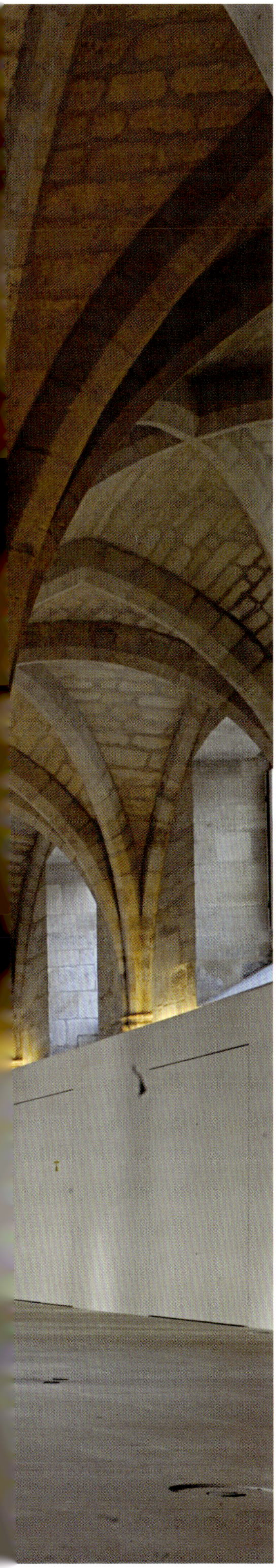
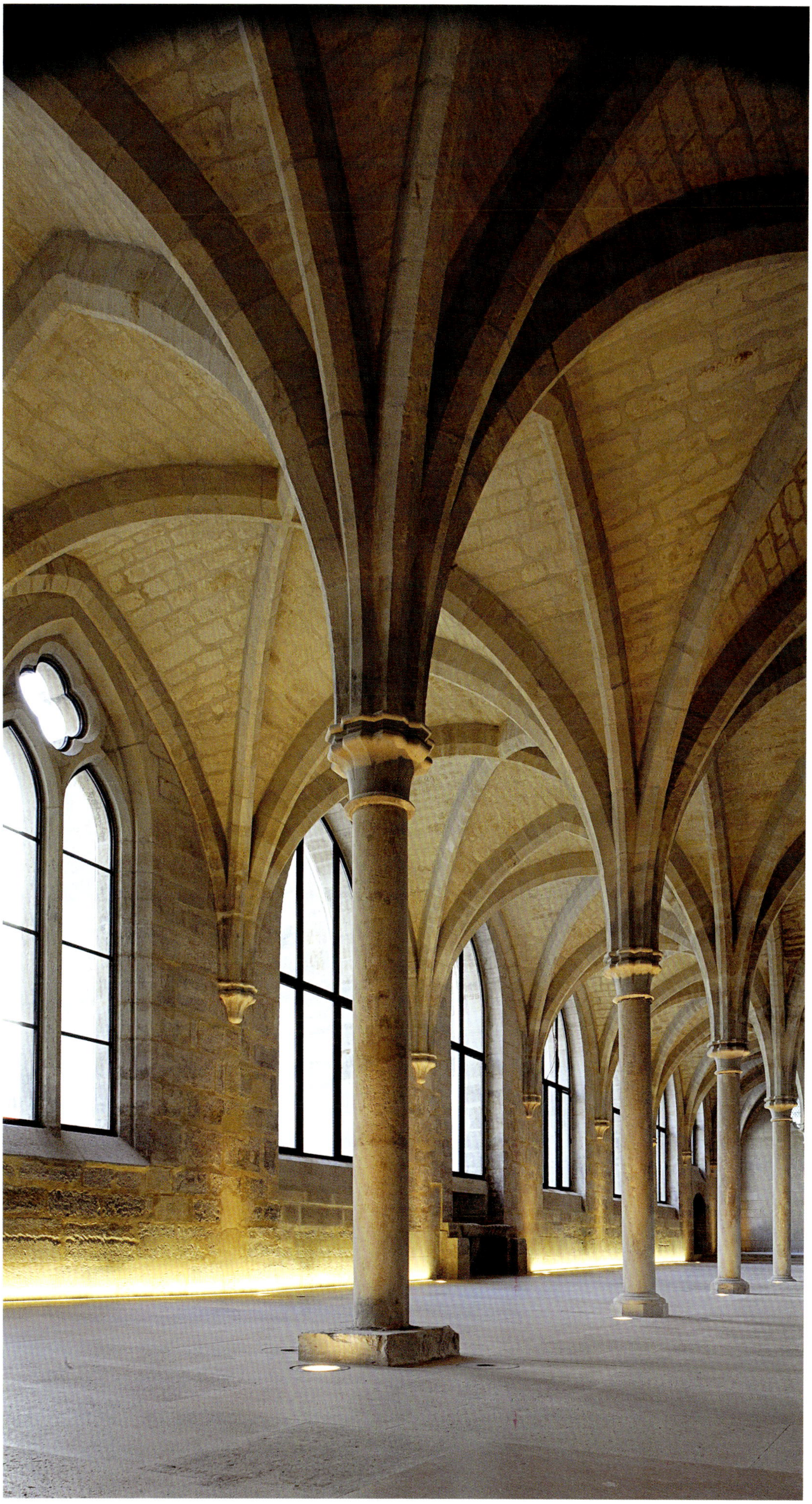

JEAN-MICHEL WILMOTTE COLLÈGE DES BERNARDINS

167

JEAN-MICHEL WILMOTTE COLLÈGE DES BERNARDINS

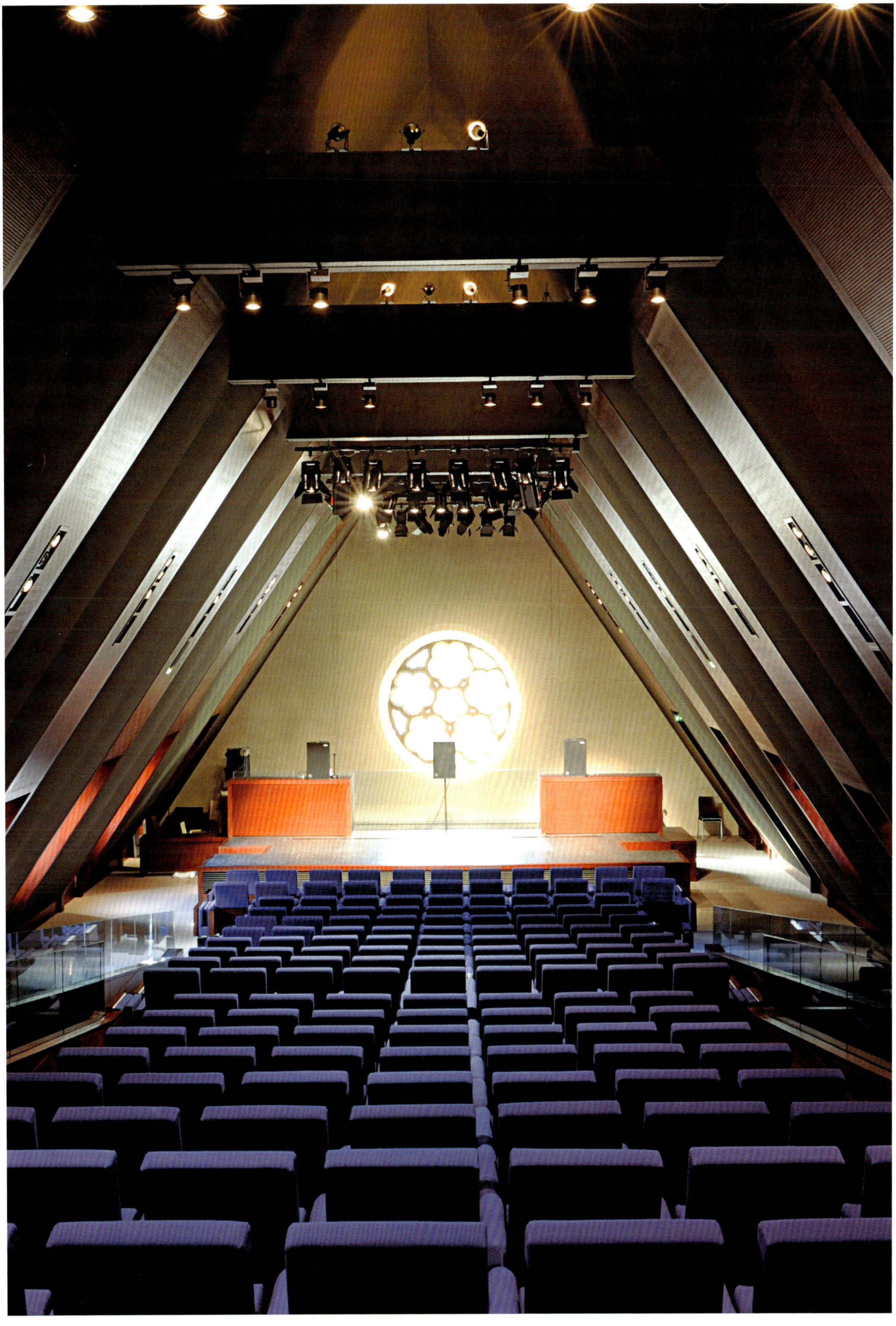

URBAN PROJECTS

JEAN-MICHEL WILMOTTE

GREATER MOSCOW PROPOSAL

Early in 2012 the city of Moscow launched an international competition for proposals for Greater Moscow, given that an area of 258 square miles (668 square kilometers)—one and a half times the size of today's city—has been allocated for expansion of the city of 12 million people.

Ten international teams were asked to make proposals for development strategies for the capital of Russia, in the vein currently being adopted for Greater Paris. The studies were conducted from January to August 2012 at the pace of one seminar per month. On September 5, 2012, a jury awarded a Franco-Russian team led by urban architect Antoine Grumbach and architects Jean-Michel Wilmotte and Sergueï Tkachenko, the mission of guiding the evolution of the extension of Moscow.

One of the guiding principles of the Franco-Russian team's plan is a focus on the Moskva River for the development of both institutional and leisure activities in the greater urban area. Like the Seine in Paris and the Thames in London, the Moskva should become a vector of the city's identity. Landscaped development of the river banks, with a constant concern for the quality of life and the valorization of existing heritage, should be accompanied by a redeployment of public transportation (here embodied by a tram line) in order to limit car traffic that today makes the quays inaccessible to pedestrians.

Today the city of Moscow is paralyzed by car traffic resulting from a lack of public transportation. That is why the winning team proposed a global vision of public transport for a metropolis that will number 14 million inhabitants by 2025. The plan calls for several rapid train lines to airports and the outskirts of Moscow (MKAD). The problems of car traffic should be eased through the intermodality of the subway network and tram lines. A new express subway line—the New Moscow Line (NML)—will efficiently tie the old city to Greater Moscow.

Although the main purpose of the Greater Moscow project is to extend the city, Grumbach and Wilmotte felt that it was more important to restructure existing lines of urban development rather than build new towns.

Location Russian Federation
Proposal date 2012
Area 258 mi^2 (668 km^2)

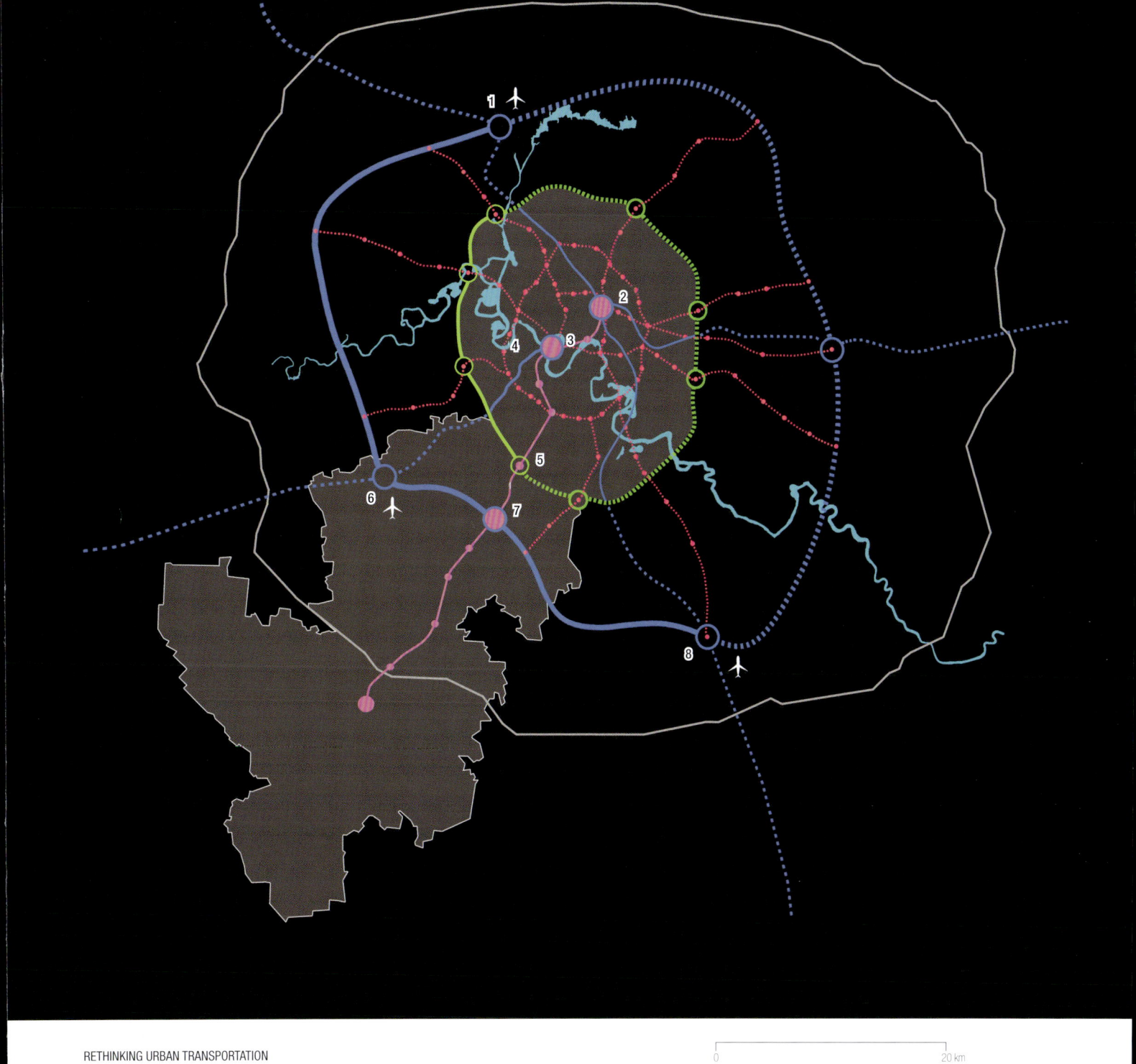

RETHINKING URBAN TRANSPORTATION

―○― Moscow Gates

High-speed train / MKAD ring road and edge
──── Phase 1: 2020–2025
▪▪▪▪▪ Phase 2

High-speed train
──── Phase 1: 2020–2025
▪▪▪▪▪ Phase 2

―•― NML metro express: 2020–2025 / NML High-speed metro: 2020–2025

⋯•⋯ Metro

──── Motorway ring road around Moscow

▰▰ Extension of New Moscow

0   20 km

1 Sheremetievo Airport
2 Three Stations Sector
3 Kremlin
4 Kievsky
5 New Moscow Gate
6 Vnukovo Airport
7 Kommunarka
8 Domodiedovo Airport

173

JEAN-MICHEL WILMOTTE GREATER MOSCOW PROPOSAL

NEW MOSCOW GATE: BEFORE/AFTER

THE MOSKVA RIVERBANK ALONG THE KREMLIN PERIMETER (BEFORE/AFTER): MOSKVA RIVER BECOMES A VECTOR OF MOSCOW'S IDENTITY

JEAN-MICHEL WILMOTTE GREATER MOSCOW PROPOSAL

STITCHING THE CITY TOGETHER: THREE STATIONS SECTOR (BEFORE/AFTER)

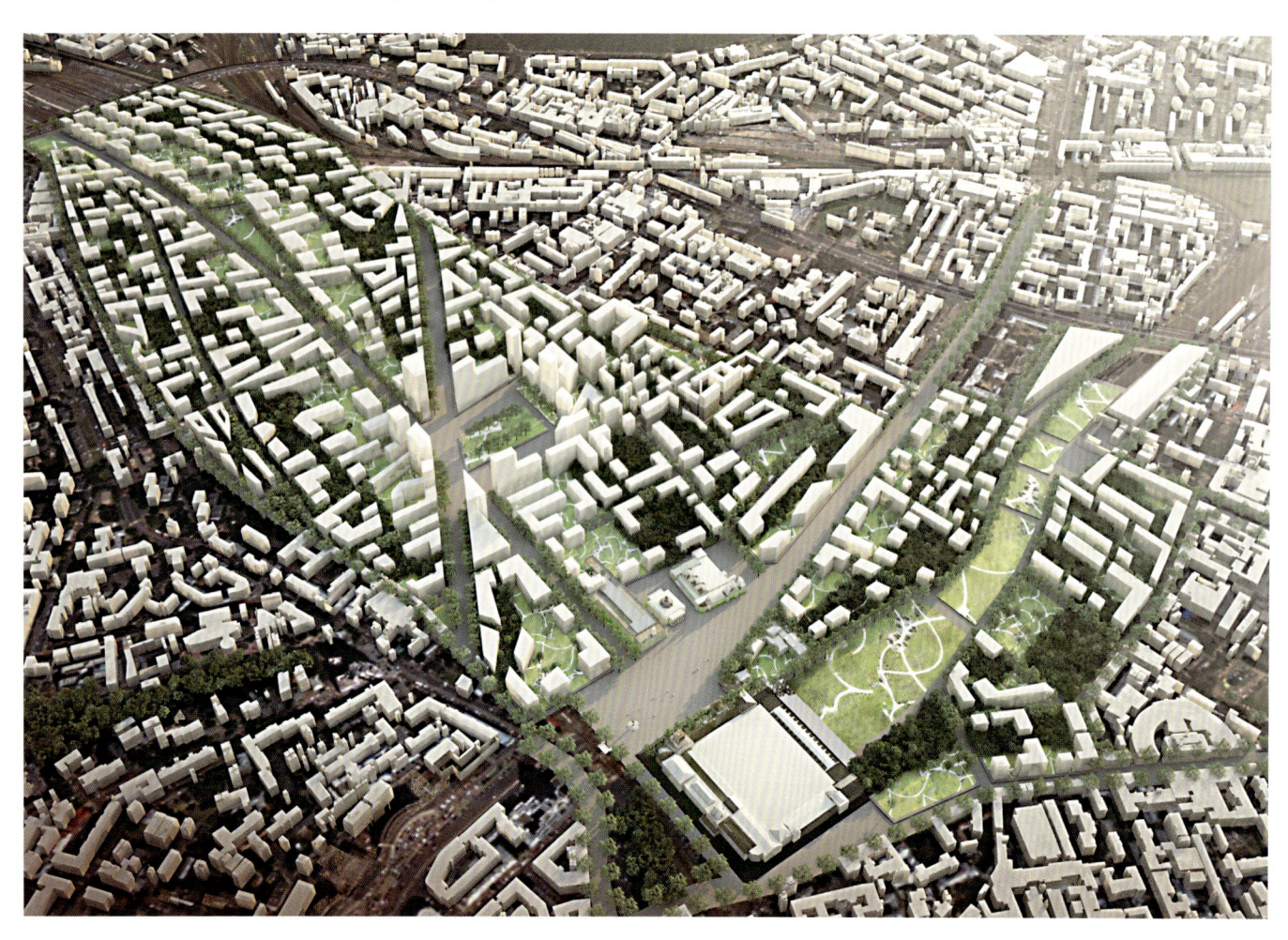

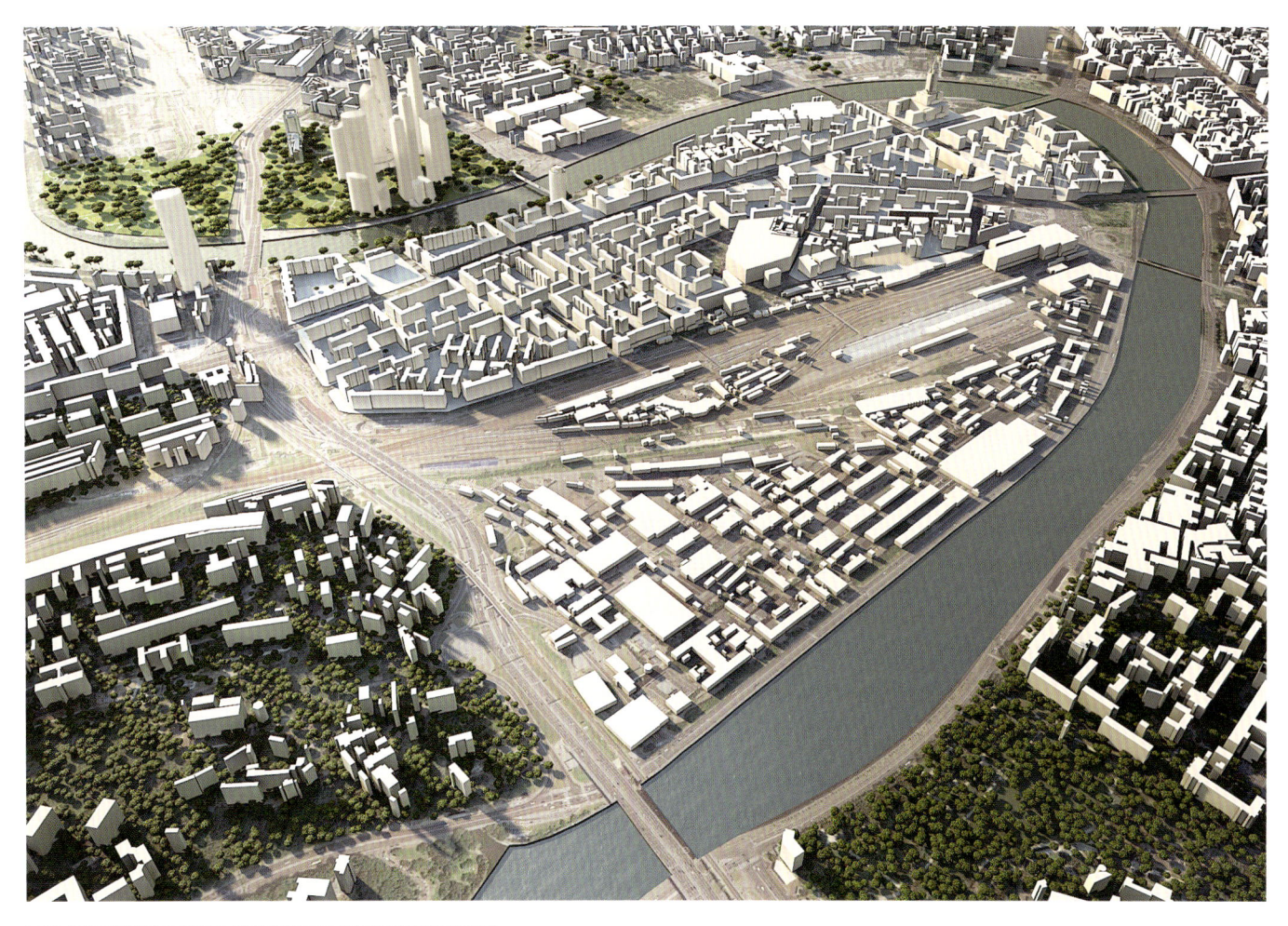

STITCHING THE CITY TOGETHER: KIEVSKY TRAIN STATIONS (BEFORE/AFTER)

JEAN-MICHEL WILMOTTE

ALLÉES JEAN-JAURÈS

The largest avenue in Nîmes, now named Allées Jean-Jaurès, was laid out in 1753 by Jacques Philippe Maréchal, a military engineer for King Louis XV, to channel water from the Jardins de la Fontaine down a mile-long (1.6-kilometer-long), 200-foot-wide (61-meter-wide) promenade, planted with four rows of European nettle trees. Unfortunately, its appeal was eroded as it steadily became an unregulated parking lot.

As local citizens wanted to reclaim this remarkable feature, Wilmotte suggested turning it into a pleasant meeting place. It functions as an extension of the Jardins de la Fontaine, notably the central pedestrian strip where leafy and stony stretches alternate in a homogeneous composition, which nevertheless hosts a wide variety of uses, ranging from a playground to gathering spots to temporary market stalls.

The kiosks and pergolas adorning the central pedestrian strip of the broad Allées Jean-Jaurès in Nîmes play on the motif of the leaves of the age-old nettle trees lining it. Composed of perforated sheet iron back-lit by LEDs, the façades enliven the avenue by providing delicate lighting that evokes Provençal lace. "We wanted to channel the energy of the Jardins de la Fontaine, restoring the original identity to the avenue so that people would feel good there, and would go there more willingly," says the architect.

The Allées begin at the foot of the gardens, where a series of ornamental pools have become an enjoyable spot swiftly accepted by the citizens of Nîmes. The materials used include sand-blasted concrete (for the sidewalk), concrete slabs, stone slabs, and paving stones made with natural stone from Croatia (for the central walkway), and wooden duckboard (for the terraces).

Location Nîmes, France
Completion date 2013, competition-winning project
Area 1 mile (1.6 km)

LOCATION MAP

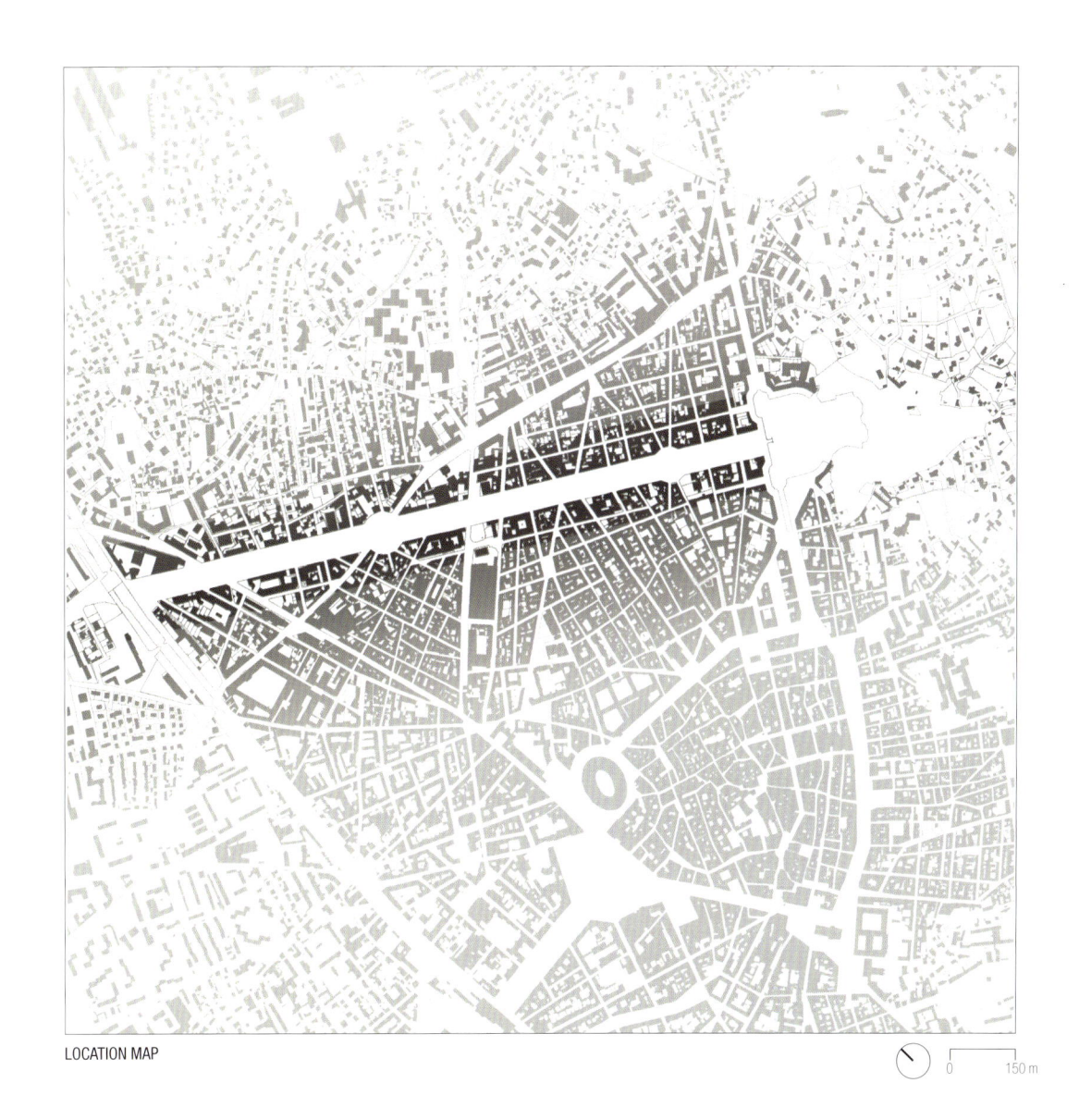

0 150 m

SEQUENCE 1

1 Pond
2 Dry-deck fountain
3 Duckboard & benches
4 Lawn
5 Ground-cover plants
6 Pavement: Concrete and stone
7 Mature hackberry
8 Shrub

0 20 m

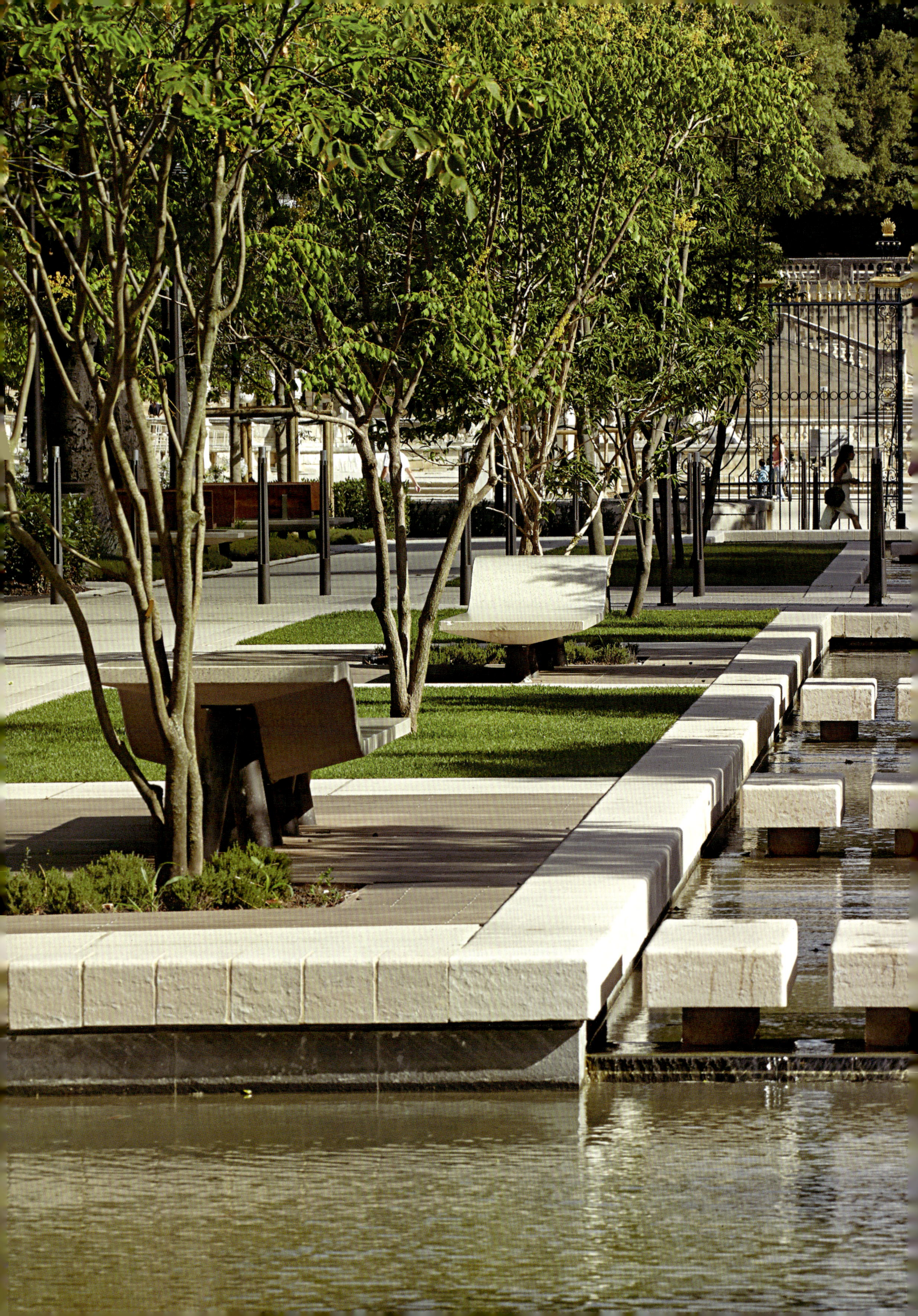

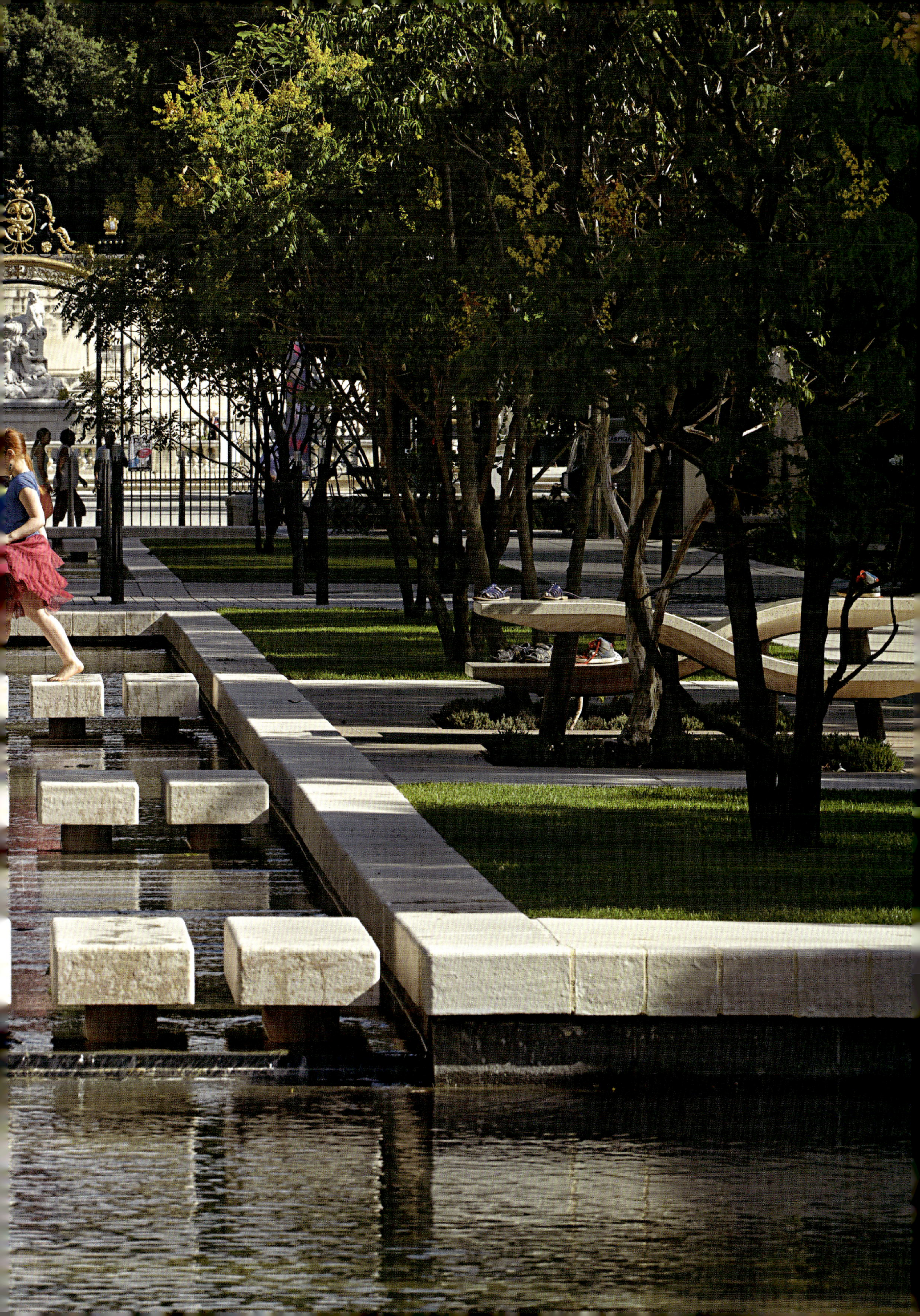

JEAN-MICHEL WILMOTTE ALLÉES JEAN-JAURÈS

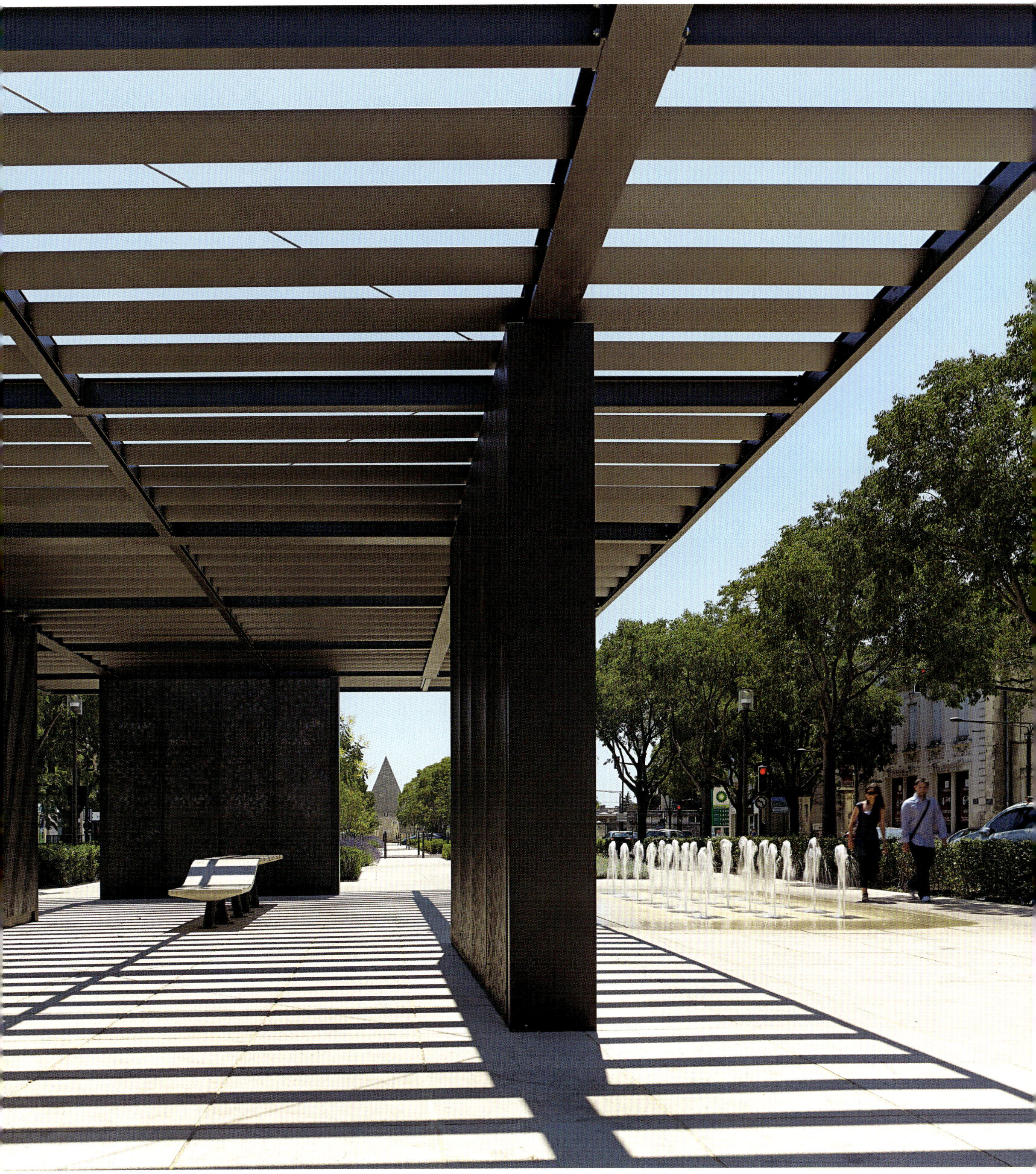

MUSEUMS

JEAN-MICHEL WILMOTTE

PAVILLON DES SESSIONS, MUSÉE DU LOUVRE

At the instigation of President Jacques Chirac and the tribal art dealer Jacques Kerchache, both the Louvre and the French state itself moved toward giving 'primitive' art its rightful place within the country's museums. They preferred the term 'Arts premiers,' meaning 'first arts' or 'primal art,' to the more pejorative 'primitive' label.

Jean-Michel Wilmotte was the winner of the competition to redesign the Pavillon des Sessions of the Louvre on the first floor on the Seine side of the palace for these collections. "The work for the Louvre's Department of Primal Arts," said Wilmotte, "represented a watershed in our way of envisaging museum design—it meant clarifying space to the maximum, so that the works would come to the fore."
On April 13, 2000, the Pavillon des Sessions was unveiled as a branch and a 'preview' of the future Musée du Quai Branly, then being built to regroup several French museums of primal arts.

Some 15,070 square feet (1,400 square meters) of exhibition space was devoted to 108 masterpieces of the arts of Africa, Asia, Oceania, and the Americas, selected by Kerchache. This was the first time that 'primal arts' had been displayed on the same premises as the glamorous 'icons' of Western art housed in the Louvre. Wilmotte's team was concerned about maintaining an appropriate link with the rest of the Louvre, even as it adapted the pavilion to the works and respected the historic dimensions of the building.

The softly lit Pavillon des Sessions presents the visitor with a clean, open, space, simplified volumes, and limited spatial divisions. The minimalist display cases were conceived architecturally, and are deliberately spacious with respect to the size of the work on show, helping to bring out the sacred feeling to the objects—the eye can appreciate the full dimension of each sculpture. This was the first time that Wilmotte had adopted such an approach, based on optimal transparency, in which lighting was no longer incorporated into the display case, but handled from a flexible overhead system able to create a source of light anywhere in the room.

Location Paris, France
Completion date 2000
Area 15,070 ft^2 (1,400 m^2)

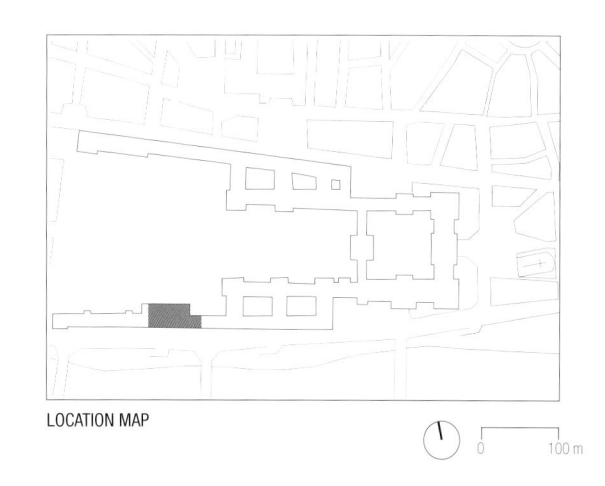

LOCATION MAP

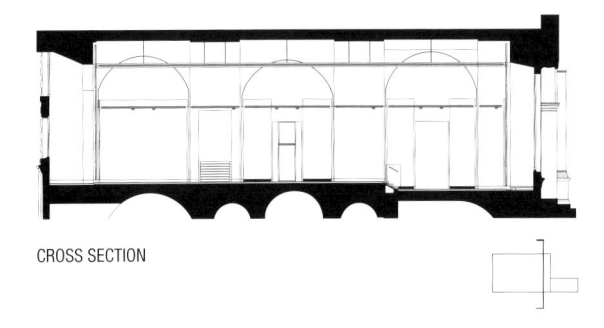

CROSS SECTION

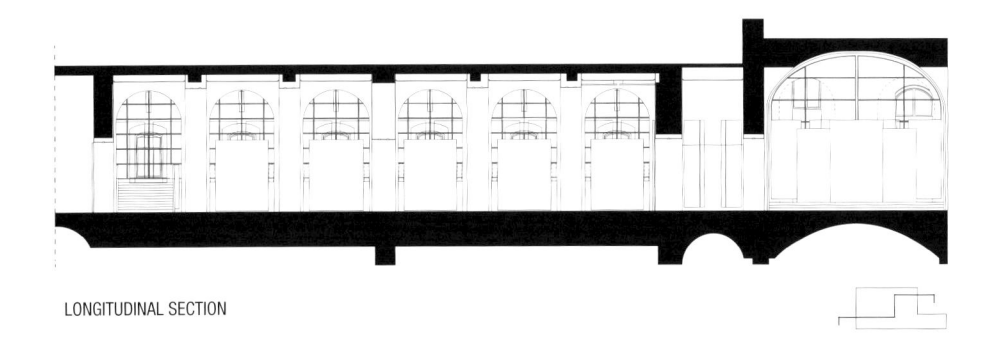

LONGITUDINAL SECTION

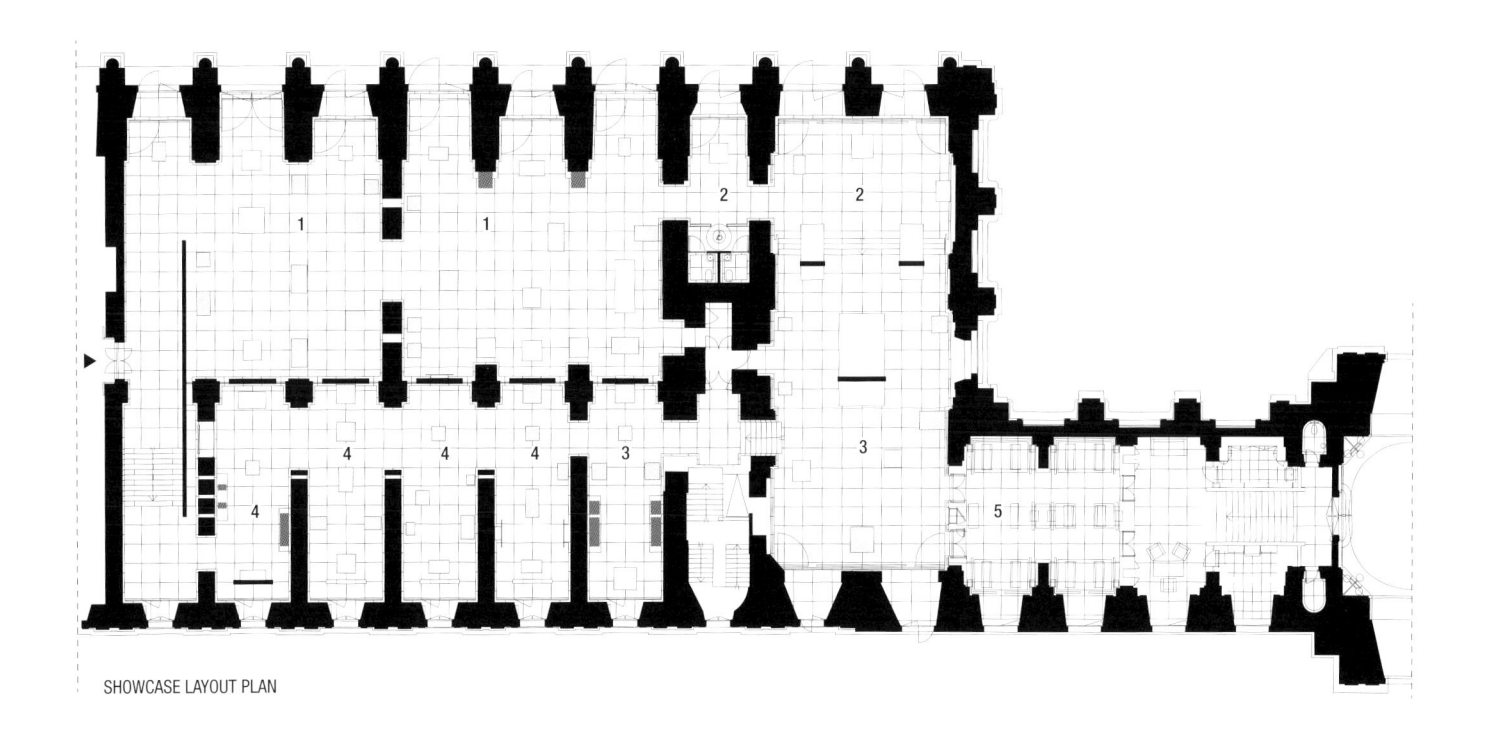

SHOWCASE LAYOUT PLAN

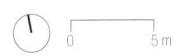

1 Africa
2 Asia
3 Oceania
4 America
5 Multimedia area

0 5 m

Wall monted showcase
Free-standing showcase
Podium
Suspended glass panel protection
Free-standing wall display

187

Océanie

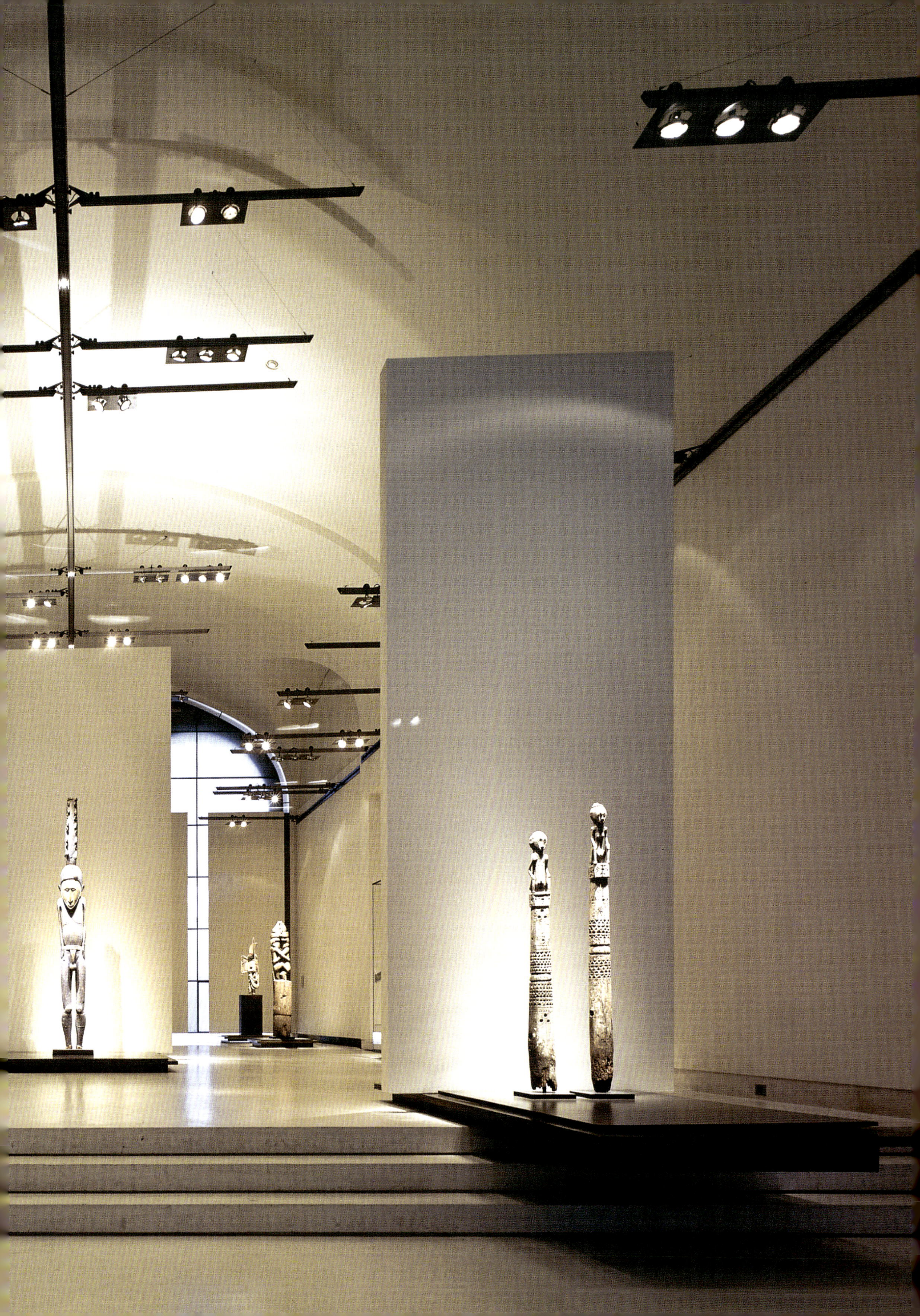

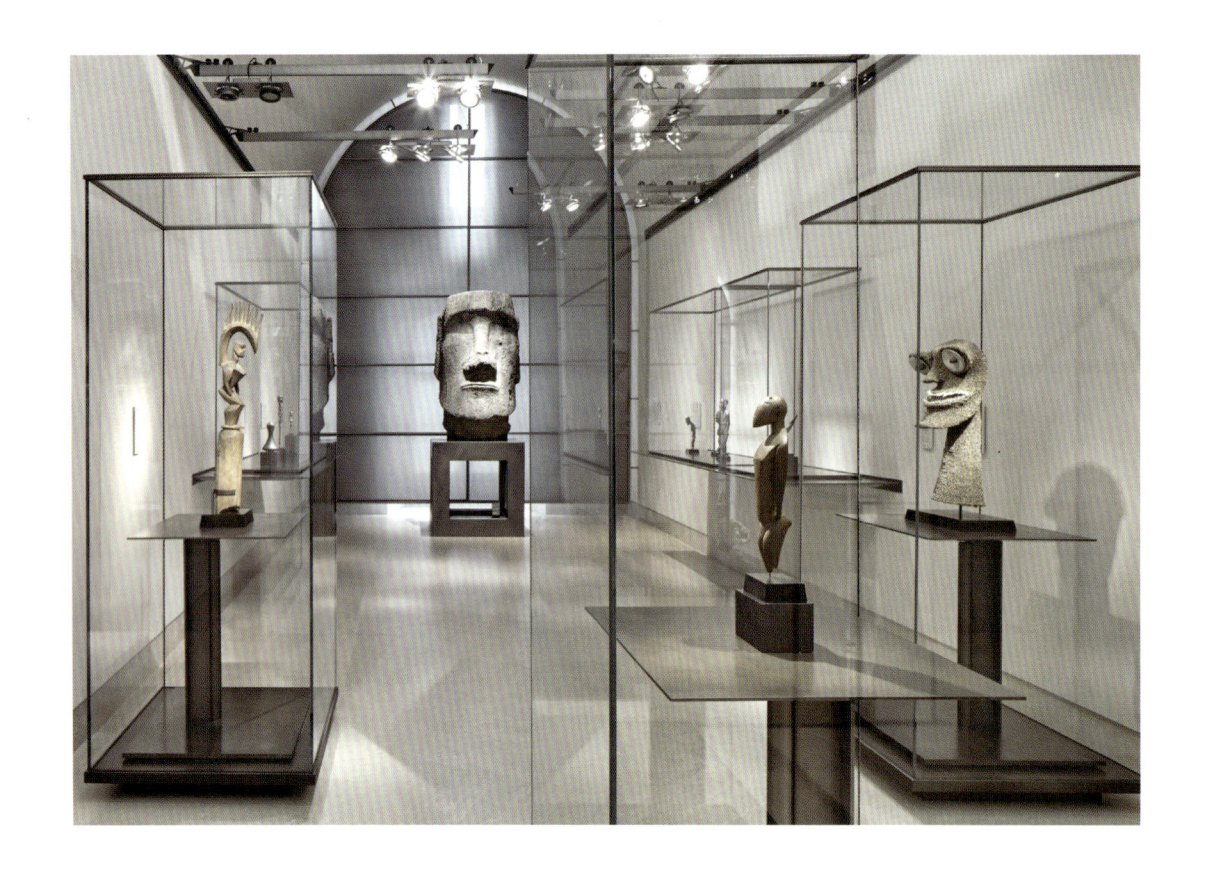

JEAN-MICHEL WILMOTTE PAVILLON DES SESSIONS, MUSÉE DU LOUVRE

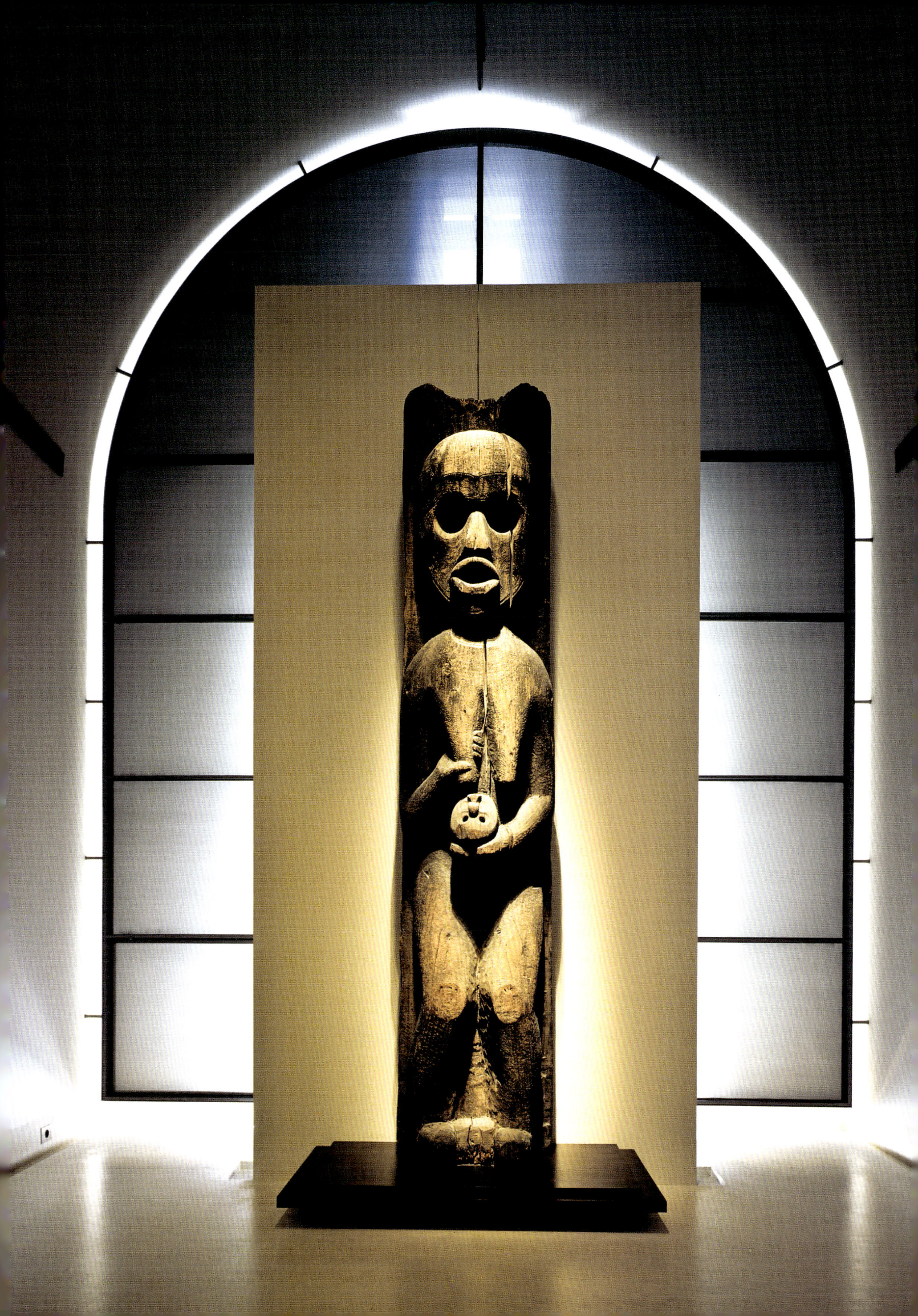

JEAN-MICHEL WILMOTTE

GANA ART CENTER

Jean-Michel Wilmotte's first built work in South Korea, the Gana Art Center, is a 32,550-square-foot (3,024-square-meter) facility. The reinforced concrete building devoted to the exhibition of contemporary art makes use of Italian beige limestone cladding and wood. The client was the art dealer Ho-Jae Lee and the facility includes a boutique, restaurant, and an open-air theater.

Located at Pyeongchang-dong, an outlying residential area in the hills to the north of the city, the Gana Art Center is on a sloped site that opens to the upper side for the amphitheater. The four-story structure is partially underground. Artificial lighting dominates the galleries located in blind volumes. Glazed corridors form balconies above the sunken amphitheater. The landscape thus penetrates into the heart of the composition, spilling down from wooded slopes. Timber decking is used for exterior surfaces.

The first building was completed in one year, and an auction room clad in copper that is intended to contrast with the light stone of the gallery building, was then built on a neighboring site. Three years later a third building intended as a place for secure storage was added, one street away. This three-story structure includes an angled exhibition space.

Black brick, one of the architect's favourite materials, alternates with large panes of dark tinted glass to form a kind of Oriental lantern. The buildings are all within sight of each other and seem to be connected through their design elements. Shortly after the completion of the Gana buildings, the same client returned to an earlier idea, which had been to create an art center in Insa-dong, an upscale area near the center of Seoul.

Location Seoul, South Korea
Completion date 1998
Area 32,550 ft^2 (3,024 m^2)

LOCATION MAP

SECTION

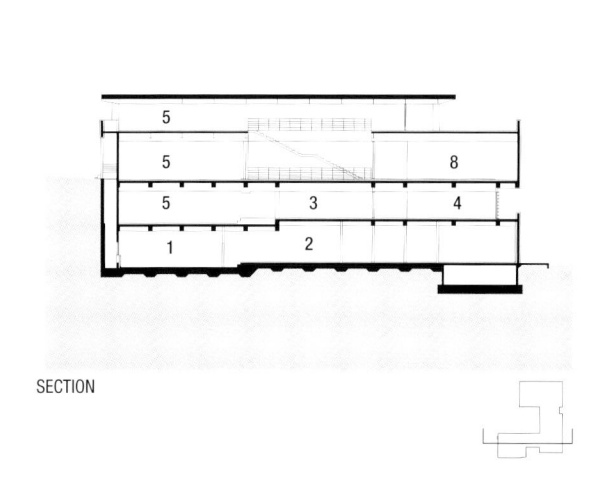

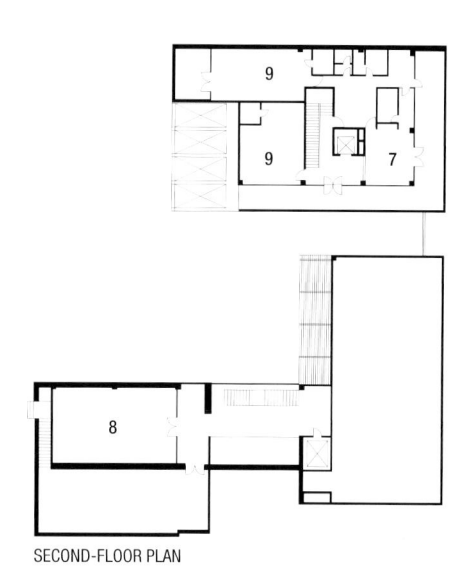

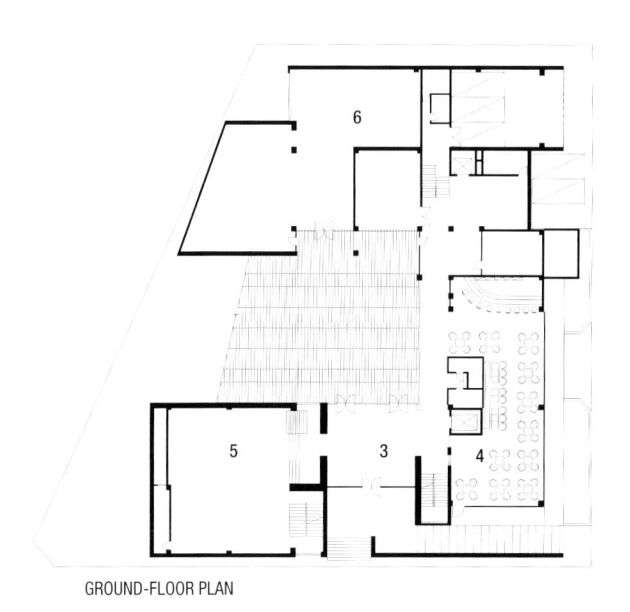

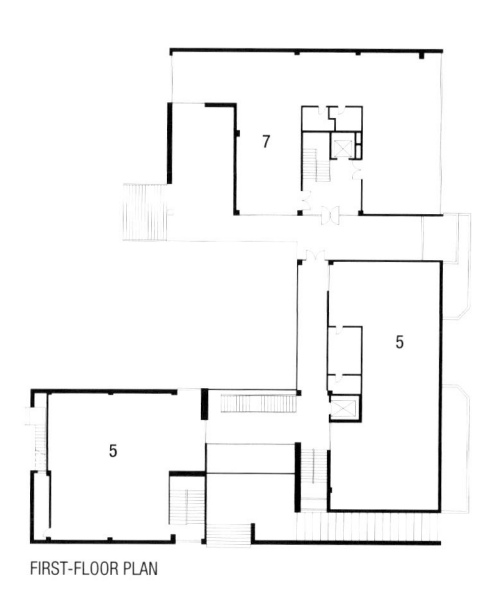

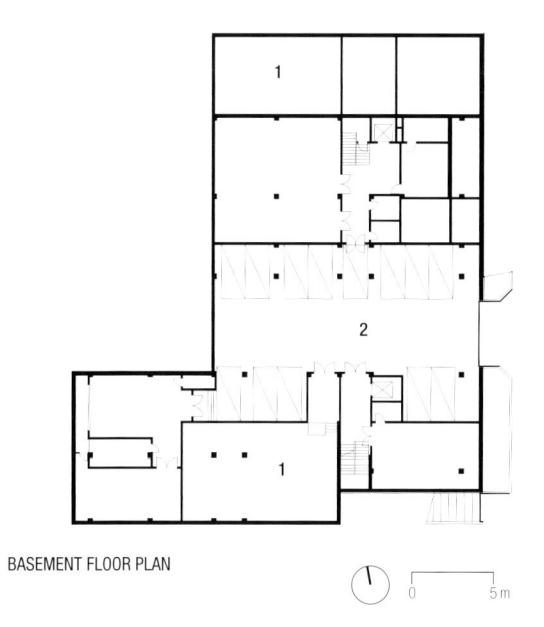

SECOND-FLOOR PLAN

GROUND-FLOOR PLAN

FIRST-FLOOR PLAN

BASEMENT FLOOR PLAN

1 Storage areas
2 Garage
3 Main entrance
4 Café
5 Permanent exhibition
6 Giftshop
7 Office
8 Temporary exhibition
9 Bedrooms

JEAN-MICHEL WILMOTTE   GANA ART CENTER

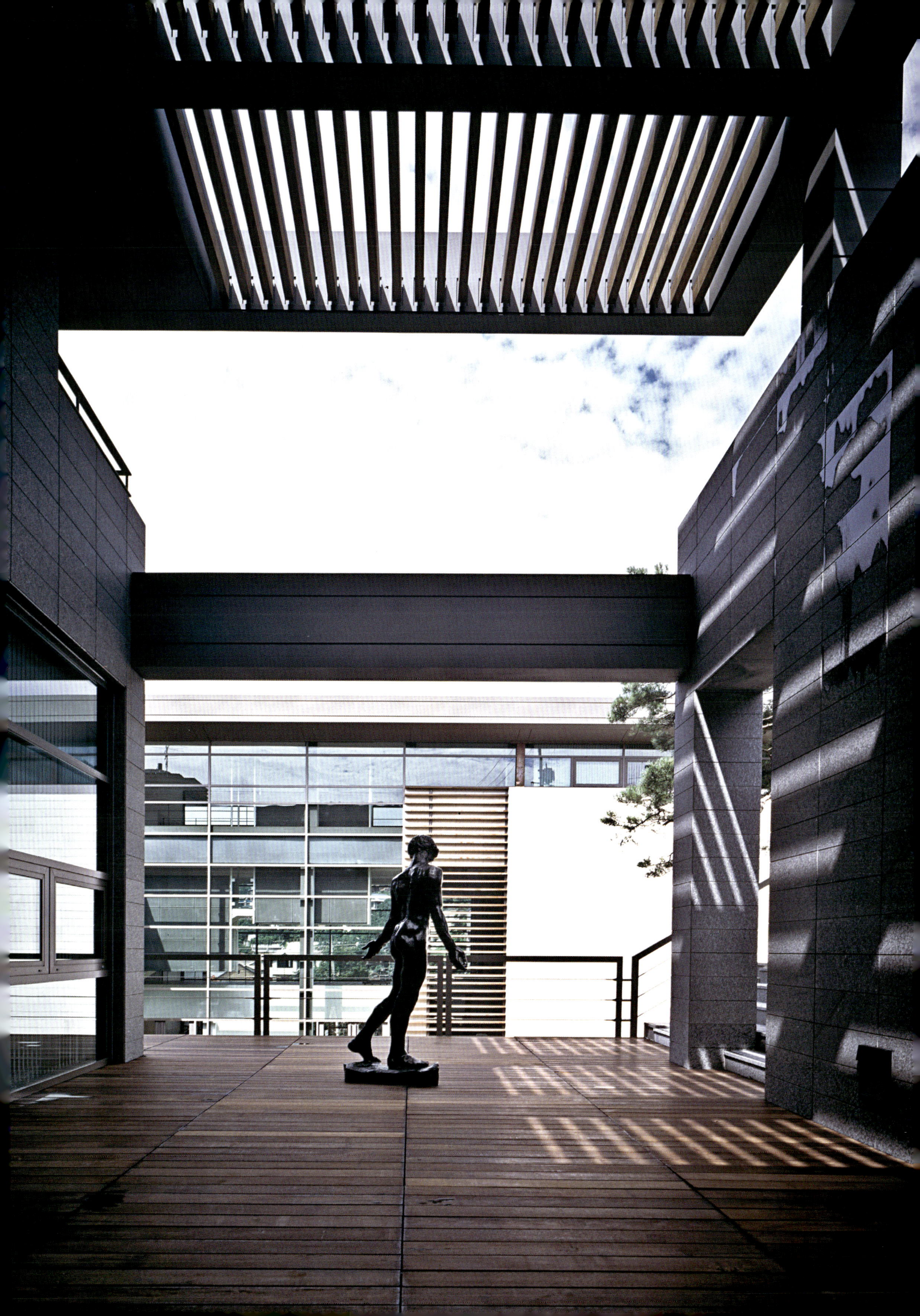

JEAN-MICHEL WILMOTTE

PRESIDENT JACQUES CHIRAC MUSEUM

This project involved the refurbishment, interior design, and subsequent extension of the museum intended to display about 200 of the 6,500 gifts received by Jacques Chirac during his two terms as President of France (1995–2007). It is located in the President's native Corrèze region of southwestern France. The reinforced concrete structure is clad in Corrèze pink granite, oak, and natural slate roofing. The first phase offered a floor area of 16,145 square feet (1,500 square meters) in 2002 with the second phase in 2006 adding a further 40,550 square feet (3,767 square meters).

Jean-Michel Wilmotte recalls that after two hours spent visiting the site, he had found his course of action, without further hesitation. Backed against a small wood, large farmhouse-like volumes sit together in a rural composition in phase with the landscape. A marsh area was remodeled into a meadow by the landscape architect Michel Desvigne, with a large pond surrounded by reed beds in the hollow. Wilmotte explains that the initial brief did little more than to put forward the idea of a museum. His role was thus to develop the concept in form and content, until the nomination of a curator.

The display, following a geopolitical scheme chosen in accord with the President, distinguishes the five continents and follows cartographic and chronological order. In Phase I, two main buildings, inspired in form and scale by the building that formerly stood at the entrance to the site were built. The museum itself occupies the second building, while the first is devoted to a temporary exhibition. Phase 2 proceeded with the construction of a similar third volume, in continuity with the earlier, and the medieval tower on the site, which serves as a beacon for the museum at the end of the enlarged terrace, over the new storage spaces. The tower is used as a library open to the public, rising up three levels around a central void.

Location Sarran, France
Completion date 2002 (Phase 1), 2006 (Phase 2)
Area 56,695 ft² (5,267 m²)

LOCATION MAP

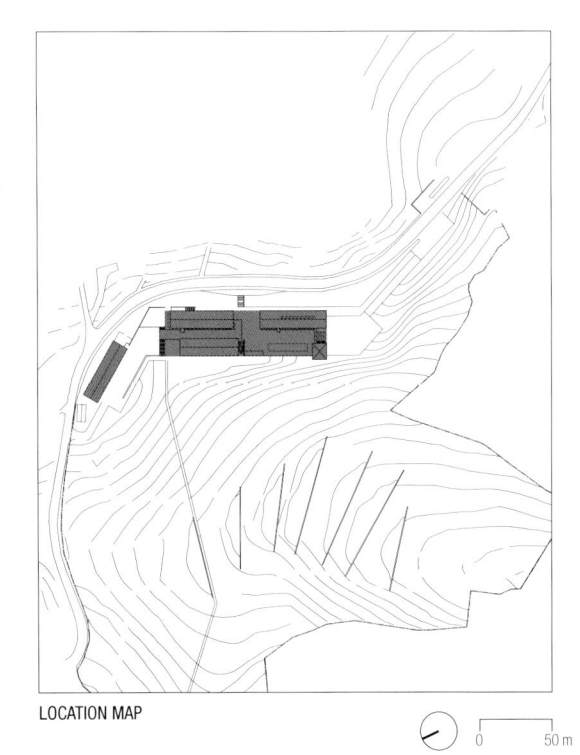

CROSS SECTION

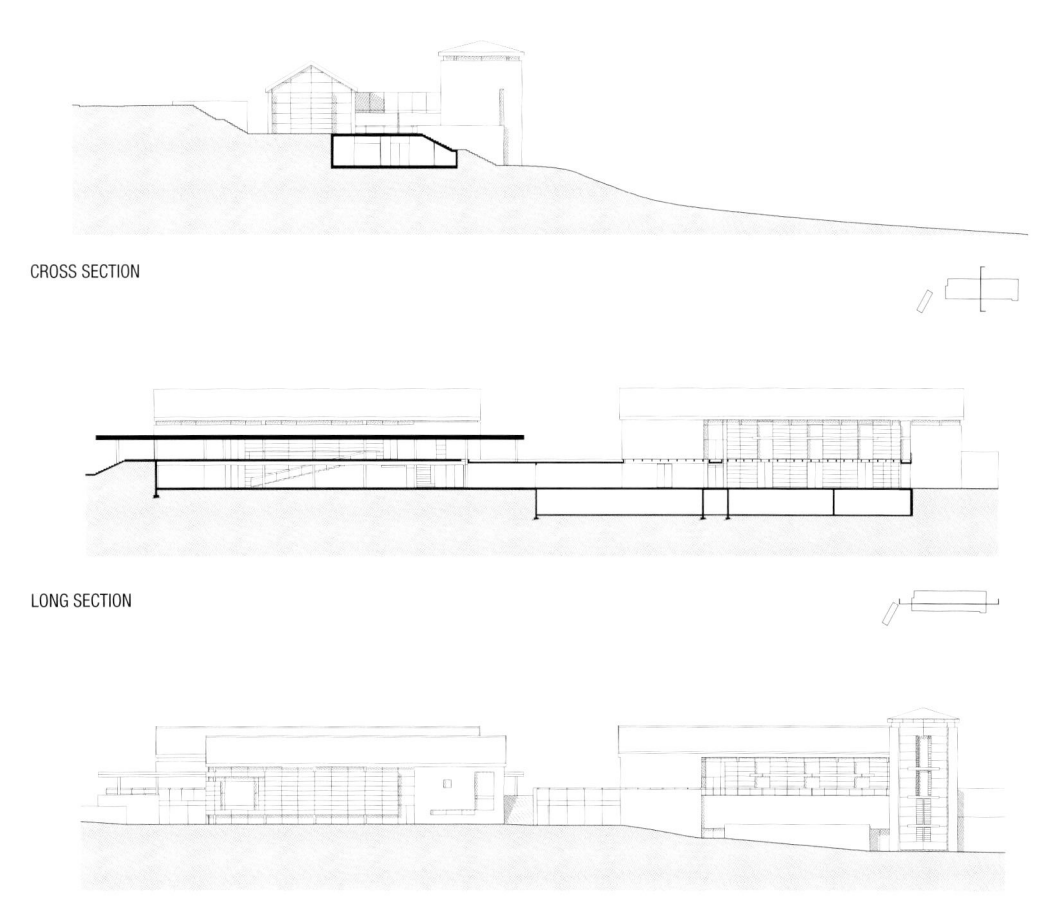

LONG SECTION

WEST ELEVATION

GROUND-FLOOR PLAN

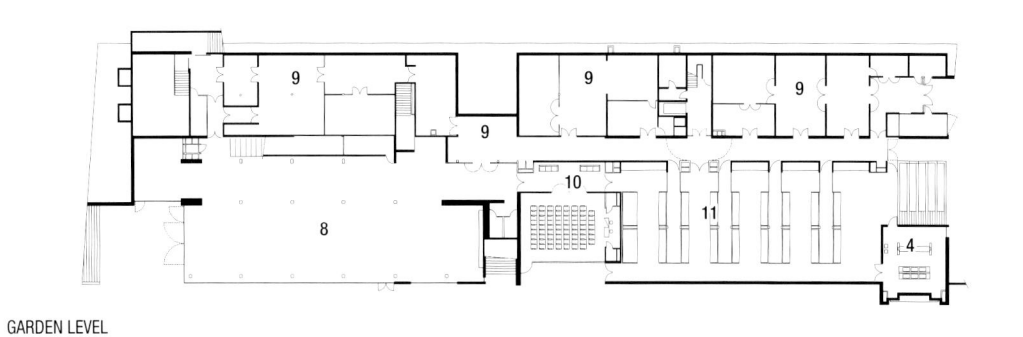

GARDEN LEVEL

1 Entrance
2 Bookshop
3 Cloakroom
4 Permanent exhibition
5 Library
6 Activities room
7 Office
8 Temporary exhibition
9 Conservation studio
10 Conference room
11 Storage for public

0   10 m

197

JEAN-MICHEL WILMOTTE PRESIDENT JACQUES CHIRAC MUSEUM

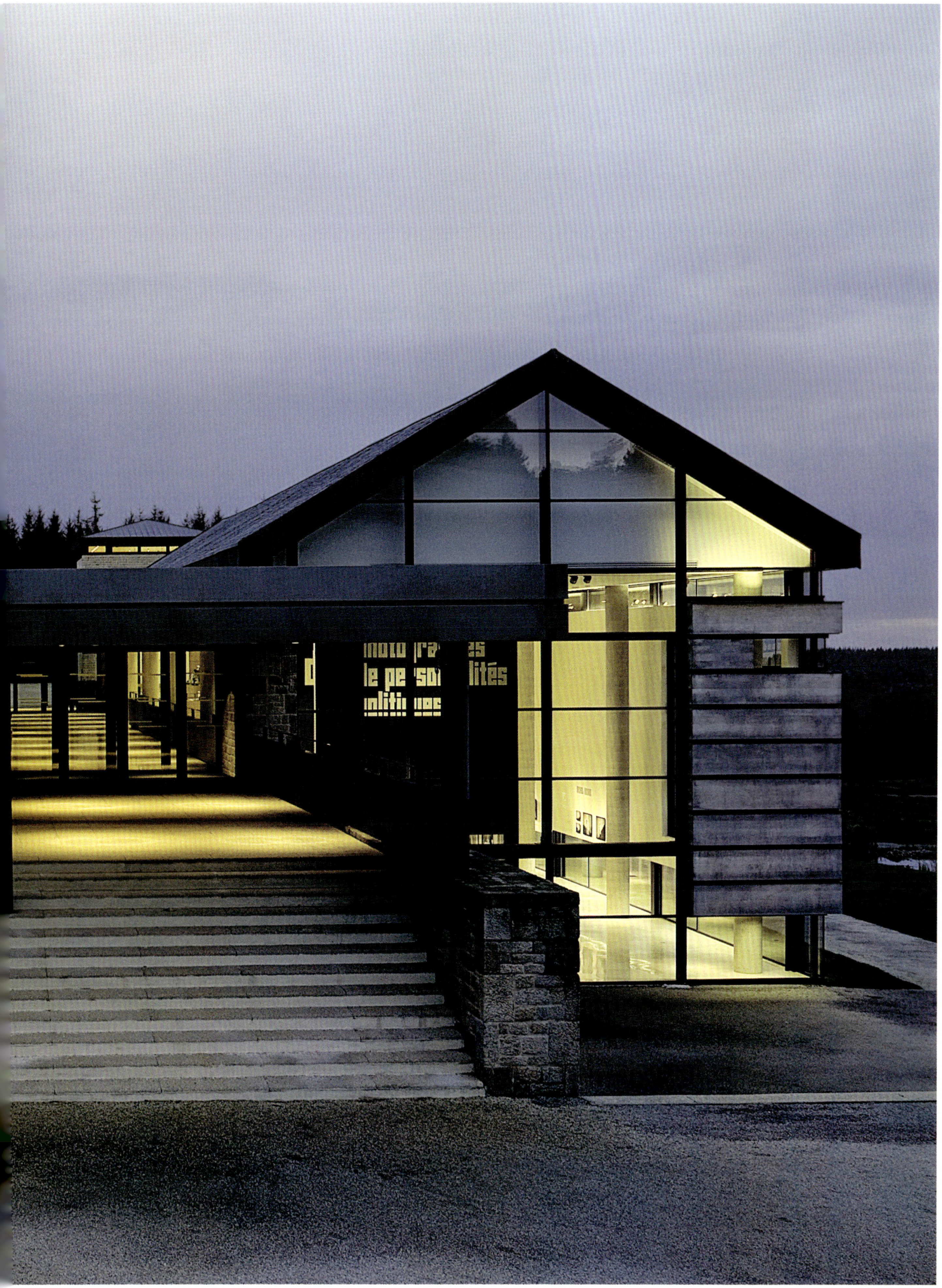

JEAN-MICHEL WILMOTTE PRESIDENT JACQUES CHIRAC MUSEUM

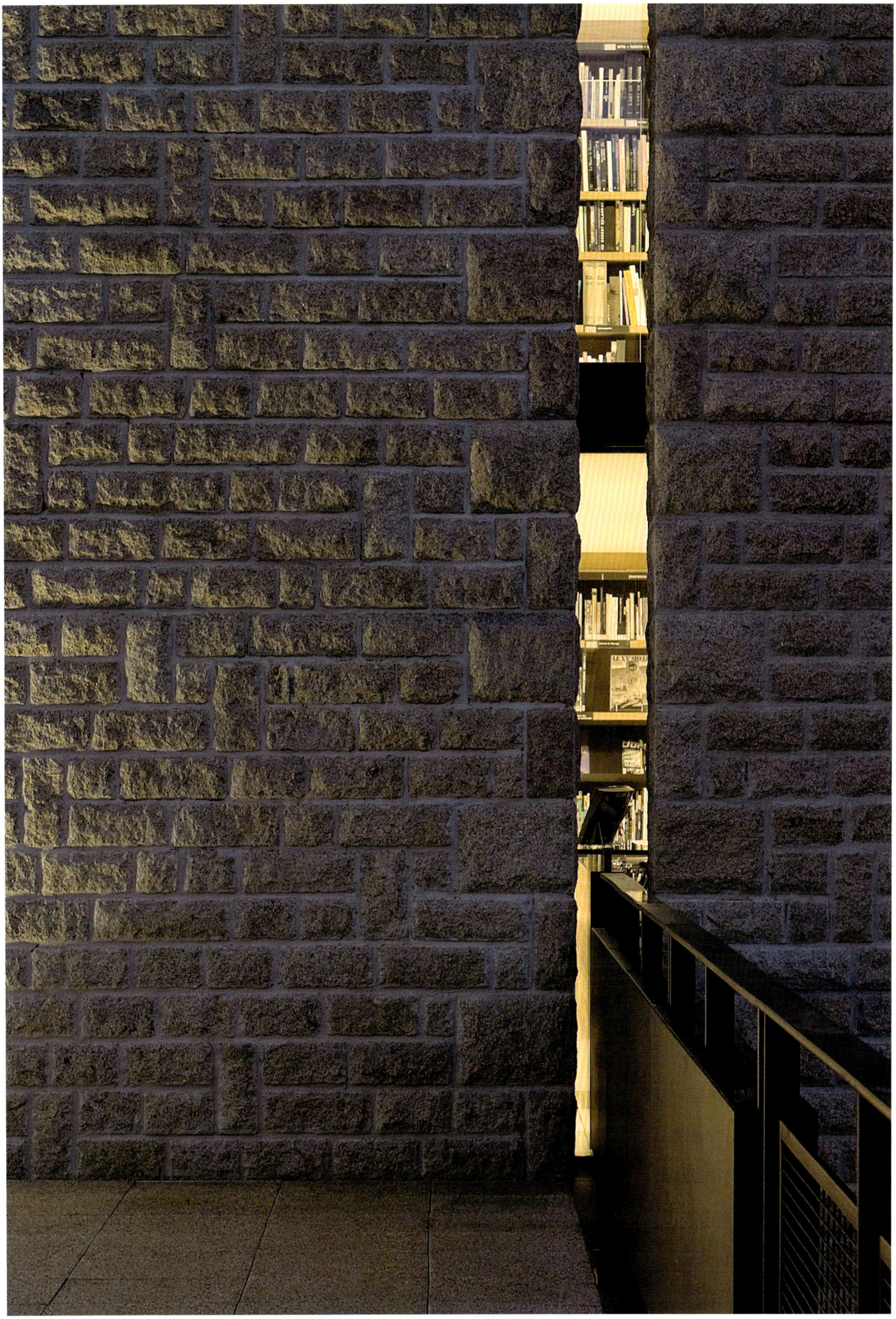

JEAN-MICHEL WILMOTTE

ULLENS CENTER FOR CONTEMPORARY ART

For this art gallery project, Jean-Michel Wilmotte rehabilitated and refurbished a 80,730-square-feet (7,500-square-meter) 1950s industrial building. The structure itself is in reinforced concrete and the architect added fine epoxy resin floors and painted walls. The Center includes a large exhibition hall of 21,530 square feet (2,000 square meters), as well as two smaller ones, a book shop, bar/cafeteria, documentation center, VIP space, restaurant, 135-seat amphitheater and 3,015 square feet (280 square meters) of office space. Ceilings reach as high as 31 feet (9.6 meters), giving the contemporary art displayed all the space it needs.

Guy and Myriam Ullens are art lovers who built up a considerable collection of Chinese art, one of the largest of its kind in the world, with more than 1,300 pieces by several generations of artists working in diverse media, including masterpieces of sculpture, painting, installation, and video. Their Center is located in the so-called 798 Area in the Dashanzi District of Beijing, a former industrial zone.

The Guy & Myriam Ullens Foundation was created in Switzerland in 2002, and is an active supporter of the Chinese art world. It sponsors events and exhibitions of Chinese art all over the world, including the Venice Biennale Chinese projects in 2003 and 2005, lends pieces from its collection to museums and art centers, and organizes exhibitions.

Wilmotte based his intervention on the intrinsic qualities of the building, removing elements added after the original construction. Doorways are 24 feet (7.4 meters) high and a brick chimney rises 110 feet (34 meters) structure the space. The configuration of the complex is based on two large nave-like spaces, set side by side. In the first area, the entrance, bookshop and cafeteria, the amphitheater, and the smaller exhibition galleries of 2,155 square feet (200 square meters) and 3,015 square feet (280 square meters) occupy the ground floor. The documentation area and VIP zone are on the mezzanine level. The second nave has the very large open area for performances and exhibitions and was left as free as possible.

The natural overhead lighting is diffused along the central axis and is associated with indirect artificial light creating a homogenous brightness in the space. The entire installation was conceived to meet the highest international standards for the exhibition of art.

Location Beijing, China
Completion date 2007
Area 80,730 ft² (7,500 m²)

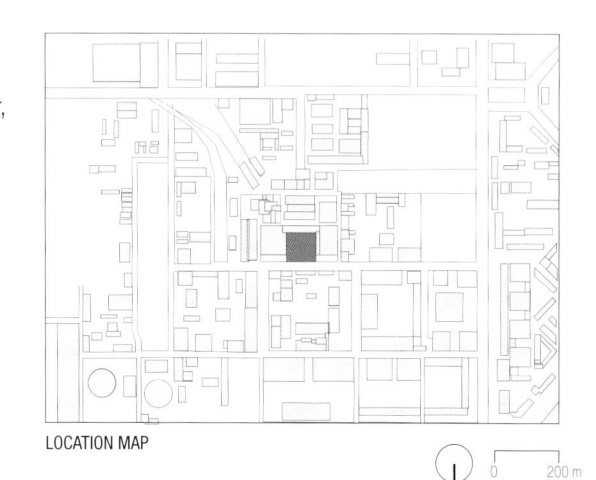

LOCATION MAP

CROSS SECTION

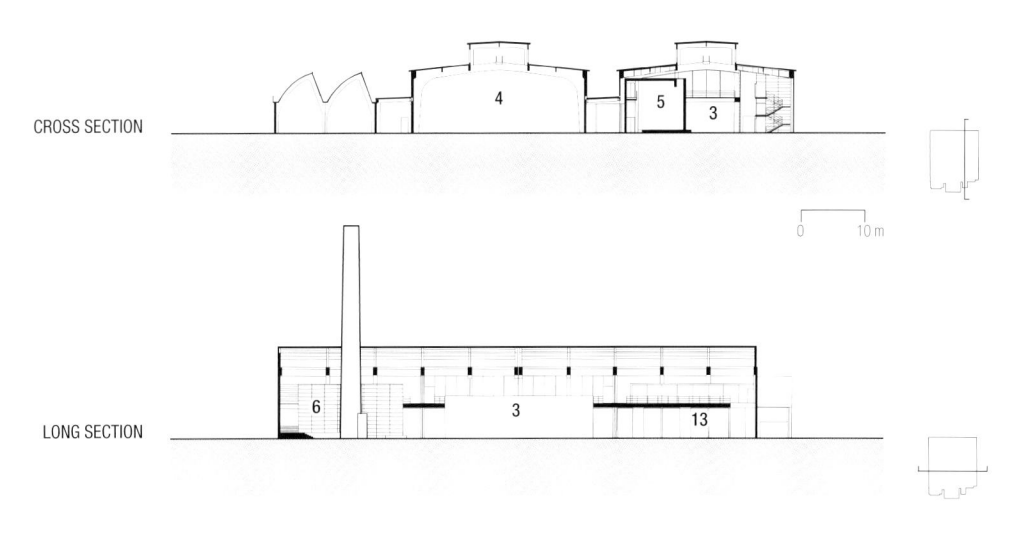

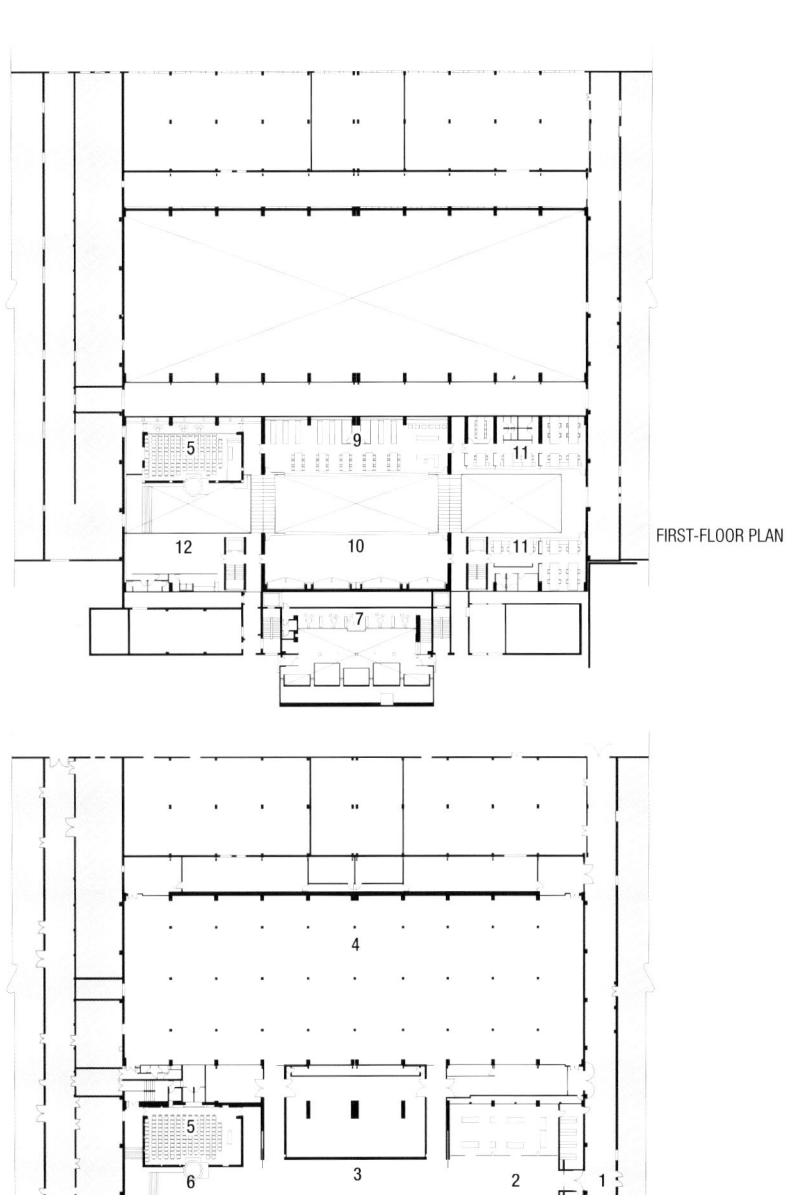

LONG SECTION

FIRST-FLOOR PLAN

1 Main entrance
2 Bookshop
3 Gallery
4 Main gallery
5 Conference room
6 Bar
7 Restaurant
8 Kitchen
9 Library
10 VIP room
11 Office
12 Private dining room
13 Entrance hall

GROUND-FLOOR PLAN

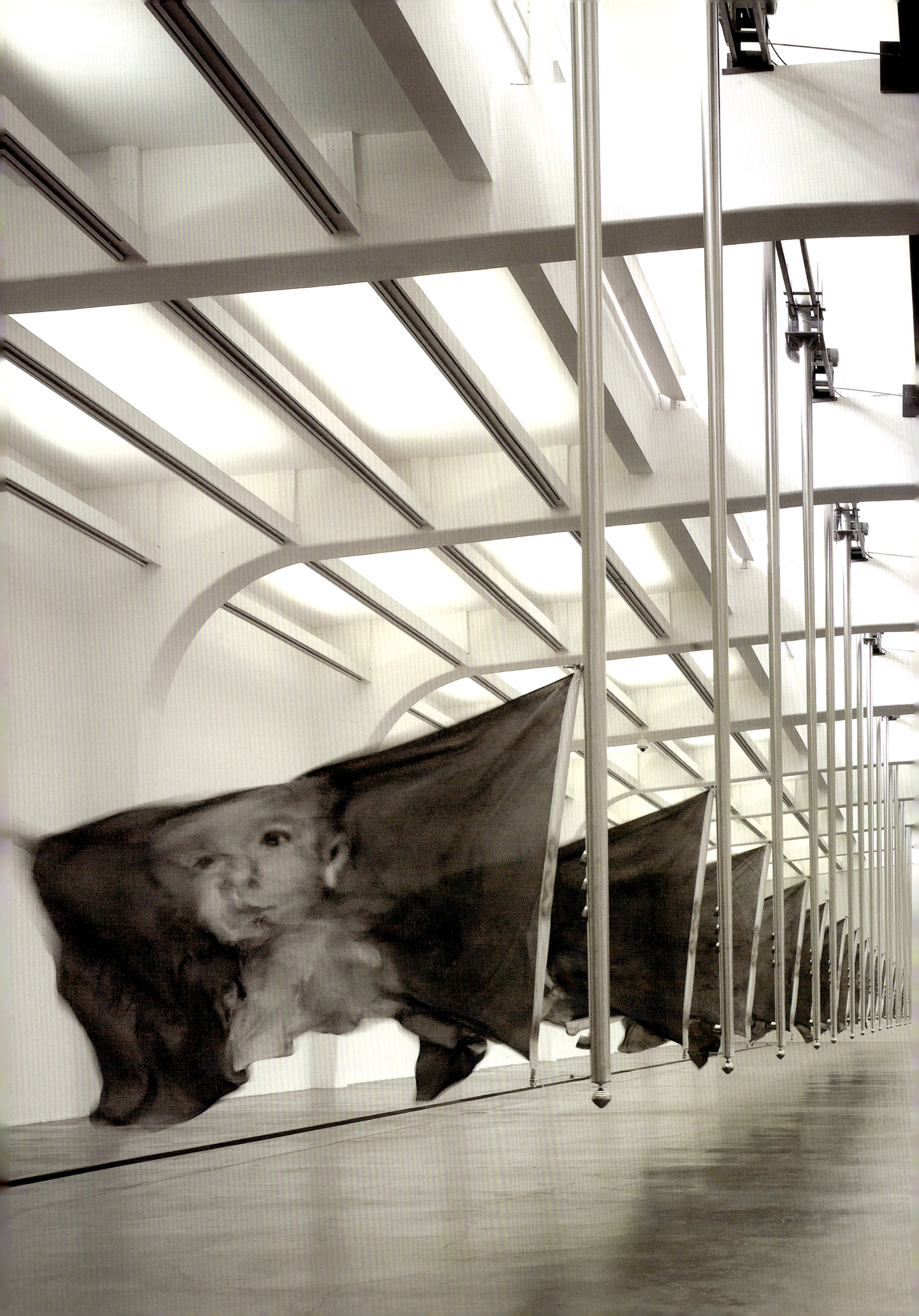

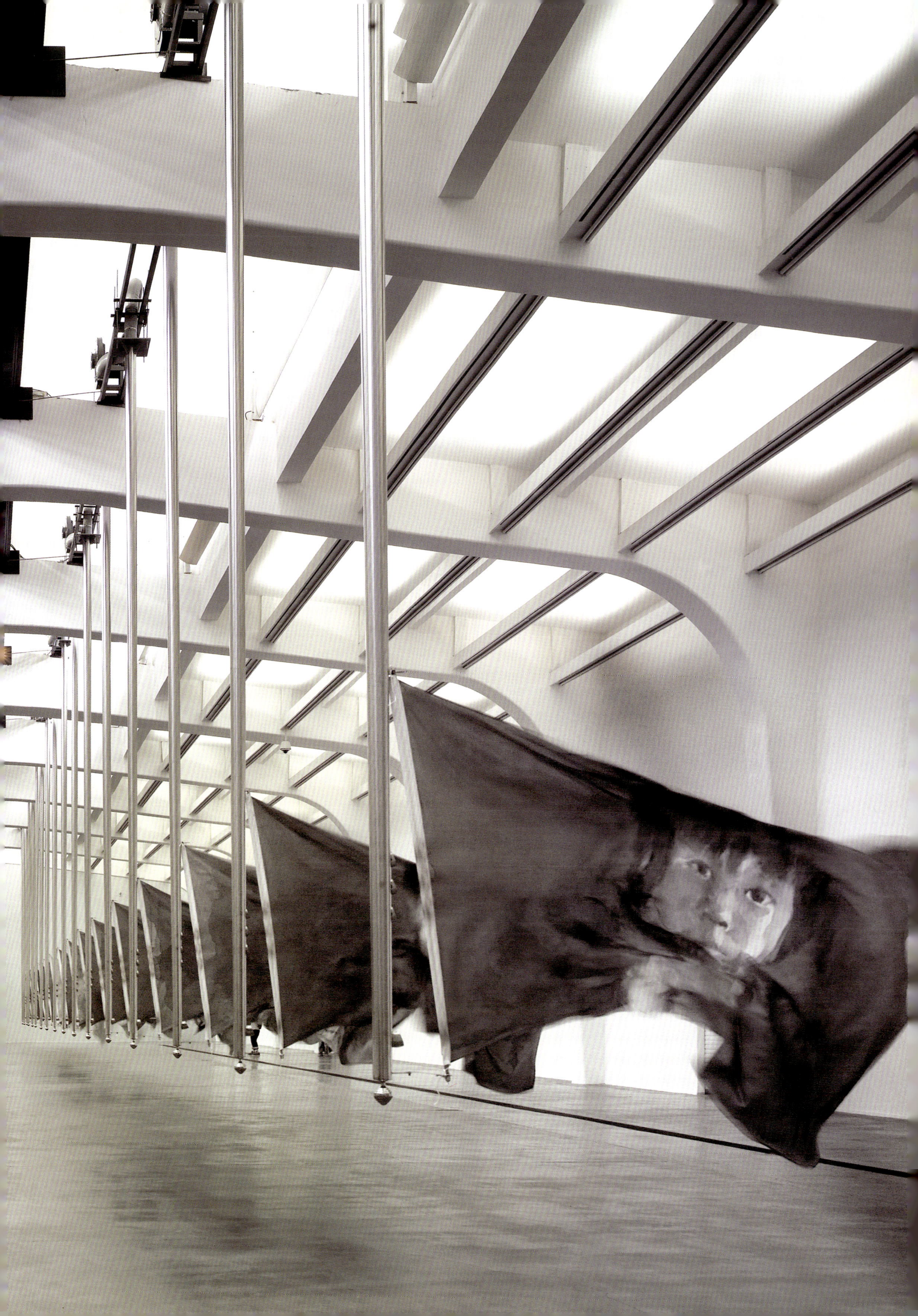

JEAN-MICHEL WILMOTTE   ULLENS CENTER FOR CONTEMPORARY ART

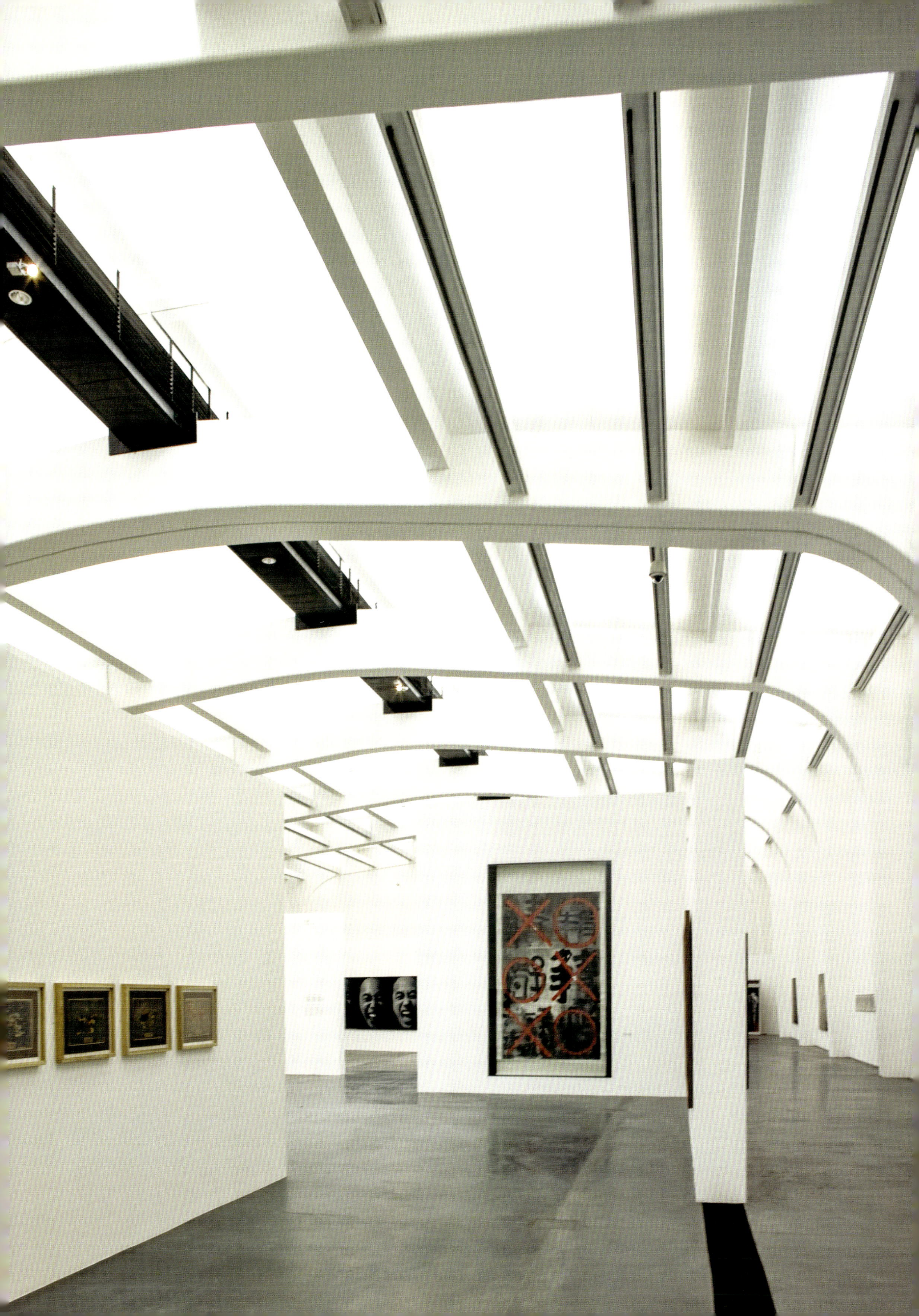

JEAN-MICHEL WILMOTTE

MUSEUM OF ISLAMIC ART OF QATAR

Working with I. M. Pei on Qatar's first major museum, located on an artificial island at the end of the Corniche opposite West Bay, Jean-Michel Wilmotte was in charge of the design of the interior display galleries. The two men had previously worked together on the Grand Louvre project in Paris.

Because the client was frequently expanding the collections, the display design had to be as flexible as possible. The galleries with a floor area of 17,225 square feet (5,250 square meters) are organized in a regular geometric pattern, with open views from gallery to gallery. This preserves the purity of organization of I. M. Pei's design. Each gallery has a number of showcases on the walls, with the central spaces left free for the installation of masterpieces in bespoke showcases.

By their size and highly technical nature, the showcases designed by Wilmotte & Associés Architectes are exceptional and unique. The 70 different types of showcases are very large in order to accommodate any type of object, or groups of smaller objects. The glass showcases have no vertical metal frames, so they seem to disappear around the objects. Inside the showcases each object is a star, center stage, spot-lit. The objects appear to be floating in space. This is achieved with dark surrounding colours, and a meticulously planned lighting scheme often making use of fiber-optics. The architectural materials—precious wood and stone—enhance this effect. The dark colours of Louro Faya and Porphyry disappear for the benefit of the object. At the same time, the rich subtleties of their textures accentuate the architecture more than flat surfaces. Also, materials are arranged differently in each gallery to facilitate orientation.

The scheme also includes the very flexible 2,295-square-foot (700-square-meter) Temporary Exhibition Gallery. The Bookshop is designed as a continuation of I. M. Pei's atrium. Display cases and small alcoves are hidden inside the walls. Furniture was designed specifically for the Museum of Islamic Arts by Wilmotte, including the tables and chairs in public spaces and the office furniture. The materials used for the furniture—wood, leather, and metal—were selected for their durability.

Location Doha, Qatar
Completion date 2008
Area 17,225 ft^2 (5,250 m^2)

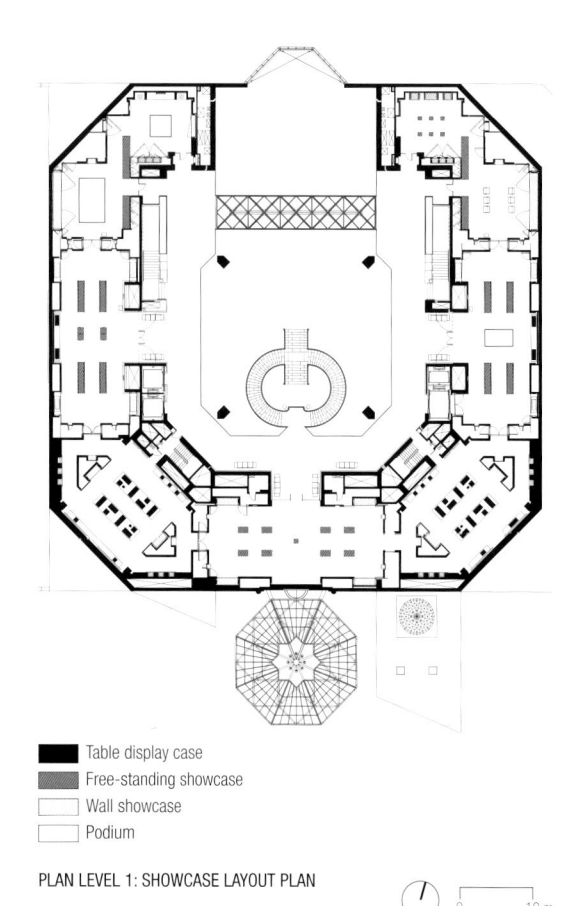

- Table display case
- Free-standing showcase
- Wall showcase
- Podium

PLAN LEVEL 1: SHOWCASE LAYOUT PLAN

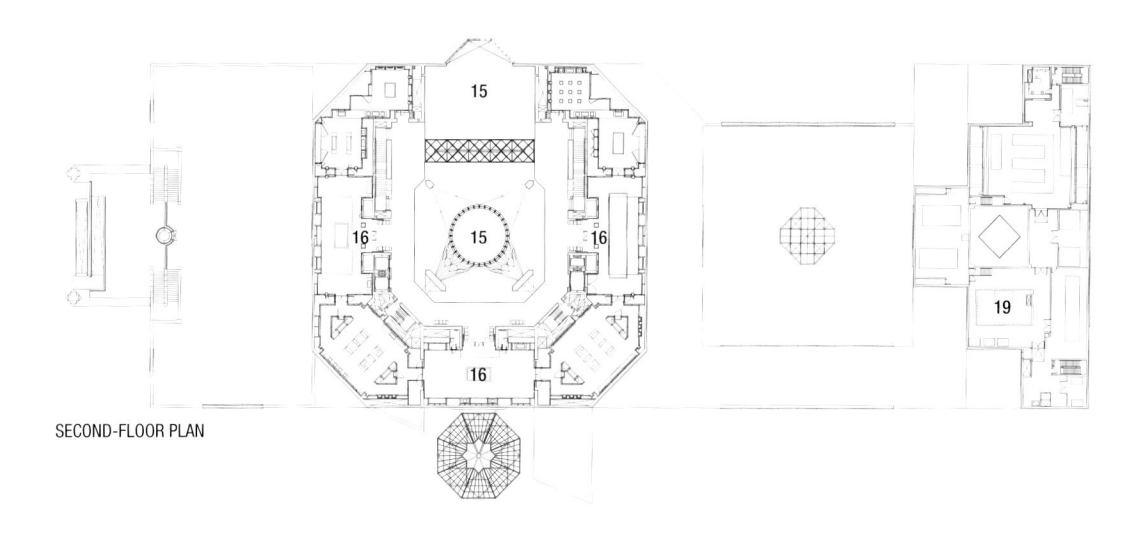

SECOND-FLOOR PLAN

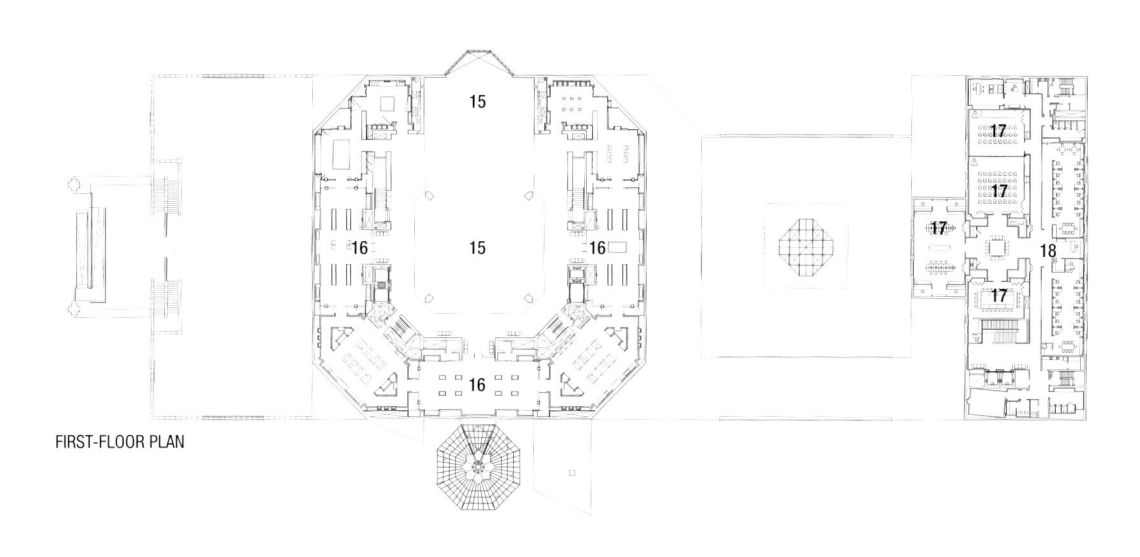

FIRST-FLOOR PLAN

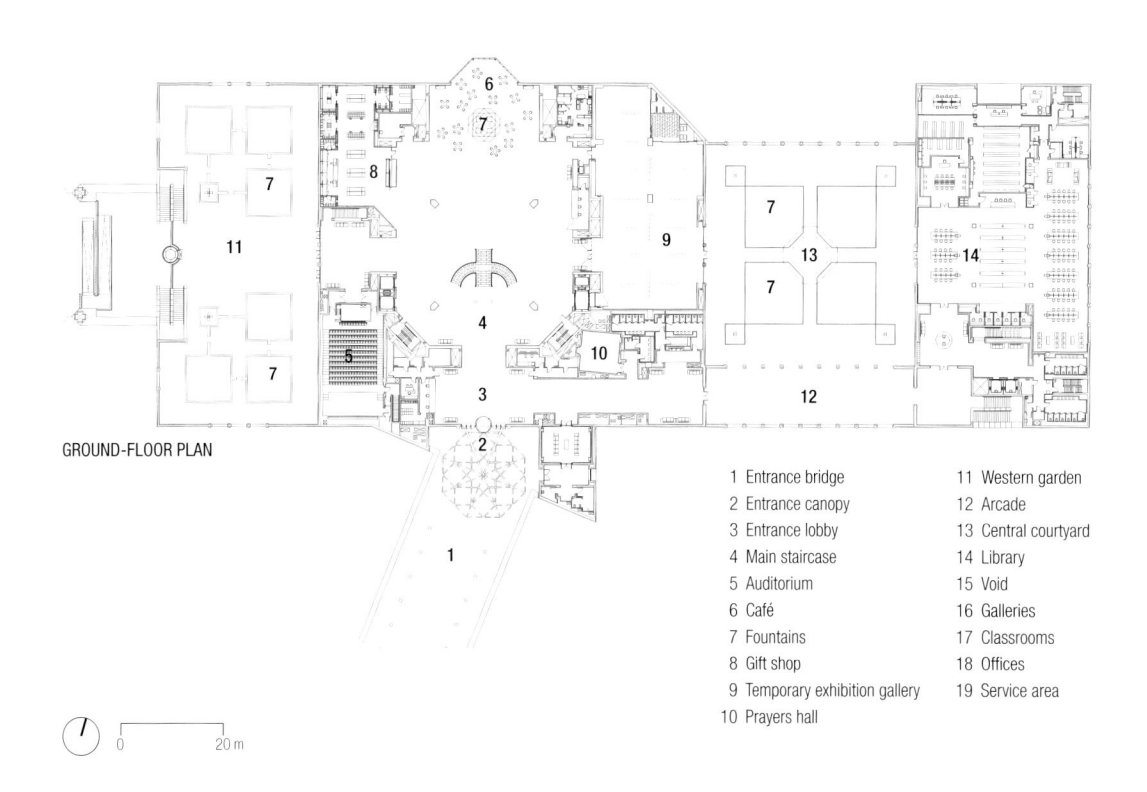

GROUND-FLOOR PLAN

1 Entrance bridge
2 Entrance canopy
3 Entrance lobby
4 Main staircase
5 Auditorium
6 Café
7 Fountains
8 Gift shop
9 Temporary exhibition gallery
10 Prayers hall
11 Western garden
12 Arcade
13 Central courtyard
14 Library
15 Void
16 Galleries
17 Classrooms
18 Offices
19 Service area

0   20 m

JEAN-MICHEL WILMOTTE MUSEUM OF ISLAMIC ART OF QATAR

211

JEAN-MICHEL WILMOTTE MUSEUM OF ISLAMIC ART OF QATAR

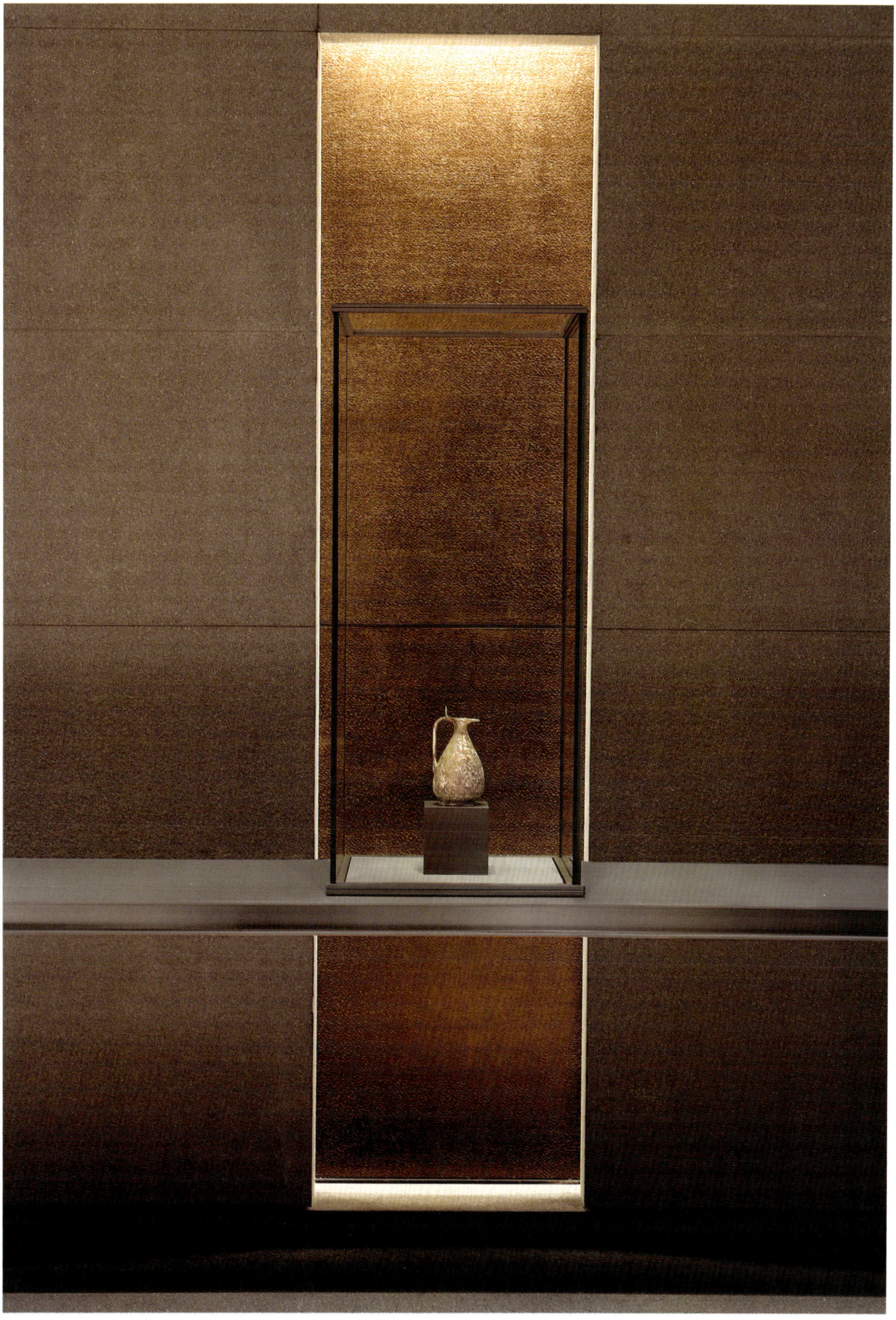

JEAN-MICHEL WILMOTTE

MUSÉE D'ORSAY REFURBISHMENT

Jean-Michel Wilmotte won a 2009 competition to refurbish museum areas and the book and gift shop with a total floor area of 23,680 square feet (2,200 square meters), including the fifth-floor 13,270-square-foot (1,233-square-meter) Impressionist Gallery of the famous Paris Museum, as well as a temporary exhibition gallery located on the same level. The Musée d'Orsay, installed in a former train station of the same name built by the architect Victor Laloux (1898–1900), boasts the largest collection of Impressionist art in the world.

The concept behind the renovation entailed reclaiming the original volumes of the space while managing the incidence of natural light on the works and creating more fluid circulation, simultaneously offering a more flexible and more complete presentation of the collection.

Wilmotte sought to retain the relatively unique quality of the existing volumes even as he created a dialogue between natural and artificial light. Dropping the ceilings on the sides made it possible to combine a human scale in contact with the works with a monumental scale expressed by the original structure in the middle of the gallery space, while taking advantage of overhead light.

Floors are laid with dark wood, while the walls are painted a delicate slate gray that allows the chromatic subtlety of the paintings to emerge. The sculptures are protected and magnified by discreet but ample display cases. Central partition walls were added for the display of key artworks.

Location Paris, France
Completion date 2012
Area 23,680 ft² (2,200 m²)

▓ Free-standing showcase
☐ Service duct and free-standing display
☐ Podium
⌐ ⌐ Water block bench by Tokujin Yoshioka

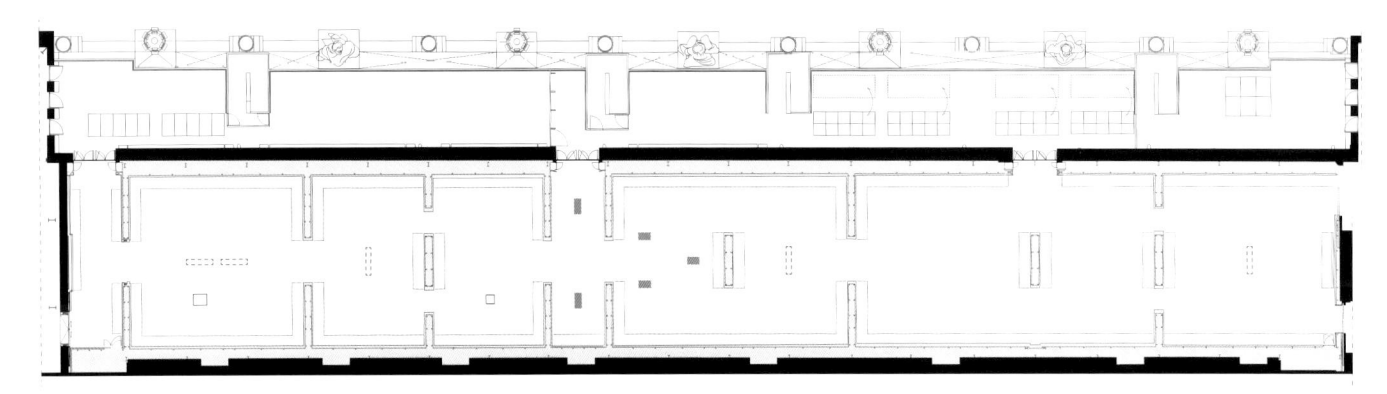

SHOWCASE PLAN

0   10 m

CROSS SECTION

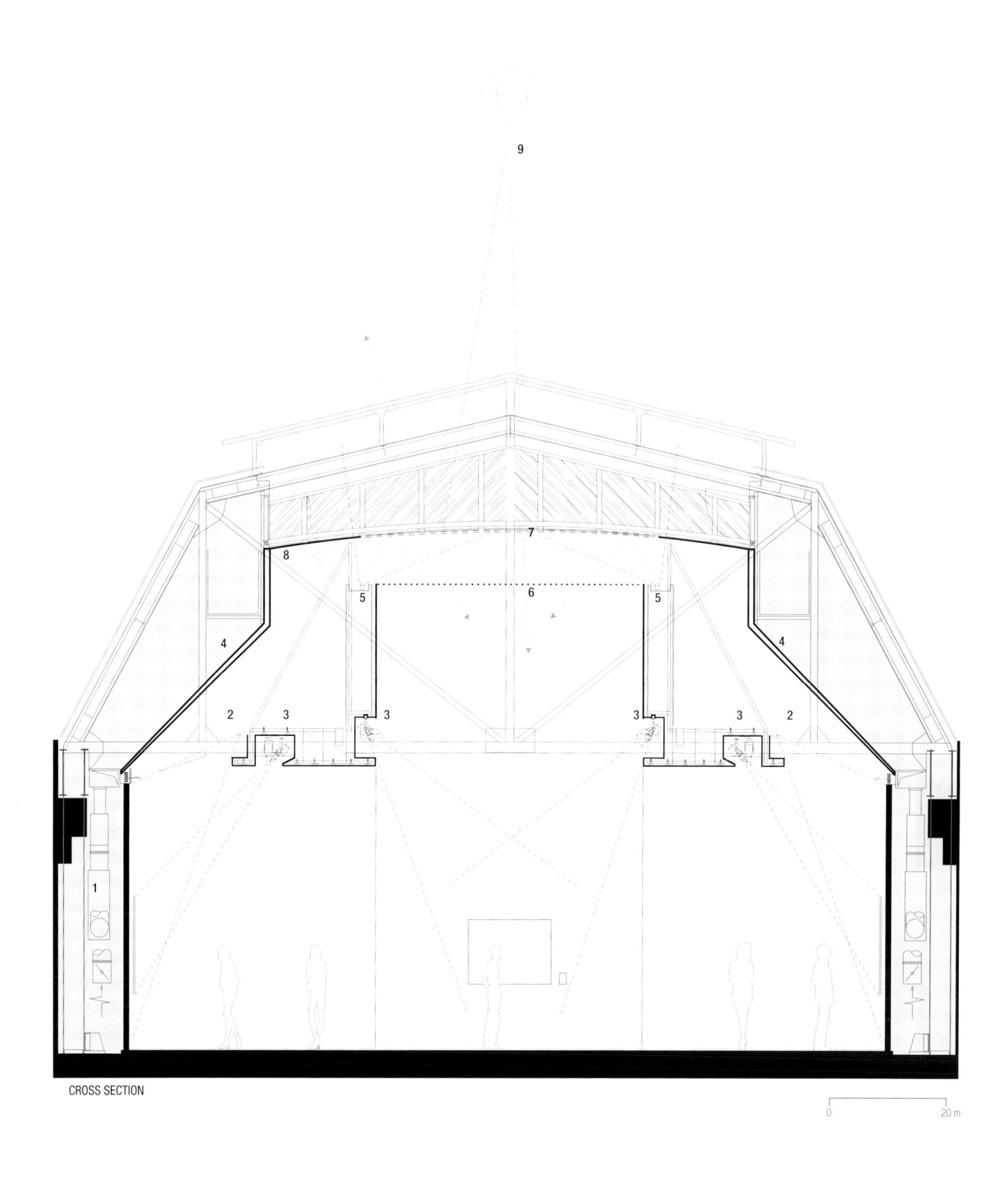

0   20 m

1 Service ducts
2 Wall washer lighting
3 Spotlight
4 Black opaque membrane
5 Indirect lighting
6 Metal grid ceiling
7 Double film: Reflective top film / light-filtering bottom film
8 Smoke extraction
9 Natural lighting

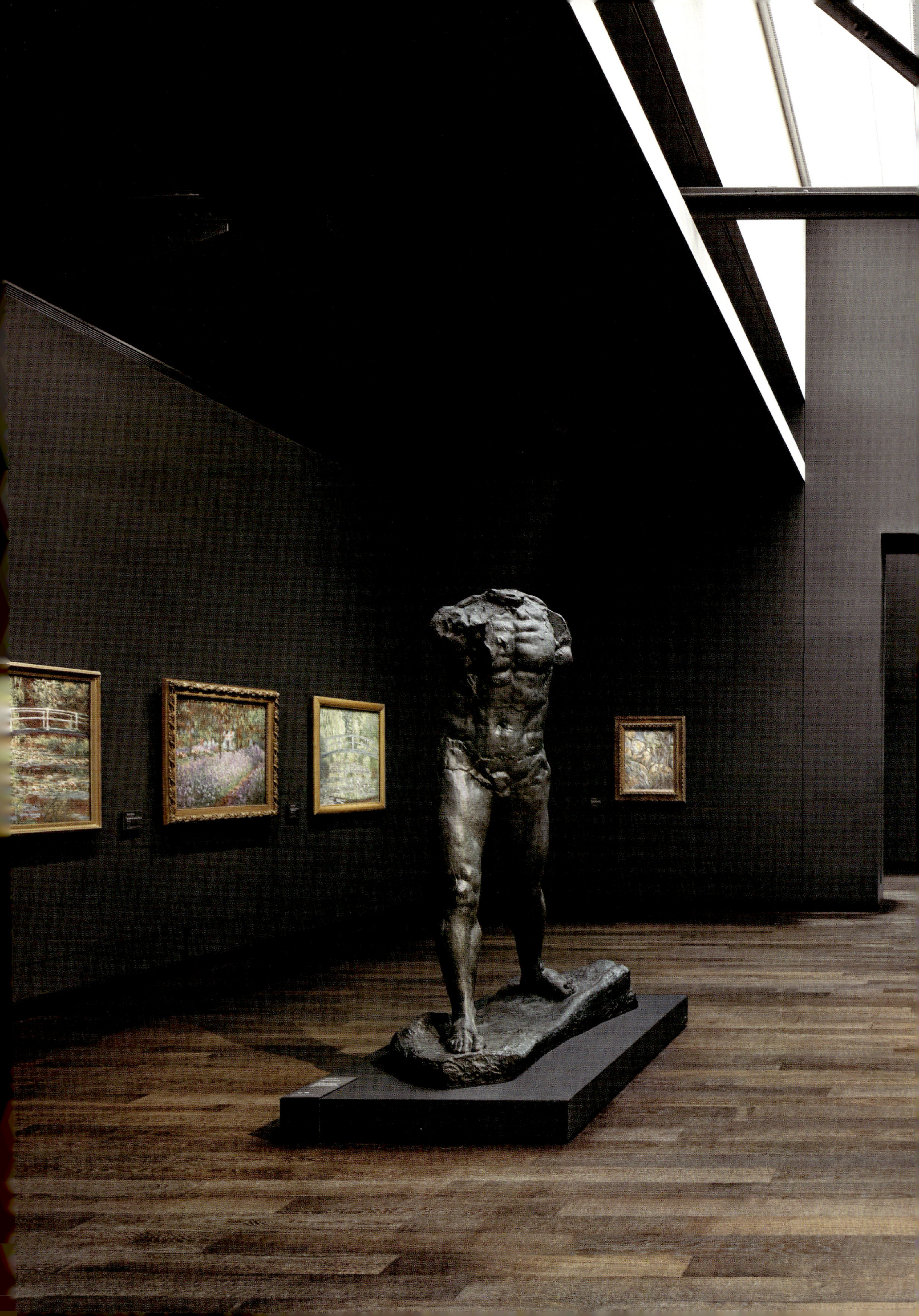

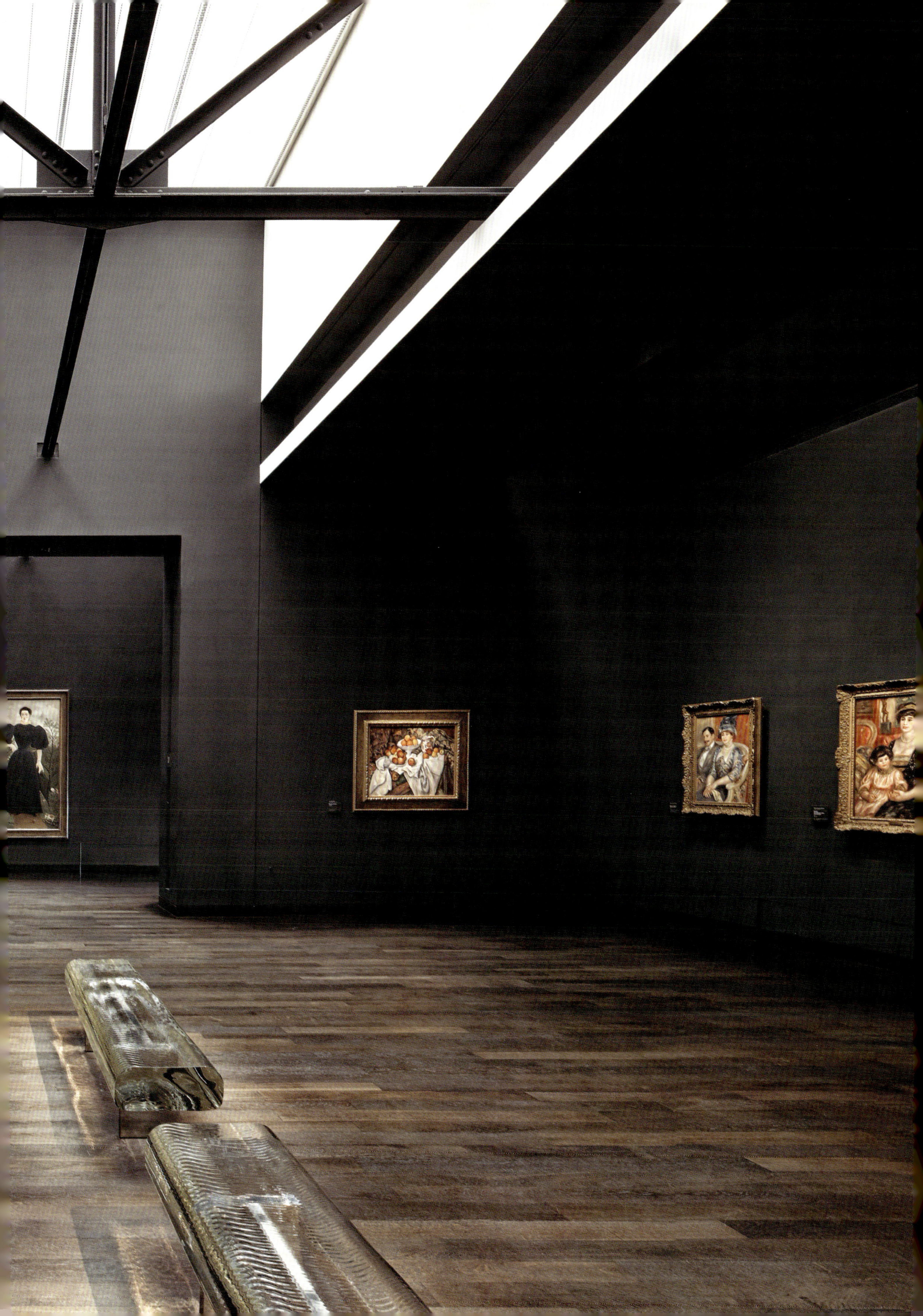

JEAN-MICHEL WILMOTTE MUSÉE D'ORSAY REFURBISHMENT

Collection Mollard
Mollard Collection | Colección Mollard

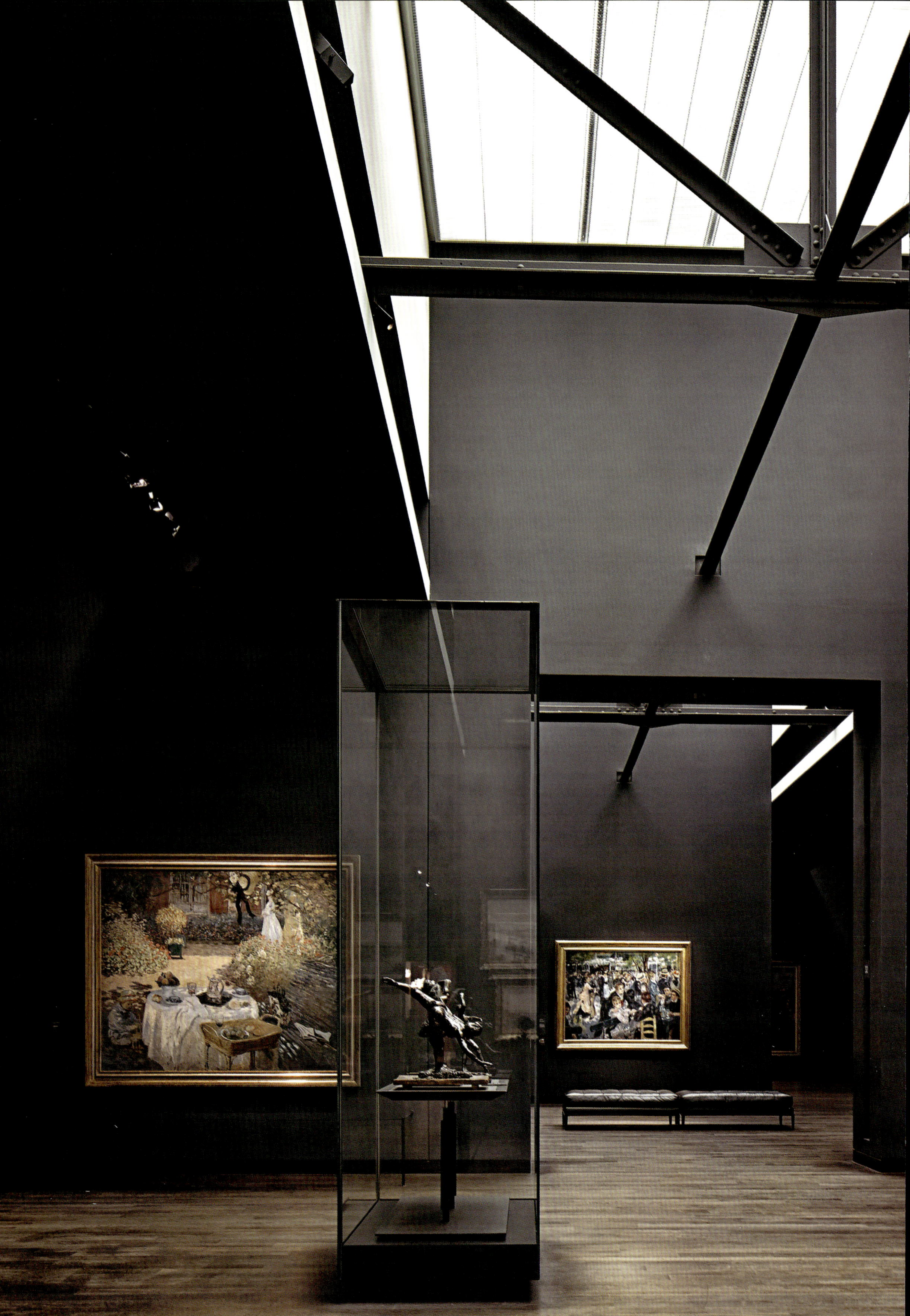

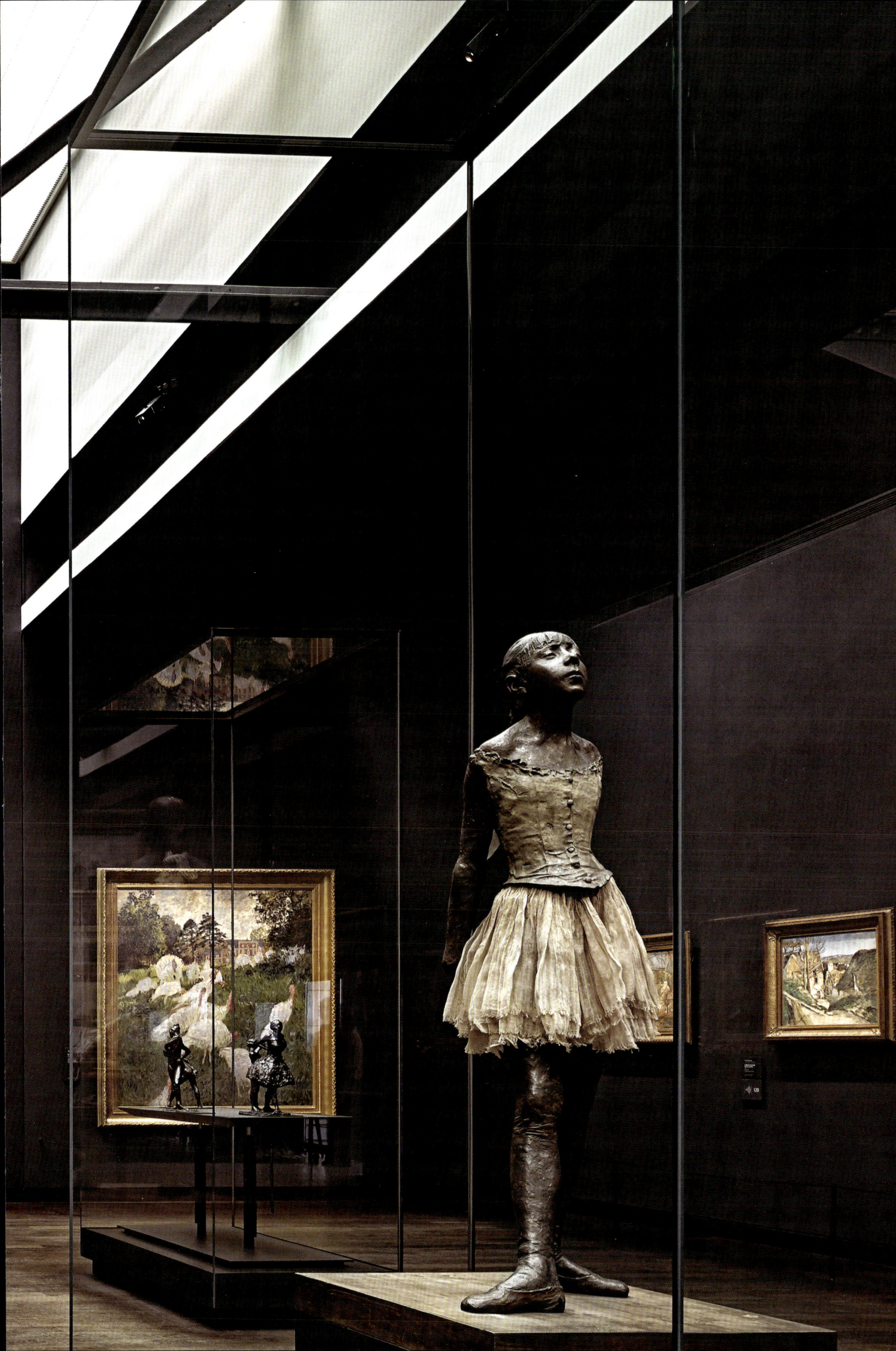

JEAN-MICHEL WILMOTTE

SURSOCK MUSEUM

Designed by Wilmotte & Associés Architectes in collaboration with the Lebanese architect Jacques Aboukhaled, the refurbishment and the extension of the Sursock Museum was conceived to be as discreet as possible, relying in part on an underground extension. The Neo-Moorish Sursock Museum, built as a villa in 1912, is one of the last remaining old homes in the upscale district of Achrafieh, now dominated by modern architecture.

Originally conceived in 1998, the project was put on hold by the years of conflict in Lebanon and updated beginning in 2008. Underground areas of the 91,495-square-foot (8,500-square meter) museum (75,350 square feet [7,000 square meters] of which is new) include a temporary 22-foot-high (7-meter-high) exhibition gallery. Overhead natural lighting is used where possible complemented by a daylight-color LED system. Wilmotte employed a sand-colored Egyptian natural stone, a glass and aluminum curtain wall, Corian and bleached oak veneer panels.

The existing garden's plan was realigned with the building entrance. A line of trees interrupted by paths restores symmetry and welcomes a contemporary concrete, metal, and glass building, which houses a library, cafeteria, and a car lift. The esplanade in front of the museum is organized around a central path surrounded by six skylights. This mineral garden paved with stone hosts sculptures throughout the year. In order to create the new exhibition spaces, as well as a storage area, parking spaces, 160-seat auditorium, and media library, it was necessary to dig more than 65 feet (20 meters) down, without weakening the existing building—a real challenge, which was managed by the local associate architect. Since 1961, the museum has been organizing a 'Salon d'Automne,' which allows artists to exhibit their work, while also permitting the institution to constitute a remarkable collection of original art works.

Location Beirut, Lebanon
Completion date 2015
Area 91,495 ft² (8,500 m²)

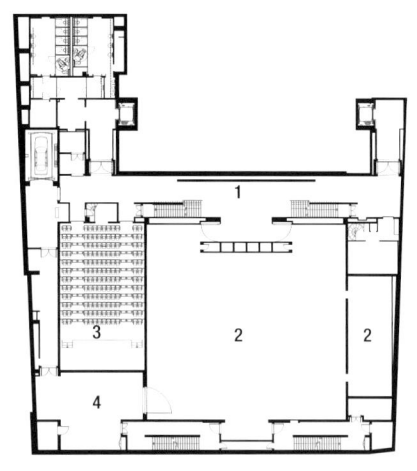

LEVEL −2 (UNDERGROUND) FLOOR PLAN

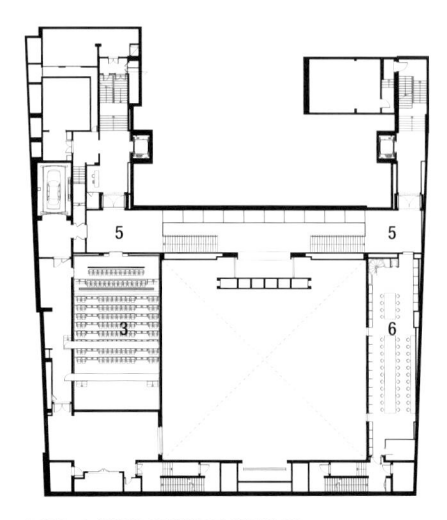

LEVEL −1 (UNDERGROUND) FLOOR PLAN

CROSS SECTION

GROUND-FLOOR PLAN

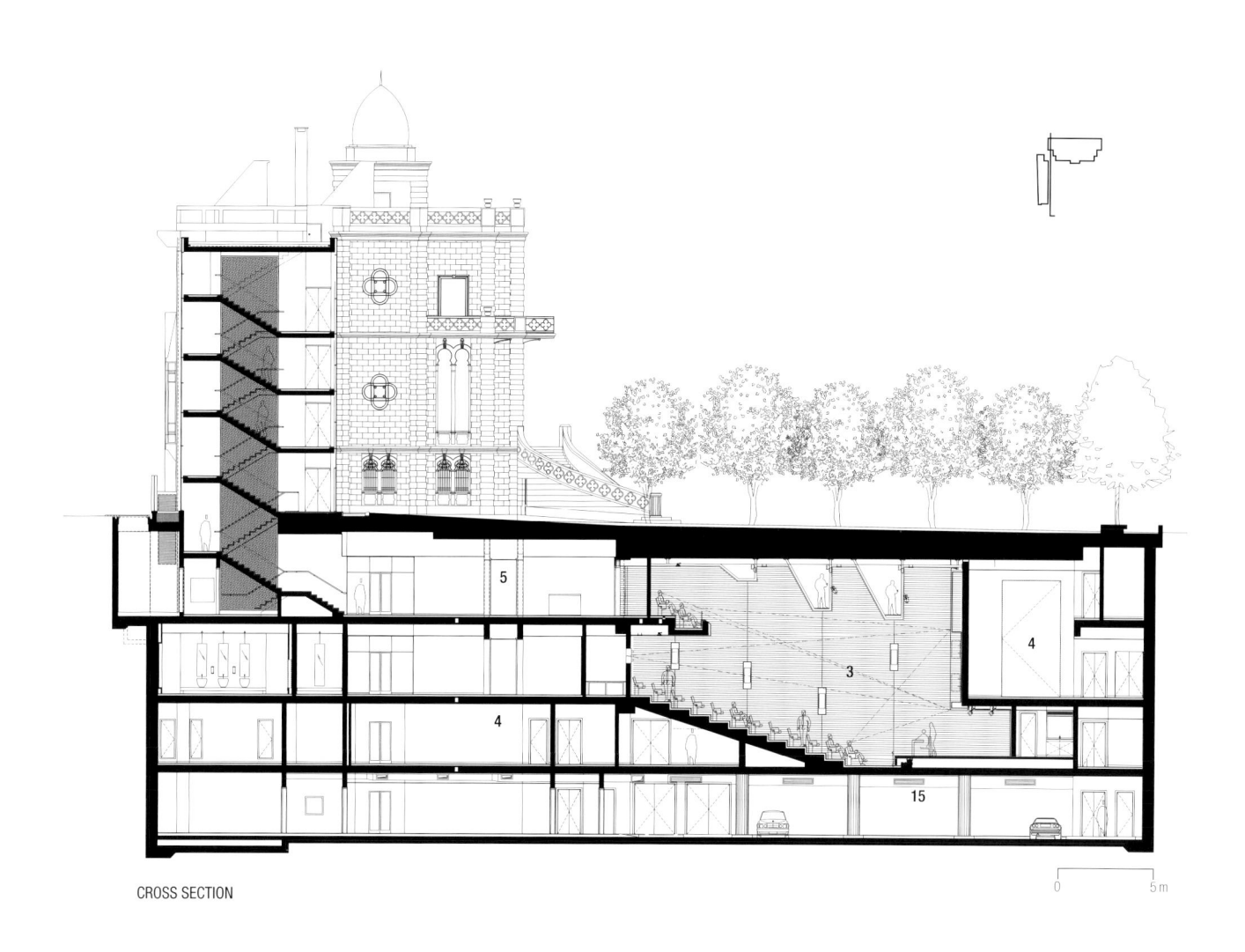

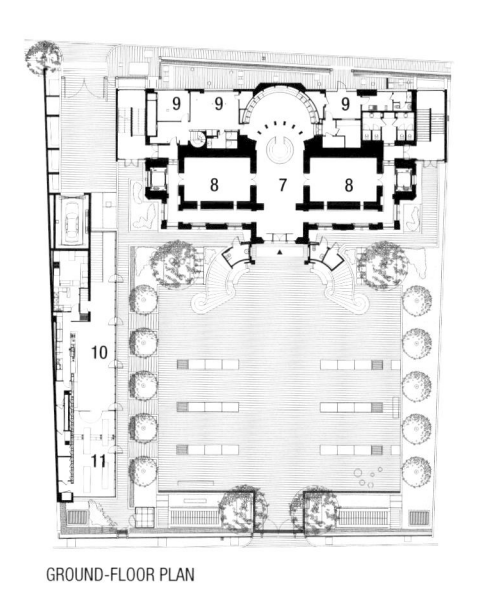

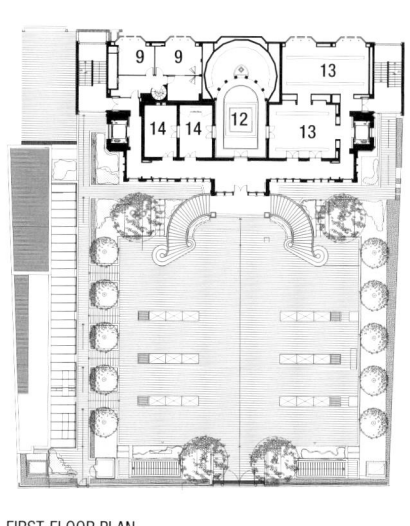

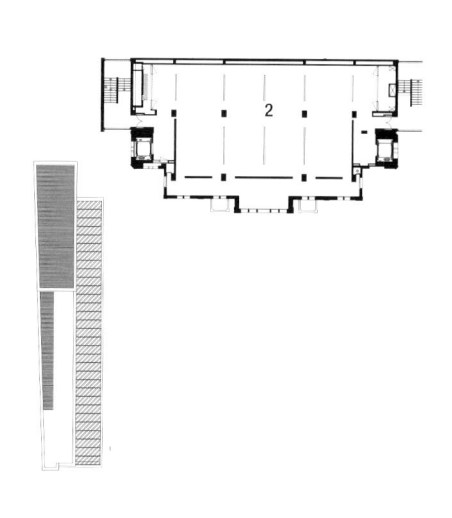

FIRST-FLOOR PLAN

SECOND-FLOOR PLAN

1 Hall
2 Temporary exhibition
3 Auditorium
4 Storage
5 Mezzanine
6 Library
7 Entrance hall
8 Galleries
9 Office
10 Restaurant
11 Bookshop
12 Arabic lounge
13 Permanent exhibition
14 Nicolas Sursock office
15 Car park

JEAN-MICHEL WILMOTTE SURSOCK MUSEUM

225

JEAN-MICHEL WILMOTTE SURSOCK MUSEUM

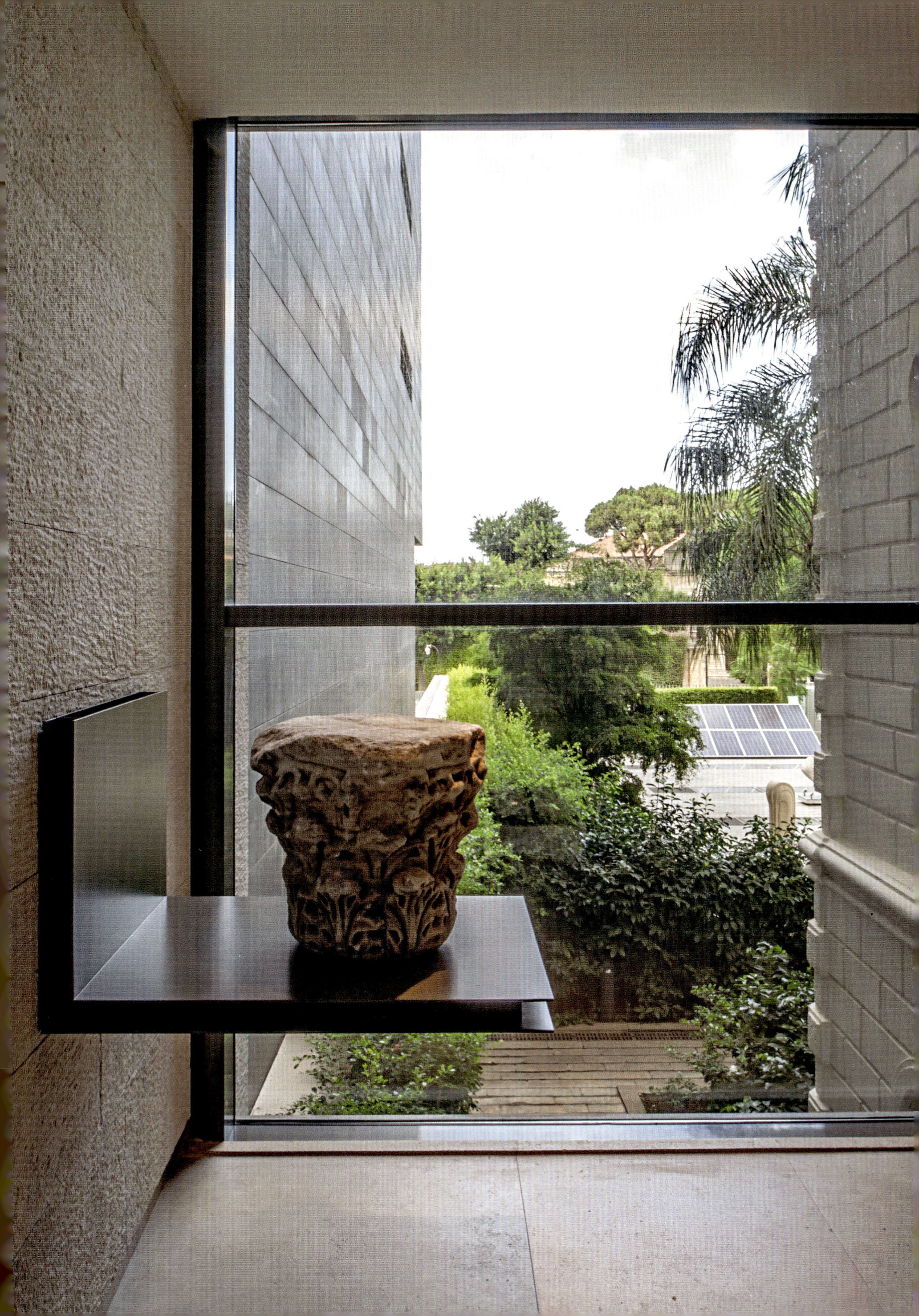

JEAN-MICHEL WILMOTTE

THE NEW RIJKSMUSEUM

The Rijksmuseum was built in 1885 by the Dutch architect Pieter Cuypers (1827–1921), in a Neo-Gothic and Renaissance style. In 2003, the Dutch government implemented a comprehensive restructure and renovation program for the Rijksmuseum, so that it would once again meet top international museum standards. A total of 129,150 square feet (12,000 square meters) of new exhibition spaces were designed by Wilmotte & Associés. The Spanish architects Cruz & Ortiz were appointed for restructuring work including the main entrance hall.

Wilmotte's brief was to restore Cuypers' original internal architecture and layout, and to design the gallery spaces so that the collection did not touch the building's walls. An additional design consideration was the collection's chronological display scheme. This ambitious arrangement required meticulous planning to successfully present contrasting works of art and artefacts side by side. The designs also had to incorporate sophisticated security measures to protect the priceless collections.

The architects intervened on four levels of the structure: the mezzanine with the Special Collections and works from the Middle Ages; Level 1 for the 18th- and 19th-century collections; Level 2 with the Gallery of Honor and the Gallery of the Night Watch by Rembrandt, as well as the highlights of the Rijksmuseum's unparalleled collection of Dutch 17th-century art; and Level 3 with pieces from the 20th century. The transparency and clarification of space introduced to the galleries by the intervention is remarkable. This was a significant undertaking in a Neo-Gothic building replete with heavy vaulting, rich ornamentation, and an architectural structure punctuated by pillars and arches. The team notably added 220 display cases that were made without vertical struts, and with anti-reflective glass and fine anthracite metal.

Wilmotte designed a unique LED-based lighting system for the museum, developed with Philips Lighting, called Lightracks. The main color palette of the galleries is a range of five hues of gray. The Rijksmuseum is by far the leading museum of the Netherlands, and one of the great museums of the world—all the more so thanks to the recent work of Jean-Michel Wilmotte.

Location Amsterdam, The Netherlands
Completion date 2013
Area 129,150 ft² (12,000 m²)

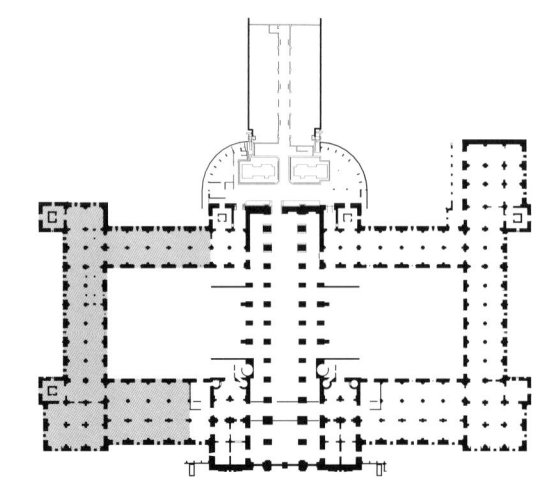

ENTRY LEVEL SHOWING THE LOCATION OF SPECIAL COLLECTIONS

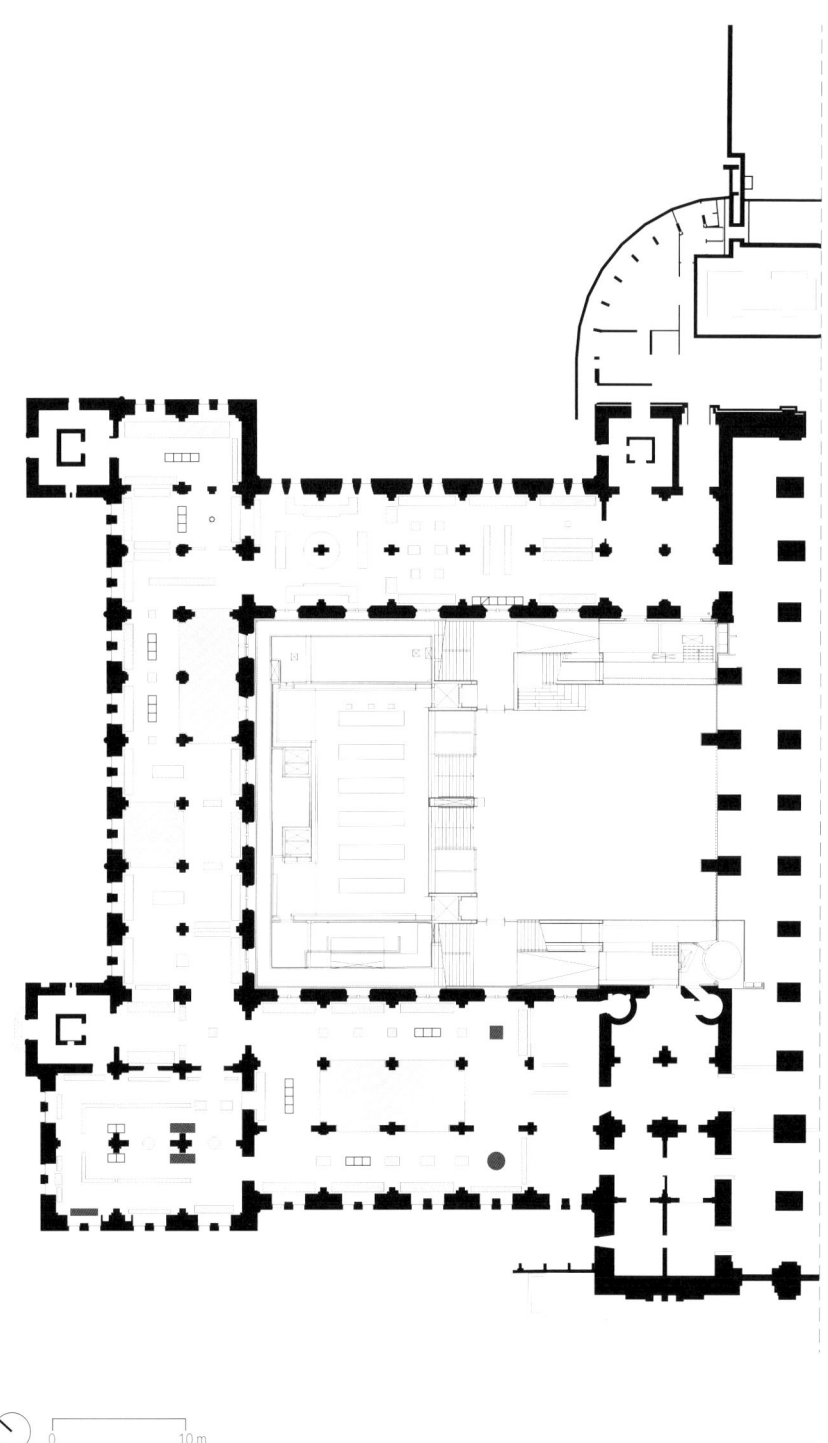

SHOWCASE LAYOUT PLAN OF SPECIAL COLLECTIONS

Podium
Free-standing showcase
Bench

229

JEAN-MICHEL WILMOTTE   THE NEW RIJKSMUSEUM

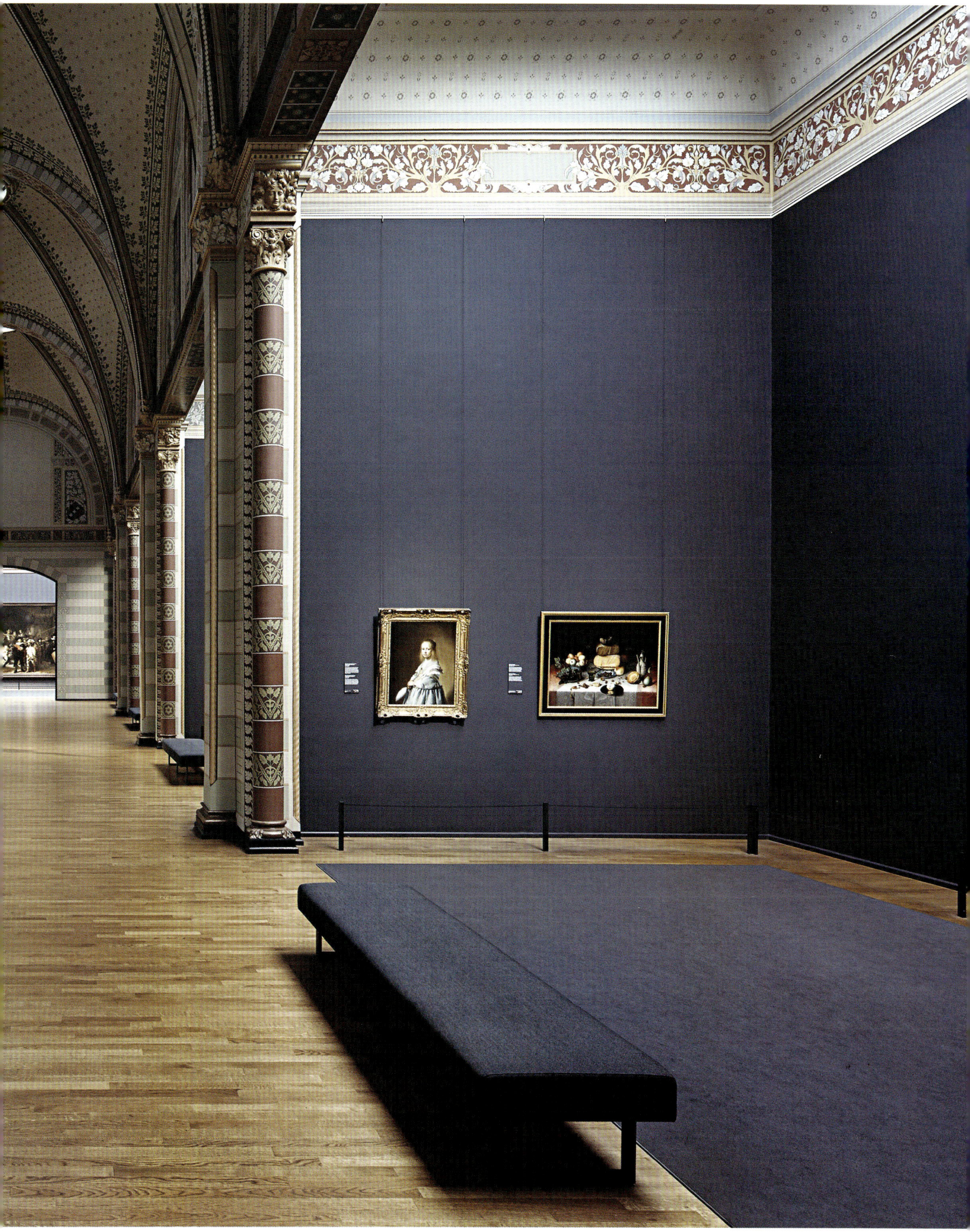

JEAN-MICHEL WILMOTTE   THE NEW RIJKSMUSEUM

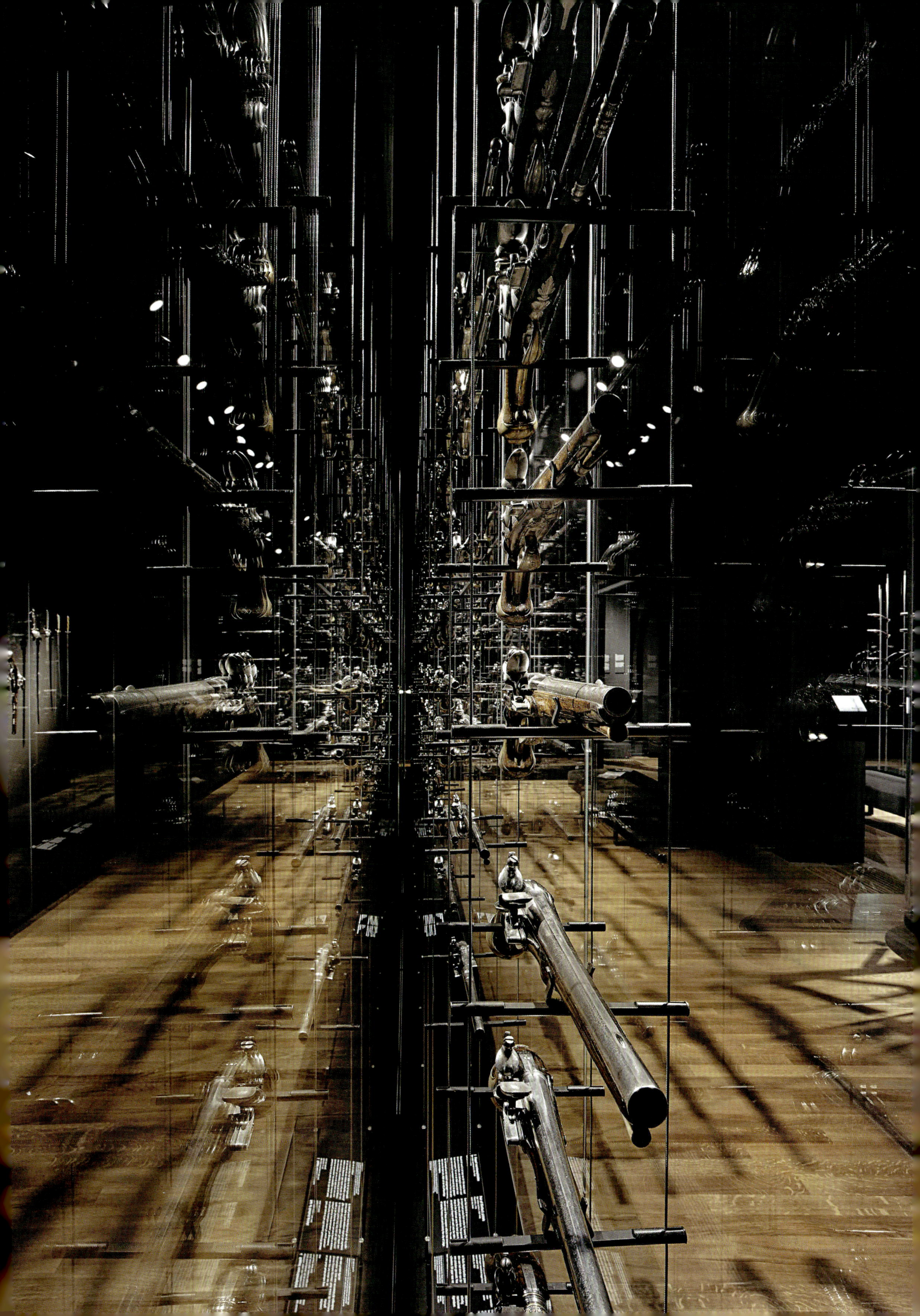

JEAN-MICHEL WILMOTTE THE NEW RIJKSMUSEUM

234

235

JEAN-MICHEL WILMOTTE

WILMOTTE & ASSOCIÉS ARCHITECTES

Wilmotte & Associés Architectes is an international, multicultural and multilingual practice founded in 1975 by the architect, urban planner, and designer Jean-Michel Wilmotte.

Based in France, the United Kingdom, Italy and South Korea, Wilmotte & Associés Architectes currently employs 254 architects, urban planners, museum design specialists, and interior designers of 25 nationalities, all driven by the same passion for exploration, knowledge-sharing, and creativity. Spun out of the architecture firm, the design studio Wilmotte & Industries SAS—including six designers—explores 'environmental design', and has developed a strong reputation in the worlds of industrial and object design.

For more than 40 years, from Dallas to Paris, from Rio de Janeiro to Seoul, taking in London, Dakar, Venice, and Moscow, they have traveled around the world discovering new lands of opportunity.

Jean-Michel Wilmotte and his collaborators are leading more than 100 projects in 27 different countries, from the biggest to the smallest, from the most spectacular to the most ordinary, with the same fervor from the initial sketch to completion.

For instance, the practice has recently completed the Russian Orthodox Spiritual and Cultural Center and Station F Start-Up campus in Paris (France),the headquarters of Unilever group in Rueil-Malmaison (France), the Center for Arts of the International School of Geneva (Switzerland), the Allées Richaud & Allées Foch high-end residential buildings in Versailles (France), the Cultural Center of Daejeon (South Korea), the 36,200-seat Allianz Riviera Stadium in Nice (France), the London headquarters of Google and JCDecaux (United Kingdom), the Ferrari Sporting Management Center (Formula 1) in Maranello (Italy), a Convention and Exhibition Center in São Paulo (Brazil), and an ecological park in Baku (Azerbaijan) for the 2015 European Games.

Other recent commissions for the practice include the refurbishment of the Lutetia hotel and the Gare d'Austerlitz in Paris, the Congress Center of Metz, the new ArcelorMittal headquarters in Luxembourg, the European University of Saint Petersburg (Russia), new districts in Libreville (Gabon), residential towers in Moscow (Russia), an office tower in Dakar (Senegal) as well as the UN headquarters for West Africa in Diamniadio (Senegal).

In these projects, which are both innovative and sustainable, design always takes into account landscaping, lighting, materials, and finishes, while being respectful of the local and historic context of the site.

The studio also shares its knowledge, as well as its high standards and values, with students and young architects, by awarding the Prix W. This architectural competition, dedicated to the combination of contemporary and traditional architecture (architectural grafting), is organized by the Wilmotte Foundation, established in 2005, which awards, publishes, and also exhibits the work of its laureates during the Venice Biennale of Architecture, in its own gallery.

Since 2010, Wilmotte & Associés Architectes has been one of the world's 100 largest architectural firms according to WA100, a study published annually by the *British Building Design* magazine, and was ranked 70th in 2018. The practice has received many distinctions and awards, including the 2014 International Architecture Award for the Allianz Riviera Stadium in Nice (France), the Best European Museum Award in 2015 for its intervention at the Rijksmuseum (Amsterdam, Netherlands), the urban planning award in the Grands Prix de la Région Capitale 2016 for the start-up campus Station F, or the European Urban Planning Award in 2016, given by the European Council of Spatial Planners for the strategic planning of Grand Roissy, where Wilmotte & Associés Architectes developed the new strategy plan for the motorway linking Paris and Roissy.

ADDRESSES

Wilmotte & Associés SAS
68, rue du Faubourg Saint-Antoine
75012 Paris
FRANCE

Wilmotte & Industries SAS
59, rue de Charonne
75011 Paris
FRANCE

Wilmotte UK Ltd
133, Oxford Gardens
London W10 6NE
UNITED KINGDOM

Wilmotte Italia Srl
Cannarregio 3560
30121 Venice
ITALY

Fondation d'entreprise Wilmotte
10, rue Sainte-Anastase
75003 Paris
FRANCE

www.wilmotte.com

JEAN-MICHEL WILMOTTE

PROJECT DATA

New Buildings

GANA ART CENTER
- City/Country: Seoul/Republic of Korea (South Korea)
- Completion date: 1998
- Client: Gana Art Center
- Area: 32,550 ft² (3,024 m²)
- Architect: Wilmotte & Associés
- Associate architect: Total Design
- W&A's project manager: Fabrice Drain
- W&A's team: Laurence Vandongeon, Alain Aubert, Astrid Courtois, Agathe de Kergos
- W&A's program: Construction of exhibition spaces devoted to contemporary art; interior design, and museography
- Building structure: Reinforced concrete
- Building materials: Italian beige limestone, wood

LEE HOUSE
- City/Country: Seoul/Republic of Korea (South Korea)
- Completion date: 2005
- Client: Private
- Area: 3,745 ft² (348 m²)
- Architect: Wilmotte & Associés
- Associate architect: Tetra Architects & Engineers
- Landscape architect: Neveux-Rouyer
- W&A's project manager: Eric Kittler
- W&A's program: Construction and interior design of a private house
- Building structure: Reinforced poured-in-place concrete
- Building materials: Tamped concrete

PANGYO RESIDENCE
- City/Country: Seongnam, Seoul/Republic of Korea (South Korea)
- Completion date: 2005
- Client: IB Housing
- Area: 104,300 ft² (9,690 m²)
- Architect: Wilmotte & Associés
- Associate architect: Tetra Architects & Engineers
- Landscape architect: Neveux-Rouyer
- W&A's project managers: Nicolas Gilsoul/Jong-Ki Min/Bénedicte Ollier
- W&A's team: Jong-Hoon Shin, Eva Meinhardt, Colleen Caulliez
- W&A's program: Construction of luxury apartment complex, seven buildings of four levels each (36 apartments in total); basement garages
- Building structure: Reinforced concrete
- Building materials: Italian white marble from Carrara, black Korean traditional brick for the ground, wood lattice, water

SIGNAL TOWER
- City/Country: La Défense, Paris/France
- Competition date: 2008
- Client: EPAD
- Area: 1,237,850 ft² (115,000 m²)
- Architect: Wilmotte & Associés
- Landscape architect: Neveux-Rouyer
- W&A's project manager: Ralf Levedag
- W&A's team: Peter Hatzmann, Ossisane Caldicote, Lorenzo Gaetani, Miguel Pinto, Alexandra Fraczek, Barbara Jeanrond
- W&A's program: Design of a 284-story ecological tower comprising offices, residential, hotel, tourist residence, shops and facilities

BRAIN AND SPINE INSTITUTE

City/Country	Paris/France
Completion date	2010
Client	ADREC CHU Pitié Salpêtrière
Area	246,495 ft² (22,900 m²)
Architect	Wilmotte & Associés
W&A's project manager	Bettina Hoeptner
W&A's team	Fiona Copstick, Véronique Bouysse-Lacroix, Cristina Cordera, Alexandra Fraczek, Eugène Mathe
W&A's program	Construction of a building, including laboratories, patient bedrooms, human-imaging sector, and offices
Building structure	Reinforced concrete post-and-beam structure
Building materials	Gray-tinted glass curtain wall

MONTE CARLO VIEW TOWER

City/Country	Monaco
Completion date	2012
Client	Michel Pastor Group
Area	107,640 ft² (10,000 m²)
Architect	Wilmotte & Associés
Associate architect	Alexis Blanchi
Landscape architect	Véronique Viale
W&A's project manager	Eric Kittler
W&A's team	Hector Montero, Tiphanie Priami Rasse, Rafik Samir Hamdi
W&A's program	Construction of a 19-story, 200-foot-tall (61-meter) high-rise tower
Building structure	Reinforced concrete
Building materials	Composite panels made of aluminum honeycomb with Moleanos natural stone surface and stainless steel profile façade)

EPADESA CORPORATE HEADQUARTERS

City/Country	Nanterre/France
Completion date	2012
Client	BNP PARIBAS Promotion Immobilière
Area	161,460 ft² (15,000 m²)
Architect	Wilmotte & Associés
Landscape architect	Jean-Michel Rameau
W&A's project manager	Ralf Levedag
W&A's team	Cristina Cordera, Peter Hatzmann, Ossisane Caldicote
W&A's program	Construction of an office building
Building structure	Reinforced concrete, posts and bearing façade
Building materials	Aluminum front, double-glazed windows with solar control, wood decking
Awards	Pyramide d'argent 2012, Pyramide de Vermeil 2012

BARRISTERS TRAINING COLLEGE

City/Country	Issy-les-Moulineaux/France
Completion date	2013, competition-winning project
Client	Bouygues Immobilier
Area	94,185 ft² (8,750 m²)
Architect	Wilmotte & Associés,
Landscape architect	Neveux-Rouyer
W&A's project managers	Ralf Levedag, Charles Moliner, Olivier Chaubin
W&A's team	Jitendra Jain, Ludovic Thomas, Romain Gauthier, Christian Chehaiber, Woytek Sepiol
W&A's program	Construction of a public law school for 1,900 students
Building structure	Concrete and metallic structure
Building materials	Stone, wood, glass, steel, aluminum, hammered concrete

ARTS CENTER, INTERNATIONAL SCHOOL OF GENEVA

City/Country	Geneva/Switzerland
Completion date	2014, restricted competition
Client	Foundation of the International School of Geneva
Area	50,915 ft² (4,730 m²)
Architect	Wilmotte & Associés
Associate architect	Brodbeck & Roulet (Marcel Hart, Daniel Zambon, and Mario Morgado)
Landscape architect	Gilbert Henchoz
W&A's project manager	Laurent Peyron
W&A's team	Edin Mujezinovic, Guillaume Renaud
W&A's program	Construction of an art center including a 400-seat multi-purpose auditorium, and a 200-seat theater
Building structure	Reinforced concrete
Building materials	Concrete, Linit U-profile glass by Lamberts

ALLIANZ RIVIERA STADIUM

City/Country	Nice/France
Completion date	2013, competition-winning project
Client	City of Nice
Area	35 acres (14 hectares)
Architect	Wilmotte & Associés
W&A's project managers	Ralf Levedag/Marco Punzi
W&A's team	Ossisane Caldicote, Louis Lafargue, Nicolas Lundström, Woytek Sepiol, Gabriela Richaud, Cristina Cordera, Peter Hatzmann, Véronique Bouysse-Lacroix, Jintendra Jain, Kuns Liu, Frank Avril, Julia Mille, Paul Bardon, Claire Rovella, Ilaria Ceccherini, Marine Gigout,

JEAN-MICHEL WILMOTTE PROJECT DATA

	Agathe Bensa, Delphine Baldassini, Fred Bequelin, Lucie Sorrenti, Emmanuel Brelot, Jean-Luc Wagner, Marleen Homan, Céline Bourret, Edouard Debré, David Guyon, Anne-Claire Grassler, Xavier Turk, Cyril Lancelin, Guillaume Renaud, Romain Gauthier, Ali Nazemi, Alekos Santantonios, Gilles Sagot, Yong-Ki Hong, Seung Ki Kim, Alban Danguy des Déserts, Marc Dutoit, Vincent Leroy, Vanessa Adolphe
W&A's program	Construction of a 35,000-seat stadium (UEFA approved) with multi-purpose facilities (sports and concerts), in a seismic zone
Building structure	Concrete structure and triangulated timber/steel frame
Building materials	Spruce, steel, concrete, ETFE
Awards	International Architecture Award 2014

QUADRANS BUILDINGS

City/Country	Paris/France
Completion date	2017, competition-winning project
Client	SAS CorneOuest Promotion (Linkcity)
Area	992,440 ft² (92,200 m²)
Architect	Wilmotte & Associés
Landscape architect	Neveux-Rouyer
W&A's project managers	Ralf Levedag/Jean Claude Antonio
W&A's team	Frédéric Poinet, Hwan-Chul Kim, Xenia Spektor, Vassil Kaykov, Jean-Baptiste Heisse, Olivier Carminati, Lorraine Bertrand, Bettina Hoeptner, Ossisane Caldicote, Vincent Carbillet, Fiona Copstick, Francesca Gulizia, Raimundo Parraga, Romain Rivaux, Ludovic Thomas, Céline Bourret, Edouard Riou, Marie Lhuillier, Alexandre Maréchal
W&A's program	Construction of four office buildings and a landscaped park for the Quadrans service campus on the site of the new French Ministry of Defence
Building structure	Reinforced concrete post-and-beam structure
Building materials	Concrete, stone, stainless steel, Corten steel, composite panels, thermo-coated aluminum, frame curtain wall, exterior glazing slide-in, terrace in exotic wood (ipe)

6 PANCRAS SQUARE, GOOGLE HEADQUARTERS

City/Country	London/United Kingdom
Completion date	2015, restricted competition by invitation—winning project
Client	BNP Paribas Real Estate
Area	531,740 ft² (49,400 m²)
Architect	Wilmotte & Associés
Executive architect	Adamson Associates
Landscape architect	Townshend Associates
W&A's project managers	Malte Mager (competition)/Pablo Lambrechts
W&A's team	Benoit Sanson, Luca Vernocchi, Dhiren Patel, Matthew Brookes, Miguel Pinto, Hugo Loureiro, Carlos Manns, Romain Gauthier
W&A's program	Construction of an office building and interior design of public areas
Building structure	Reinforced concrete (basements and ground floor)/steel construction with metal decks (other floors)
Building materials	Terracotta, anodized aluminum, concrete, glass

DAEJEON CULTURAL CENTER

City/Country	Daejeon/Republic of Korea (South Korea)
Completion date	2014, competition-winning project
Client	City of Daejeon
Area	98,275 ft² (9,130 m²)
Architect	Wilmotte & Associés
Associate architect	Shinwha Architects & Engineering
W&A's project manager	Michael Levy
W&A's team	Yujong Choi, Yuhui Shi, Fiona Copstick, Mark Zerkaulen, Guillaume Renaud
W&A's program	Construction of a cultural center including a 350-seat theatre, an exhibition hall, a music studio, offices, and parking lot
Building structure	Reinforced concrete
Building materials	Aluminum panels and glass

FERRARI SPORTING MANAGEMENT CENTER

City/Country	Maranello/Italy
Completion date	2015
Client	Ferrari S.p.A.
Area	258,335 ft² (24,000 m²)
Architect	Wilmotte & Associés
Associate architect	Studio Quaranta
W&A's project manager	Ralf Levedag
W&A's team	Erica Bonomi, Lorenzo Gaetani, Nicolas Lundström, Giovanna Mancini, Matthew Brookes, Ossisane Caldicote, Warren Nicoud

W&A's program	Construction of the new Ferrari sporting management center devoted to the design and assembly of Ferrari Formula 1 racing cars
Building structure	Reinforced concrete
Building materials	Silk screened glass panels (ground floor façade), double-skin glass façade (upper floor façade)

RUSSIAN ORTHODOX SPIRITUAL AND CULTURAL CENTER

City/Country	Paris/France
Completion date	2016
Client	Russian Federation
Area	50,105 ft² (4,655 m²)
Architect	Wilmotte & Associés
Landscape architect	Louis Benech
W&A's project manager	Ralf Levedag
W&A's team	Louis Lafargue, Thérèse Leroy, Véronique Bouysse-Lacroix, Nicolas Lundström, Cyril Lancelin, Ossisane Caldicote, Warren Nicoud, Romain Rivaux, Romain Gauthier, Guillaume Renaud, Alekos Santantonios, Ali Nazemi, Jean-Baptiste Coursault, Gilles Sagot, Alexandre Thai
W&A's program	Construction of a cultural center, a cathedral, a spiritual center, and a primary school
Building structure	Reinforced concrete
Building materials	Massangis natural stone, glass, gold leaf

PRIVATE CHALET

City/Country	France
Completion date	2015
Client	Private
Area	6,460 ft² (600 m²)
Architect	Wilmotte & Associés
Associate architect	Pascal Chatron-Michaud
Landscape architect	Neveux-Rouyer
W&A's project managers	Eric Kittler/Bertrand Leridon
W&A's team	Romain Nowak, Tiphanie Priami Rasse, Romain Gauthier, Alban Danguy des Déserts
W&A's program	Construction of a wood contemporary chalet
Building structure	Reinforced concrete, wood frame construction
Building materials	Textured stained oak, slate from Portugal, sheet metal

EIFFAGE CORPORATE HEADQUARTERS

City/Country	Vélizy-Villacoublay/France
Completion date	2015
Client	Eiffage Immobilier
Area	258,335 ft² (24,000 m²)
Architect	Wilmotte & Associés
Landscape architect	Neveux-Rouyer
W&A's project manager	Jean-Fançois Patte
W&A's team	Jean-Baptiste Heisse, Pierre Floch, Pierre Calame, Nancy Chidiac, Bénédicte Ollier, Romain Gauthier
W&A's program	Construction of the new Eiffage headquarters comprising offices, exhibition hall, library, company cafeteria, car park
Building structure	Concrete structure and steel frame
Building materials	Aluminum panel cladding, ventilated curtain wall, raw concrete
Awards	BIM d'Or 2014

BLEU CIEL TOWER

City/Country	Dallas/USA
Completion date	2017
Client	Harwood International
Area	461,000 ft² (42,800 m²)
Architect	Wilmotte & Associés
Associate architect	Harwood Design Factory LLC
Landscape architect	Uchiyama Design Studio/Halff D+PC, Inc
W&A's project manager	Ralf Levedag
W&A's team	Louis Lafargue, Nicolas Lunsdström, Matthew Brookes, Ossisane Caldicote, Warren Nicoud
W&A's program	Construction of a 33-floor, 370-foot-tall (115-meter-tall) high-rise tower, including 158 luxury apartments
Building structure	Reinforced concrete
Building materials	Concrete, aluminum, glass, reconstituted stone

GIROFLÉES TOWER

City/Country	Monaco
Completion date	2020
Client	Michel Pastor Group
Area	226,040 ft² (21,000 m²)
Architect	Wilmotte & Associés
Associate architect	Rainier Boisson
Landscape architect	Jean Mus & Compagnie
W&A's project manager	Ralf Levedag
W&A's team	Louis Lafargue, Claire Davisseau, Tudor Zamfirescu, Alban Danguy des Déserts, Ossisane Caldicote, Warren Nicoud

JEAN-MICHEL WILMOTTE   PROJECT DATA

W&A's program	Construction of a 22-floor, 425-foot-tall (130-meter-tall) residential high-rise tower, and six parking floors	Interior architect	SM Design/Jouin Manku
		Landscape architect	Neveux-Rouyer
		W&A's project manager	Christian Oudart
		W&A's team	Jean-Luc Perrin, Fabienne Dumant
Building structure	Reinforced concrete	W&A's program	Restructuration of an office complex into a 5-star hotel including 99 rooms and 32 suites. First luxury hotel to receive HQE certification in France.
Building materials	Stainless steel, stone, glass		

Renovation Projects

LA RÉSERVE, RAMATUELLE

City/Country	Ramatuelle/France		
Completion date	2009		
Client	Michel Reybier		
Area	89,340 ft² (8,300 m²)	Building structure	Reinforced concrete post-and-beam structure
Architects	Wilmotte & Associés	Building materials	Concrete, natural stone (façade on the street), natural stone and lime plaster (façade overlooking the garden)
Landscape architect	Neveux-Rouyer		
W&A's project manager	Anne-Claude Morand Dessart		
W&A's team	Jérôme Collet, Mio Shibuya, Chantal de Pelsmaeker		
W&A's program	Refurbishment of a 1970s building into a five-star hotel and spa, including seven rooms and 16 suites	Awards	Exclusive 'Distinction Palace' rating
Building structure	Reinforced concrete		
Building materials	Coating concrete, dry stone, natural stone (flooring), wood decking		

CHÂTEAU PÉDESCLAUX

		City/Country	Pauillac/France
		Completion date	2015
		Client	Domaine Château Pédesclaux
		Area	82,880 ft² (7,700 m²)
		Architects	Wilmotte & Associés
Awards	Wallpaper Design Awards 2011, exclusive 'Distinction Palace' rating	Associate architect	Atelier d'architecture BPM (Arnaud Boulain)
		Landscape architect	Neveux-Rouyer
		W&A's project manager	Laurent Brunier

JEAN PIERRE RAYNAUD STUDIO

City/Country	Barbizon/France	W&A's team	Elise Malisse, Angéline Geslain, Pierre-Yves Kuhn, Jean-Sébastien Pagnon, Romain Gauthier, Ali Nazemi
Completion date	2010		
Client	Jean Pierre Raynaud		
Area	2,585 ft² (240 m²)		
Architects	Wilmotte & Associés	W&A's program	Extension and refurbishment of Château Pédesclaux vineyards: creation of a cellar
Landscape architect	Neveux-Rouyer		
W&A's project manager	Philippe Pingusson		
W&A's program	Restructuration and extension of an old Normandy-style house as an artist studio	Building structure	White reinforced concrete (barrel warehouse in the basement) and bronze metallic structure (vat room on ground and first floor)
Building structure	Stonework covered in plastered filler imitating the freestone (an existing and partially conserved provisions at the back of the building), steel structure and glass curtain wall (new part of the building facing the wood)	Building materials	Black quartz concrete, bronze anodized aluminum strips (vat façade), glazed transparent front with large dimension glass panel, white concrete slabs, American walnut floor
		Furniture	Wilmotte & Industries and Victoria Wilmotte (tasting room)
Building materials	Steel, aluminum, glass		

MANDARIN ORIENTAL HOTEL

City/Country	Paris/France		

SUMMIT HOUSE, JCDECAUX UK HEADQUARTERS

Completion date	2011	City/Country	London/United Kingdom
Client	Société Foncière Lyonnaise, Mandarin Oriental Hotel Group	Completion date	2016
		Client	DF Real Estate
Area	236,805 ft² (22,000 m²)	Area	69,965 ft² (6,500m²)
Architects	Charles Letrosne (1930s)/ Wilmotte & Associés	Architects	Wilmotte & Associés
		Landscape architect	Townshend Associates

W&A's project managers	Miguel Pinto/Pablo Lambrechts
W&A's team	Jean-Luc Wagner
W&A's program	Extension, refurbishment, interior design and re-cladding of JCDecaux offices
Building structure	Existing concrete structure, extension and alterations in steel
Building materials	Rendered concrete, aluminum, glass

STATION F START-UP CAMPUS

City/Country	Paris/France
Completion date	2017
Client	SDECN (Xavier Niel)
Area	365,975 ft^2 (34,000 m^2)
Architects	Eugène Freyssinet (1927), historical listed building/Wilmotte & Associés
Chief architect for historic monuments	2BDM Architectes
W&A's project manager	Jean-François Patte
W&A's team	Charlotte Bertrand, Jean Besson, Pierre Calame, Nancy Chidiac, Florian Giroguy, Théo Kirn, Marie Leyh, Carmen Villarta, Romain Queroy, Romain Gauthier, Alekos Santantonios, Ali Nazemi, Gilles Sagot, Jean-Baptiste Coursault, Cyril Lancelin, Guillaume Renaud, Ludovic Rubrecht, Alban Danguy des Déserts, Alexandre Thai
W&A's program	Renovation to turn a monumental hall used for train-truck transfers of freight, built in pre-stressed concrete in 1927 by engineer Eugène Freyssinet, into a digital start-up hub
Building structure	Pre-stressed concrete
Building materials	Steel, wood, glass
Furniture	Wilmotte & Industries

COLLÈGE DES BERNARDINS

City/Country	Paris/France
Completion date	2008
Client	Association diocésaine de Paris
Area	53,820 ft^2 (5,000 m^2)
Architect	Wilmotte & Associés
Chief architect for historic monuments	Hervé Baptiste
Landscape architect	Neveux-Rouyer
W&A's project managers	Emmanuel Brelot/Xavier Turk
W&A's program	Renovation of 13th- and 15th-century buildings, including the creation of two auditoriums and a library
Building structure	Solid stone ancient structure, new roof with steel frame supporting the upper two floors; the entire load is supported by 300 sub-surface concrete micro-pilings
Building materials	Saint-Maximin natural stone, steel joinery
Awards	European Union Prize for Cultural Heritage, 2010 (Grand Prix)/Europa Nostra Awards (conservation)

Urban Projects

GREATER MOSCOW PROPOSAL

City/Country	Moscow/Russia
Completion date	2012, competition-winning project
Client	City of Moscow
Area	258 mi^2 (668 km^2)
Architect	Wilmotte & Associés
Architect planner	Antoine Grumbach
Russian associate architect	Serguei Tkachenko
W&A's project managers	Charles Moliner/Anne Speicher/Jean-Pierre Franco Lucio
W&A's team	Edouardo Iannicelli, Noémie Masson, Cyril Lancelin, Romain Gauthier, Guillaume Renaud, Gilles Sagot, Romain Queroy
W&A's program	Master plan and mobility concept of Greater Moscow

ALLÉES JEAN-JAURÈS

City/Country	Nîmes/France
Completion date	2013, competition-winning project
Client	City of Nîmes
Area	1 mile (1.6 km)
Architect and urban designer	Wilmotte & Associés
Associate architect	Carré d'Archi
Landscape architect	Neveux-Rouyer
W&A's project managers	Marie-Noëlle Passa/Anne Labroille/Marc Dutoit
W&A's team	Ana Claudia Correa Diaz
W&A's program	Urban design of Nîmes' largest avenue (1 mi-long [1.6 km], 200 ft wide [61 m])
Materials	Sand-blasted concrete (sidewalk), concrete (parking area), concrete and stone slabs and paving stones made with natural stone from Croatia (central walkway), wooden duckboard (terrace)
Urban furniture	Wilmotte & Industries
Awards	Nominated project for the 2013 Urban Design Award (Moniteur Group), Victoire du paysage 2016 'Grand Prix du Jury'

JEAN-MICHEL WILMOTTE   PROJECT DATA

Museums

PAVILLON DES SESSIONS, MUSÉE DU LOUVRE
City/Country	Paris/France
Completion date	2000, competition-winning project
Client	Etablissement public du Grand Louvre
Area	15,070 ft^2 (1,400 m^2)
Architect	Hector-Martin Lefuel (1860s–1870s)
W&A's project manager	Alain Desmarchelier
W&A's team	Racha Kayali
W&A's program	Museography
Showcase	Wilmotte & Associés

PRESIDENT JACQUES CHIRAC MUSEUM
City/Country	Sarran/France
Completion date	1998–2002 (Phase 1) & 2002–2006 (Phase 2)
Client	Conseil général de la Corrèze
Area	Phase 1: 16,145 ft^2 (1,500 m^2); Phase 2: 40,550 ft^2 (3,767 m^2)
Architect	Wilmotte & Associés
Associate architects	J. Parquet/D. Chassary (Atelier Centre); Nissou-Parquet
Landscape architect	Michel Desvignes
W&A's project manager	Emmanuel Brelot
W&A's team	Xavier Turk, Alain Thibault, Yoo-jung Kim, Hélène Lecarpentier
W&A's program	Refurbishment, interior design and subsequent extension of the museum to conserve gifts received by Jacques Chirac during his two terms as President of the French Republic
Building structure	Reinforced concrete
Building materials	Correzian pink granite, oak, coating, roofing natural slate

ULLENS CENTER FOR CONTEMPORARY ART
City/Country	Beijing/China
Completion date	2007
Client	Ullens Center for Contemporary Art
Area	80,730 ft^2 (7,500 m^2)
Architect	Wilmotte & Associés
Associate architect	MADA s.p.a.m.
W&A's project manager	Emmanuel Brelot
W&A's team	Xavier Turk, Moochol Shin, Jérôme Peuron, Myun Kim, Ho Keun Kwon
W&A's program	Rehabilitation and refurbishment of a 1950s industrial building into an art gallery
Building structure	Reinforced concrete
Building materials	Fine epoxy resin (floor resin), painted wall

MUSEUM OF ISLAMIC ART OF QATAR
City/Country	Doha/Qatar
Completion date	2008
Client	State of Qatar
Area	17,225 ft^2 (5,250 m^2)
Architect	I. M. Pei Partnership Architects
Landscape architect	Michel Desvignes
W&A's project manager	Emmanuel Brelot
W&A's team	Fabian Servagnat, Xavier Turk, Emilie Oliviero, Moochol Shin
W&A's program	Museography and book shop/gift shop furnishing
Showcases	Wilmotte & Associés

MUSÉE D'ORSAY REFURBISHMENT
City/Country	Paris/France
Completion date	2011, competition-winning project
Client	Etablissement public du Musée d'Orsay
Area	23,680 ft^2 (2,200 m^2)
Architect	Victor Laloux (1898–1900)
W&A's project managers	Emmanuel Brelot/Xavier Turk
W&A's program	Museography and bookshop/gift shop furnishing
Showcases	Wilmotte & Associés

THE NEW RIJKSMUSEUM
City/Country	Amsterdam/Netherlands
Completion date	2013, competition-winning project
Client	Rijksmuseum in partnership with the Ministry of Education, Culture and Science, and the Rijksgebouwendienst
Area	129,150 ft^2 (12,000 m^2)
Architects	Pierre Cuypers (1885); Cruz y Ortiz (renovation)
W&A's project manager	Marleen Homan
W&A's team	Vanessa Adolphe, Marc Dutoit, Anne-Claire Grassler, Flore Lenoir, Domenico Lo Rito, Dji-Ming Luk, Emilie Oliviero, Bénédicte Ollier, Alekos Santantonios, Céline Seivert
W&A's program	Museography
Furniture and showcases	Wilmotte & Associés/Wilmotte & Industries
Awards	Leaf Awards 2014, "international interior design" category

SURSOCK MUSEUM

City/Country	Beirut/Lebanon
Completion date	1998–2015
Client	Nicolas Ibrahim Sursock Museum
Area	91,495 ft^2 (8,500 m^2)
Architects	Unknown/Wilmotte & Associés
Associate architect	JA Designs (Jacques Aboukhaled)
W&A's project managers	Alain Desmarchelier/Emmanuel Brelot
W&A's team	Ho Keun Kwon
W&A's program	Extension and refurbishment
Building structure	Reinforced concrete
Building materials	Egyptian natural stone, curtain wall (glass, aluminum), Corian, panel veneered in bleached oak

JEAN-MICHEL WILMOTTE

MAJOR PROJECTS

Projects in progress

France

Antibes, Carrefour retail—refurbishment, 312,155 ft² (29,000 m²)

Jouy-en-Josas, HEC Campus—construction, 968,750 ft² (90,000 m²)

Ferney-Voltaire, Shopping Center—refurbishment and extension, 430,555 ft² (40,000 m²)

La Plagne Aime 2000, Hotel, residences, leisure center, retail—urban, architectural and landscape project, 581,250 ft² (54,000 m²)

Lyon, Les Terrasses de la Presqu'île—urban renewal, 6 acres (2.4 ha)

Marseilles, Giptis Research Institute—construction, 237,880 ft² (22,100 m²)

Metz, Congress Center—construction, 164,690 ft² (15,300 m²)

Neuilly-sur-Seine, American Hospital of Paris—construction of K building, 168,995 ft² (15,700 m²)

Nice, Carrefour retail—extension, 172,225 ft² (16,000 m²)

Nice, IKEA store and residential—construction, 581,250 ft² (54,000 m²)

Orly, Coeur d'Orly—offices and retail, construction, 602,780 ft² (56,000 m²) (Askia offices, 193,750 ft²—18,000 m², 2015)

Paris, Lutetia hotel, 5-star—refurbishment, interior design and furniture design, 203,870 ft² (18,940 m²)

Paris-Saclay, Servier Laboratories—construction, 484,375 ft² (45,000 m²)

Paris-Roissy—modernization of A1 motorway between Paris and Roissy, 12 mi (20 km)

Poissy, PSG training center—construction, 699,655 ft² (65,000 m², interior) and 1,722,225 ft² (160,000 m², exterior)

Roquebrune Cap-Martin, Vista La Cigale hotel, 5-star—refurbishment, 113,020 ft² (10,500 m²)

International

Congo (Republic), Loango, Slavery Memorial—construction, 199,130 ft² (18,500 m²)

Iran, Mashhad, International terminal of Mashhad Airport—construction, 398,265 ft² (37,000 m²)

Italy, Milan-Carrefour Paderno retail—construction, 430,555 ft² (40,000 m²)

Gabon, Libreville—masterplan and architecture, residential, offices, retail, coastline and marina, 268 acres (107 ha)

Luxembourg, Arcelor Mittal headquarters—construction, 570,487 ft² (53,000 m²)

Mauritius, Beau Champ-8 villas—construction, 107,640 ft² (10,000 m²)

Monaco, Les Giroflées tower (residential)—construction, 226,040 ft² (21,000 m²)

Romania, Bucharest, Bioparc—masterplan, 143 acres (57 ha)

Russia, Moscow-Greater Moscow—development strategies, 258 mi² (668 km²)

Russia, Moscow, Red October (residential)—refurbishment, 441,320 ft² (41,000 m²)

Russia, Moscow, Red Side 2 towers (mixed use)—concept design, 1,114,065 ft² (103,500 m²)

Russia, St Petersburg, European University—refurbishment, 91,495 ft² (8,500 m²)

Saint-Tropez, Cheval Blanc-La Pinède hotel, 5-star (LVMH)—refurbishment and extension, 30,675 ft² (2,850 m²)

Senegal, Dakar, Mixed-use tower—construction, 340 ft high (104 m high), 222,815 ft² (20,700 m²)

Senegal, Dakar, Palace of Arts—refurbishment, 64,585 ft² (6,000 m²)

Senegal, Diamniadio, UN headquarters—construction, 430,555 ft² (40,000 m²)

USA, Dallas, Bleu Ciel tower (residential)—concept design, 461,000 ft² (42,800 m²); 5 towers (offices, residential, retail), 3,235,630 ft² (300,600 m²)

Projects completed since 2015

France

Paris, Gare du Nord—masterplan, 917,625 ft² (85,250 m²), 2016

Paris, Quadrans building—construction of offices on the site of the new Ministry of Defence, 992,440 ft² (92,200 m²) (Phase 1 completed in 2015, 492,985 ft² [45,800 m²]/Phase 2 completed in 2018, 499,445 ft² [46,400 m²])

Paris, Russian Orthodox Spiritual & Cultural Center—construction, 50,105 ft² (4,655 m²), 2016

Paris, Schlumberger headquarters—refurbishment, 43,055 ft² (4,000 m²), 2017

Paris, SMA headquarters and Okko hotel—construction, 419,790 ft² (39,000 m²), 2017

Paris, Station F Start-Up Campus—refurbishment, 365,975 ft² (34,000 m²), 2017

Rueil-Malmaison, Green Office, Unilever Headquarters—construction, 378,735 ft² (35,000 m²), 2015

Pauillac, Château Pédesclaux Winery—construction and extension, 82,880 ft² (7,700 m²), 2015

Versailles, Les Allées Foch—construction, 66,735 ft² (6,200 m²), 2015

Versailles, Les Allées Richaud—refurbishment and construction, 205,590 ft² (19,100 m²), 2015

Vélizy-Villacoublay, Eiffage headquarters—construction, 258,335 ft² (24,000 m²), 2015

International

Azerbaijan, Baku, Baku Park for the European Games, 40 acres (16 ha), 2015

Brazil, Rio de Janeiro, Grand Mercure hotel, 4*—construction, 21,530 ft² (20,000 m²), 2015

Brazil, São Paulo, São Paulo Expo—construction, 1,065,625 ft² (99,000 m²), 2016

Italy, Maranello-Fiorano, Ferrari Sporting Management Center—construction, 258,335 ft² (24,000 m²), 2015

Lebanon, Beirut, Sursock Museum—refurbishment and interior design, 91,495 ft² (8,500 m²), 2015

South Korea, Daejeon, Cultural Center—construction, 98,275 ft² (9,130 m²), 2015

United Kingdom, King's Cross Central—Google London Headquarters—construction, 531,735 ft² (49,400 m²), 2015

United Kingdom, London, JCDecaux London Headquarters—refurbishment, 69,965 ft² (6,500 m²), 2016

South Korea, Seoul, Incheon International Airport, Terminal 1—interior design, 3,229,175 ft² (300,000 m²), 2000/Terminal 2—interior architecture concept and Art consultant, 4,090,286 ft² (380,000 m²), 2018

Other major projects

France

Bordeaux, Congress Center—refurbishment and extension, 117,325 ft² (10,900 m²), 2003

Clichy, L'Oréal headquarters—refurbishment and extension, 161,460 ft² (15,000 m²), 2014

Issy-les-Moulineaux, Barristers Training College—construction, 94,185 ft², (8,750 m²), 2013

Nanterre, EPADESA Corporate Headquarters—construction, 161,460 ft² (15,000 m²), 2012

Nice, Allianz Riviera sustainable stadium—construction, 581,250 ft² (54,000 m²), 36,200 seats, 2013

Nîmes, Allées Jean-Jaurès—urban design and furniture design, length 1 mile (1.6 km), width 200 ft (60 m), 2013

Paris, Avenue de France—urban design and street furniture, 2004

Paris, Collège de France—refurbishment and extension, 276,630 ft² (25,700 m²), 1998–2004

Paris, Collège des Bernardins—refurbishment and interior design, 53,820 ft² (5,000 m²), 2008

Paris, ICM (Brain and Spine Institute—construction, 246,495 ft² (22,900 m²), 2010

Paris, Maison de la Mutualité—Refurbishment, 139,930 ft² (13,000 m²), 2012

Paris, Mandarin-Oriental hotel, 5-star —refurbishment, 236,805 ft² (22,000 m²), 2011

Paris, Musée d'Orsay—refurbishment of 3 Impressionist galleries, 23,680 ft² (2,200 m²), 2011

Paris, Musée du Louvre:
—Grand Louvre, temporary exhibition galleries, shops, restaurants, 1988–1990
—Pavillon des Sessions, Department of Primitive Arts, interior design, 15,070 ft² (1,400 m²), 2000
—The Richelieu wing, interior design and specific furniture, 54,465 ft² (5,060 m²),1993
—The Rohan wing, interior design, 10,765 ft² (1,000 m²), 1999

Paris, Tramway des Maréchaux Sud, RATP T3—urban furniture, 2006

Ramatuelle, La Réserve hôtel, 5-star hotel-spa—refurbishment and interior design, 89,340 ft² (8,300 m²), 2009
Rueil-Malmaison, Schneider Electric headquarters—construction, 365,975 ft² (34,000m²), 2008

Saint-Estèphe, Château Cos d'Estournel Winery—refurbishment and extension, 57,048 ft² (5,300 m²), 2008

Sophia-Antipolis, SophiaTech Campus—construction, 197,520 ft² (18,350 m²), 2012

International

China, Beijing, UCCA—refurbishment of a plant into a Contemporary Art Center, 80,730 ft² (7,500 m²), 2007

Italy, Forlì, San Domenico Museum—refurbishment and interior design, 53,820 ft² (5,000 m²), 2006

Monaco, Monte Carlo View Tower, residential—construction, 107,640 ft² (10,000 m²), 2012

South Korea, Seoul, Gana Art Center—construction, 32,550 ft² (3,024 m²), 1998

South Korea, Seongnam, Pangyo—construction of 36 flats, 104,302 ft² (9,690 m²), 2005

The Netherlands, Amsterdam, The New Rijksmuseum—interior design and museography, 12,915 ft² (12,000 m²), 2013

Portugal, Lisbon, Chiado Museum—refurbishment and museography, 36,600 ft² (3,400 m²), 1994

Qatar, Doha, Museum of Islamic Art—interior design and museography 17,225 ft² (5,250 m²)

Switzerland, Geneva, International School—construction of Arts Center, 50,915 ft² (4,730 m²), 2014

JEAN-MICHEL WILMOTTE

AWARDS

2017   GESTE D'OR, *Architecture, Materials and Research Grand Prix*, awarded to Station F, the world's biggest start-up campus, Paris, France.

2017   PYRAMIDES D'OR, *First Achievement Award*, awarded to the Quai de la Borde residence project in Ris-Orangis.

2017   CNCC TROPHY AT SIEC 2017, *design of a retail park award*, awarded to L'Avenue 83 project in La Valette-du-Var.

2017   PYRAMIDES D'ARGENT ILE-DE-FRANCE, Low Carbon building Award, awarded for the Épicéa residence project in Issy-les-Moulineaux.

2017   PYRAMIDES D'ARGENT ILE-DE-FRANCE, First Achievement Award, awarded for the Quai de la Borde residence project in Ris-Orangis.

2016   5E ÉDITION DES VICTOIRES DU PAYSAGE, *Grand Prix du Jury* awarded to the Allées Jean-Jaurès project, Nîmes, France.

2016   Jean-Michel Wilmotte was rewarded by a BFM Awards for his whole career.

2016   GRANDS PRIX DE LA RÉGION CAPITALE, *Urban design prize* awarded to the rehabilitation of the Halle Freyssinet into Station F, the world's biggest start-up campus, Paris, France.

2016   GRAND PRIX EUROPÉEN DE L'URBANISME awarded by the European Council of Town Planners for the territory of the Grand Roissy. Wilmotte & Associés is associated to this project through the requalification of the A1 motorway linking Paris to Roissy.

2016   JANUS DU COMMERCE, awarded by the Institut Français du Design to L'Avenue 83 retail park, La Valette-du-Var, France.

2016   iF DESIGN AWARD (PRODUCT), awarded by the International Forum Design GmbH, GRAFA lighting system manufactured by Artemide.

2016   PIERRES D'OR, Programme category, awarded to the refurbishment of the Halle Freyssinet into Station F, the world's biggest start-ups campus, Paris, France.

2015   TROPHÉES DU LOGEMENT ET DES TERRITOIRES, Sustainable programme of the year prize awarded to Quai de la Borde residential building, Ris-Orangis, France.

2015   PRIX NATIONAL DE LA CONSTRUCTION BOIS (National Prize of the Wooden Construction), 2nd prize awarded to the Allianz Riviera stadium, Nice, France.

2015   GRAND PRIX DU RAYONNEMENT FRANÇAIS (French Influence Award), cultural influence prize awarded to Jean-Michel Wilmotte, Paris, France.

2015   BEST EUROPEAN MUSEUM, awarded by the European Museum Forum to the Rijksmuseum, Amsterdam, Netherlands.

2015   PYRAMIDES D'ARGENT ILE-DE-FRANCE, Prix Spécial du Jury, Refurbishment and transformation of the former royal hospital of Versailles into residential, retail, cultural spaces and offices, Versailles, France.

2015   PYRAMIDES D'ARGENT MIDI-PYRÉNÉES, Prix d'Immobilier d'Entreprise awarded to Safran office buildings, France, Toulouse.

2015   14th edition of the PRIX AMO (ARCHITECTURE & clients) LIEU DE TRAVAIL ARCHITECTURE ENVIRONNEMENT, Special prize awarded for the refurbishment and modernization of the L'Oréal group headquarters, Clichy, France.

2014   BIM D'OR (BUILDING INFORMATION MODELING AWARD awarded to the Campus Pierre Berger, Eiffage headquarters, Velizy-Villacoublay, France.

2015   LES ÉTOILES DE L'OBSERVEUR DU DESIGN awarded for the design of URBA, street lamp manufactured by Thorn.

2014	LE GESTE D'OR has distinguished the rehabilitation of the Halle Freyssinet into Station F, the world's biggest start-up campus, Paris, France.	2004	IF DESIGN AWARD awarded by the International Forum Design for the lighting system *PhaosXeno* LED manufactured by Zumtobel.
2014	LEAF AWARDS, International Interior Design category, awarded by Leaf International to The New Rijksmuseum, Amsterdam, The Netherlands.	1997	PRIX CITEC awarded to the exhibited collection at the CITEXPO 97 show, Montpellier, France.
2014	INTERNATIONAL ARCHITECTURE AWARD, awarded by The Chicago Athenaeum & The European Center of Architecture Art Design and Urban Studies to Allianz Riviera stadium, Nice, France.	1996	EUROPEAN PARKING AWARD awarded in Budapest by the European Parking Association to the Parking des Célestins (Lyon Parc Auto), Interior design: J.-M Wilmotte, M. Targe, D. Buren, Lyon, France.
2013	LES ÉTOILES DE L'OBSERVEUR DU DESIGN, "Made in France" prize awarded to the kitchen appliances LA CORNUE W manufactured by La Cornue.	1995	LA LAMPE DE TRENTE ANS during the 30th edition of the International Lighting exhibition at Porte de Versailles, Paris, France.
2013	JANUS DE LA CITE, Éco Design mention, awarded by the Institut Français du Design to the Paris dustbin Bagatelle manufactured by Seri.	1994	GRAND PRIX NATIONAL DE LA CREATION INDUSTRIELLE awarded by the French Ministry of Culture.
2012	GOOD DESIGN AWARD awarded by the Athenaeum-Museum of Architecture and Design to the ATOLLO washbasin manufactured by Rapsel.	1992	PRIX D'AMENAGEMENT ET D'URBANISME, public space category awarded by the Publisher *Le Moniteur des Villes* for the urban renewal of the city of Agde with the creation of specific furniture, France.
2012	PYRAMIDES D'ARGENT ILE-DE-FRANCE, Prix de l'immobilier d'entreprise awarded to Via Verde building, EPADESA headquarters, Nanterre, France.	1991	OSCAR DU DESIGN awarded by the *Nouvel Economiste* for the Espace Technal, Toulouse, France.
2011	GOOD DESIGN KOREA awarded by the Korea Institute of Design Promotion to Samsung group for the Samsung Raemian village project, Yongin, South Korea.	1990	PRIX EUROPA NOSTRA awarded to the refurbishment of the Grenier à Sel as the best example of European renovation and heritage conservation, Avignon, France.
2011	MAN OF THE YEAR, awarded to Jean-Michel Wilmotte by the wine magazine *La Revue du Vin de France* for the Château Cos d'Estournel winery, Saint-Estèphe, France.	1990	MEDAILLE D'ARCHITECTURE INTERIEURE awarded by the Académie d'architecture, Paris, France.
2011	WALLPAPER DESIGN AWARDS, BEST NEW HOTEL prize awarded to La Réserve 5-star hotel-spa, Ramatuelle, France.	1989	PRIX S.A.D (Salon des Artistes Décorateurs), France.
		1989	Elected DESIGNER OF THE YEAR during the International Furniture Exhibition in Paris, France.
2010	PRIX EUROPA NOSTRA awarded for the best example of European renovation and heritage conservation for the refurbishment of the Collège des Bernardins, Paris, France.	1988	LE LIN D'OR award, Milan, Italy.
		1985	LAMPE D'OR awarded during the International Lighting Exhibition in Paris for the Washington lamp.
2010	TROPHÉE D'OR OF FESTIVAL FIMBACTE awarded to André Malraux Médiathèque, Béziers, France.		
2009	STRATEGIES, GRAND PRIX DU DESIGN 2009 Commercial architecture Prize awarded to the Docks 76 retail park, Rouen, France.		
2007	PYRAMIDES D'ARGENT ILE-DE-FRANCE: Grand Prix Regional awarded for the residential programme Résidences du Mail at Bois d'Arcy, France (Real Estate Developer: Promogim) & PRIX DE L'ESTHETIQUE IMMOBILIERE awarded for the residential programme *Côté Coeur* à Issy-les-Moulineaux, France (Real Estate Developer: Sefri-Cime).		
2006	ARTURBAIN.FR award during the Robert Auzelle seminar with the support of Dominique Perben, Ministry of Transports, Equipment, Tourism and Sea, awarded for the Place de la Libération, Dijon, France.		
2006	IF DESIGN AWARD awarded by the International Forum Design for the lighting systems *iWay* and *iRoad* manufactured by iGuzzini.		

Jean-Michel Wilmotte—Honors and Roles

Member of the *Cercle Pierres d'Or* since 2016

Member of the *Académie des beaux-arts*, Architecture department since 2015

Member of the board of Directors of the BBCA (low-carbon building) association since 2015

Administrator of the *Arts Décoratifs*, Paris, since 2008

Dean of the University of Architecture of Hongik, South Korea 2006–08

Chevalier de l'Ordre National de la Légion d'Honneur 1999

Grand Cross of *Ordem do infant dom Henrique*, awarded by the President of Portugal Mário Soares 1994

Chevalier de l'Ordre National du Mérite 1994

Commandeur des Arts et des Lettres 1992

Chevalier des Palmes Académiques 1986

JEAN-MICHEL WILMOTTE

SELECTED BIBLIOGRAPHY

By Jean-Michel Wilmotte
'Dessin d'acier, dessein sublimé' in *Guide de la réhabilitation avec l'acier à l'usage des architectes et des ingénieurs*, Saint-Aubin, CTICM, 2010, pp. 6–7.
Dictionnaire amoureux de l'Architecture, Paris, Editions Plon, 2016, p. 787.
'L'acier est bien vivant' in *Guide de la réhabilitation des enveloppes et des planchers*, Eyrolles, Paris, 2014, p. 7.
'Question de bon sens' in *Architecture Intérieure des Villes. Interior, urban, design*, Le Moniteur des Villes, Paris, 1999, pp. 14–15.
'Regards émotions…' [sur Jean Lurçat], in *Jean Lurçat (1892–1966): Au seul bruit du soleil*, Cinisello Balsamo (Italy), Silvana Editoriale, 2016, p. 15.
'Retrouver Venise' in *Venezia, la scomparsa*, Paris, Editions Xavier Barral, 2017, p. 5.
Wilmotte, J.-M., Jodidio, P. 'Voir l'espace autrement' in *Connaissances des Arts*, n°480, February 1992, pp. 70–79.

Monographs
Alvarez, J. *Wilmotte*. Paris, Editions du Regard, 2016.
Bony, A., Jodidio, P. *Wilmotte. Design: 1975–2015*, Munich, Prestel, 2019 [forthcoming book].
Direction de la Culture et de l'Animation de la ville de Saint-Quentin, Jean-Michel Wilmotte, architect/designer, Saint-Quentin, 2002, Catalogue of the 'Jean-Michel Wilmotte, architecte/designer' exhibition.
Grisoni, J., Loubeyre J.-B. *Wilmotte, L'instinct architecte*, Le Passage, Paris, 2005.
Institut culturel français, *Wilmotte, Elogio dell'evidenza*, AFAA, 1996. Catalogue of the Italy traveling exhibition (Florence, Rome, Forli, Bari), June 1996–August 1998.
Lamarre, F., Tournaire P. (photos), *Jean-Michel Wilmotte, Architectures à l'œuvre*, Le Moniteur, Paris, 2008.
McDowell, D. *Jean-Michel Wilmotte, Architecture-Écritures*, Aubanel, Geneva, 2009.
Meier, R. (foreword), Barré, F. (preface) *Wilmotte. Réalisations et projets*, Le Moniteur, Paris, 1993 (reprinted 1995).
Pradel, J.-L. *Wilmotte*. Electa Moniteur, Milan, Paris, 1989.
Rambert, F. *Jean-Michel Wilmotte*, Editions du Regard, Paris, 1996.
Wilmotte & Associés, *Projets Récents Futurs*, London, PUSH, 2009.
Wilmotte, J.-M., Virilio, P. (foreword) *Architecture Intérieure des Villes, Interior, urban, design*, Le Moniteur des Villes, Paris, 1999.

Works About Wilmotte & Associés' Projects
Amar, M., Bianchi, F. *Maison de la Mutualité*, Paris, 2012.
Banque de Luxembourg. *Architects–Arquitectonica*, Blue Print Extra 12, London, 1994.
Besacier, H. Désveaux, D., Meyronin, B., Rambert, F., Collomb, G. (foreword), LPA (François Gindre), Groupe 45 (Georges Verney Caron), *Ceci n'est pas un parc* [Lyon's car parks], Libel, 2010.
Bony, A. *Meubles et décors des années 80*, Editions du Regard, Paris, 2010.
Colbert Management & Conseil, *Les Demeures Anahita by Wilmotte*, Colbert Management & Conseil, Paris, 2016.
Crespolini, C., Godon, P. [Rouen] *Métrobus*, éditions La Vie du Rail, Paris, 1995.
Dagen, P., Béret, C., Lévy, B.-H. *Paix. Clara Halter – Jean-Michel Wilmotte*. Editions Cercle d'Art, Paris, 2005.
Desmoulins, C. (dir.), *Le Collège des Bernardins, Histoire d'une reconversion,* Editions Alternatives, Paris, 2009.
Dutertre, P. 'Place du Grand-Jardin, gare routière à Chelles' in *Paysages urbains, une France intime*, le Moniteur, Paris, 2007, pp. 90–91.
Engel, P. *Guide de la réhabilitation des enveloppes et des planchers*, Eyrolles, Paris, 2014.
Engel, P. *Guide de la réhabilitation avec l'acier à l'usage des architectes et des ingénieurs*, CTICM, Saint-Aubin, 2010.
Engel, P., Berlanda, T., Bruno, A., Mazzolani, F. 'Rénover et réinvestir l'existant' in Construire en acier, N° 3+4, 2010, pp. 4–17.
Engel, P., Koolhas, R. (foreword) *Manuel de la réhabilitation avec l'acier à l'usage des architectes et des ingénieurs*, Presses de l'EPFL, Lausanne, 2017.
Eric Mazoyer, E., Du Govic, N. *Paroles d'architectes*, Bouygues Immobilier, 2002.
Henriques da Silva, R. (dir.), *Obraçom: Museu do Chiado. Historias vistas e contadas*, Instituto Português de Museus, Lisbon, 1995.

Hugonot, M.-C. 'Jean-Michel Wilmotte: spécialiste de la diversité' in *Habiter la montagne. Chalets et maisons d'architectes*, Editions Glénat, Grenoble, 2016. pp. 58–67.

'Jean-Michel Wilmotte, Hotel de Nell and La Réserve Ramatuelle' in *The design hotels book 2016*, Design Hotels AG, Berlin, 2016, pp. 230–234/252–255.

Jodidio, P. 'Chalet Greystone. Courchevel, France' in House with a view, residential mountain architecture / Vue d'en haut, residences de montagne, Victoria (Australia), Images Publishing, 2008, pp. 246–249.

Jodidio, P. 'Château de Méry-sur-Oise' in *Connaissance des Arts*, special issue, 2001.

Jodidio, P. 'Jean-Michel Wilmotte. Frejus St Raphaël Community heater. Tour du Ruou house' in *Architecture in France*. Taschen, Cologne, 2006, pp. 184–191.

Jodidio, P. 'Jean-Michel Wilmotte: Ullens Center for contemporary Art (UCCA)' in *Architecture Now 6*, Cologne, Taschen, 2009, pp. 546–551.

Jodidio, P. 'Jean-Michel Wilmotte: Bordeaux Lac Convention Center' in *Architecture Now 3*, Taschen, Cologne, 2004, pp. 534–539.

Jodidio, P. 'Jean-Michel Wilmotte: Contemporary Art Center, Hamon Donation' in *Architecture Now 2*, Taschen, Cologne, 2002, pp. 566–571.

Jodidio, P., Lammerhuber, L. (photos), Museum of Islamic Art, Doha, Qatar, Munich, Prestel, 2008.

Jodidio, P. 'Lyon: le Musée des beaux-Arts' in *Connaissance des Arts*, special issue, 1994.

Jodidio, P. 'Wilmotte. Muséographie' in *Connaissance des Arts*, special issue, 1994.

'L'acier de fond en comble [Collège des Bernardins]' in *Construire en acier*, N° 3+4, 2010, pp. 30–35.

Lamarre, F. 'L'œuvre au noir [Restructuring of Lyon's customs building]' in *Europe, acier, architecture*, n°8, April 2008, pp. 40–43.

Leloup, M., *De la Halle Freyssinet à la Station F*, Paris, Editions Alternatives, 2017.

Maubant, J.-L. *Lyon: la ville, l'art et la voiture*, Villeubanne, Art/Edition, 1995.

Mc Dowell, D. 'Un coin d'ombre et de douceur sur la plage' [about Ramatuelle's villa by Jean-Michel Wilmotte], in *Jean Mus: jardins méditerranéens contemporains*, Editions Ulmer, Paris, 2016, pp. 164–171.

Mollard, C., Le Bon, L. *L'art de concevoir et gérer un musée*. Antony: Editions du Moniteur, 2016.

Müller, D. 'Multi-faceted: Museum of Islamic Arts in Doha/Qt' in *Professional Lighting Design*, n° 68, Sept./Oct. 2009, pp. 33–39.

Peyrel, B., Quinton, M. *Altarea Cogedim: Regards de créateurs* [Wilmotte: Cœur d'Orly, Promenade de Flandre (Roncq), Site Safran (Toulouse), l'Avenue 83 (Toulon-La Valette)], Editions de la Martinière, Paris, 2014.

Wilmotte, J.-M., Pradel J.-L. (foreword), *Mémoire d'empire. Trésors du Musée national du Palais de Tapei. Mise en scène par Wilmotte*, Arles, Actes Sud/AFAA, 1999.

Zabalbeascoa, A. 'Jean-Michel Wilmotte's architecture studio, Paris, 1991' in *The architect's office*, Barcelona, Editorial Gustavo Gili, 1996. pp. 172–175.

Publications by the Fondation Wilmotte

Catalogue of the Prix W

Prix W 2018. Fort de Villiers, Paris, Fondation Wilmotte, 2018.
Prix W 2016. Pondorly, Paris, Fondation Wilmotte, 2016.
Prix W 2014. Tower of London, Paris, Fondation Wilmotte, 2014.
Prix W 2012. Industrial site in Venice, Paris, Fondation Wilmotte, 2012.
Prix W 2010. Depot of the archives of the Bibliothèque nationale de France in Versailles, Fondation Wilmotte, Paris, 2011.
Prix W 2009. Water tower in Latina, Fondation Wilmotte, Paris, 2009.
Prix W 2007. Minoterie Lepoivre, éditions Jean-Michel Place, Paris, 2007.
Prix W 2006. Château Barrière, éditions Jean-Michel Place, Paris, 2006.

Exhibition Catalogues

Bruno, A., Wilmotte J.-M. (editorial), Jodidio, P. Fare, Andrea Bruno: Disfare, Rifare Architettura. Da Rivoli a Bagrati, Paris, Fondation Wilmotte, 2014. Exhibition catalogue, Venice (Italy), from September 18, 2014 to January 30, 2015.

Calandre, P. Isola Nova, Paris, Fondation Wilmotte, 2014. Exhibition catalogue of photographs by Philippe Calandre. Venice (Italy), from December 18, 2013 to May 20, 2014. London (United Kingdom), from September 13, 2014 to November 15, 2014.

Delangle, F. (photos), Wilmotte, J.-M., Ponti, S. (texts), Venezia, la scomparsa, Paris, Editions Xavier Barral, 2017, p. 136 Exhibition catalogue of photographies by Frédéric Delangle. Venice (Italy), from May 11 to November 26, 2017

Galassi, G. (photos), Ginapri, L.(text) Elogio della Luce: visioni del Razionalismo italiano, Fondation Wilmotte, 2015. Exhibition catalogue of photographs by Gianni Galassi. Venice (Italy), from November 7, 2015 to February 28, 2016.

EXHIBITIONS DEDICATED TO JEAN-MICHEL WILMOTTE'S WORK

'Etat d'Esprit'
Institut Français d'Architecture/Paris (France), from November 19 to December 13, 1986.

'Jean-Michel Wilmotte'
Yamagiwa Inspiration Gallery/Tokyo (Japan), June 1–10, 1992. *Exhibition of Wilmotte's furniture, urban furniture and architecture*

'Novator 93'
Saint-Martin-ès-Aires Chapel/Troyes (France), from June 17 to August 31, 1993. *Exhibition of lighting items*

'Jean-Michel Wilmotte'
Rouen (France), May 1994. *Photographs of Wilmotte's urban furniture and architecture. Exhibition organized by Rouen's SIVOM for the occasion of the presentation of 22 Rouen's Metrobus stations design*

Jean-Michel Wilmotte at 'Art du Jardin' Fair
Saint-Cloud (France), from May 30 to June 3, 1996. *Projects of benches and street lights designed for Hess Form + Licht*

'Jean-Michel Wilmotte'
Seoul Art Center/Seoul (South Korea), September 3–28, 1996. *Exhibition of selected works*

'Jean-Michel Wilmotte'
Modern Art Museum/Taipei (Taiwan), Autumn 1996. *Exhibition of selected works*

'Jean-Michel Wilmotte'
Tokyo Bunkamura/Tokyo (Japan), Spring 1997. *Exhibition of selected works*

'Jean-Michel Wilmotte au Salon des Maires et des collectivités locales'
Parc des Expositions/Paris (France), November 19–21, 1996. *Exhibition featuring benches and street lights designed by Wilmotte for Hess Form + Licht in the auditorium and the main walkway of the Paris Parc des Expositions at Porte de Versailles*

'Architecture intérieure des villes'
68, rue du Faubourg Saint-Antoine, Paris (France), from November 18, 1997 to 1998. *Presentation of urban design projects by Jean-Michel Wilmotte and staging of the new urban furniture collection designed for Hess Form + Licht company*

'Esterni – Interni'
Doge's Palace/Venice (Italy), from September 25 to October 28, 1998. *Exhibition of selected works*

'Elogio dell' evidenza'
French cultural institutes/Florence, Rome, Forli, Bari (Italy), from June 18, 1996 to 30 August 30, 1998. *Exhibition of selected works. Itinerary exhibition supported by the AFAA (Ministry of Foreign Affairs) and the French Cultural Institute presented in several cities of Italy*

'Architecture intérieure des villes'
Gana Art Gallery/Seoul (South Korea), from September 4 to October 4, 1999. *Exhibition of a selection of urban planning projects and urban furniture*

'Fonte de ville'
L'Arc Scène Nationale/Le Creusot (France), from October 8 to December 19, 1999. *Exhibition featuring benches and street lights designed by Wilmotte for Hess Form + Licht, and presentation of photographs: interplay of light and shade*

'Jean-Michel Wilmotte – Selected projects'
Hôtel de Région/Le Puy-en-Velay (France), 2002. *Exhibition of selected works in architecture, museography, urban planning and design*

'Jean-Michel Wilmotte – Selected projects'
French embassy/Athens (Greece), 2004. *Exhibition of selected works in architecture, museography, urban planning, and design*

'Nouvelle ligne de mobilier urbain pour Hess'
Bordeaux (France), 2004. *Exhibition of a new line of urban furniture during the Week of Architecture*

'Jean-Michel Wilmotte, architect/designer'
Galerie Saint-Jacques, Saint-Quentin (France), from April 19 to May 15, 2002. *Exhibition of selected works in architecture, museography, urban planning and design. Jean-Michel Wilmotte received the title of 'Citizen of Honor of Saint-Quentin'*

'Wilmotte UK Launch Event'
London (United Kingdom), 2009. *Exhibition of selected works in architecture, museography, urban planning, and design*

'Utopies et Innovations'
Saint-Louis (France), 2010. *Presentation of the Wilmotte Foundation and selected works of Wilmotte & Associés*

Designer's days, Opening of the 'Galerie d'actualités Wilmotte'
Galerie d'actualités Wilmotte/Paris (France), from May 31 to June 4, 2012. *Presentation of the new collection of high-end kitchen equipment designed for La Cornue W; presentation of the Nice Stadium project and Eclatec lighting installation on the Passerelle des Arts*

'Design for U.S.' Paris Design Week 2012
Galerie d'actualités Wilmotte/Paris (France), September 10–16, 2012. *Presentation of the new furniture collection designed for American company Holly Hunt*

'Aplat by wilmotte'
Galerie d'actualités Wilmotte/Paris (France), January 2014. *Presentation of a concept of high-performance and environmentally friendly architectural paints, named 'Aplat by Wilmotte,' in partnership with Jefco, manufacturer of professional paintings*

'Architecture Passions, 40 ans de créations Wilmotte & Associés'
Espace Richaud/Versailles (France), September to November 27, 2016. *Presentation of Wilmotte & Associés design practice and a number of selected projects*

Exhibitions organized by the Wilmotte Foundation

'Prix W 2012'
Wilmotte Foundation/Venice (Italy), from September 29 to November 25, 2012. *Exhibition of the winning projects of the Prix W 2012 award & presentation of a selection of Wilmotte & Associés' projects*

'Otto mani e un occhio: Nasser Bouzid, Jean-Gabriel Coignet, Côme Mosta-Heirt, François Perrodin, Marin Kasimir'
Wilmotte Foundation/Venice (Italy), from May 31 to November 24, 2013. *Exhibition dedicated to four sculptors and one photographer*

'Isola Nova. Philippe Calandre'
Wilmotte Foundation/Venice (Italy), from December 18, 2013 to May 20, 2014. Wilmotte UK/London (United Kingdom), from September 13, 2014 to November 15, 2014. *Presentation of a series of new islands in Venice inhabited by large industrial structures mixed with fragments of traditional Venetian architecture*

'TraFumetto e gioco: disegniveneziani. Matteo Alemanno, Marco Maggi e Francesco Nepitello'
Wilmotte Foundation/Venice (Italy), from April 5 to May 20, 2014. *Presentation of original drawings from the author of strip cartoons Matteo Alemanno, and also Venetian games*

'Prix W 2014: Design a cultural and events center for the Tower of London'
Wilmotte Foundation/Venice (Italy), from May to September 2014. *Exhibition of the winning projects of the Prix W 2014 award*

'Andrea Bruno: Fare, Disfare, Rifare Architettura, da Rivoli a Bagrati'
Wilmotte Foundation/Venice (Italy), from September 18, 2014 to January 30, 2015. *Retrospective of Italian architect from Turin Andrea Bruno's work*

'Relectures. Alessandra Chemollo'
Wilmotte Foundation/Venice (Italy), from May 7 to October 25, 2015. Wilmotte UK/London (United Kingdom), from June 8 to November 30, 2016. *Exhibition of some of Jean-Michel Wilmotte's projects in Museum design, interpreted by Alessandra Chemollo, photographer*

'Elogio della luce [Praise of light]. Gianni Galassi'
Wilmotte Foundation/Venice (Italy), from November 7, 2015 to February 28, 2016. *Gianni Galassi captures the purity of the Italian rationalist architecture through magnificent and almost abstract photographs*

'Prix W 2016: Pondorly, design of a new arc de Triomphe for Paris'
Wilmotte Foundation/Venice (Italy), from May 6 to September 15, 2016. *Exhibition of the winning projects of the Prix W 2016 award*

'Russian Orthodox Cathedral of Paris'
Wilmotte Foundation/Venice (Italy), from February 18 to March 2, 2017. *Presentation of the Russian Orthodox Cathedral of Paris designed by Wilmotte & Associés*

'Venezia, la scomparsa. Frédéric Delangle'
Wilmotte Foundation/Venice (Italy), from May 11 to November 26, 2017. *Commissioned by Jean-Michel Wilmotte, presentation of French photographer Frédéric Delangle's work dedicated to a new vision of Venice in 36 original prints*

Exhibitions commissioned by Jean-Michel Wilmotte

'Elogio dell' ombra. Bruno Romeda'
68, rue du Faubourg Saint-Antoine/Paris (France), from January 28 to February 17, 1993. *Presentation of Italian sculptor Bruno Romeda's work*

'The ruins of Detroit. Yves Marchand & Romain Meffre'
Wilmotte UK/London (United Kingdom), from February 27 to April 27, 2012. *Presentation of the photographs of Detroit, Michigan by French photographers Yves Marchand and Romain Meffre*

'Art in progress. Leonora Hamill'
Wilmotte UK/London (United Kingdom), from February 15 to March 28, 2013. *For the first time in the United Kingdom, presentation of an exhibition dedicated to British photographer Leonora Hamill's work, winner of the 'Prix HSBC pour la Photographie (2012)'*

'Wild Surfaces. Edith Marie Pasquier'
Wilmotte UK/London (United Kingdom), from June 19 to July 26, 2013. *For the first time in the United Kingdom, presentation of British photographer Edith Marie Pasquier's work*

'Le temple du Soleil. Patrizia Mussa'
Wilmotte UK/London (United Kingdom), from May 22 to September 20, 2015. *Presentation of the photographs of the Grande Motte made by Italian artist Patrizia Mussa*

'Ubiquity: 2. Miguel Chevalier'
Wilmotte UK/London (United Kingdom), from April 13 to June 15, 2018. *Interactive visual installation by Miguel Chevalier*

JEAN-MICHEL WILMOTTE

CREDITS

All location maps, plans and drawings are by Wilmotte & Associés, redrawn by Pauline Henry, Antonio Marino, and Donata Buzinskaite.

New Buildings

Lee House © Pascal Tournaire 18–20; © Ki-Hwan Lee 21

Pangyo Residence © Ki-Hwan Lee 24–5, 26; © Pascal Tournaire 27

Signal Tower © Roomservice 3d – Niels Kretschmann 30–1, 32, 33

Brain and Spine Institute © Didier Boy de la Tour 36–7, 38, 39

Monte Carlo View Tower © Milène Servelle 42 (top), 43; © Pascal Pronnier 42 (bottom)

Epadesa Corporate Headquarters © Didier Boy de la Tour 46–7

Barristers Training College © Didier Boy de la Tour 52; © Nicolas Fussler 50, 51, 53

Arts Center, International School of Geneva © Adrien Barakat 56–7

Allianz Riviera Stadium © Milène Servelle 60–5

Quadrans Buildings © Antoine Huot 68–9; © Nicolas Fussler 70–1

6 Pancras Square, Google Headquarters © Steve de Vriendt 74, 75; © Edmund Sumner Partnership 75, 76

Daejeon Cultural Center © Ki-Hwan Lee 80–1, 82, 83

Ferrari Sporting Management Center © Milène Servelle 86–7, 88, 89

Russian Orthodox Spiritual and Cultural Center © Alessandra Chemollo 92–3, 94, 96–7; © Mario Fourmy 95

Private Chalet © Milène Servelle 100–3

Eiffage Corporate Headquarters © Nicolas Fussler 106–9

Bleu Ciel Residential Tower © Joseph Haubert 112; © Wilmotte & Associés 113

Giroflées Tower © Wilmotte & Associés 116, 117

Renovation Projects

La Réserve Hotel, Ramatuelle © Jacques Denarnaud 122–3, 127; © Grégoire Gardette 124, 126 (top); © Manuel Zublena 125, 126 (bottom)

Jean Pierre Raynaud Studio © Françoise Huguier/VU' 130–1; © Philippe Chancel 132–3

Mandarin Oriental Hotel © Didier Boy de la Tour 136–7, 139; © Guillaume Maucuit Lecomte 138

Château Pédesclaux Winery © Rodolphe Escher 142–3, 144; © Anaka 145

Summit House, Jcdecaux UK Headquarters © Edmund Sumner Partnership 148–51

Station F Start-Up Campus © Patrick Tourneboeuf 154–61

Collège des Bernardins © Pascal Tournaire 164, 165, 167; Géraldine Bruneel 166 (top), 169; Pierre-Olivier Deschamps/VU' 166 (bottom); Guillaume Maucuit Lecomte 168

Urban Projects

Greater Moscow Proposal © Wilmotte & Associés, Antoine Grumbach and Sergueï Tkachenko 173, 174, 176, 177; © Wilmotte & Associés, Antoine Grumbach, Sergueï Tkachenko and Atelier Villes et Paysages 175

Allées Jean-Jaurès © Didier Boy de la Tour 180–1, 183; © Dominique Marck 182

Museums

Pavillon des Sessions, Musée du Louvre © Didier Boy de la Tour 188–9, 191; © Alessandra Chemollo 190

Gana Art Center © Pascal Tournaire 194; © Jung Chea Park 195

President Jacques Chirac Museum © Didier Boy de la Tour 200 (top); © Pascal Tournaire 198–9, 200 (middle and bottom), 201

Ullens Center for Contemporary Art © André Morin/Yan Pei-Ming 204–5; © Pascal Tournaire 206–7

Museum of Islamic Art of Qatar © Lois Lammerhuber 210, 212, 213; © Zed Photography 211

Musée d'Orsay Refurbishment © Alessandra Chemollo 216–21

Sursock Museum © Emmanuel Brelot 228–9; © Géraldine Bruneel 230, 231

The New Rijksmuseum © Alessandra Chemollo 230–1, 233; © Julien Lanoo 232, 234–5

INDEX OF PROJECTS

6 Pancras Square, Google Headquarters 72–7

Allées Jean-Jaurès 178–83

Allianz Riviera Stadium 58–65

Arts Center, International School of Geneva 54–7

Barristers Training College 48–53

Bleu Ciel Residential Tower 110–13

Brain and Spine Institute 34–9

Château Pédesclaux Winery 140–5

Collège des Bernardins 162–9

Daejeon Cultural Center 78–83

Eiffage Corporate Headquarters 104–9

Epadesa Corporate Headquarters 44–7

Ferrari Sporting Management Center 84–9

Gana Art Center 192–5

Giroflées Tower 114–17

Greater Moscow Proposal 172–7

Jean Pierre Raynaud Studio 128–33

La Réserve Hotel, Ramatuelle 120–7

Lee House 16–21

Mandarin Oriental Hotel 134–9

Monte Carlo View Tower 40–3

The New Rijksmuseum 228–35

Musée d'Orsay Refurbishment 214–21

Museum of Islamic Art of Qatar 208–13

Pangyo Residence 22–7

Pavillon des Sessions, Musée du Louvre 186–91

President Jacques Chirac Museum 196–201

Private Chalet 98–103

Quadrans Buildings 68–71

Russian Orthodox Spiritual and Cultural Center 90–7

Signal Tower 28–33

Station F Start-Up Campus 152–61

Summit House, Jcdecaux UK Headquarters 146–51

Sursock Museum 222–7

Ullens Center for Contemporary Art 202–7

Every effort has been made to trace the original source of copyright material contained in this book. The publishers would be pleased to hear from copyright holders to rectify any errors or omissions.

The information and illustrations in this publication have been prepared and supplied by Wilmotte & Associates. While all reasonable efforts have been made to ensure accuracy, the publishers do not, under any circumstances, accept responsibility for errors, omissions and representations express or implied.